POLICE IN INDIA
PROBLEMS AND PERSPECTIVES

POLICE IN INDIA
PROBLEMS AND PERSPECTIVES

By

Dr. Krishna Mohan Mathur

Foreword By

K.P.S Gill

GYAN

ISBN : 978-81-212-0350-0

Published, 2018

Published by

Gyan Publishing House
5, Ansari Road
Daryaganj, New Delhi-110002
Phone: 011-47034999, 9811692060
www.gyanbooks.com
E-mail: books@gyanbooks.com

Printed at: G. Print Process, Delhi.

FOREWORD

I am very happy to introduce the book *Police In India - Problems and Perspectives* written by Dr. Krishna Mohan Mathur. The Police are the only government functionaries who are available seven days a week, twenty-four hours a day to respond to the citizens' need for help and assistance when they are in distress or victims of crime. The Indian Police System has been under tremendous pressure after independence to meet the growing demands of the democratic urges of our developing society. Collective violence and terrorism have thrown the greatest challenge to the country particularly in states like Punjab, Jammu & Kashmir and Assam. According to the author "the menacing cloud of terrorism and violence in Punjab and J & K, the continuing insurgency in the North-East, the growing discontent in the vast tribal belt of Madhya Pradesh, Orissa, Bihar and West Bengal, rising wave of rioting and tensions have thrown serious challenges to the police". State Police Force and the members of Central Police Organisations are working very closely to fight terrorism and secessionist movements in India. Indian Police and Para-Military Forces have achieved success to a large extent in maintaining the unity and integrity of the country. In the present book Dr. K.M. Mathur has covered very important areas of police work. The author has recommended that "Police should be given additional vehicles, more sophisticated equipment and weaponry, better communication and better training so as to improve its mobility, fire power, and ability to flash messages instantly and to perform its duties in a more effective manner. Police requires more meaningful, and job-oriented training to bring about much needed change in its outlook, orientation and behaviour." Collective violence, terrorism, unrest and offences against women, are matters of great importance to all the citizens of the country. Organisational matters like personnel policies, police training, police morale, police leadership, police role and police culture have been analysed by the author in the work. He has given the history and development of Central Reserve Police Force in a separate chapter and has brought out its outstanding role in an analytical manner. I am sure his book will provide very useful insider's view to the readers. Policing a democracy is never easy nor uncontroversial. The task therefore is to improve the quality of policemen to make them as humanitarian, effective and responsive to the nation's needs. The role of the police is inevitably more difficult in a secular, social democratic republic which has a large population beset by and is often divided along caste and communal lines.

I strongly recommend the book not only to police officers but to all citizens of the country who would like to know about problems of the police. The author has covered a vast area in his book and has made valuable contribution to the subject. I would commend this publication as a very useful reference to the social scientists, policy makers and the public in general. I hope the readers will find book educative, interesting and useful in forming their views about the police.

Director General of Police Punjab **K.P.S. GILL, I.P.S.**
Chandigarh

PREFACE

THE Police forms a microcosm of many of the dilemmas endemic in human society. How a secular socialist democratic society should police itself is one of the more interesting and intractable problems to be solved by democracy. In early primitive societies, where violations of behaviour could breed vendettas elders of the community undertook a police function. But as the society grew more diverse and complex, the ordinary citizen became less inclined or willing to police his neighbour and increasingly devolved his responsibilities on to full-time scapegoats labelled police-officers. The modern functions and performance of the police therefore call for clear as well as cool consideration. But policemen like deviants also must be studied not as a group but as individuals; not in isolation, but in the context of their contemporary community. Police must change with society. Police are the cutting edge of the rule of law and they are the instruments therefore of one of the Government's sacred charge. Police has generally been viewed as an instrument of system maintenance and its entire effectiveness is judged by the skill and efficiency it displays in this respect. Police organisations have to open out and allow research scholars to analyse, study and expose the police problems and dilemmas to the public. Policing is both a science and an art. The explosive growth of literature on police during the last four decades leads one to question the heritage, present condition and the future of the police as a separate discipline of knowledge. All over the world police studies need to be carried out on scientific lines to understand the background of policing and the challenges which are being faced by the police organisations. The present book therefore can be considered one of such efforts to uncover the problems and perspectives of the police. The present study has endeavoured to outline origin and development of science of Policing and has tried to formulate the general theories of police science. The author suggests that the police science should be introduced as a subject at school, college and university as a separate discipline of knowledge. The study has made some indepth study on topics like collective violence, terrorism, agrarian unrest, police morale, Central Reserve Police Force, police leadership, police training, police culture and personnel policies in police. Changing role of police in India has been analysed both from the point of view of an insider and a research student. Offences against women and children as a part of study of victimology have been brought out in the book. The police mandate has to be creatively adopted and moulded into a new police culture befitting a democratic society which is wedded to the ideals of social justice.

It is the earnest belief of the author that the present study will give the correct perspective to the people, the academicians and practising police leaders who are keen to know the problems of police. To provide the appropriate background the book traces the historical background, of the institution of the police around the world and provides the brief history of the development of the literature on police science. An effort has been made to bring new insights and approaches to an area that is too often discussed in hackneyed and polarized over-simplifications. This work does not claim to be either exhaustive or comprehensive because the time required for further study and proper research have been the constraining factors.

I express my heart-felt gratitude to Shri K.P.S. Gill, I.P.S., Director General of Police, Punjab, for writing the foreword of this book. My thanks are due to Director General, C.R.P.F., Director, Bureau of Police Research and Development, Director, S.V.P. National Police Academy, Hyderabad and Director, Internal Security Academy, Mount Abu. I express my deep sense of sincerity and regard to Dr. B. Varma, Retired Director, Internal Security Academy, Mount Abu, and Prof. P.D. Sharma, Head of Political Science Deptt. Rajasthan University, Jaipur who have been sources of intellectual inspiration to me. Prof. S.R. Maheshwari of I.I.P.A. New Delhi, Prof. R.K. Arora and Prof. Ram Ahuja of Rajasthan University also need special mention. M/s B.N. Mullik, K.F. Rustomji, N.S. Saksena, G.C. Shinghvi, P.R. Raj Gopal, S. Venugopal Rao and many other senior police officers deserve my thanks for enriching my knowledge of the subject by their scholarly view-points and opinions and personal-interaction with me on many occasions. I am also beholden to many friends with whom I had the privilege of discussing various aspects of the work. I want to give my special thanks to Shri. P. Sudhakaran who has typed out the book with utmost care and excellence with a cheerful smile. The Library staff of N.P.A. Hyderabad and I.S.A. Mount Abu also deserve my sincere thanks.

My family's contribution in completion of this book is beyond measure. My wife Prabha Mathur and children Shikha, Pragya and Shiv Shubhang encouraged me immensely by sparing me from all domestic liabilities and commitments for devoting full attention to complete the work. Shikha and Pragya have also given many suggestions on my articles and have helped me in editing the manuscript at the initial stages. The book is an oblation to the Almighty Lord Shiva whose benevolent Mercy, Blessings and Grace, have remained the divine force behind my endeavours.

I am also thankful to the Editor of Indian Journal of Public Administration for granting permission for allowing re-printing of the article in the form of a Chapter in this book. My deep sense of gratitude to the Editor of Indian Journal of Public Administration."

CONTENTS

CHAPTER-1

BACKGROUND TO POLICING

THE PRESENT form and function of any police organisation is linked to the history of its development, the present cultural definition of its purpose and extent of its legitimate control and authority and the ways in which the organisation symbolizes how it carries out its charter. [1] For a proper understanding of any police organization, it is necessary that its historical evolution, prevailing socio-political conditions, and state of development of society are analysed. The development of police organisations and their expansion have often coincided with and been explained by major "law and order" crises or social unrest within the society. The origin of police in all societies can be traced to the need for social control. Social control is that mechanism by which a community or group operates as a whole and maintains a changing equilibrium. Social control is the sum total of a cultural pattern, social symbols, values, ideas or ideals, by which a society brings its members into conformity to the approved pattern of social behaviour. Police as law enforcing agency is an important institution of that social control which has existed in some form or the other in all societies in all ages. Even in most ancient India we find some codified laws enforced by the agents of the state. Police in ancient India can be known and studied through various scriptures, codes, inscriptions contemporary works of literature and art etc. The concept of governance in ancient India were of *Dharma* and *Danda* and there were functionaries to ensure the operation of "Danda". The Mahabharata speaks of *Gramadhipati* and the Buddhist Jatakas mention *Gramabhojaka.* Kautilya's "Arthashastra" refers to a detailed police organisation, a "Sangrahana" for 10 villages, a "Kharvatika" for 200 villages, a "Dronamukha" for 400 villages and a "Sthaniya" for 800 villages. [2] Kautilya has mentioned ancient police institution to save human society from "Matsanyaya" by following "DANDANITI" that is the law of regulating human conduct by punishment. [3] Kautilya has mentioned Eighteen Tirthas in the Arthashastra and given description of many varieties of police functions of that time. *Dauvarika* was the warden of police and was responsible for keeping strict vigilance on the management of the royal palace. *Antarvansika* was probably a lady police officer whose function was to maintain vigilance on the harem of the king. The *Dandapal*, the *Durgapal* and the *Antahpala* were uniformed officers who used to discharge a good deal of police duties in addition to some military type of duties. *Dandaparika* and *Kotapala* were all uniformed employees who used to perform police duties. The *Antahpala* was the guardian for the safe upkeep of the roads and was responsible for keeping the roads free of robbers. A critical survey of history would show that "Police in embryo" existed in all societies in some form or the other. There are clear indications that the ancient civilizations of Egypt and Assyria had some machinery to enforce their social laws. There was a police in ancient Sumeria although its duties are not known, the Egyptian Pharoahs had police, both to maintain law and order and to check political enemies. Classical Greece had a police force in every city state and Rome developed the concept of urban police to a level far ahead of the time. The present day *Vigili Urbani* may quite legitimately consider themselves as the successors of the Imperial Roman *Vigiles Urbis*. The concept of police is not the same throughout the world. The modern police force appeared in the early 19th century during Napoleon's rule in France. Napoleon gave Europe the first really modern police organisation, a professional and efficient para-military force, the Gendarmerie; and the first political police Fouche's Hante police. [(4)] In the Vatican City State the traditional police force is the Guard (Guardia Svizzera) formed in 1506 by Pope Julius II as his personal bodyguards and retained by his successors.

The development of the police in early societies in many countries is rather obscure and it is very difficult to say anything with definiteness about its origin and development. The Persian or Archaemenian empire under Cyrus and Darius is well known to have promulgated the laws through law bearers. The Greeks enacted many laws but their enforcement is known to have been very poor. Perhaps the only evidence of a police force in these city-states was the Scythian archers in Athens introduced and established by Peisistratus. [(5)] When Augustus built an empire in Rome an effective police system was given to the world. Augustus created a mysteriously large body of vigiles consisting of policemen and firemen. The vigiles of Augustus Claudius, the police system which Constantine introduced in the Byzantine Empire in the third century A.D., the system of police in Islamic Empires or the introduction of the "Missi Dominici" of Charlemagne in France are some of the early examples of ruler appointed Police. The Islamic rulers of Ommayid and Abbaside dynasties evolved a police system which consisted of a large force of detective police and spies, Charlemagne made his pioneering contribution to police systems by introducing the Gendarmerie who were, to begin with, armed civilians to enforce the laws in France. The word "Police" as an organised police force in the modern connotation was used in about 1829. [(6)] All over the world police organisation developed in a very gradual manner. Australia's first real police force was created in Sydney in 1810 and a criminal investigation was added to it from 1827. Historically Australia has a dual system of policing; a centralised common-wealth force and various state police forces. The formation of a police force in Tasmania can be dated back to 1804 when the first chief constable was appointed. In Austria, Vienna had its first police force in the form of a citizen's watch from 1221. A Day and Night watch was formed in 1531. City police forces in the modern sense were first organised in 1782 and brought under centralised command in Austria in 1789. In Austria a secret police force also existed from 1713 and a military police watch from 1775. In Brazil by 1567 a civil guard existed in the main coastal towns but the first modern police was the municipal police force created in Rio de Janeiro in 1808. In Canada, the Royal North West Mounted police was formed in May 1873. Later the Canadian police forces have been reorgainsed in four categories; the Royal Canadian Mounted police, a federal force, the provincial police forces and the transport police forces controlled by the Canadian railway companies and National Harbour Board and the municipal police forces. In Denmark the first full time police force was created in Copenhagen in 1590 and many other towns formed municipal police forces during the 17th century. In France a permanent night watch force existed in Paris from the sixth century. The Gendarmerie was formed in the 12th century as the Marechanssee, the Royal authority to enforce military law throughout the country. A national police force was created in France by Royal Edict in 1699. The first civilian policeman (Sergents de ville) appeared in Paris in 1829. The Gendarmerie Nationale is the model for most of the world's para-military, Police Forces. Police history in Italy goes back to the Roman Empire which had the first full time police force in the modern sense in Europe. Italy has at present three National police forces; the state police, the Corps of Carabineers and the Treasury guards. The Corps of Carabineers is incharge of the maintenance of public order, crime investigation, anti-terrorist duties and military police work. In Japan the first modern professional police force was created in 1871. A police bureau (Keihoryo) was formed in 1874 to supervise all the police activity in Japan. In Japan there are special Riot Police Units (Kidotai) which are equipped with latest specialised equipment for control of civil disturbances. The first police force in South Africa's history was the Dutch organised watch, formed in about 1655 and limited to guard duties. Law enforcement was added to its functions in 1657. In 1825 the British colonial administration organised Cape constabulary. In Spain, local police forces existed from about the

12th Century and were consolidated during the 16th and 17th Century. Police forces in the modern sense were created with the formation of the carabineers (Carabineros) in 1829 and the Civil guard (Guard a civil) in 1844 in Spain. In the U.S.S.R. Cheka was created in December 1917 as the first political police force which acted as the sword and shield of the party. In the United Kingdom there were constables policing the towns from the 13th century although they were more military men than police men. In England and Wales watchmen were appointed in towns and cities to guard the gates under an ancient system of watch and ward authorised by the statute of Westminster of 1285. Henry Fielding established a group of paid trained detectives in 1749 and will go down in the history of British police as having made outstanding contributions to the development of police system. [7] In 1752 Government paid him money to establish a paid force known as the Bow Street Police. Henry Fielding built up a little force of Volunteers to keep the streets of that part of London safe and Fielding's great idea was to prevent crime, not to arrest criminals. He had three branches in his police, the foot patrol, the horse patrol and the detective. [8] The disorder in the metropolitan areas of Britain in the late eighteenth and early nineteenth centuries as a result of the urbanisation and the pauperization of the landless peasant was a focal point for the development of the modern British police system. [9].

In Japan the police system recommended by Kawaji Toshiyoshi in 1874 and introduced by him continued till 1947 with of course necessary changes to suit the new developments. Gabriel Nicolas de La Reynie (1625-1709), can be called the father of great Paris police which was organised and developed under his dynamic leadership after March 1667. Louis Lepine remained as Prefect of Police of Paris from 1893 to 1913 (except for a break of 2 years 1897-1899) provided a very active and worthy leadership to the Paris police. The first full time police force was formed in the U.S.A. in Philadelphia in 1833. The Texas Rangers were the first state police force in the U.S.A. to be formed in 1835. The first police force in the United States, organised in the New York city in 1845 was patterned consciously on the then new Metropolitan Police of London. [10] The American police did not simply inherit the English model intact. Indeed the police model that took root in the United States was attired by several features of the American society and of the police response to them. One of the most salient aspect of police organisations in the United States is their local character. Policing in the U.S.A. is action oriented, disdainful of the general "Stay at home public", heavily involved with weaponry and its use and is essentially characterised by ethnic pluralism. The primary characteristic of police organisation in America is its diversity. [11] There are 40,000 separate police agencies in the United States ranging in size from one man or two man departments in small towns to New-York's Force of 30,000. The salaries and the ranks of the American police are not standardised. C.I.A. (Central Intelligence Agency) was established by National Security Act 1947. F.B.I. (Federal Bureau of Investigation) was formed in July 1908 by Charles J. Bonaparte. The Immigration and Naturalization service was created in March 1891 in the U.S.A.

In all societies law enforcement is a highly visible activity and generally law enforcement agencies reflect the cultures which have produced them and in turn play a part in maintaining their social values and the overall social fabric. Police is "intimately related to the community in which it is located and in which it serves. The personnel of the department are drawn from the community and have a personal involvement in the life and values of the society." [12] The nature of duties and functions of the police differ from societies to societies, countries to countries. Functions of police in totalitarian societies are different from duties and powers of police in free societies. The Cheka of U.S.S.R. is organised with the object of "Putting into practice the dictatorship of the proletariat." The Cheka, according to Dzerzhnisky was "the Vanguard for fighting counter revolutionaries and the enemies of the people." Under Stalin the militia was brutal but fairly honest. "In the Stalin era the police respect for the laws of the Soviet Union was far less than that in the Tsarist regime. The police was ruthless and brutal and a by-word for terror." [13] Many Russian novelists have written about the police under the Tsars. The finest description is in Anton Chekhov's short story "The Chameleon" in which police Inspector Ochumelov is painted as a docile servant of the rich sections of society. The police, by the very nature of their functions, are an anomaly in a free society. They are invested with a great deal of authority under a system of government in which authority is reluctantly granted and when granted, sharply curtailed. [14] In a free and democratic society, the strength of a democracy and the quality of life enjoyed by its citizens are determined in large measure by the ability of the police to discharge their duties. A democratic and free society looks to its police to prevent people from preying one another; to provide a sense of security; to facilitate movement; to resolve conflicts; and to protect the very processes and rights such as free elections, freedom of speech, and freedom of assembly -- on which continuation of a free society depends.

Police themselves have done little to describe the full range and importance of their multifarious activities and duties. Police and police work have often been received with ambivalence and ambiguity by the people. [15] The police are the only agency available seven days a week, twenty-four hours a day to respond to the citizen's need for help and assistance. To view police activity solely from the standpoint of law enforcement is perhaps to miss the crux of the role of the police in the community. The principal function of the police is to promote peace in the community. [16] Elaine Cumming, Ian Cumming and Laure Edel in their study found that more than half of the calls made to the police appeared to involve requests for help in personal and inter - personal matters. [17] The most sophisticated explanation of the myriad duties assigned to police has been developed by Egon Bittner who argues that the capacity of the police to use coercive force lends thematic unity to all police activity. "Whatever the substance of the task at hand, whether it involves protection against an undesired imposition, caring for those who cannot care for themselves, attempting to solve a crime, helping to save a life, abating a nuisance, or settling an explosive dispute, police intervention means above all making use of the capacity and authority to overpower resistance to an attempted solution in the native habitat of the problem. [18] Generalisations in police work beyond certain limits are difficult because police work differs from one country to another, one society to another and one community to another. Not only do variations in demands made upon the police result from demographic factors -- such as the make-up, stability and density of the population; communities also tend, over a period of time, to develop different styles of policing that in turn, serve to screen out or reinforce what a community consequently expects of its police. [19] If one penetrates beyond the generalisations about what the police do (such as maintain law and order, prevent crime, serve the aged and the children, protect the weak), if one goes beyond the literal descriptions of how police spend their time (such as locating missing persons, directing traffic, carrying out patrolling, attending calls for help) one can clearly find out the following multiple objectives of the police:

"(1) To prevent and control conduct widely recognised as threatening to life and property (serious crime).

(2) To aid individuals who are in danger of physical harm such as the victim of a criminal attack.

(3) To protect constitutional guarantees such as right of free speech and assembly.

(4) To facilitate the movement of people and vehicles.

(5) To assist those who can't care for themselves; the intoxicated, the addicted, the mentally ill, the physically disabled, the old and the young.

(6) To resolve conflict, whether it be between individuals, groups of individuals or the individuals and their government.

(7) To identify problems that have the potential for becoming more serious problems for the individual citizen, for the police or for government.

(8) To create and maintain a feeling of security in the community."[20]

(9) Regulation and control of private morals and public decencies of life.

(10) To carry out other social service duties to the community to which it belongs.

Recognition of the full magnitude and complexity of police functions and the many conflicting objectives of police organisations, the need for upgrading the quality of the police personnel becomes quite imperative and urgent. In a modern democratic and developing society, the duties and responsibilities of the police are generally to --

" (1) Promote and preserve public order;

(2) Investigate crimes and where appropriate, to apprehend the offenders and participate in subsequent legal proceedings connected therewith;

(3) Identify problems and situations that are likely to result in commission of crimes;

(4) Reduce the opportunities for the commission of crimes through preventive patrols and other appropriate police measures;

(5) Aid and cooperate with other relevant agencies in implementing appropriate measures for prevention of crimes;

(6) Aid individuals who are in danger of physical harm;

(7) Create and maintain a feeling of security in the community;

(8) Facilitate orderly movement of people and vehicles;

(9) Counsel and resolve conflicts and promote amity;

(10) Provide other appropriate services and afford relief to people in distress situations;

(11) Collect intelligence relating to matters affecting public peace and crimes in general including social and economic offences, national integrity and security; and

(12) Perform such other duties as may be enjoined on them by law for the time being in force." [21]

In examining the contents of police work in five countries namely Britain, India, Israel, the Netherlands and the United States one finds that in all the five societies police perform both social control and social support tasks. Many thinkers have said that social integration is one of the functions of police in all societies. In modern society police are deeply involved in the social integration process. Social integration can be understood on several levels, individual (psychological), small group (social psychology) and societal (sociological). According to Bayley in Japan so many of the people the police see regularly and to whom only they attend, are defeated, bedraggled, and helpless. Some have been abused by their own vices, some by circumstances they could not control. All are pitiful and lost, the hope gone out of their lives." [22] According to John Clark police work contributed to the overall unity, and welfare of a society. "[23] Egon Bittner has held that the vastly preponderant majority of police manpower, time and resources is and must be allocated to activities that have either nothing or only very little to do with law enforcement in the strict sense of the term. He concluded that police research has demonstrated that police work, far from being the kind of low grade occupation it is brought out to be, in fact involves the exercise of judgement and skill in handling problems of great complexity and importance. [21]

A sociology of police is developing and will continue to grow and significant benefits for police are to be expected from the promotion of the discipline in a police context.

During the last three decades police claims to professionalism have been asserted on the basis of professional specialised training and expertise based on a systematic body of knowledge and lengthy basic training. " In recent years police science has emerged as a subject of study in many Universities in America. It is not difficult to construct a syllabus of considerable breadth, depth and relevance to police work." [25] Sociology, politics, economics, criminology, penology, public administration, comparative police studies, police principles and ethics, police strategy, forensic science, criminalistics, laws and legal system are some of the core subjects constituting police science. Police as an academic branch of knowledge is at once both science and an art. It is a science to the extent that recognised scientific methodology, as applied in other social sciences, is adopted in an attempt to determine general concepts and principles about the working of the human mind. It is an art in so far as these concepts and principles are used in an attempt to understand and predict the behaviour of individuals or groups of individuals. Use of forensic science knowledge make police a science but the art of interrogation makes it an art. Thus police as a branch of knowledge is at once both science and art. In investigating any crime, the investigator has to use available scientific tools and techniques, but he has to learn the subtle art of investigation to reach to the bottom of the crime and criminal activity. Science and art have common pursuit and both shared the same values of social control and common good. Science and art are both necessary to make the life whole. In police work no dividing line can be drawn and all concepts and actions have to be understood in totality of the socio-political environment. Police science is gradually developing into a more systematic and richer branch of knowledge. Certain new trends are visible in police work which have brought silent revolution in policing. The increased use of fire arms, the general acceptance of new technological developments and the growing intrusion on individual privacy despite various legal safeguards have brought the policing revolution. Modern scientific techniques are being used to deal with rising crime rate and the still increasing civil protests at home and abroad. Modern technology is being employed as an aid to greater effectiveness. There has been a rapid advance in forensic techniques. The huge growth in technological equipment has outstripped the law designed to protect the citizen. "In the 1980s the technopoliceman has a wide range of equipment at his disposal. A helicopter fitted with video equipment can pick out individual faces at a demonstration, a fibre optic camera with a lens not much bigger than a biro tip can be inserted into rooms under surveillance, telephones can be tapped and mail opened." [(26)] Forensic science has taken the modern technological policeman into the laboratory world of microscopes and spectrum analysis while computer technology has opened vast vistas of quick retrieval of crime records. Police today rely overwhelmingly on technology and equipment. Mobility of the police has undergone tremendous change with the use of motor transport and police helicopters. Para-military character of police is increasing all over the world with the increase in insurgency and terrorism. The growth of specialisation and professionalism have become necessary due to the technological advances and the requirements of the time.

The management of police organisations has become a very challenging and complex task although not all police managers may see it that way. To what extent managerial action can improve the functioning of the organisation is a question which requires analysis and diagnosis of all those factors which contribute towards present levels of performance. Detailed examination and anlaysis of the nature of police system reveals how police managers must contend with a variety of problems in their attempts to shape and direct police work. Bureaucratic systems, monetary constraints, social demands, crime pattern, Police mandate and objectives, community demands and the dilemmas inherent in the policing, all contribute to the challenge facing the police manager. Police Chiefs today have full responsibility on their shoulders for decisions taken by various subordinates in an organisational context in which chiefs do not have much control. "The ability of the senior ranks to make rules that prescribe proper behaviour and then hold subordinates responsible for failing to comply with them can too easily insulate senior echelons from responsibility for organisational policies, procedures and practices implemented by their subordinates." [27] Independently of changes in the size and number of police forces, there has been an absolute increase in the sheer number of police personnel and this fact alone places a great onus upon police managers. Police managers are virtually the leaders who are responsible for planning, organising, staffing, directing and guiding police operations in their respective areas. When a police manager is required to perform managerial type activities and operating type activities simultaneously, he generally gives priorities to the operating work. The police manager's role demands a knowledge and understanding of the psychological aspects of management. Problem analysis and decision making are probably the most important issues that the police manager faces. The police managers have to be realistic and accept the fact that conflict is an ingredient of every police organisations. In recent years there is great emphasis on management training for senior and middle level police officers yet the managerial theories as applicable to police organisations have to be formulated and tested in various organisational contexts.

Police science is a newly developing branch of knowledge which has yet to find wide acceptance and academic recognition. The social sciences have demonstrated their practical value for police work. The sociological research and studies can lead to improved public understanding of and confidence in the police, based upon independent and objective study. The police themselves can learn about various sociological ideas and concepts from comparative research. Police organisations have to open out and allow research scholars to analyse, study and expose the police problems and dilemmas to the public. Police organisations have to develop a scientific temper and progressive outlook to keep pace with the changing time. The science of policing is gradually coming up of age. Because of the radical contributions made by the sixties and the seventies to the policing and to crime control, foundations to a science of policing has been laid down. [28] The police science today covers a vast field of knowledge dealing with general law enforcement, criminalistics, crime investigation and interrogation, police systems, police administration, police personnel management, police technology and forensic science. The maturation of police science can be brought about by bridging the separation of basic and applied research on police through synergetic relationship between police theory and police practices. [29] Policing is both a science and an art, science and art have common pursuits. Both are vital and necessary to make police administration effective and efficient. Police science is today under study by political thinkers, public administrators, police functionaries and social scientists in many advanced countries. Police administration is not applied mechanics but a living and breathing organism shaped by the political, economic and social trends of the community and the ethos of the police. The explosive growth of literature on police during the last four decades leads one to question the heritage, present condition and the future of the police as a discipline of knowledge. The amorphus body of research by social scientists and the writings of a large number of police leaders and practitioners in various countries constitute in a very meaningful sense a coherent and systematic discipline and have helped in making police a developing new science. [30] Police science is still in its nascent stage and has yet to develop into a broad based social science. "Studies in police science in India are still in a stage of infancy. Very few scholars and social science researchers have devoted their energy and expertise to understand the socio-administrative realities of democratic governance in a plural society of India's size and diversities." [31] All over the world police studies need to be carried out to understand the background of policing and the challenges which are being faced by the police organisations in various nations of the world. Studying closely the police history of the different countries, one invariably comes across the figure of a leader who emerged at the critical time and provided required leadership to the police organisation. Felix Edmindovich Dzerzhnisky of the USSR, J.E. Hoover of U.S.A., La Reynie of France, Kawaji Toshiyoshi of Japan, Samuel B. Steel of Canada, F.E. Louwage of Belgium stand out as founding fathers and pioneers of policing.

Notes and References

1. Peter K.Manning and John Van Maanen (1978) (Ed) -- *Policing: A view from the Street*, (Goodyear Publishing California), p.I.
2. Second Report of the National Police Commision, (Dharma Vira Report)Government of India, August 1979, p.10.
3. Kautilya's *Arthsashtra.* Book I chapter III
4. John Andrade (1985) -- *World Police and Para-military forces*, Mac Millan p. ix.
5. Sharad Chandra Misra (1970) -- *Police Administration in India*, p.3.
6. J.F. Moylan (1929) -- *Scotland Yard and the Metropolitan Police*, London, p.I.
7. John L. Sullivan -- *Introduction to Police Science*, p.10.
8. Richard Harrison (1954) -- *The Story of World's Police*, Phoenix House Ltd. London, pp 13-14.
9. C. Reith (1956) -- *A New study of Police History*, Oliver and Boyd *London*, p.25.
10. T. Fleming (1970) -- *The Policeman's Lot*; American Heritage 21 (2); 4.
11. Norman L. Weiner (1981) -- "Policing in America", in *Modern Policing* (Ed) David W. Pope and Norman L Weiner.
12. Withan A. Westley (1970) -- *Violence and the Police - A Sociological study of Law, Custom and Morality*, p.19.
13. N.S. Saksena -- "Police in the Soviet Union", *The Hindustan Times*, November 29, 1987.
14. Herman Goldstein (1977) -- *Policing a Free Society*, p.I.
15. Paul G. Shane (1980) -- *Police and People.*, p.2
16. Quinney R. (1970) -- *The Social Reality of Crime*, Boston, p. 113.
17. Elaine Cumming, Ian Cumming and Laura Edel (1965) -- "Policeman as Philosopher, Guide and Friend". In *Social Problems* 12, p. 285.
18. Egon Bittner (1970) -- *The Functions of the Police in Modern Society*, p.40.
19. For further reinforcement of this point see Wilson's *Varieties of Police Behaviour*, 1968.
20. Herman Goldstein, *op.cit.* p.35.
21. Second Report of the National Police Commission (Dharm Vira Chairman). Govt. of India August 1979. p.18. Para 14.51.
22. D.H. Bayley (1978) -- *Forces of order. Police Behaviour in Japan and the United States*, Berkeley, California, p.31.
23. John Clark (1967) -- *Police - A Social Study*, Oxford, p.126.
24. E. Bittner (1975) -- "Police Research and Police Work". In E. Viano (Ed). *Criminal Justice Research*, Heath.

25. Norman J. Greenhill (1981) -- "Professionalism in the Police Service". In *Modern Policing* (Ed) David W. Pope and Norman L. Weiner -- p.60.

26. Sarah Manwaring-white (1983) -- *The Policing Revolution*, p.84.

27. P.A.J. Waddington -- "The Role of the Police Committee, Constitutional arrangements and social realities." *Local Government Studies* (September - October 1984) p.37.

28. David John Farmer (1984) -- *Crime Control - The Use and Misuse of Police Resources* -- Plenum Press New York.

29. Dr. K. M. Mathur -- "Is there a Police Science? Search for an Answer", Papers presented at XIX All India Police Science Congress, Shillong, November 5-8, 1985, p.79.

30. *Ibid*,.

31. Dr. P.D. Sharma (1987) -- Foreword to the book *The Problems of Police in a Democratic Society* written by Dr. K.M. Mathur. Foreword p. vii, R.B.S.A Publishers, Jaipur.

CHAPTER-2

ORIGIN AND DEVELOPMENT OF "SCIENCE OF POLICING"

WHILE ATTENDING the All India Police Science Congress, regularly as a participant, the author raised a debate. "Is there a Police Science?" in one such Congress session held at Shillong in 1985. Search for an answer led the author to take up serious research on the development of the "Policing as a Science." As a branch of specialised knowledge, "Police-Science" is in its infancy. It is still a mixture of philosophy, history and art of "Policing" and the writings on the subject are still largely descriptive and analytical. At its best it is an objective and systematic approach to the various facets of policing. New generalisations and research studies on police are beginning to provide the kind of theoretical framework that is necessary for evolving and formulating new eras of knowledge. We are on the verge of great discoveries of knowledge relating to policing and in the past two decades the basic foundations of a new discipline have been laid. No modern society can survive without police and the policeman occupies a most valuable position in a civilized society. Police science tries to consolidate, systematize and organise the discipline which provides the skills, knowledge, expertise and practical art of carrying out the professional work assigned to the policemen in different societies of the world. The aims of Police science are: (1) to make police officers realize the significance of their job, (2) to teach them technical, human and conceptual skills required to perform the job of police man, (3) to inculcate the desirable attitudes so as to harmonize individual, group and social needs and aspirations, (4) to inculcate appropriate behaviour so as to enable them to deal with various developing situations, (5) to psychologically and physically prepare the policeman to learn to live under tensions and pressures of police work and to develop appropriate responses to them, (6) to provide a value-system and a philosophy for the police man, (7) to understand the limitations of the role of police as a social control agency and as a part of criminal justice system, (8) to develop the professional areas of police work as a social service organisation, (9) to study the origin and development of crime and criminological tendencies in human beings, (10) to develop various other areas of knowledge which indirectly or directly impinge or are related to police work. Police science is related to the art and science of social surgeon (Police) who has to carry out surgical operations in social setting to control and contain crime, disorder and social durance.

When police has to make interventions in various social situations to preserve law and order, the police, acting as social surgeons have to be detached, unemotional, scientific, cautious, observing all the precautions at their disposal with effective command and judgement to take a correct decision for police intervention. Charles Raith aptly calls the 'Police' "the Blind eye of History" and deplores the failure of history to study the effect which the police system of a country produces on its development in all spheres -- political, economic and social. Studying closely the police history and police system of the different countries, one can easily think of a new branch of knowledge which should include a systematized and well documented knowledge of the subject of police. Enormous literature on police in the form of books, monographs, articles, reviews and the like stands as a clear testimony to the fact that police science as a scientific and comprehensive study of all the relevant aspects of police, has not yet fully evolved and that an integrated set of theoretical formulations or conceptual frameworks are yet to be worked out. Keeping this significant point in his view the author has tried to deal with some aspects of the theoretical study of police science and to trace its historical development as a new scientific discipline.

This chapter presents a brief methodical account of the basic principles and generalisations of police science. It contains the core ideas that today constitute an appreciable working consensus among police scientists. Police science brings together the results of a great amount of empirical investigations through field observations, surveys, historical and cross-cultural comparisons and other matters pertaining to police systems, police practices, police philosophy and police concepts as have been developed by different police thinkers so far. Police science training and higher education can make police more flexible, less hostile, less prejudicial, less authoritative and more humane and considerate. Development of police science will significantly increase the knowledge of police problems of the public and will bring public closer to the police. For proper recognition as a separate discipline, police science has to enrich its academic contents by building up concepts, thoughts generalisations, models and theories which can find universal acceptance. A good codification, classification and presentation of all available material on police science in a systematic manner on scientific lines is the need of the hour and this chapter is an effort in the same direction.

Is the police science rich enough as a professional branch of knowledge by itself. For any recognised professional discipline, four things are needed--

(a) knowledge, identifiable philosophy, general theories and concepts;

(b) skills and techniques needed for practitioners;

(c) professional commitment for larger professional objectives and code of conduct;

(d) the scientific temper and progressive outlook to build up the knowledge in a systematic manner.

The burden of giving "police science" its due recognition as full-fledged discipline of knowledge lies with the academicians, social scientists and the police writers, police leaders and managers. Science, according to Garner, may be described as "a fairly unified mass of knowledge relating to a particular subject, acquired by systematic observation, experience or study". The scientific character of a study can be assessed by the scientific method applied in the study. Science of policing is now slowly emerging as a fairly unified mass of knowledge relating to police work acquired and documented by scientific observation, parctical field experience and study of police working in various societies. Science of policing is the historical, structural, political, social and psychological analysis of police in its varied perspectives. Science of policing is the science of "law enforcement" and "social control" over social deviants. It is also a science dealing with security of the society from its internal threats and law-breakers. Science of policing is distinctly separate from military science, criminology and penology and deserves to be treated as a separate and independent social science.

The word 'Police' in its broadest sense means that species of governmental activity which has for one of its chief objects -- the protection of the lives and property of the persons within the state and to detect and bring criminals to justice. The old notion, entertained at one time by certain persons that a police officer has to be a "bully" and a "strong muscleman" for keeping everyone in his place by loud voice, if not by actual force, has now become largely outdated. Today we frequently have the picture of the policeman politely escorting an elderly lady or a child across the street or cheerfully giving required help, guidance or information to a stranger or perhaps in his spare time serving as a sponsor for a Boy's club. The Englishman has long regarded any London Bobby as his personal friend, guide and philosopher. The nature of a police officer's work requires him to be informed on many different subjects from criminal law, scientific criminal investigation, interrogation, detection, arrest etc., etc. The police officer's calling is a very old one but it is just in the process of developing into a profession. The subjects required to be learnt by police are many and developed at different times in different countries. Today policing has been termed as Police Science for the purpose of christening the body of knowledge as a separate branch of social sciences.

Although policing is relatively a young and developing branch of knowledge, its problems are age-old and thoughtful men of all periods of history have attempted to find solutions to the policing problems of their age. Police, like other young social sciences, is yet to be accepted as an academic discipline throughout the world. The functions, duties, responsibilities and expectations from the police are continuing to expand yet the development of literature on police in the past has been rather slow. Science is an accurate and quantitative description of events in a systematic manner. Science is an attempt at handling of related data in order to establish hypotheses, theories and verifiable laws. Police to a great extent fulfils the above requirements and can be considered a Social Science. The science of policing like other social sciences, has overlapping interests with its neighbouring sciences such as political science, public administration, sociology, psychology, and history. Many promising opportunities for studies can be ahead where police science blends with other social sciences. The science of policing has grown up as an academic discipline during the last four decades. Police Science is a systematic branch of knowledge which studies the behaviour and experience of the police personnel in a given socio-political system.

The science of policing is a young and fast developing branch of systematic knowledge about police. Police science has the following essential characteristics of a social science.

1. As a social science police science studies facts and realities about police. Its subjects are facts not ideals, realities of life not abstract formulations. It deals with policing in different societies.

2. Universalism -- Police exists in some form or the other in all human societies and it has certain common elements. Coercive power of the society is generally a distinguishing feature of police in all social systems.

3. Verifiable -- Police science has certain limitations in forming laws and principles but police theories prove true of every verification and re-verification. Finger-prints of no two individuals are similar can be verified at any time.

4. It employs the scientific method -- Police science employs the scientific methods of enquiry such as case history, questionnaire, interviews, observation, etc. In police science, there are various sociological methods which are being used by researchers to-day.
5. Police science delineates cause-effect relationships. Police science finds an answer to 'how' as well as 'why' of various human activities and relationships related with police work.
6. Objectivity -- Police science provides an unbiased and objective study.
7. Police science is both theoretical and applied science.
8. Police science is both a rational and an empirical science.
9. Police science is a social and not a natural science.
10. Police science is a categorical and positive science and not a normative science.

The science of policing aims at providing with:

1. a realistic understanding of the mission of law enforcement;
2. a first hand view of law enforcement in action;
3. exploration of various specialised areas of law enforcement required in modern day policing;
4. multi-disciplinary approach to the study of criminal behaviour, law enforcement, forensic science, criminology, and other police concerned subjects;
5. study of administration of police in various socio-political systems;
6. analysis of the sociology of policing in its various facets, and anomic phenomena such as assassinations, riots, and demonstrations and directs attention to the entire gamut of police administration within a society.

"Police science" needs to be studied for the following reasons --

1. No society, whatever its state of development can survive and maintain social discipline without the presence of the institution of police in some form or the other.

2. Policing in some form or other is essential for all societies and all political entities for the survival and continuance of certain accepted social norms and practices in daily life.
3. Police has a crucial role to play in modern life and no activity of human beings can go on unhampered unless there are regulatory restrictions and effective enforcement of laws of the society.
4. "Policing" as a science will help in building up professionalism in police organisations and will provide more useful service to the society.
5. Police in the third world countries are required for internal security duties and for ensuring smooth progress of development works and schemes.

The science of policing deals with various aspects of "policing" and primarily is concerned with a theoretical and practical understanding of the police in a systematic and scientific manner. It gives us theoretical and applied perspective of the police work. Police science provides us with a scientific and inter-disciplinary approach to the police subjects and is basically concerned with how the dicta of police work are learnt and transmitted from generation to generation of policemen.

Social Sciences -- A Disintegrating Family of Inter-Disciplinary Areas

"Social Sciences" is a broad term and refers to that group of sciences which are studies in human behaviour in their various perspectives. The social sciences deal with the most complex phenomena of all. It is difficult enough to understand the human individual apart from his social behaviour; it is all the more baffling to try to bring order and simplicity into the intricate pattern of social inter-action. Sociology, economics, political science, anthropology, public administration, psychology are some of the well accepted social sciences. Anthropology, the science of man; economics, science of economic behaviour; political science, the science of political behaviour, are all part of social sciences. During the last few decades social sciences are having a disintegrating family of inter-disciplinary areas, giving recognition gradually to new sciences. Psychology as a separate science was recognised near the end of the last century and it is usually credited to Wilhelm Wundt(1832-1920). A study of human activity in a social setting under which man lives; the family, the community and the larger society with all its political, economic and social institutions cannot be studied from any single standpoint, a number of different fields of inquiry have developed such as history, anthropology, economics, geography, political science, sociology and other specialities. Taken together these are known as "social sciences". As methods of study became more sophisticated and tools of enquiry were refined; it was inevitable that specialisations gave birth to new disciplines and approaches. All social sciences have two foci of interest--basic research and applied research. Basic research is concerned with the quest for knowledge while applied research seeks to improve the human conditions by discovering something that can be put to practice. Although policing has been an integral part of all societies, specialised basic research and applied research on policing gradually led to the creation of a separate branch of knowledge. The social sciences, which until few decades ago were very limited in number now have considerably multiplied. New disciplines are emerging tending to elaborate the higher synthesis of the social sciences and to define their individual places in the universe of knowledge. Police science has been accepted in the United States of America and in some other developed countries as an independent branch of knowledge because it contains essential elements of a social science. Scientific method, factual subject matter, universal applicability, vindictive nature of its laws and establishment of cause - effect relationship are the essential characteristics of a social science. Viewed in this perspective, Police science can be accepted as a newly developing science. Social sciences proceed upon the assumption that man is the central figure and being related to the study of complex man the social sciences have comparatively less exactness. Social sciences investigate laws related to man or man's socio-economic or political behaviour. The basic elements of social sciences cannot be separated analytically and because of their lesser exactness, social sciences can make comparatively fewer predictions. Social sciences provide comparatively lesser scope for measurement of subject matter and therefore objectivity is achieved with difficulty in social sciences. Police Science is gradually emerging as an independent social science. In the United States of America there are more than 85 universities which offer master's degree in police science and criminology and there are more than 58 universities which offer Doctorate degrees (Ph.D.) on police science and criminology. Police science as a subject is also covered in public administration which is also being considered a separate social science. Each social science has developed more or less distinctive techniques, instruments, routines and areas of knowledge. One is entitled to call any branch of knowledge as a science if its theories are progressively refined and tested by observation and if the ideals of objectivity and exactness guide inquiry. Police science shares with other social sciences the task of scientific exploration of human behaviour in its given socio-economic and political setting. There is no hard and fast division between one social science and another nor there should be any. There are however important differences of emphasis that mark off one discipline from another. Police science is primarily concerned with - developing an empirical science of "Policing" and trying to apply scientific methods of research to build up theories and models. Police science is a social and not a natural science. Police science is both a rational and an empirical science. Comte held that society is a totality and its study should be done as a whole. According to Comte, sociology is the sole social science but sociologists today do not agree with Comte's theory. There can be no denying that police science is gradually emerging as a separate discipline and it has its necessity and utility in the present age of division of labour and specialisation. Police science can be regarded neither as the handmaid nor the mistress of the social science but as their sister. Police science covers various aspects of police administration in various politico-social set-up and studies crime and criminals in its multi-dimensional viewpoints. Police science is the science of law enforcement and "security of the State". Police science is also like military science, a branch of knowledge whose application is needed by field officers to enforce laws and regulations of the state and to secure safety and security for the citizens against criminals and law offenders.

Police science has no quarrels with public administration, criminology, political science or forensic science. Police science has its own independent literature as do other complementary disciplines of knowledge. Police science has like every other discipline, its philosophers, elucidators, theoreticians, surveyors and its charlatans. Police science is no exception to the broad pattern of other disciplines. Every discipline interfaces with those at its periphery--police science also interfaces with politics, management, public administration, criminology and other allied social sciences. Those who believe that police work can and ought to be reduced to a science and that its organisation and management merely require an applied social technology, thereby demonstrate neglect of, or indifference to the nature of the activity which police officers undertake. [(1)] All police education and training should endeavour to promote the growth of a new science and art of policing which is required in the way of excellence in police work around the world.

Police Science: The Applied and the Normative Areas

'Police-Science' aims to understand various facets and phenomena related to the functions of police in relation to a given socio-political structure in its all aspects. How to investigate a crime, how to interrogate a suspect, how to make police arrangements for fairs and public functions, how to enforce laws and arrest offenders, how to carry out preventive and pro-active patrolling and surveillance and all practical aspects and applied areas of police science. Just as our present day society is complex, so is policing. Most police agencies define police role as generally under following five major headings:

(a) Police as a law enforcement agency.

(b) Police as an arm of the executive government.

(c) Police as the protector of rights and liberties of citizens.

(d) Police as a social service and agents of social change.

(e) Police with a role in political development. [(2)]

Police science deals with not only applied art of policing but also with the normative aspects of the profession. Like all professions, code of conduct has been made for police officers almost in all countries. Knowledge of the police job, insistence upon high quality of professional ethics by senior peer groups, rigorous organisational discipline within the profession and a system of inbuilt incentives and professional disapprobation are some of the well-known normative areas of police profession. From genuine professionalism stems genuine service and professionalisation in its ultimate produces more effective policing. [(3)] Policing is a prestigious and valued responsibility involving considerable skills, knowledge and expertise at a variety of tasks under frequently trying circumstances. Police often complain that the public does not perceive them this way. Probably proper and fuller development of "science of policing" will give the public some concrete ideas about their difficult and challenging professional tasks. Police profession should mature by researching and perfecting their methods of operations, by modernizing their technologies, by emphasizing and demanding the strictest admission standards and training possible and by having the self-discipline and self-consciousness to realize the importance of their idealized forms in the public mind. Policeman as a friend, philosopher and guide to the common man should be one of the ideals of police profession. Nothing could advance the police profession faster than a radical shift in the attitude on the part of the police leaders and administrators. Police managers must come to grips with new social thinking, new social values and new social ethics so that police profession may fulfil its social responsibilities and may achieve the public service ideal both in form and substance. [4]

Police Professionalism will help in Developing the Science of Policing

Policing is now accepted as an altruistic profession along with medicine, nursing and teaching. [5] Before the police as a formalised institution and a paid profession came into existence the task of policing in most countries was a co-operative community effort. [6] During the medieval period in England mode of policing was done through the mutual pledge system which encouraged responsibility among local citizens and their associations to maintain law and order and perform watch and ward duties. Gradually policing has been developed as a full time profession with its own code of conduct and professional training.

Distinction Between Police Science and Criminology

According to E.H. Sutherland and D.R. Cressey, the science of criminology "includes within its scope the processes of making laws, of breaking laws and of reacting towards the breaking of laws." [7] In criminology the sociology of law, criminal etiology and penology are studied in depth. The major concern of the sociology of law is to critically examine the impact of various legal systems upon crime and we also investigate the effects of present law upon crime and study the possible reforms in the laws in order to prevent and control the occurrence of crime. The department of criminal etiology studies the social and personal factors responsible for the occurrence of crime and growth of criminals. Police science studies much more than criminology alone because it covers police administration, police procedures and police techniques in various socio-political systems and why crime and criminals continue to operate therein.

Is there a "Science of Policing"?--Some Nagging Doubts

The science of policing has not been so far given the proper status of a science in the classics of knowledge -- *Encyclopaedia Britannica*, *International Encyclopaedia of Social Sciences* or in *Everyman's Encyclopaedia*. The science of policing is a new and developing one that can be defined as " the science dealing with investigation of crime". [8] According to many thinkers, the science of policing at its present stage of development cannot be considered a full-fledged science. Although some police administrators prefer to think of police work as a science, [9] it is very much of a folk art taught and learned on the streets. [10] The science of policing is a social science which is concerned with police work in its total ramifications. The scope of science of policing extends not only to the police duties, responsibilities and problems but also to the society and state where policing is carried out. The science of policing is not regarded as a science by many thinkers because in their opinions --

(1) "Police thinkers do not agree on principles, methods and conclusions on the various police subjects.

(2) "It lacks continuity of development.

(3) "Future course of action cannot be predicted in the science of policing.

(4) "Experiments are not possible.

(5) "The contents of police science are wide, uncertain, diffused and complicated.

(6) "It is not possible to reach a uniform principle or universal conclusion through observation or experiments". [10a]

There are definite elements of truth in the above mentioned arguments, but the science of policing like sociology and political science, can be described as a fairly unified mass of knowledge relating to a particular subject, acquired by systematic observation, experience or study. Without being an exact science, the science of policing has been responding to the needs of the time and is approximating itself to the claim of being called a "social science".

Police administration is not applied mechanics, but a living, breathing organism shaped by the political, economic and social trends of the time and the country. Policing, in one form or the other has always existed in all societies and various concepts of policing developed in due course of time in accordance with the nature and genuine disposition of the people of various countries. The science of policing is the newly developing science with inter-disciplinary approach which studies all branches of knowledge relating to police work in its total ecological context and also concerns with investigation of crime, detection of offenders and role of police as a public service agency. August Vollmer asserted the need for a professional training to policeman comparable to that of the lawyer or the physician.

Professionalism can produce more effective policing to the people in general. Professionalism in the police service requires professional autonomy, specialisation, technical skills, professional commitment and social value of the police work. Professionalism requires expertise based on a systematic body of knowledge, high standards of admission, lengthy inservice training, pride in membership, functional exclusiveness, specialisation and vocational commitment to the police service.

The science of policing is gradually coming up of age. Because of a radical contribution made by the sixties and seventies to policing and to crime control, foundations to a science of policing has been laid down. [11] Compared with the primitive level of knowledge of police matters less than two decades ago, the beginning has been significant.

At the present stage of development of science of policing it is too ambitious to conceive that it is possible to identify and develop a coherent body of systematic theory which is substantially independent of other social sciences and will concern itself only with science of policing. Science of policing however should adopt a holistic concept of the meaning of knowledge. The acquisition of knowledge in science of policing must be perceived as a synthesising exercise rather than as a specialising one. The science of policing is, unlike other disciplines an action-oriented social science which is engaged in the task of implementation of public politics. Police work should be analysed and studied as a generic process with universal applications.

The Nature and Scope of the Science of Policing

Science of policing is today under study by political thinkers, public administrators, police functionaries, researchers and sociologists in the United States of America and other advanced countries as a new developing science. Police leaders in many countries claim police as a full-fledged science. Every practitioner of a profession or vocation naturally seeks to elevate the public image of his work, not for status or ego satisfaction alone but to set higher standards of performance for his chosen vocation. Police profession has, by now developed a fair amount of scientific literature with a wide ranging knowledge, information, skills in various related fields, particularly in areas such as ballistics, fingerprint analysis and detection work. But an average working police officer is not yet a police scientist; he is a practitioner of a craft whose individual performance and contribution to the broad mission of the police has to be individually judged. Judged by the standards of performance of 95 per cent police personnel, police work is still only an art and a craft. But it is high time the police profession should march towards the goal of making and building the police science. It was Colquhoun who made a great statement in 1795 in his treatise, heralding a new police era in the following words :- "Police in this country may be considered as a new science; the properties of which consist not in the judicial powers which lead to punishment, and which belong to Magistrates alone; but in the prevention and detection of crimes and in those functions which relate to internal regulations for the well ordering and comfort of civil society." [12] (Treatise on the police of the Metropoles - Preface.) In recent years police science has emerged as a subject of study in many American universities with a syllabus of considerable breadth, depth and relevance to police work. Comparative police studies, police principles and ethics, police strategy, management and administration constitute the core study of police science. Criminal law, criminology, penology, forensic science and criminalistics provide additional subjects for police science syllabus.

The science of policing can be a systematic study with an inter disciplinary approach to the various problems of policing and analysis of police personnel from supra-disciplinitarian angle. The nature and scope of science of policing can include the following in the opinion of the author :-

(1) The science of policing can constitute a supra-disciplinary effort focusing on police administration, police activities, police procedures and police personnel.

(2) It can be based on researches with analytical approaches and draw its findings, theories, hypotheses and concepts from behavioural sciences, management science, social sciences and other modern areas of study.

(3) Using pure and applied research methodology, science of policing can be concerned mainly with improving "Policing" through the use of systematic knowledge, structural rationality, organised activity and objective thinking.

(4) In common with all applied scientific knowledge, the science of policing can be instrumental-normative in principle and can gradually develop its own concepts and theories.

(5) Police science can constitute a new body of systematic and empirical knowledge about "policing" and "police professionals". It can cover the cross disciplinary knowledge involved in the formulation, analysis, implementation and evaluation of police problems. Its boundaries cannot be precise and can cut across traditional academic disciplines

such as political science, sociology, psychology, management science, public administration and behavioural science.

The science of policing can build systematic knowledge which should seek to analyse police activities, police problems and police professionals in an objective, scientific and systematic manner. The science of policing can be developed through analytical and evaluative research on various aspects of police work. Description oriented researches, explanation oriented researches, criticism oriented researches and evaluation oriented researches on "policing" have ultimately resulted in publication of useful literature on the subject. Now-a-days scientific analysis, operational research, management science, model building, statistical techniques and methodologies are applied in police research. The science of policing today covers a vast field of knowledge dealing with general law enforcement, criminalistics, corrections, crime investigation and interrogation, criminology and penology, crime prevention, traffic, commercial investigation, police communication, police intelligence and security operations, police management, police administration and police personnel management.

The maturation of the science of policing can be brought about by bridging the separation of basic and applied research on police through synergetic relationship between police theory and police practices. The specialist/generalist dichotomy can be rendered irrelevant with the emergence of police scientists who would be specialists in general approach and method. Inter-disciplinarity in policy research can eventually given way to supra disciplinarity and would result in development of professionals trained in police science. During the last thirty years a new field of knowledge called "Police Science" has been taking shape. Police administration is dramatic, colourful and centrally related to the processes of governance and struggles over wealth, power and prestige, with control of the police frequently determining which values should be stressed and which groups should receive advantages. The science of policing is a young science dealing with the fast developing field of new knowledge about what constitutes the essence of policing and what are the mechanics by which police are controlled. The science of policing can be a systematic study of police work, police role and all knowledge that is required for the police profession.

The science of policing has been so far treated as a part of Public Administration or social science but gradually it is becoming customary for some universities in the U.S.A. to offer Graduate and Master's Degree with "Police Science" as a major subject. This new developing science is actually building its own knowledge from a cluster of inter-disciplinary fields. When the term "Science of Policing" is mentioned, one is inquisitive to find out who originated police science. Police is an old profession and no society can exist without some institution of social control. Kautilya's classical work *Arthasastra* written in about B.C. 310 for the first time provides valuable knowledge of police functions and police organisations. It was Rollin M. Perkins who wrote his *Elements of Police Science* (The Foundation Press in Chicago) in 1942 where the science of policing was first recognised as an independent field of knowledge. *Modern Law Enforcement and Police Science* by E.W. Williams and Dr. Samual J. Saden (Charles C. Thomas 1967) *Police Science for the Young American* by V.A. Leonard and *Introduction to Police Science* by John L. Sullivan (Mc Graw Hill, New York 1971) are some of the books, having title of police science though these books have not dealt with the definition, scope or the history of police science.

The explosive growth of literature on police during the last four decades leads one to question the heritage, present condition and future of the discipline of policing. The amorphous body of research by social scientists and the writings of a large number of police leaders and practitioners in various countries constitute in a very meaningful sense a coherent and systematic discipline and have helped in making policing a developing new science. The science of policing today is only in its infancy. O.W. Wilson(1972), Joseph Wood (1973), Fosdicks(1916), (1920), (1958) and Vollmer(1937) are some of the prominent police scientists who have recognised the need for a separate discipline for police professionals and have in their own ways contributed to the development of the science of policing. Sleeman, Dzerzhnisky and Edgar Hoover have made valuable contribution to the development of the science of policing. Le-Reynie of France deserves the credit for setting up in Paris "an effective and efficient metropolitan police force". Charles Rowan and Richard Mayne as the first Commissioner of Metropolitan Police, London worked out the philosophy and organisational structure of London police and gave its principles and guidelines which gained universal acceptance. Kawaji Toshiyoshi made valuable contribution to the development and growth of police organisation in Japan. Samuel B. Steel made useful contribution to the evolution of the North-West Canadian Mounted police. August Vollmer of USA, Louis Lepine of France, Scholer of Austria and Louwage of Belgium have also made valuable contributions in their own ways in the development of police systems. Edward Richard Henry, former IGP of Bengal (1891-1901) contributed to the development of scientific investigation through his work on finger prints. Shri B.N. Mallik has made pioneering contribution by giving "philosophy for the police" and by writing a number of original books on police and allied matters. His book *World's Great Policemen* has greatly contributed to the development of science of policing. Dr. Anand Swarup Gupta, S.K. Ghosh, Dr. P.D. Sharma, S.C. Misra, Venugopal Rao, S.M. Diaz, G.C. Shinghvi, N.S. Saksena, P.R. Rajgopal, Dr. K.M. Mathur, J.C. Madan and K.F. Rustomji have also made useful contributions to the development of literature on police administration and science of policing.

The Expanding Frontiers of the Science of Policing

The subject cannot retain or build its academic standing unless its pioneers and thinkers are studied, analysed and scrutinised by some researchers. The police thoughts were developed by police officers who practised the profession and wrote their reminiscences and biographies. Police practitioners and police leaders at times wrote certain instructions, orders and guidelines for their subordinate police officers and some police thoughts owe their origin to them. Some administrative thinkers also at times made valuable contributions to police thoughts in their writings on public administration. University professors who taught police subjects in various police *academies* or universities have also given their ideas and contribution to the science of policing. Recently a large number of researchers have started carrying out research studies on police problems. It is not possible nor perhaps necessary to review the entire literature available on police. However, certain broad generalisations and bird's eye view of the history of police thoughts have been attempted in this chapter.

Historical analysis seeks discovery of ways in which a particular aspect of reality of police as an institution has been shaped by earlier forces and events. In the context of policing, one is obliged to identify the forces which gave rise to police and policing as we see them today. History of police thoughts can be reviewed from chronological order tracing the writings on police from ancient times to the present day.

Police literature can be divided into following broad sections --

(1) Biographies, reminiscences and experiences of police officers in general.

(2) Police systems and organisation including history of police in various countries.

(3) Police administration and police laws including police procedures, its role in Government, its relation with local government and legal enactment.

(4) Police operations, powers, functions and duties and modern aids to the police.

(5) Police personnel including recruitment and training, leadership, motivation, police ethics and behaviour, job performance, unions and police uniforms.

(6) Police fight against crime with the help of forensic science, medical jurisprudence and other technological advances.

(7) Police and society including police image and corruption.

(8) Miscellaneous police writings including paramilitary forces and their role as police agent.

(9) Police technology, computerisation in police and other scientific advances.

(10) Victimology is another developing branch of police science.

Kautilya--the Father of Police Science

Kautilya can be considered father of police science as he did pioneering work in the field of the science of policing. According to Kautilya, detection of crime and arrest of the suspicious, protection of civil population and prevention of illegal acts were the basic function of the police. Thus he can be considered the first police thinker. Kautilya devoted much of his attention to the position of spies in the field of politics and enjoined some obligations to villagers in providing security measures. Kautilya has given an elaborate system of espioange prevalent in his time and can be considered the father of intelligence and espionage. Kautilya's *Arthashastra* refers to a detailed police organisation -- a "Sangrahana" for 10 villages, a "Kharvatika" for 200 villages and a "Sthaniya" for 800 villages. [13] The classical source Kautilya's *Arthashastra* written in about B.C. 310 by Kautilya (Chanakya) the reputed minister of King Chandra Gupta Maurya, provides valuable information on the police and administration of justice. In Kautilya's *Arthsasthra* there is insistence on rigorous proof of guilt, the need for objective and scientific investigations and provisions of adequate safeguards against false accusations and miscarriage of justice. Kautilya devoted a whole chapter to the techniques of criminal investigation, criminal intelligence, forensic science and medicine, the personality traits of the criminals and methods of interrogation and thus did the pioneering work in the field of police science. He enunciated a progressive penal policy [14] and reiterated the wholesome principle of ensuring compensation to victims of crime. He thus did pioneering work in the field of victimology and criminology.

THE HISTORICAL DEVELOPMENT OF POLICE SCIENCE

(1) The Period of early thinkers (up to 1900)

A critical survey of ancient Indian epics would show that "Police Science in embryo" existed in ancient and medieval India and Kautilya can be considered the "father of the Police Science". The earliest reference and mention of a functionary doing policing, like watch and ward against thieves, is available during the Vedic era (see Kane, P.V.(1946) --*History of Dharma Shastra*, Vol. III). The *Rigveda* speaks of the spies (SPASAM) of Varuna. They sit down around him (1.24.13). They are indeceived and wise (VI-675) in the *Artharva Veda* (VI 164). According to the mythological belief Varuna's spies descending from heaven traverse the world, and through "thousand eyes they look over the earth" (Besides Varuna spies are attributed to Mitra (VIII-613) to Agni (VI 43), to Soma (D-73.4), to demons combated by Indra (1.37.8) and to the Gods in General (x 10.8) according to P.C. Chakravarti as mentioned in his book *The Arts of War in Ancient India,* Chapt. VIII. The *Rigveda* and *Atharva Veda* have mentioned certain kinds of crime and punishments known to the Vedic people and have mentioned about criminal justice system.

In Chanakya's *Arthashashtra* there is a detailed description of "police organisation" and "system of espionage" and he deserves to be called "the father of Police Science". He touched upon the techniques of criminal investigation, criminal intelligence, forensic science and medicine and methods of interrogation.

In B.C. 1800 great Indian saint and law giver Manu classified offences under eighteen heads, twelve of which related to civil and contractual obligations while the rest were criminal offences. Insult (*Perushya*), violence (*Sahasa*), theft (*Stheya*) and adultery were the criminal offences punishable by the State. Manu gave the *Dandaneeti* (science of punishment) and recommended institution of prison. The word "police" was first used by the French in 1660s to describe something akin to the modern usage. The word first appeared in English in 1714 when Commissioner of Police was appointed in Scotland Yard. If we carry out a historical analysis of published literature on police, we find that Patric Colquhoun wrote " A treatise on the commerce and police on the River Thames" in 1800 A.D. and later "A treatise on the Metropolis" (London) in 1806. In 1829 John Wade published A *Treatise on Police and the crime of the Metropolis*. In 1844 W.A. Sleeman wrote *Rambles and Recollections of an Indian Official* (London). In 1849 the Central Police Station at Scotland Yard were connected with a telegraph line. In 1850 Allan Pinkerton founded his own detective agency and is thus considered the founder of largest detective agency in the world. In 1873 Edward H. Savage publised his book *Police Records and Recollections of Boston by Daylight and Gaslight.* Edward Savage began the practice of taking home convicted criminals in lieu of their being sent to prison thus becoming the father of probation. In 1878 telephone was first installed in a police station in Washington in 1878. In 1885 Augustine Costello wrote *Our Police Protectors*. In his book author made an admirable study of police department including sketches of its most prominent personalities. In 1887 George Walling wrote *Recollections of a New York Chief of Police*. In 1887 John J. Flinn and John E. Wilke wrote *History of Chicago Police*. In 1891 Augustine Costello wrote *History of Police department or Jersey city.*

In 1894 Arthur C. Crawford wrote *Reminiscences of an Indian Police official.* During this period most of the writings are reminiscences of police officers or were books dealing with history of small police forces. In 1880, Alphonse Bertillon, Chief of the Criminal Identification Bureau of the Paris Police had developed the "Bertillon system" of Anthropometry (physical measurement) as the principal means of identification later utilised by the police throughout the world. The system remained popular till 1903. The death knell of Bertillon system was sounded in 1903 when Wills and Wilhim West, two American convicts were found to have identical measurements in the same prison. [(15)] In 1910 Henry system of classifying fingerprints was adopted. 1829 is an important year in the history of police science when the famous Metropolitan London police was formed by Sir Robert Peel. Peelian reform brought modern policing to the world. The twelve tenets of Peelian reform have become a legend all over the world. These tenets placed the police under government control for the first time and organised them along military lines. In 1839, Marine Police Force was incorporated in the Metropolitan Police Force as the Thames Division. The Fingerprint system for criminal investigation and the identification of criminals was invented in 1948 by Edward Henry, Inspector General of Police in Bengal (India). In 1899, the automobile was used in Police Work for the first time in Akron, Ohio, USA.

(2) The Early Nineteenth Century Thinkers (1900-1950)

During the period from 1900 to 1950, the science of policing was developed by many thinkers and writers. In 1900, dogs' training for police work was originally developed in Belgium. In 1901, Capt. W.L. Malvilla Lee wrote *A History of Police in England and Wales.* Green Garrow wrote his book *In the Royal Irish Constabulary* in 1905. In 1906 William Mc. Adoo wrote his book *Guarding a City* (New York) Facsimili transmission was introduced for police work in 1908 from Paris to London. August Vollmer introduced formal police training in 1908 in the USA. In 1916, first scientific crime laboratory in the USA was set up under the direction of a full-fledged forensic scientist. Regular police women were first appointed in Metropolitan police London in 1916. In 1909, W.A. Gayer wrote *Stepping stones to Police Efficiency*. In 1910, Leonhard Felix Fuld wrote *Police Administration - a critical study of police organisations in the United States and abroad.* In his dissertation he viewed crime and police as variables which could be manipulated through administrative tools. In 1911, Edmund Charles Cox wrote *Police and Crime in India.* In 1912, Gould Bury wrote *Life in the Indian Police.* In 1915-16, Raymond B. Fosdick wrote *European Police Systems* and in 1920 he wrote *American Police Systems*. He was a young civilian who became actively interested in police administration and wrote the above mentioned two authentic books on police systems. In 1920s police communication with teletype-writers was introduced for the first time. In 1920s the technique of identification of firearms on the basis of striated marking on bullet jacket was introduced. In 1921, the first modern polygraph was constructed by John A. Larson in California. In 1921, the first lie detector machine was built for use in criminal investigation. Sir Edward Henry between 1903-18 was instrumental in development of "the new science of Fingerprints". During his life time the new science of fingerprints was pioneered in India as a form of legal identification and later "the Henry system" was the standard finger printing technique used in Europe and America. (16) In 1915, Raymond Fosdick held that without a comparatively high ratio of police to population the beat system could not be effective. He wrote that Boston probably had the best police force in the country and held that the smaller the police force, the larger the beat, thus lessening the extent of personal contact between public and the police. (17) Arthur Wood wrote *Crime Prevention* in 1918 and *Policemen and Public* in 1919. S.M. Edward wrote the *Bombay City Police* in 1923 and *Crime in India* in 1924. In 1925, Bruce Smith wrote *The Police State*. In 1926, Sir William Nott Bower wrote his book *Fifty two years of a Policeman.* In 1929, August Vollmer became the first professor of Police Administration in the world by accepting the appointment at the University of Chicago. In 1929, J.F. Moylan wrote *Scotland and Metropolitan Police*. In 1930, Vollmer was responsible for creating the University Fingerprint and Identification Bureau at the University of Chicago and this was the first state Bureau in the U.S.A. In 1931, Cornelius Willemse wrote *Behind the Green Lights.* Vollmer was a pioneer in new concept of traffic law enforcement, the use of scientific crime detection procedure, the development of a motorized police force, use of research in determining the proper assignment of police manpower to patrol beats and professionalism in police service. In 1932, John Court Curry brought out his book on the Indian Police. In 1933, Cornelius Willemse published *A Cop Remembers* and Farlicq wrote *French Police from within.* In 1934, Fred Gilbert Blackeslee wrote *Police Uniforms of the World*, and William Charles Gwynn wrote *Imperial Policing*. Glover also brought out his work *English Police - its origin and development* in 1934. Alwyn Solmes in 1935 published his book *English policeman 1871-1935*. August Vollmer in 1936 published *Police and Modern Society* and Sir Basil Thomson wrote *Two Storeys of Scotland Yard.* In 1934 Daimbr-Dinz corporation began developing bullet proof windshields and windows for his automobile and armoured car was made available for Hitler by 1938. In 1936, Maurice Tomlin published *Police and the Public* and Kishan Puri published his *Memoirs of the Marwar Police (Jodhpur State)* in the same year. In 1942, O.W. Wilson wrote *Police Records - their installation and use* and in 1943 Charles Reith wrote *British Police and the Democratic Ideal.* In 1942, Rollins M. Perkins edited and published *Elements of Police Science* in which articles of many well-known American police thinkers were included. In 1944, James Mills wrote *Scottish Police an outline of their powers and duties* and in 1948 Moylan published his book *The police in Britain.* Audial surveillance and electronic waves dropping was perfected during Second World War. In 1949 H. Scott wrote the famous book entitled *Police Problems of today.* Rollin M. Perkins, the Frank C. Rand Professor of Law in Vanderbit University U.S.A. wrote *The Elements of Police Science* in 1942. *Elements of Police Science* covered criminal investigation, detection of counterfeit money, police courtesy, on the witness stand, maulage, photography, fingerprints, first-aid, revolver shooting, the law of arrest, traffic safety and criminal law and thus laid the foundation of Police Science.

(3) The Expansion Period (1950-1965)

After World War II hundreds and eventually thousands of institutions were established across the United States of America and many of which instituted police science programmes. Four year programmes resulting in Master's degree were also started. In 1950, J.N. Dwivedi published his book *Police Powers and Duties.* In 1951, J.M. Hart published his book entitled *British Police.* In 1952, O.N. Nilson wrote *Police Planning* and R.L. Holcomb wrote *Police Patrol.* In 1953, Gour D. Douglas wrote a *Study of Police Employment and Training in Kansas,* G. Howard wrote *Guardians of the Queen's Peace.* In 1954, Joshua H. Eagel wrote *Police Stations planning and specifications.* R.S. Kaushal wrote *Police and the Public;* S.T. Hollins wrote *No Ten Commandments Life in the Indian Police.* In 1955, C.C.H. Moriarty wrote *Police procedure and administration* and H.S. Dewhurst wrote *The Rail, road Police.* In 1956, Raymond E.Cliff wrote *A Guide to modern Police thinking,* P.N. Ashenhust wrote *Police and the People;* Charles Reith published *A new study of police history;* Reynolds wrote *Police headquarters* and Tom Fallon wrote *River Police.* In 1957, Richard Harrison wrote *the C.I.D. and the F.B.I.,* S.Wollin and R.M. Slausser edited *The Soviet Secret Police,* Beveridge wrote *Inside The C.I.D,* Gabard E. Caroline and John P. Kenney wrote *Police writing,* Wilson wrote *Police Planning;* Dr. L. Korken wrote *Ethics in Police Service,* Phillip John Stead wrote *The Police of Paris* and W.H. Parker wrote *Parker on Police.* In 1958, John Griffin wrote *Statistics essential for police efficiency.* In 1959, A.C. Germann wrote *Police Personnel Management,* Alan Garfitt wrote *The book for Police* and P.B. Weston wrote *Police promotion quizzer.* In 1958, V.R. Krishna Iyer published his book *Police in a welfare State.* In 1959, John Coatman wrote *Police;* Thomas M. Frost wrote *A forward look in police education,* John P. Kenney wrote *Police Management Planning* and K. Krishna Murthi wrote *Police powers and duties.* In 1960, Bruce Smith wrote *Police systems in the United States,* G.E. Berkley wrote the *Democratic Policeman;* Foran wrote *the Kenya Police* and John. A. Gardiner wrote about *Traffic and the Police variations in the law enforcement policy.* For the first time in 1960 helicopters were used for traffic surveillance and in 1970s for general police work. In 1961 G. Douglas Courley and Allen P. Bristow wrote *Patrol Administration,* Higgins Lois Lundell wrote *Police Woman's Manual,* Allen Bristow and E.C. Gabard wrote *Decision making in Police Administration.* In 1962, A.C. Germann wrote *Police Executive Development;* Charles Reith *wrote the Blind eye of history - a study of the origin of the present police era;* Epstein wrote *Inter-Group relations for*

Police officers; Frank Elmas wrote *the Police as a Career;* J.E. Curry and Glen D. King wrote *Race Tensions and the Police;* Mary Holman wrote *The police officer and the child,* Cland R. Sowle edited *Police power and individual freedom- the Quest for balance.* In 1963, Allen Z. Gammage wrote *Police Training in the UnitedStates;* Arther Siegal, Philip J. Federman and Douglas G. Shultz wrote *Police Human Relations Training;* and G. Douglas Courley wrote -- *Police and the Public.* In 1964, Fred J. Cork wrote *the F.B.I. Nobody knows*; J. Delarue wrote *The history of the Gestapo,* Nelson A. Watson edited *Police and the Changing Community;* Camer wrote *The World's Police*; Juby E. Towler wrote *The Police role in racial conflicts,* V.A. Leonard wrote *Police organisation and Management,* Richard H. Blum edited *Police Selections*, Joseph H. Fichter wrote *Police handling of arrestees;* Ben Whitaker wrote *The Police* and Michael Banton wrote *The Police in the community.* In 1965, C.V. Hearn wrote *A duty to the Public - a frank assessment of today's police force;* James Brennan and Donald W. Olmstead wrote *Police work with delinquents - analysis of a training programme;* S.K. Ghosh wrote *Police and the Public;* S.C. Consul wrote *Laws relating to Police personnel in India;* William H. Hewitt wrote the *British Police Administration;* Robert W. Hodge wrote *The Public, the Police and the administration;* and Geoffry Marshall wrote *Police and Government - The state and account ability of the English Constable.*

Police Vehicles - Ever since the first organised law-enforcement agencies were formed, the need for some form of transport has been recognised. Motor cycles, cars, jeeps, aircrafts and helicopters are used as police transport in various countries. The police became mechanised towards the end of the 19th century with the introduction of the bicycle which enabled the patrolling officer in sparsely populated area to cover a much larger beat. In 1899, the automobile was used in police work in Akron Ohio, the USA but police mobile for patrolling were introduced in 1910 in Berkeley by August Vollmer. It was not until after World War I that the automobile was introduced for police work. The Chief of Police reluctantly exchanged his pony and trap for a Ford, a Renault or a bull nose Morris and as the motor vehicles grew on the road, so the need for motorised patrols began to make itself felt. It was in the United States that the motor car first really came to be accepted for police work. Patrol cars did not make any great impression on British policing system until after 1945 and in France there are still many more motor cycles used than the patrol cars. The history of airborne police follows very much the same pattern with the United States leading the way, both in fixed wing aircraft and helicopters. [18] The French Gendarmerie Nationals has a number of helicopters.

West Germany, Indonesia, Japan and a number of countries now use helicopter for police work.

Central Reserve Police has been deployed throghout the country on law and order duties as can be seen from the following table:

State Wise Break Up CRPF Deployment 1989-90

S.No.	State	Total coys deployed			
		As on 1-1-89	As on 1-7-89	As on 1-1-90	As on 1-7-90
1.	Andhra Pradesh	18	6	6	6
2.	A & N Islands	3	2	2	2
3.	Arunachal Pradesh	22	17	17	17
4.	Assam	12	33	17	20
5.	Bihar	5	5	11	6
6.	Chandigarh	17	21	21	21
7.	Delhi	63	66	65	45
8.	Gujarat	7	1	1	1
9.	Haryana	8	8	8	2
10.	Jammu & Kashmir	27	36	56	122
11.	Manipur	21	21	21	20
12.	Mizoram	8	7	7	5
13.	Meghalaya	5	8	5	4
14.	Nagaland	10	3	3	6
15.	Punjab	191	189	174	194
16.	Pondicherry	2	1	1	1
17.	Rajasthan	8	12	14	14
18.	Sikkim	3	3	3	3
19.	SriLanka	13	13	1	-
20.	Tamil Nadu	7	-	-	6
21.	U.P.	5	5	5	11
22.	West Bengal	16	16	16	10
23.	Tripura	22	19	17	17

(4) Modern Police Thinkers (1966 to present day)

Era from 1966 can be called an era of police professionalism and specialisation. One of the more seminal works regarding the social psychological dimension of police work is the theoretical model of police cynicism developed by Nederhoffer (1967). Recent major works have addressed the issue of primary functions of police and have begun to piece together a pattern from the complexities and contradictions in the police mandate. (Skolnick, Wilson, Banton and Manning). Police, according to Manning, are confronted with an impossible mandate. In 1968, the U.S. Congress passed the omnibus Crime Control and Safe streets Act of 1968. The Act established the Law Enforcement Assistance Administration (LEAA) and Law Enforcement Education Programme (LEEP). LEEP provides loans to students pursuing a university education directly related to law enforcement and grants to police officers enrolled in law-enforcement related courses. By 1975 there were 1105 police science programmes in U.S. From 1966 onwards, there has been tremendous increase in police literature. On the average about 200 books are being published every year on police and allied subjects particularly in the USA, the U.K., India, Japan and other countries.

The era of Police Technology

The 70s and 80s represent a period in which the focus of attention shifted in large measure from the individual to group and entire police systems.

Charles R. Swanson and Leonard Territo have summed up these Police Scientific Technologies as under :-

1. Automatic Vehicle Monitoring (AVM) system which employs computer technology to show the actual location of each patrol car and result in more rapid responses to call for services and enhanced officer staety.
2. Distribution of hidden video cameras and automatic police signalling devices at various locations to combat commercial robberies and burglaries.
3. Development of quality control measures designed to improve and maintain performance of police laboratories, analysing evidence in criminal cases.
4. Use of anti-fencing or 'sting' operations with a view to identifying the receivers of stolen property, the apprehension of violators, the recovery of property and general disruption of stolen property markets.

5. Introduction of computer technology to perform a variety of tasks, including the preparation of crime statistics, crime analysis, personnel scheduling and record keeping.

6. Sensitivity to the need of victims and witnesses serving to improve the administration of justice. [18-a]

The General Theories of Police Science

Some of the most commonly accepted theories of police science are enumerated below:

1. Police, in some form or the other, existed in all societies and communities from time immemorial.

2. Policing forms an important system of 'Social Control' over the deviant behaviour of the members of the society.

3. There is great scope for discretion in law enforcement. Total and full enforcement of all laws by the police is neither desirable nor feasible.

4. Police, being the strong arm of the government, is generally the visible representative of the government. In a more symbolic sense police are the visible manifestations of public authority, of the existence of laws and the sanctions that can be imposed upon those who violate them.

5. In all societies, police activities are effected in many predictable ways by the socio-political environment in which the police operates. National culture and socio-political environment play important roles in police behaviour.

6. The problems of police regulations are shaped by a web of inseparable elements -- popular morality, political culture, the public's search for diversion and pleasure, social structure and economic infrastructure of the community.

7. Some amount of corruption is prevalent in all police organisations because police powers are bound to generate some corrupt practices. The exact incidence of corruption is generally linked to organisational policy and level of public reactions to such corruption.

8. The behaviour of individual policeman is shaped by the individual's career aspirations, his individual family background, organisational sub-culture and general socio-political milieu

in which he operates. Police perceptions of their role and of the behaviour required of them both as individuals and as an institution, appear to vary depending on the political context.

9. Police activities are generally ramified and varied in nature. The different activities which might be selected for analysis are large in number. Police are a diffuse topic for study, not a researchable explicandum.

10. The political culture of a community acts as a constraint on the style of law enforcement which is adopted. (J.J. Tobies - "Police and Public in the United Kingdom". In *Police Forces in History* of George L. Mosse. p.103). Police system is a sub-system of the criminal justice system. Criminal justice system is a sub-system of the governments. Administrative system is a sub-system of general political system of public administration. Thus police system represents a mere segment of the administrative sub-system of the wide political-social universe.

11. Police service today extends much beyond mere routine police duties of investigation, prosecution and intelligence work, "it has also as its objective the welfare of the individual and the society". Broadened concept of social responsibilities on the part of the police has given new horizons to the positive policy of police service. [19]

12. In most of the communities, the role of the police has been misunderstood and misconstrued. There is role dilemma in police work and in many societies police have been assigned "an impossible mandate". The police are viewed as performing a variety of contradictory roles.

13. The goals, objectives, philosophies and mission of law enforcement are generally kept vague and ambiguous. Paramount among these are the ambiguity surrounding the police functions and the numerous conflicts and contradictions inherent in police operations. [20]

14. In most of the societies including democratic ones, policemen are perceived to have coercive and restrictive duties which tend to control the rights and values of the citizens and tend to curtail human dignity. The more the police officer attends to his duties in sincere manner as both an instructor and a servant of society "the more likely it is that he will encounter severe criticism". [21]

15. Police organisations can usefully employ some of the modern management techniques and there is a great scope for adopting management techniques to police work and administration.

16. Crime is a socio-politico-economic phenomena and police alone cannot prevent it. There is an increasing rate of crime all over the world in its prevention. Crime is eternal as eternal as society. Crime cannot be abolished. Police can only have a marginal influence upon social control, which is a function of many other agencies and attributes of the social structure.

17. Police technology is an application of scientific principles, devices and methods to the functions of law enforcement. There is an immense scope for use of police technology in enhancing the professionalism in the police service. In 1889, the automobile was used in police work. Facsimile transmission (tele-photography) was introduced to police work in 1908. In 1920s, the technique of identification of firearms on the basis of striated markings on bullet jacket was introduced. In 1960s helicopters were used for traffic surveillance and in 1970s for general patrol work. New police technologies are bound to increase professionalism in police work.

18. In all societies, police are ultimately responsible and accountable for their performance to some agencies. The concept of police accountability is closely linked with the police image in the society.

19. Basic research is needed in many police fields for a proper analysis of crucial issues. Research is useful for measuring effectiveness, efficiency, workload and quality of police work. Basic research can provide the guidance for (1) more fully understanding the police business (2) improving its basic operations and their impact on the society. Police organisation has its own direct action and indirect action environments as given in the diagram.

DIAGRAM SHOWING POLICE ENVIRONMENTS

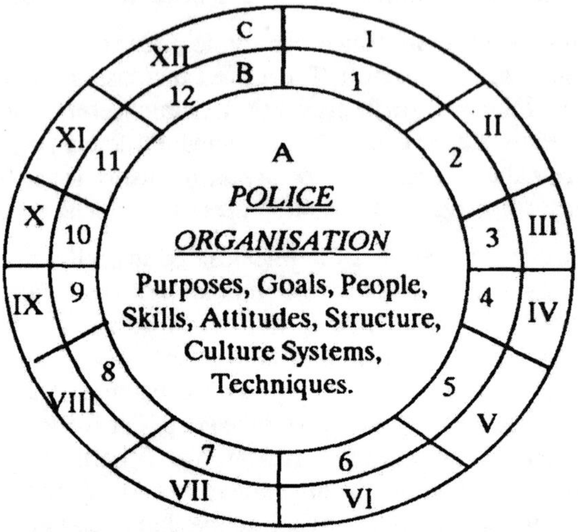

A - Structures, culture, techniques, systems, technologies, Forensic Sciences.

B - Factors in Direct Action Environment.

(1) Citizens
(2) Weaker Sections
(3) Juvenile delinquents
(4) Pressure groups, mobs
(5) Mass Media, Intelligence
(6) Political parties, trade unions
(7) Laws, Government
(8) Courts, Bars
(9) Other enforcement agencies
(10) Fundamentalists, terrorists
(11) Organised criminals, dacoits
(12) White collar criminals.

C - Factors in Indirect Action Environment.

(1) Constitution, national ideology
(2) Education, social structure
(3) Population growth, pluralism
(4) Culture, Change in moral values
(5) Economy, financial resources
(7) Unequal distribution of wealth, materialism
(8) Other national agencies
(9) International law, trade
(10) International crime and terrorism
(11) International enforcement agencies
(12) International relations press.

20. The ultimate objective of all efforts to improve the police is to increase their capacity to deliver high quality services to the government and the community and to equip them to do so in ways that are consistent with and support to high values which the society cherishes.

21. Police, in all societies, as law enforcing agencies, are aware that it must have greater support from prosecutors, law courts, correctional agencies and the people they serve if crime is to be curbed and controlled effectively. The most efficiently administered police agency will falter unless the community it serves genuinely supports it. Conversely a supportive community, intensely interested in reducing crime, will be ineffective if the police agency is complacent or incompetent. Vigorous cooperation is necessary.

22. There is a higher rate of criminality among the rulers compared to the general population although the criminality among the rulers tends to decrease dramatically with the restriction of their power through democratic constraints. [22]

23. There are no measurable and quantifiable indices of police effectiveness. The most usual indices of police effectiveness -- although they are not the only measures of good policing --are the number of indictable offences known to the police as a measure of their preventive success and the percentage cleared up as a guide to their detective skill -- although this includes only those cases able to be proved in the law-court. [23]

24. The internal security challenges particularly of terrorism and law and order administration are of great concern to the police all over the world. [24] Internal security training, research and reforms have to be carried out all over the world to keep police effective and capable of handling these challenges. All over the world police officers face challenges of law and order and internal security.

25. The pressures on policing are numerous. " There are countless things invisible, countless subtle pressures that act on police from day to day, year in and year out, in shape what they do and determine who they are. "[25] Political, economic, social, legal and ethical pressures always prevail on policing. Besides there are intra-departmental, extra-departmental and inherent pressures on policing.

26. There are so may rules, regulations, laws, Acts, by-laws and instructions involved in police work that even a most conscientious police officer cannot help but break at least a few of them during any normal tenure of a police officer. In many police organisations, many police officers are guilty of committing marginal crimes and there are also organisational deviance in certain police departments due to various reasons.

27. There are various styles of policing and these styles of policing are shaped by multiple situational and personal factors such as the values and priorities (and personality) of the individual police officer, the demands of the police work, the various political, social, legal and economic pressures brought to bear on the officers. According to Wilson there are "watchman", legalistic and a service style. [26] Five common styles of individual policing are "safe", "producing", "crime-fighting", "avoiding" and "street policing". [27] There are few "pure" examples of any one style of policing and generally there is a subtle mixture of various styles although there may be a pre-ponderance of any one style of policing.

28. Police are generally attuned to power games and power struggle and are experts at bureaucratic manipulation and pressuring. Policemen all over the world are required to deal with matters involving subtle human conflicts and profound legal and moral questions without being allowed to give the subtleties and profundities anywhere near the consideration they deserve. Bittner points out that all police departments employ some officers who like to harass people solely on the basis of their own gratuitous fascination with power and tend to assign these officers disproportionately to districts populated by alienated and powerless people. [28]

29. Bayley and Mendelsohn has given an interesting following list of "minority" attributes applicable to police officers. [29]

    (a) They are thought of in stereotypes;

    (b) They present a uniform appearance to non-police;

    (c) They have a low status in the community that is incongruent with their high self-image;

    (d) They are regularly treated to verbal and physical abuse;

    (e) They are convinced that they are systematically misunderstood;

(f) They are conscious of being protrayed in the media in a simplistic, detracting manner.

(g) They live in an environment of attitudes that seems quixotic and uncertain.

(h) They are respected in principle but not in fact and are expected to know their place and not be too pushy or offensive.

(i) In search of support, they turn inward on their own families and colleagues. They fear that people outside their community cannot be relied to be fair and impartial.

Police are often considered a necessary evil whose control should be limited, whose organisation should be fragmented and whose numbers should be minimal. However, all over the world there is constant increase in police numbers and there is proliferation of police organisations.

Police Science should be introduced as subject at the School, College and University levels as a separate subject

Police Science should be introduced as a full-fledged subject at university level and at school/college level. Bureau of Police Research and Development with the assistance of National Council of Educational Research and Training, should prepare books on police science which should be introduced in high school and in the plus-two syllabus of the Central Board of Secondary Education as a first bold step to educate children about police working. In consultation with University Grants Commission and Indian Council of Social Science Research, Bureau of Police Research and Development should get suitable literature prepared on police science so that it may be introduced as separate subject in Bachelor of Arts and Master of Arts degrees. In the United States, police science as a separate subject has been recognised in a number of universies even for Master of Arts and Ph.D. Degrees. A committee of delegates should visit some universities of the U.S.A. and should submit specific recommendations to the next Police Science Congress regarding the modalities and literature already available abroad on police science as a separate subject. Bureau of Police Research and Development, in consultation with universities and colleges should prepare text books on the following subjects before police science can be recognised as a full-fledged subject :

(1) Police Administration and procedure;

(2) History, origin and development of Police in various countries of the world.

(3) History of Police thoughts and thinkers;

(4) Criminal Investigation and police operations;

(5) Police weapons and uniforms;

(6) Traffic control and Road safety;

(7) Police Record Systems and statistics;

(8) Delinquency and crime prevention;

(9) Criminology and Penology;

(10) Forensic Science;

(11) Commercial and Industrial Security;

(12) Police, Society and the Government;

(13) Police, Social Service and Social Legislation;

(14) Modern management of Police organisations.

At present a number of foreign books are already available on various subjects and some of the good foreign books can be published as Indian editions. History of Police thoughts and thinkers is one subject on which, to the best knowledge of the author, no book or even article is available at present. Shri B.N. Mullik has done the most pioneering job in this field by bringing out a book entitled *World's Great Policemen*. In this book an attempt has been made to analyse the lives of seventeen prominent police personalities and find out what were the qualities which made them great. He divided these policemen into two categories viz. those who made history and those who were leaders and pioneers. There is a vast scope for research in this almost virgin field and in the first instance about forty prominent police thinkers of the world should be selected for indepth study of their contribution to police science. Collaboration with Indian universities and particularly departments of sociology, political science and public administration can be sought for research in this unexplored but rich field. There is a growing need for making the subject of Police Science and Administration a part of the university curriculum at least in some selected universities of India.

Osmania University, Hyderabad in India have done a pioneering job by introducing one optional paper on "Police Administration" as a part of Public Administration for Master's Degree. Other universities of India should also introduce "Police Administration" as a paper for Master's Degree in Public Administration. Recently Jammu & Kashmir University has started a paper on Police Administration. According to Normal J. Greenhill, to start with we should have(1) graduate qualification in police science as a necessary qualification for a fully professional grade of senior officers and (2) a diploma in police science as a necessary qualification for middle ranking officers (Sub-Inspectors).

University Grants Commission should accept in principle the proposal to have "school of police studies" in all universities of India in a phased programme of the years.

National Police Academy, Hyderabad can prepare training programmes for following six levels :

1. Primary School level
2. Higher Secondary School level
3. High School level
4. Ten Plus Two (intermediate level)
5. Graduate level
6. Post-Graduate level.

Just as we have military science as a subject, police science as a separate subject can be introduced at various levels. Suitable material for each level can be prepared by a committee of experts. At primary school level, police as a friend and guide can be projected who should be contacted for help. At higher secondary school level, traffic police, patrolmen and working of police outposts/police stations can be introduced. Thus for each higher level of education the scope of police studies can be widened and more subject matter can be introduced. At high school level, it can form part of civics and social studies. There is a long felt need for a school of police studies and an interdisciplinary approach to studies will be favoured.

Immediate need to develop Police Science and consolidate available literature

Proper documentation of available police literature is an urgent need. Police science can get the proper recognition in universities and colleges only when adequate literature is made available on various aspects/branches of police science and scientific documentation and consolidation of police literature is carried out on scientific lines. Police Science Congress should encourage police officers and other social scientists to carry out pure and applied research on various aspects of police science. In some selected universities 'chairs' for the police science should be started and eminent social scientists having interest in police science or retired senior police officers having aptitude for research and teaching should be selected as professors for the newly developing police science. Bureau of Police Research and Development can encourage basic research on police science by instituting fellowship at National Police Academy, Hyderabad and Internal Security Academy, Mount Abu. More and more scientific research should be carried out to bring out uniform principles, methods and procedures in police science. Policing had to be professionalised by developing Police science so that it may meet the challenges of a fast developing technocratic society. The International Association of Chief of police, the American Bar Association, the National Advisory Commission on Criminal Justice standards and goals, the Police Foundation and the Law Enforcement Assistance Administration are some of the organisations of United States of America who have worked towards this goal.

In the opinion of the author the following suggestions will go a long way in making "Police Science" more acceptable to the academic world of universities:

1. History of police science should be prepared by properly evaluating the original contributions made to this newly developing science by various police officers, social scientists and other scholars of eminence.
2. Original contributions to the police science made by various police practitioners, and police administrators in various countries should be recognised and evaluated on scientific lines.
3. Police as a subject should be gradually introduced to the students at various levels. At primary, secondary and higher secondary levels of education also, police as a service oriented organisation should be introduced to the students so that they may develop correct perspectives about police.
4. In some selected universities "Pre-degree Certificate in Police Science" should be awarded to those who study police science for two years course after Matriculation. Similarly "Degree Course in Police Science" can be started in selected universities. Police science as an optional subject can be introduced at Matriculation level. Necessary literature for such subjects should be prepared by the national level police institutions of the country.

5. International bibliography on selected police literature should be prepared and made available as a priced publication to the universities.

6. Certain selected police officers and police scientists should be sent abroad to visit existing "Departments of Police Science". More than hundred fifty programmes are being offered by more than fifty colleges and universities in the United States of America. The Bureau of Police Science, started at Iowa University, Iowa City, USA can be one of the important places to be included in the proposed foreign trip.

7. There is a need for international cooperation for bringing out "A Journal of Police Science" in which research papers, articles and surveys on police science can be published periodically.

8. Police science can flourish only if we involve academicians and universities. Hope for the future rests primarily upon a renewed emphasis on university professional education.

9. Positive police philosophy, professional specialisation, decentralisation, accountability, autonomy, modernisation, and professional code of conduct can be the main elements of the professionalisation of police. The time is fast approaching when the profession of police will be recognised as one to which no one will be admitted without a special certificate or diploma or degree to be issued only after a period of preparation, education and training to that now required in such fields as medicine and law. It means that new applicants will be selected from those thoroughly prepared in advance to take profession. Like other professional man, the police officer needs knowledge, high standards of ethics and personal conduct and an understanding of his role in the overall scheme of things.

Notes and References

1. David Bradley, Neil Walker and Roy Wilkie (1986) -- *Managing the Police, Law, Organisation and Democracy*, p.4.

2. Dr. K.M. Mathur (1987) -- *Administration of Police Training in India*, Gian Publishing House, New Delhi, p.32.

3. The Royal Commission on Police London - 1962, quoted by Pope and Weiner (1981) -- *Modern Policing*, London, pp. 65-67.

4. Dr. K.M. Mathur (1987) -- *Problems of Police in a Democratic Society*, RBSA Publishers, Jaipur, p.51.
5. A.C. German (1976) -- *Law Enforcement: A Look into the future -- The police chief*, p.24.
6. Ralph. A. Olmos (1974) -- *An Introduction to Police Community Relations* -- Charles C. Thomas, Publisher, Springfield Illinois, USA. p.5.
7. Sutherland E.H. and D.R. Cressey -- *Principles of Criminology*.
8. *A Supplement to the Oxford English Dictionary* Vol. III. p.622.
9. For example see O.W. Wilson and Roy C. Mclaren (1972) -- *Police Administration*, New York, McGraw Hill.
10. Richard J. Lundman (1980) -- *Police Behaviour - A sociological perspective*, Oxford University Press 1980 p.174. (10 a) Dr. K.M. Mathur -- "Is there a Police Science - Search for An Answer", All India Police Science Papers 1985, Shillong.
11. David John Farmer (1984) -- *Crime Control - The use and misuse of Police Resources*, Plenum Press, New York.
12. Colquohoun - *Preface to Treatise on the Police of the Metropolis*.
13. *Second Report of the National Police Commission*, Govt. of India, Aug. 1979, p.10.
14. R. Shama Sastry (1915) -- *Kautilya's Artha Sastra*.
15. Henri Souchon, -- "Alphonse Bertillon." In P.J. Stead(Ed) *(1968) -- Pioneers in Police went on strike*, (London Weidenfold Nicholson, app.2.
16. Thomas A. Reppetto (1978) -- *The Blue Parade*, The Free Press, New York, p.89.
17. Fosdick -- *American Police Systems*, pp. 121-22.
18. Wilson and McLaren (1983) -- *Police Administration - Structures, Processes and Behaviour*, Macmillan Co, p.8.

18a. Dr. K.M. Mathur - "Is there a Police Science - Search for An answer", All India Police Science Congrees 1985, Shillong.

19. Wilson and McLaren (1972) -- *Police Administration*. Mc Graw Hill, New York, p.6.
20. Herman Goldstein (1977) -- *Policing a Free Society*, Cambridge Mass Ballinger p.8.
21. G.F. Berkley (1969) -- *The Democratic Policeman*, Beacon Boston, p.6.
22. P. Sonokin and Walter A. Lunden -- *Power and Morality*. For further elucidation of the concept see S. Venugopal Rao (1977) -- *Power and Criminality*, Allied Publishers, Introduction pp. IX - XIX.
23. Ben Whitaker -- *The Police in Society*, p.73.
24. For full development fo the concept please see Dr. K.M. Muthur (1989) -- *Internal Security--Challenges* and *Police in a Developing Society*, RBSA Publishers
25. James F. Ahern (1972) -- *Police in Trouble*, New York.

26. James R. Wilson (1968) -- *Varieties of Police Behaviour, The management of Law and order in Eight Communities*, Cambridge.

27. Adrian Kinnane (1979) -- *Policing:* Nelson Hal Chicago, pp.75-76.

28. Bittner -- *The Functions of Police in Modern Society,* pp. 99-100.

29. D. Bayley and H. Mendelsohn (1969) -- *Minorities and the Police; Confrontation in America*, The Free Press, New York, p.54 quoted by Adrian Kinnane -- *Policing,* p.157.

CHAPTER - 3

COLLECTIVE VIOLENCE -- GENESIS AND RESPONSE

"WE REALLY understand very little about the origins and causes of human violence in all its daunting variety." [1] Violence is in simple terms the extreme form of aggression. Aggression denotes a "behaviour aimed at the injury of some object" [2] and is an act that delivers noxious stimuli to another person. Violence involves not only overt application of force resulting in an injury or destruction of person(s) or property or reputation but also overt threat of injury that may result in trauma to the victim. Violence invariably includes all types of behaviour either threatened or actual, that result in or are intended to result in damage to property or destruction or injury or death of an individual and thus have serious social implications. Violence in a modern society is a purposive social act negatively resorted to realise certain ends and interests in violation of the existing normative order of the society. Violence has been the most dramatic force in the corpus of myth and legends of people living in various cultures and societies in all ages. During the last 45 years India has witnessed many types of tribal, ethnic, communal, political, agrarian and collective violence on very large scales in various parts of the country. Giving labels to episodes of collective violence on the basis of a single cause or factor, communal, agrarian, caste based, election violence etc. is highly misleading because eruption of collective violence, almost invariably takes place on account of a multiplicity of causes. The causes of violence in a society tend to be varied, complex and deeply rooted in the community's historical, political and cultural development. Modernisation, accompanied by urbanisation, secularisation and industrialisation may often lead to societal violence in a pluralistic society committed to the ideology of economic growth and development. As a result of modern communications and technology, an international flow of revolutionary ideas and certain modes of violence have become accepted methods for correcting perceived social injustice. Rapid social change brings with it new expectations and as a consequence new frustrations leading to violence. [3] The Radical New Left Philosophy from Sorel, Sartre to Fanon has shown a tendency to transform macabre of murder and the morbidity of killing and bloodshed into a civilized man's sacred ritual for the redemption of the fallen. The nihilistic phenomenology of violence believes that "violence, like Achilles Lance, can heal the wound that it has inflicted." [4]

Violence can be defined as the illegal employment of methods of physical coercion, excessive, unjustified and unrestrained force, outrage, profanation or injury. The essence of violence is the inflection of uncalled for injury on other people, this injury may be mental or physical, violence can also be defined as the "illegal employment of methods of physical coercion for personal or group ends". Violence manifests itself in several ways and in varying degrees and is not infrequently, the most vital element which shapes decisions in present day society. Agitations, hartals, strikes, bandhs, gheraos, insurgencies, fasts, self-immolations, coercive public protests, all constitute integral parts of the syndrome of violence. Communal riots, linguistic agitations, labour strikes, demonstrations, looting and arson, assault and stabbing, tampering of telecommunication, attacks on tram cars, buses, petrol pumps, brick-batting, bayonet attack, shooting with fire-arms, attacks on police, destruction of public property are the main forms of violence which are committed in present day society. Unfortunately, violence according to Professor Sidney Hook, accompanies most mass movements today for three important reasons -- firstly, violence is dramatic and concentrates the attention of the community; secondly, violence is an involuntary act under the impulse of crowd mind in the face of resistance and in a sensitive situation any appearance of resistance is enough to spark off violence. "Any systematic and consistent refusal to use violence, no matter how extreme the provocation, would doom every movement of social reform to futility if it were faced by an intransigent foe whose liberty of action was not bound by the fetish of non-resistance." [(5)] Violence is a universal phenomenon and is present in some degree and in some form in every kind of social arrangement. Violence symbolizes the outward manifestation of participation of a newly awakened political group into the world of politics and at times violence acts as a "Danger Signal". [(6)] Violence makes the community "see" a socio-political evil and draws the attention of the political leaders in a powerful and dramatic way to the community's deep seated feelings of disgust and frustration. Violence servies as a "storm signal" on the political horizon and is often the "mid-wife" of change as the history of Chartism in England shows. Mass violence provides a tension - release to pent up mass frustration and an escape from the boredom of disgusting human existence. As Bernard Crick puts it, "Boredom is the only illegitimate child of conformity and physical violence becomes its inevitable bastard." Criminal violence, suicides, murders, riots and civil disorders are various forms of violent human behaviours. The existence of at least two more individuals or group in a conflict situation are necessary for violence to be committed creating two identities perpetrators of violence and victims of violence. Social violence assumes its true meaning when heightened emotions and sentiments of the people such as anger, revenge, hatred, frustration, envy and the like gather instrumental potency. The psychological perspective of group behaviour of violence has been studied by certain psychologists as an unconscious or irrational behaviour (See particularly Gustav Lepton (1960), S. Freud (1922), John David and Herbert Harari (1960), H. Edward Ransford (1968) Neil J. Smelsar (1962) and H. Blumer (1969). Social violence by a group is at times aimed at the task of fulfilling certain individual and mutual needs (See particularly Richard A. Berk (1974), Howard Raiff (1959, 1970), Herman Chernoff and Sincoln Moses (1959), Tom Hyden (1967) and Robert M. Fogeler (1971).

Professor Sidney Hook has enumerated three reasons for collective violence in mass movements. Firstly group violence is dramatic and concentrates the attention of the community by making a powerful emotional appeal to the heroic sentiments of sacrifice, honour and courage. Secondly, whatever be the nature of the social process, its ultimate constituents consist of a series of individual actions by individual man driven under the impulse of "crowd-mind" or "group-mind". Thirdly, "the threats of violence have won occasional concessions which would hardly have been granted out of admiration for the non-resistant spirit". Violence is often the "mid-wife of change" and the history of all countries show that violence is a universal phenomenon. Violence acts as a "Danger signal" and group violence, not infrequently, serves as a "storm signal" on the political horizon. The gap between the rich and the poor has undoubtedly increased growing frustration and sense of deprivation among the poor and the weaker sections giving rise to the militant class war psychology. Rising expectations, mass poverty, inadequate housing, rising prices of essential commodities combined with universal suffrage and rapid politicization of the masses provide an explosive environment for group violence. Unplanned growth of large industrial cities with their vast slums, their insanitary conditions and their uprooted humanity provide another breeding ground for group violence. The anonymity of enslummed urban masses serves as an effective cover for group violence. Radicalism whether of the Right or the Left finds it easy to foment group violence. Group violence quickly mobilizes the energies of the people; it is interesting to participate in; the anonymity of the crowd gives the participants a sense of security, group violence provides a tension-release to pent up frustrations, they provide an escape from the boredom of existence and a refreshing distraction in the uneventful dull life of the urban masses. Violence manifests itself in several ways and in varying degrees. Collective violence posing threat to law and order can be conveniently categorised into the following :

1. Communal violence
2. Caste violence
3. Industrial labour unrest
4. Separatist movement and insurgency causing violence including ethnic violence
5. Political terrorism causing violence
6. Agrarian tensions and riots
7. Student violence
8. Election violence and political violence like anti-reservation violence
9. Dacoities and group violence
10. Apparently transient disturbances and violence including linguistic violence
11. Police violence/state violence.

Violence within the context of law and order is generally limited to rioting as defined under section 146 IPC. Sectarian violence, whether perpetrated in the name of caste, religion, region or language is different from class conflict. The analysis of social violence can be easily linked to the economic, social, psychological and political process of change which are associated with the transition from a traditional underdeveloped economy to a modern developed economy, a traditional feudal class based society to a secular and modern society.

Causes of Violence

While individual violence may be explained in terms of deviant behaviour, the collective violence is reflected in racial riots, communal disturbances, insurgencies and wars between communities and nations. Social scientists conceptualize the conflict situations ultimately resulting in violence in terms of four concepts of "prejudice, discrimination, social tension and social violence". Most frequently prejudice and discrimination mutually reinforce each other as in the case of high caste and weaker sections or between two language groups (Bengali and Assamese). The various theories explaining the phenomenon of violence in man are as under:

Biological theory : It stipulates that human violence is instinctive -- as is the violent behaviour of animals or that it is caused by genetic irregularities. According to Konrad Lorenz while many animals kill for food, only rats and humans kill their own kind in anger. [7]

Anthropological theory : Anthropologists account for violence by stressing the different cultural norms generally termed as "sub-culture differences" which govern another. Feelings of frustration and injustice in ethnic minorities, religious groups and certain sections of society ultimately lead to violence.

Psychological theory : Violence can be a normal response to provocation or it can be a response that is consistent with norms supporting its use and so forth. The psycho-pathological theories focus on aggressor's psychological personality characteristics and pathological disorders as the chief determinants of violence. On the level of socio-psychological level, there are theories like frustration - aggression theory, Perversion Theory, Motive Attribution Theory and Self Attitude theory. On the level of socio-cultural or sociological analysis there are theories like structural theory, System tension Theory, Anomic Theory, Theory of Sub-cultures of violence, Resource Theory, Social Learning theory, Symbolic Interaction Theory and Exchange Theory. [8] According to Freud, the death instinct is centred in the "Id" (the unconscious reservoir of instinctual, biological drives) and must be controlled by the "Ego" (the self) and the "Super Ego" (that portion of mind concerned with the social norms). Freud believed that violence is linked to a human impulse to return to the inorganic state known as the death instinct. [9] In another psychological theory propounded by Erich Fromm, human aggression stems from the character of individual personalities. The three potentially aggressive personality types are characterized in Fromm's theory "the Sadistic" who compensates for real or imagined impotence by seeking absolute control over others; "the Necrophiliac" who is driven to destruction and annihilation by hatred for life and "the Bored" who displays a lack of interest not only in other people and things but in himself as well. [10] Seeds of violence are planted early in life by incidents in individual's personal life history.

The Social Learning theory : Albert Bandura and Richard Walters have formulated a social learning theory of aggression that focuses on the initiation, especially by children of aggressive role models to which they are exposed. Violent behaviour is acquired by man merely by watching and imitating the violent behaviour of others and it is a learned behaviour.

The Frustration Aggression theory: The frustration aggression theory maintains that violent behaviour results from the frustration of purposeful activity. [11] Violent behaviour is the result of the interference which is caused to an on-going activity and interference causes frustration which in turn leads to violence.

Sociological theory: P.K. Paul, in his article "Why do People Riot?" has held that human violence is the result of (a) a severe conflict of social values between the dominant and minority groups; (b) a hostile belief system held by the aggrieved group based considerably on reality; (c) a failure of communication between the aggrieved and dominant groups of a society and (d) a failure in social control resulting from either over-control or under-control. [12] Weber argued that the legitimate use of violence is restricted to the State. A great deal of the violence in our society is related to fundamental and deep-seated value conflicts. From the sociological view point, violence is the outcome of many variables of a social order. In his classic study *Suicide,* Emile Durkheim observed that so long as society remains unchanged the number of egoistic, altruistic and anomic suicides remain the same. [13] Neil J. Smelser has enumerated the following six essential conditions for violent collective behaviour in his book *The Theory of Collective Behaviour*:

1. Structural conduciveness
2. Structural strain
3. A generalised belief system
4. Precipitating factors
5. Mobilisation for action by leaders
6. Ineffective social control.

Relative Deprivation theory: One of the major exponents of relative deprivation theory defines relative deprivation as:

"Actors' perception of discrepancy between their value expectations and their environment's apparent value capabilities. Value expectations are the goods and conditions of life to which people believe they are justifiably entitled. The referents of value capabilities are to be found largely in the social and physical environment: they are the conditions that determine people's perceived chances of getting or keeping the values they legitimately expect to obtain." [14]

"A sense of suddenly worsening deprivation, injustice or oppression, is often a major precondition of violence. De-Tocqueville, in *L'Ancien Regime et la Revolution,* was probably the first to articulate this hypothesis:

"It is not always by going from bad to worse that a country falls into a revolution. It happens most frequently that a people, which had supported the most crushing laws without complaint, and apparently as if they were unfelt, throws them off with violence as soon as the burden begins to be diminished. The state of things destroyed by a revolution is almost always somewhat better than that which immediately preceded it; and experience has shown that the most dangerous moment for a bad govenment is usually that when it enters upon the work of reform... The evils which were endured with patience so long as they were inevitable seem intolerable as a hope can be entertained of escaping from them. The abuses which are removed seem to lay bare those which remain, and to render the sense of them more acute; the evil has decreased, it is true, but the perception of the evil is more keen."[15] Four basic models of relative deprivation have been explored and refined by modern theorists[16] -- (i) capabilities remaining static while expectations rise, (ii) rising capabilities overtaken by rising expectations; (iii) the so-called J-curve situation, in which capabilities keep pace with expectations for a period and then suddenly drop behind; and (iv) general socio-economic malaise which may cause a dramatic fall in capabilities while expectations remain constant. Some writers on relative deprivation theory shrewdly broaden their concept of deprivation to encompass values and rights. Felik Gross, for example, gives high priority to the role of mass perceptions of ethnic and political oppression and injustice, and he argues that historically it is periods of intense politico-ideological tensions rather than those marked by inequalities which are most conducive to violence.[17]

Multi Causative theory : We frankly recognise the lack of any adequate general scientific theory of the necessary and sufficient conditions for constantly recurring in the recorded history of conflict and challenging both our attention and our powers of explanation and analysis: (i) ethnic conflicts, hatreds, discrimination and oppression; (ii) religious and ideological conflicts, hatreds, discrimination and oppression; (iii) socio-economic relative deprivation; (iv) stresses and strains of rapid modernisation tending to accentuate;[18] (v) perceived political inequalities, infringements of rights, injustice or oppression; (vi) lack of adequate channels for peaceful communication of protests, grievances and demands (e.g. denial of franchise or other rights of participation, representation or access to media); (vii) existence of a tradition of violence, disaffection and popular turbulence; (viii) the availability of a revolutionary leadership equipped with a potentially attractive ideology;[19] (ix) weakness and ineptness of the government, police and judicial organs (e.g. under-reaction, over-reaction;

(x) erosion of confidence in the regime, its values and institutions afflicting all levels of the population including the government; (xi) deep divisions within governing elites and leadership groups. [20]

Violence in Indian Society

David H. Bayley has analysed the anatomy of public violence in India and categorised it into three categories : (a) the violence of Remonstrance; (b) the violence of Confrontation and (c) the violence of Frustration. [21] David H. Bayley has summarised the attributes of each major forms of violence as under the following nine headings: (See Appendix-'B') Procession and public meetings, hartals and strikes, fasts, courting of arrests, riots, are various forms which exhibit violence of Remonstrance. Communal riots, and violence against weaker sections fall into category of the violence of Confrontation. Burning of buses and trains, student violence, looting of fair price-shops, hijacking of buses, sabotage, political murders etc. fall in the category of the violence of Frustration. "In India, whether violence comes from remonstrance or confrontation, much of its momentum comes from frustration as the circle of participants widen. The rickshaw drivers, hooligans, street urchins and unemployed young men join not because they indentify with the initial cause but because violence appeals to their personal predicament." [22] Group crime which stem from the widespread discontentment within a pluralistic society develops into waves of violence regardless of legal scruples. The violators are not ordinary but ideological criminals who gravely disturb peace and tranquillity through use of violence to remedy group grievances in defiance of law. Hartals, bandhs, gherao, self-immolations and political terrorism has converted the politics of agitation into politics of mass violence. [23] The Naxalite type of political terror and violence, the growing public disorders in Assam, violent activities of upper classes against weaker sections of the society are all manifestations of violence in a developing society.

The law and order administration has to understand the pathology of mass violence and must answer relevant questions pertaining to each dimension of violence. First--there are politico-economic-social agitations which result in mass violence. The second manifestation of violence is that of communal riots between minority and majority groups, between weaker sections and upper sections of the society. The third manifestation of violence is that of students and younger group. The fourth dimension of violence, is that of insurgents of Nagaland, Mizoram and Manipur and Naxalite violence of political extremists. The fifth manifestation of violence is that which is indulged by the armed gangs of dacoits and outlaws of Rajasthan, Madhya Pradesh and U.P. The latest form of violence is that of terrorists and extremists and urban guerrillas. Organised, calculated and brutal violence by small groups is the most disturbing feature of the contemporary political scene in India and buses and trains, posts and telegraphs, the government property, telephone exchange, university and college premises are the usual targets. Unfortunately one of the attractions of mass violence is the capacity of violence to dramatize and intensify the issue. Mass violence has become a national phenomenon in India. "Today violence erupts in all parts of the country -- organised and massive in the cities, sporadic and individual in the villages -- but the character and causes of violence are not the same everywhere. There are similarities between the Communist-led-secular, organised violence of Bombay and Calcutta; linguistic and regional violence as in Bombay in 1956 and Mysore in 1966; tradition-rooted violence as in Madras under D.M.K. inspiration in 1965 and the anti-cow-slaughter agitation in Delhi in 1966." Mass violence by hostiles/insurgents in Nagaland, Mizoram and Manipur and Naxalites movement in West Bengal, Andhra Pradesh and Orissa also form part of the national phenomenon." [(24)]

Political Violence

The immediate causes of political violence in the country in the recent past are mainly (1) increasing political instability; (2) sharply deteriorating economic conditions of the people; (3) rise in and spread of consciousness among the people that they are not getting justice; (4) gradual break of links between the political parties and people (many of the agitations taking place outside the framework of the political parties); (5) nearly complete collapse of the party system (horse trading is the main feature) and (6) increasing dependence of the Government upon police and armed forces to maintain itself. Political violence, according to Paul Wilkinson, "is either the deliberate infliction or threat of physical injury or damage for political ends or it is violence which occurs unintentionally in the course of severe political conflicts". Political violence is very difficult to classify and analyse because it frequently involves the interaction and effects of the actions of a whole group or a whole community involving a multiplicity of motivations, political considerations, psychological effects and subjective evaluations. Mass political violence can be in the shape of riots or street violence, armed rebellion or resistance, state of mass terror and repression, civil war, limited war, revolution or counter-revolution depending on the intensity of violence. Small group political violence can be found in the shape of isolated acts of sabotage or attacks on property, isolated assassination attempts, political gang warfare and feuds, political terrorism, localised or small scale guerrilla operations, international or transnational terrorism and guerrilla raids on foreign states. [25] Acts of political violence can be murder, kidnapping and other forms of terrorism such as bombs, arson and robbery. Political violence is a singularly clumsy and ambiguous mode of communication and it is extremely difficult for its promoters and perpetrators to control it once it is started. Most political violence serves both instrumental and expressive functions simultaneously but unfortunately the immediate physical effects of political violence -- death, maiming, destruction -- are irreversible and cannot be atoned. Paul Wilkinson has classified political violence into following nine categories : [26]

	Types	*General aims or purposes*
1.	Inter Communal	Defence or furtherance of alleged group interests in conflicts with rival ethnic or religious groups.
2.	Demonstrative	Expression of anger and protest can be used to persuade Govt. to remedy grievances.
3.	Praetorian (man of like rank a member of emperor's body-guards)	Used to coerce change in government leadership and policy.
4.	Repression/Retributive	Quelling actual or potential opposition and dissent.
5.	Resistance	To oppose and prevent a Govt. establishing authority and executing its laws.
6.	Terroristic	Use of systematic murder and destruction, or threats of murder and destruction to terrorise targets or victims into conceding the terrorists' political aims.

7.	Revolutionary	Overthrow of existing political system and its replacement by a new regime; note that leaders of this type of violence are often prepared to exploit all types of political violence including war.
8.	Counter-Revolutionary	
9.	War	To gain political ends by means of military victory over opponents.

Types of political violence mentioned above however are rarely to be found in their pure form in the real world and in most countries inter-communal, remonstrative, praetorian and repressive violence have brought endemic unstability to the liberal states. Unfortunately, criminal gangs and anti-social elements often exploit political violence.

"The explosion of mass violence poses a grave threat to the internal security of our developing economy. Violence and popular radicalism can drive the country like gaderene sevine into the depths of chaos; it is a threat to democratic way of life. Massive concentration of population in unplanned cities, growing unemployment, a quantitative expansion of the educational system, the poignant sense of rootlessness of people, rising trend of prices, erosion of moral and social values, religious fundamentalism have all led to frustration, anger and violence in Indian society". (27) The last four decades have registered a large volume of manifest violence, with the concealed violence remaining more or less unabated in certain parts of the country. The volume of manifest violence which is the product of the ferment of social change coming over large segments of Indian society is not inevitable and could have been reduced with appropriate and effective responses and institutional arrangements with a little planning, foresight and timely intervention. The emergence of organised crime in Bihar, U.P., Bombay, Gujarat and the newly evolved political-criminal nexus are the new challenges which cannot be easily met with the traditional instruments of crime control. (28) According to U.S. Presidential Commission of 1967, "organised crime involves thousands of criminals working within structures as those of any large scale corporation subject to laws more rigidly enforced than those of legitimate Government. Its actions are not impulsive but the results of intricate conspiracies in order to amass profits." Since long the Mafia kings of Dhanbad have been enjoying political patronge in Bihar and Uttar Pradesh. Problems related to organised crime and resultant violence are not of a nature which would be easily amenable to the traditional handling of crime by the police.

There has been an extraordinary spurt in the growth of violence during the last two decades. According to one estimate about 12000 persons were killed during the five years from 1980 to December 1985 through inter-communal violence and related security operations. Communal violence both in terms of intensity and frequency has been on the increase. "If large numbers applaud the patently illegal blinding of criminals in Bhagalpur and a Station House officer in U.P. is lynched and his body dismembered by a yelling mob within yards of his police station because he insists on executing a Court's order, if an engineer and his son are killed for refusing to award a contract against rules; if gun-totting bands of *hoodlums* over-run polling booths at the instigation of persons in responsible positions; if even school examinations cannot be conducted without the presence of the armed police; if large groups incensed by a Supreme Court judgment go on the rampage; if legislators threaten to gherao the Governor to prevent him from addressing the budget session and if mobs storm a legislature building, it is time for all Indians to sit up and ponder." [29] Today the transformation of the rural society from a harmonic to a disharmonic system has given rise to agrarian unrest and consequent violence in rural areas. Social violence has important political dimensions in India in the context of mobilisation of masses for political demonstrations, agitations and sometimes public violence by vested political parties. Terrorism in Punjab and Kashmir is almost certainly political in nature and is causing maximum loss of life and property in the country today. In Punjab alone 359 persons were killed in terrorist violence in 1984, 63 in 1985, 420 in 1986, 810 in 1987, 1994 in 1988 and 1162 in 1989 according to an official estimate. The whole of Kashmir valley has been also in the grip of violence and curfew had to be imposed in major cities and towns of Kashmir valley as a precautionary measure. After five days Kashmir militants released Rubiya, daughter of Union Home Minister in exchange for five colleagues in December 1989. The escalation of violence in the Srinagar valley is in large part a pre-emptive move by militants to foil the steps the State administration has initiated to flush them out and seize, their arms caches. [30] The militants killed seven police officials and police firing claimed at least 20 lives when government buildings were burnt or were rocked by blasts. [31]

Police Violence

"In certain professions like the police, the inherent brutality in men is apt to be enhanced and reinforced by the milieu in which they function and the sub-cultural traits they acquire in constant confrontation with violence. More important it is the sense of frustration and failure to control crime through socially approved channels of administration of justice which generates cynicism, higher brutality and counter-violence." [32] Case studies of instances of police violence show that most often the policemen have gone out of control under conditions of serious stresses and strains. Sometimes the police resorts to counter-violence when the policemen are killed in action or when police leadership suffers from lack of elan and crisis of authority in internal management. According to David Burnham, the use of violent force by the police can be divided into four sometimes overlapping categories. First the violent force the state legislature has authorised the police to use while making an arrest. Second the violent force that is tacitly authorised by either public or police tradition to handle such offenders as the sex criminals or the 'cop fighter'. Third the violence used by those policemen who enjoy hurting others. Fourth the violence that erupts when policemen become afraid or are under great physical or mental stress. [33] The fourth kind of violent force erupts during public riots, demonstrations and agitations when policemen are subject to brickbats and mental strain. Police have developed a sub-culture of violence and Westley's most significant finding is that at least 37 per cent of the policemen believe that it was legitimate to use violence to coerce respect. [34] Berkley, referring to socio-cultural factors prevailing in America has said: "If the American police are prone to use violent and repressive tactics, American society offiers them the means and the climate to do so." [35] Indian society can be compared well with the American society in the acceptance and even glorification of violence as a way to solve problems. Use of third degree methods of police interrogation, police firings on mobs and rioting crowds, police arrogance in behaviour and police handling of Naxalites, dacoits and insurgents in so-called encounters--all these things bring police violence as a prominent feature of police sub--culture. Dr. Nelson Watson, a psychologist on the staff of International Association of Chiefs of Police noted: "The very fact that police are the only group authorised by the state to use force tends to attract the occasional men who like to use it". In his study of the police Dr. Westley said that he found a small number of policemen "who are clearly sadists, who frequently commit brutalities repugnant to the rest of the police." However, Dr. Hans Toch, have held the view that "there are no sadist--just weak and stupid policemen who distort the hell out of the way the police normally operate". Some psychologists justify police violence as a reaction of physical fear and emotional discomforts of policemen.

Dr. Spiegal has said-- "Most cops dont's have any education, they are inarticulate. At some time when police are faced by a crowd or mob fear erupts and the individual policeman no longer seems to be able to discriminate and he strikes out at any one near him." Police training tactics and the direction given by the top commanders are considered extremely important factors in reducing police violence. Unfortunately, the govenment always honours those policemen who had gun-battles with armed criminals but not those who carry out non-violent arrest of a notorious violent criminal or those who tactfully prevent or control a violent riot without use of force or police violence. This government attitude also indirectly supports police violence as a police sub-culture. A chronicle of grisly events of police violence makes painful and disquieting reading. We had the Baghpat incident in Uttar Pradesh in the late seventies; the Mathura rape case in Maharashtra, and the dreaded Bhagalpur blindings in Bihar. According to Amnesty International Report 1978 in Andhra Pradesh the allegations are that between 300 to 500 Indians were killed by police during the year 1968-77 following arrest in staged encounters. In the words of Punjab Police Commission (1961-62) -- "Considerable evidence has been led to the effect that police make out fake encounters with criminals and shoot them because they cannot obtain sufficient evidence against them to bring them to justice before the Courts of Law." [36] The suppression of mass violence always generates more violence on the part of the government and unfortunately official violence has, according to Dr. P.D. Sharma, provoked popular violence in a non-violent society like India. The administration of order has to view according to Dr. P.D. Sharma, "and understand the concept of 'bilateral violence' in the context of existing class structure of Indian society and has to respect each life, whether it is that of the labourer or that of the police sub-inspector". [37]

Police Response

Collective violence in India could be categorised in three broad categories pertaining to communal, educational and political-economic issues. A violent bandh poses the question of protection of public and private property and maintenance of law and order in the society. The Government is placed in such situations in an unenviable position because if organisers of bandh are detained, the Govt. is branded as undemocratic and if it avoids confrontation, violence and lawlessness rule the society and organisers describe the bandhs as a total success. If police force is used to quell violence, press splash bold headlines about the orgy of police : violence on the peaceful demonstrators; if police has orders to use restraint, it is blamed for inefficiency and inaction. The dangers posed by the problems of lawlessness and group violence require, *inter alia*, evolving of porper strategies in regard to law and order administration. [38] The police administration normally responds to public violence in the following ways :

1. Imposition of section 144 or clamping of curfew;
2. Rounding up of a few miscreants and starting prosecution against those involved in violent activities;
3. Declaring assemblies as unlawful and dispersing them by use of force -- use of tear gas, lathi and ultimately firing.

The police have an impressive armoury of laws that they can use to control and head off violence. Section 30 of Indian Police Act, Section 145 of Indian Penal Code, Section 106, 107, 151, 144, 145 155, 109 of Code of Criminal Procedure and the Preventive Detention Act 1950. However, the first requirement for effectively dealing with the violence is adequate intelligence. Violence resulting from public remonstrance is describable in advance but police intelligence has to be well trained, vigilant and alive to the situation. Violence of confrontation can also be anticipated by signs of tensions building up in the community but violence of frustration is almost totally unpredictable. The job of regulating crowds and monitoring them for incipient violence is most arduous, continual and extremely difficult. The police often feel like fire watchers in a dry region, when the forests are like tinders and one careless act by a single individual may cause a holocaust beyond hope of containing. For controlling organised crime and mafia activities very innovative measures are necessary. The rapidly spreading "social poison" of organised crime might well destroy the social, political, economic and moral heart of our nation and therefore should no longer delay the setting up of joint strike forces capable of functioning all over the country and under a central agency duly empowered with all legal, administrative and procedural powers for meeting the challenge of organised crime learning from the experience of U.S.A. and Australia. The joint strike force should be composed of officers from the police, customs, excise, narcotics, income-tax and CBI and their powers should be sufficiently adequate to enable them to function effectively without being impeded by procedural constraints and departmental bottlenecks.

The existence of violence in public life thrusts the police into the limelight of public attention in an invidious role. Unfortunately, police action against public violence generally results in scandals about police excesses and police atrocities (zulums). Remarking on the charge of police brutality Pandit Jawaharlal Nehru said in Lok sabha in 1956: "The poor police is so used to being kicked and cuffed like that and always condemned. It is easy to make a charge against the police . . . . . let us punish the policeman when he is guilty or anybody else when he is guilty. But the stone thrower becomes a hero and is taken out in procession -- may be -- and the poor policeman who gets the stone on his head is a person who is guilty of zulum or atrocities" (*Lok Sabha Debates*). Due to a number of factors police are uncertain and sometimes hesitant in their handling of violent criminals and agitators. "The handling of violence is without question", as has rightly remarked by David Bayley, "the most contentious area of police activity". Increasing violence of extremist groups of society cannot be adequately dealt by the ordinary police. The entire criminal justice system needs to be involved for effectively curbing/controlling and preventing the increasing violence. It is necessary for the organisational effectiveness and survival of the police to manage both primary and secondary violence. Police resources and training have to be given due attention if police has to earn public confidence in dealing with violence. Apart from physical and technological resources, there has to be sincere and all out attempts to make the policy effective by increasing the powers of the police under the law. There has to be significant reform in the overall attitude and functioning of the criminal justice system. Better trained, alert and professionally competent armed policemen are required to deal with increasing violence. Special combat troops like commandos are required to head off violence in our society. Hijackers cannot be handled by ordinary policemen, we need highly trained young police commandos to deal with them. Hardcore insurgents, can be contained, isolated and defeated by specially trained police commandos. Government of India has taken a bold decision to train young CRP officers for police commando duties at Internal Security Academy, Mount Abu (Rajasthan).

The most basic tasks of police in dealing with effective violence are as under:-

1. Intervene in gang conflicts and violent situations by effective interposing.
2. Collect evidence, apprehend suspects and testify in courts.
3. Gather intelligence on various activities to prevent them by timely arrests.

4. Confiscate weapons and explosives/ammunitions and carry out effective show of force.
5. Obtain information about members, terrorists and impending violence.
6. Carry out effective patrolling and surveillance.
7. Riot control schemes be kept up-to-date and carry out the same whenever needed.
8. Take out heat and fury of the situation by effective crisis management.
9. Police must endeavour to use an absolute minimum of force in dealing with violence.
10. The state or federal government should be approached to provide facilities to develop non-lethal control devices for use in violent disorders.
11. Mechanical agents like rubber bullets, wooden bullets, fabric bullets, plastic projectiles and high powered water jets should be developed to supplement conventional lethal firearms for controlling violence.
12. Police must aviod "brutality" while dealing with violent situations and must exhibit a high degree of self-control during their efforts to moderate and contain violence. A high degree of training, motivation and self-control is needed for such behaviour by the police.

Whenever possible in controlling violence, authoritarian "peace-keeping" should be supplemented by "humanitarian peace-keeping" which should be characterised by openness, informality, flexibility and under-reaction. Police should rely primarily on conversation, persuasion, and social science knowledge about human behaviour. The following techniques can be used for resolving conflicts and violent situations:

1. Assemble leaders from opposing groups for negotiations and truce talks in a peaceful atmosphere.
2. Appeal to moral values and ideals and make pleas for understanding, co-operation and forgiveness among the warring violent groups.
3. Dispel false impressions and disseminate accurate information about groups and thus reduce tensions and hostile belief system.

4. Divert energies away from collective goals to individual goals.
5. Bring opposing groups together to share pleasant activities such as dance, rock concerts, picnics, etc.
6. Persuade conflicting groups to develop healthy atmosphere of trust and cooperation.
7. The vicious cycle of misunderstanding, protests and violent reactions should be broken by resolving inter-group conflicts.
8. The show of force by the police can at times have great psychological impact in management of violent situations.

Violence, disturbance of public order and requirements for special law

Shri N.S. Saksena has observed that "militarisation of law and order is like the use of narcotics, the dosage has to be continuously increased". To fight increased violence and terrorism police have to be increasingly reliant on advanced technology, diverse weapons and modern equipment. Police and security forces are being equipped with sophisticated equipment; bomb disposal teams now have a wide range of tools to detect, disrupt and disarm every sort of explosive device. In the fields of police communication, surveillance, monitoring, jamming and interception equipments are being constantly refined and modified to meet the increasing challenges of violence. To deal with violence, armed police battalions, CRPF, BSF, ITBP and other such "third force" is being created and expanding in developing countries.

As observed by National Police Commission in its third report, increasing violence is seen as the most disturbing feature of the country. Mass media particularly newspapers, publish frequent details of violent incidents involving large groups of agitators who clash with the police while articulating smoe issue of discontent and frustration. Violent crimes like murder, dacoity, robbery, rape, kidnapping, abduction and riots have increased at a very fast rate during the last three decades due to rising prices, growing unemployment, poverty, increasing migration to cities, growth of city slums, inadequate and irregular services and the stresses and strains of daily life. Population explosion, urbanisation, communal clashes, group conflicts, extremist activities have added to the growth of violence in the contemporary society. Criminal liability of individuals participating in group violence is difficult to establish under the existing laws. Article 352 of the Indian constitution read with 42nd amendment has made it possible for emergency provisions to be restricted to a part of the country which may be threatened by internal disturbances. There is definite need for an effective law to deal with violence and disturbances of public order. The National Police Commission has recommended special laws which should provide for:

(i) notification of any specific area disturbed by widespread disorder and breach of peace as a 'proclaimed area' to which certain provisions of the Act will apply;

(ii) suitable definitions of 'riotous mob', 'instigator', 'public propert' and 'sabotage' to identify crimes connected with them;

(iii) control over movements of persons in the proclaimed area;

(iv) tight control over possession and use of arms and explosives;

(v) externment of bad characters from a specified area;

(vi) preventive detention for a period not exceeding three months;

(vii) attachment of criminal liability to instigators for unlawful acts committed by riotous mobs on their instigation;

(viii) special courts to deal with offences under the Act as also other specified offences;

(ix) presumption regarding culpable mental state unless rebutted by the accused;

(x) presumptions regarding some aspects of evidence arising from documents;

(xi) tightening the provisions regarding 'bail'; and

(xii) fixing time limits for the completion of investigations and commencement of proceedings in court.

Conclusion

There is a primary need to initiate steps to reverse the movement of Indian society from fundamental negativity to fundamental positivity, from violence and aggression to harmony and cooperation. The value system of Indian society needs to be changed. The time has come when we will have to think of entire human society as one family whose members need not fight and shed blood on grounds of religion, language, culture, caste or economic considerations. The state structure– legislature, executive, judiciary and the public, mass media and the public opinion – all are responsible not only for maintaining violence-free society but also to establish social justice and harmony in the nation.

Violence is increasing in modern society and mass media and cinema are partly responsible for its excessive popularity. The social control institutions like family, school and college education, religion and ethical value-system have failed to contain and control the increasing violence. Police of future will have to deal with more and more violent agitations and incidents of social unrest. In all state police headquarters a policy planning cell should be created to work out the long range strategies of police policy towards violent disorders and political agitations. Intelligence set-up of the police organisations has to be geared up for collection of social intelligence about volatile groups and extremist organisations. Special training to the police forces to deal with violence should be arranged for all levels of police officers. During police operations against communal violence, student unrest and industrial disputes, police must act impartially, firmly and in a very humane manner. Damage of public property should be minimised by effective police intervention. The scope of Section 435 I.P.C. should be widened to cover all conceivable means employed in the damage of public property in India and deterrent punishments should be prescribed under section 425 I.P.C. for those who carry out violent activities. The organisers of public protests should be made responsible for damage of property by suitable amendment in existing laws. Police should be given adequate training and orientation to build up healthy public relations so that citizens may come forward to help the police in dealing with violent agitators. All police officers of the rank of Station House Officers and above should be permitted to hold press conferences and issue press briefings so that no rumours come out in newspapers. Mass media should be used effectively to build up public opinion against violence and extremist activities. The culture of reception rooms should permeate the police stations to educate the citizens about the problems and dilemma of police life and safeguard police image from distortion. Public must come to assist police by giving timely information and all possible assistance in police operations against volatile groups. Police officers should be actively associated in all programmes of rehabilitation of victims. The police brutalities and lawlessness can be reduced by effective intra-departmental and organisational control. Organisational control of police involves matters like quality of new entrants, their basic training, subsequent in-service training, attitudinal orientation, organisational culture, etc. Modernisation of police, provision of adequate resources, sound deployment strategy and effective leadership can go a long way in building up an enlightened police force which alone can deal with violence in a correct manner as is required in a democratic society.

Notes and References

1. Paul Wilkinson – "Social Science Theory and Civil Violence". In *Terrorism-Theory and Practice* (Ed). Y. Alexander, p.45.
2. L. Berkowitz (1962) – *Aggression : A Socio-Psychological Analysis*, New York M.c. Graw Hill.
3. Ted R. Gurr (1969) – *Violence in America - Causes and Prevention of violence*, New York, Signet Books.
4. See Jean Paul Sartre's 'Preface' to Frantz Fanon's Book (1974) – *The Wretched of the Earth*, Penguin Books, pp. 18-19, and 25.
5. Article on "Violence", in *Encyclopaedia of the Social Sciences*, Vol.XV.
6. Lewis A. Coser – "Some Social Functions of Violence", *The Annals*, (Special Number on "Patterns of Violence") March 1966.
7. Konrao Lorenz (1971) – *On Aggression*, p.229.
8. For details see Leonard Berkowitz *op. cit.*, Joffrey H. Goldstein (1975) – *Aggression and Crimes of Violence*, New York; Ram Ahuja (1985) – *Crime Against Women*.
9. Sigmund Freud (1956) – *Civilization and its Discontents*.
10. Erich Fromm - "The Erich Fromm Theory of Aggression"., *New York Times Magazine*; 27 February, 1972.
11. John Dollard (1939) – *Frustration and Aggression*.
12. P.K. Paul - "Why Do People Riot" - *Science Today*, Sept.70. Vol.5 No.3, pp. 28-33.
13. Emile Durkheim (1951) – *Suicide*, p. 304.
14. Ted R. Gurr, 'Psychological Factors in Civil Violence," *World Politics*, Vol. 20, No.2(Jan. 1968), pp. 252-53.
15. Alexis de Tocqueville, *L'Ancien Regime et la Revolution*, trans. Henry Reeve (London : John Murray 1856), pp. 322-23.
16. Ted R. Gurr – *Why Men Rebel*, Princeton: Princeton University Press 1970; James C. Davis – "Towards a Theory of Revolution", *American Sociological Review*, Vol.27 (Feb. 1962), pp. 5-19; W.G. Runciman (1966) – *Relative Deprivation and Social Justice*, London : Routledge and Kegan Paul.
17. Feliks Gross (1958) – *The Seizure of Political Power*, New York : Philosophical Library, pp. 388-90; 'Political Violence and Terror in 19th & 20th Century: Russia and Eastern Europe' in V.B. of a Report to the National Commission on the Causes and Prevention of Violence(Eds) James F. Kirkham, Sheldon G. Levy and William J. Crotty, Washington, DC, US, Govt. Printing office, pp. 421-76.
18. On this aspect see Huntirgton – *Civil Violence and the Process of Development*.
19. A point stressed by Feliks Gross – *Political Violence and Terror, op. cit.*
20. See. L.Trotsky – *The History of the Russian Revolution*, pp. 86-88.
21. David H. Bayley (1969) – *The Police and Political Development in India*, p.253.

22. *Ibid*, p.262.
23. K.M. Mathur (1987) – *The Problems of Police in a Democratic Society*, RBSA Publishers, Jaipur, p.64.
24. S.P. Aiyar (1967) – "Violence and Constitutional Government". In his book *The Politics of Mass Violence in India*, p.154.
25. Professor Samuel Huttington (1971) – "Civil Disobedience and the Process of Development" in a Delphi Paper, No.33, London, pp. 1-15 and *Political Order in Changing Societies*, New Yale University Press, 1968.
26. Paul Wilkinson (1977) – *Terrorism and the Liberal State*, p.33.
27. Dr. Krishna Mohan Mathur (1989) – *Internal Security Challenges and Police in a Developing Society*, RBSA Publishers, Jaipur, p.18.
28. For extensive detailed treatment of the subject see P.R. Raj Gopal (1988) – *Violence and Response - A critique of the Indian Criminal Justice System*, Uppal Publishing House, New Delhi, pp. 111-204.
29. J.N. Chaturvedi (1988) – "Policy and Administrative implications of Collective Violence". *In Collective Violence - Genesis and Response*, K.S. Shukla (Ed). Indian Institute of Public Administration, p.149.
30. *The Times of India*, 24th January. 1990 – "Crunch in the Valley".
31. Shekhar Gupta – "Militants Seige", *India Today* - January 31, 1990, p.22.
32. "Crime Control and Police Violence"–S. Venugopal Rao, *The Indian Express* (New Delhi), 10.1.1981.
33. David Burnham – "Police Violence", *New York Times*, July 7, 1968.
34. William A. Westley – "Violence and the Police", *American Journal of Sociology*, July 1959, p. 34-41.
35. George E. Berkley (1969) – *The Democratic Police*.
36. For further details see Punjab Police Commission (1961-62) headed by Justice Mehar Chand Mahajan, also see K.M. Mathur – "Police Lawlessness - How to Police" in *Essays on Police Community Relations* compiled by SVP NAP Hyderabad.
37. Dr. P.D. Sharma – *Indian Police - A Developmental Approach*, p. 229.
38. J.C. Kukkar "Imperatives of Law and order Administrators". In *Administration of Law & Order*, Ed. N.K. Sethi, HCM Institute of Public Administration, Jaipur, p. 141.
39. D.H. Bayley, *op. cit.*, p.264.

CHAPTER-4

TERRORISM AND HOW TO TACKLE IT

TERRORISM HAS grown enormously during the last three decades and has become an increasingly sophisticated and for many, an increasingly accepted political instrument of the extremists. Rajiv Gandhi while addressing the United Nations General Assembly has said, "Terrorism is a major challenge of our time. It has assumed new forms. The terrorists' contempt for human beings, bordered on barbarism. Terrorists were now using modern means of communication and the media to air their demands". [(1)*] Terrorism is political, goal-oriented action involving the use of threat of extra-ordinary violence, performed for psychological rather than material effects and the victims of which are symbolic rather than instrumental ··· [(2)*] Terrorism is now a big business. The latest data show the incidence of terrorist activity these days is nearly 400 per cent greater than it was in 1970. In the last two decades in the third world there has been an increase in the terrorist activities. Although terrorism is not of recent origin, its analysis began only with the incorporation of terroristic methods in the revolutionary strategy by the 19th century Russian anarchists. The most elaborate and systematic attempt at creating a philosophy or more precisely, an ideology of terror came from Jean Paul Sartre. Herbert Marcuse of the Frankfurt school of philosophy, Mikhail Bakunin, and Frantz Fanon are some of the thinkers who have supplied terrorism its rationale. The cult of terrorism is increasing all over the world. In a paper on "Terrorism in Western Europe" an official of the U.S. state department stressed that Western Europe would remain a prime target for terrorist attacks of the total of 233 attacks carried out by the Middle East terrorists during the five year period 1980-85, 32 per cent occurred in 1985. [(3)*] The Americans and the people in the West generally denounce the Palestine terrorists, the Lebanese Muslims, the Italian Red Brigades and the Baddar Meinhof of Germany as most dangerous terrorist groups. Technology provides the physical elements of contemporary terrorism -- transportation, coercion and communication. Terrorism is a powerful weapon in the psychological warfare against the state. In Paul Wilkinson's words "terrorism is more than simply a manifestation of psychopathology and more than a symptom of social discontent, oppression and injustice, though it may be both of these things as well". Terrorism creates a climate of panic and socio-political disorientation. Political terrorism is no more than coercive intimidation through instrumentalities of murder and destruction. Terrorist violence is often resorted to by criminal psychopaths who have the misguided zeal of carrying out violence for their political aims. We are witnessing in contemporary India three types of terrorism *viz.*

(i) Terrorist acts of insurgents in the North East India particularly in Tripura and Manipur.

(ii) Naxalite type of terrorist activities in Andhra Pradesh, Orissa and other states.

(iii) The secessionist variety of terrorism linked with Khalistan movement.

Terrorism has to be differentiated from the insurgency problem of north-east. An insurgent has the support of a large section of local population while a terrorist need not have such public support. The terrorist may or may not be a citizen of the country in which he operates.

Terrorism is now a global phenomenon identified with the spread of ideological vigilance and we are today in an "age of terrorism". The advances of science and technology, development of means of transport and communication, easy availability of highly sophisticated weapons, extensive publicity by mass media like television and published material, have made the present day society extremely vulnerable to unsuspected and ruthless attacks of terrorism. Terrorism today is a form of violent strategy, a form of coercion, intentional use of violence or the threat of violence. At the heart of every terrorist action, there is a cause, a political goal, a perceived injustice or denial of liberty that is as concrete to, the activist as any prime minister's notion of justice or freedom. No political rhetoric can disguise this fact, no opponent of terrorism should forget this. [(4)*] Terrorists generally penetrate atrocities and violence with the aim to produce terror at some time in their struggle. Terror, Kropotkin wrote, is "propoganda by the deed" because when a bomb explodes, the explosion draws more attention than a thousand speeches or pictures. Terror means "a state of intense fear and apprehension" and "a state of fear and submission produced by terrorist methods". According to section 2(b) of Terrorist affected areas (Special Court) Act 1984, terrorist means a person who indulges in wanton killing of persons or in violence or in the disruption of service or means of communications essential to the community or in damaging property with a view to :

(i) putting the public or any section of the public in fear; or

(ii) affecting adversely the harmony between different religious, racial, language or regional groups or castes or communities; or

(iii) coercing or overawing the government established by law; or

(iv) endangering the sovereignty and integrity of India.

The distinguishing feature of terrorism as on organised form of violence is the unwillingness to be limited by any convention, the aim remains to produce terror. [5] Terrorism refers to random or extortionate violence directed against the life, physical well-being, or freedom of government officials, and are at times even directed against the general impairment of public property and human lives. *The Encyclopaedia of Social Sciences* has defined terrorism as "a term used to describe the method or the theory behind the method whereby an organised group or party seeks to achieve its avowed aims chiefly through the systematic use of violence". Terrorism connotes a policy intended to strike with terror those against whom it is adopted. It includes the employment of methods of intimidation and the fact of terrorizing or the condition of being terrorised. Jordan Paust has defined terrorism as the purposive use of violence by the precipitator(s) against the instrument target in order to communicate to a primary target into behaviour or attitudes through intense fear or anxiety in connection with a demanded power (political) outcome. [6]* According to Central Intelligence Agency estimates deaths and injuries during the years 1968-80 in the world as a result of terrorism were as under :

Year	*Individuals killed*	*Individuals injured*
1968	35	208
1969	64	202
1970	131	212
1971	36	227
1972	157	412
1973	127	551
1974	344	1100
1975	276	748
1976	415	920
1977	261	461
1978	442	690
1979	738	664
1980	642	1078

Kidnapping, barricade hostage, letter-bombs, incendiary bombs, explosive bombing, armed attacks, hijacking by air, sea and land transport, assassination, sabotage, exotic pollution, threat, break-in, theft, conspiracy, hoax, sniping, shooting out with police, arms smuggling are some of the main terrorists activities of terrorists in the world. Terrorist kidnapping throughout the world during 1970-82 are given below:

	Event	*Total*
1.	Total incidents	781
2.	Incidents against business	376
3.	Incidents against domestic business	282
4.	Incidents against foreign business	37
5.	Incidents against U.S. business	57
6.	Total killed	174

The vast majority of terrorist kidnappings has taken place in Latin America and Europe. During 1968-82 there were 28 successful kidnappings of U.S. diplomats. Since 1969 Italian terrorist groups of various persuasions have carried out 13,000 criminal actions the most violent of which resulted in 315 murders and 1075 woundings. In Italy 25 ideologically motivated kidnappings and 487 kidnappings for ransom were recorded between 1970 and June 1982.

Terrorism can be analysed and understood with the help of five most important factors namely incentives, capabilities, vulnerabilities, intentions and legal perspective. An analyst interested in analysing terrorism might ask what political events, economic conditions, social upheavals for terrorists to take recourse to terrorism. Capabilities of terrorists may include skills and commitments of combatants, supporters and sympathisers, degree of motivation and fanaticism, degree of public support, organisational unity and cohesion, international support and availability of all types of resources like vehicles, supplies, explosives and money. Vulnerabilities can include the strengths and weakness of whole societies, the physical security given to targets, flexibility and adaptability of socio-economic, political system as a whole. Targets include VIPs, bridges, roads, railway lines, airports, vital installations, aircrafts, convoys and nuclear power plants. Intentions cover very broad spectrum and include close attention to incentives, capabilities and vulnerabilities. Intentions generally may involve broad strategies or the application of specific tactics to particular targets. Long range intentions, plans are all part of the concept. The legal perspective includes the legal system of the country, immigration laws, customs laws and other legal matters related to terrorism. Ideology, domestic material support legally available to the terrotrists and the international support are important factors in analysing terrorism in an objective manner. Aircraft hijacking is one of the most popular weapon of terrorists. Between 1961 and 1968, 66 aircrafts were hijacked all over the world. Between 1969 and 1972, 279 aircrafts were hijacked by terrorists. During 1971-81 seven aircrafts hijacking incidents took place in South Asia involving three Indian aeroplanes. On January 30, 1971 an Indian Airlines Fokker Friendship plane was hijacked by Kashmir National Liberation Front. On 10th september, 1976 Aircraft Boeing 737 of Indian airlines was hijacked by pro-Pakistani Kashmiris and taken to Lahore. Indian Airlines Boeing 737 with 117 passengers on board was hijacked on 29th September, 1981 by six pro-Khalistan hijackers led by Gajendra Singh. On July 5, 1984 Indian Airlines 405 carrying 255 passengers was hijacked to Lahore by a special squad of Akali terrorists demanding release of AISSF office bearers. Terrorism is a tangled skein of varied human motivations, actions, emotions, goals and ideologies that have employed terrorism, the multitudinous arms and tactics available to terrorists all these factors have made terrorism as a disease of the modern society which can sometimes be controlled temporarily but has no certain cure in the long run. Basically terrorism is a form of "psychological warfare", it is a form of armed conflict, it is a political weapon of coercion. Terrorism is sometimes synonymous with urban guerrilla warfare. Terrorism is also an instrument of war at ideological plane. Marighella said "Terrorism is an arm the revolutionary can never relinquish". [7] Political terrorism is the threat of violence or an act or series of acts of violence effected through surreptitious means by an individual, an organisation, or a people with a view to achieving certain well-pronounced political goals or political purposes. Terrorism generally encompasses the following ingredients and characteristics:

(1) Terrorism publicizes the terrorists' political cause.

(2) Terrorism demonstrates the capabilities of the terrorists to strike blows.

(3) Terrorism heartens sympathisers of the terrorists cause.

(4) Terrorism disconcerts the enemy.

(5) Terrorism eventually the ultimate goal -- demoralizes the enemy and paralyzes him.

(6) Conceivably, in certain circumstances, terrorism could deter political allies of the terrorists target country from assisting that country.

(7) It has a psychological effect -- it frightens the foe and emboldens the ally. [8]

(8) Terrorism is usually the weapon of the few or a group while insurgency enjoys larger base.

(9) Terrorists are "indiscriminate, essentially arbitrary and unpredictable" (Wilkinson).

(10) Terrorists are in extreme minority and tend to form cohesive groups for their protection.

(11) The pledged terrorists group is created not from a national or freely given contract or covenant but from fear.

(12) The primary aim is to destroy, not to hold territory or run government. According to Laquer, there is no known case in modern history of a terrorist movement rising to political power, although terror has been used on the tactical level by radical political parties.

(13) "The media are the terrorist's best friend. The terrorist's act by itself is nothing, publicity is all." [9]*

Terrorism has three fundamental functions as a military weapon. It demoralizes the enemy, his armed force, police and even the civilian population through assassinations, bomb explosions and this has a psychological impact. It causes material destruction by sabotage of specific targets like utilities, communications and industries. It impairs economic strength by engendering a state of psychological unease and uncertainty in economic activities. The quintessence of terrorism has been summarised by Roland Gaucher thus: "The goal of terrorism is not to kill or destroy property but to break the spirit of the opposition. A minister is assassinated; his successor takes warning. A policeman is killed, ten others tremble. High tension lines are sabotaged, the news sweeps over the country. Terrorism seeks sbove all to create a sensation -- within the ranks of the enemy in the public opinion and abroad". [10] Terrorism has, in the modern age, become a form of mass entertainment due to excessive mass publicity by television and newspapers. It has become very alluring for the frantic few to appear on the world stage of television and thus today terrorism is aimed at the people watching not at the actual victims but the drama. In a free society terrorist activities are by their very nature news worthy because they affect our lives. Betrand De Jouvenal has observed: " unfortunately only those who have themselves risen by violence know how dangerous it is to tolerate its appearance. While those who have risen by legitimate means are puzzled by the inception of violent politics and hesitate to deal with the peril in time."

The protagonists of terrorism generally have the following aims :

(1) To spread their ideological message in favour of certain revolutionary doctrines.

(2) To gain recognition and acceptance from the people as a credible force and from some foreign governments to exert international pressure.

(3) To enlist new recruits from like minded individuals and to broaden their base of power.

(4) To undermine the authority and prestige of the government and bring contempt for the estab lishment.

(5) To provide repression and over-action on the part of the government and security forces thereby making the government unpopular.

(6) To get publicity in mass media and mobilisation of public opinion in their favour.

(7) To terrorise dissident associates and avenge arrest or deaths of associates.

(8) Lenin has enumerated two different objectives of terrorist actions. The first objective is to kill individuals such as high officials and lower ranking members of the police and army. The second objective is to confiscate money from government as well as from private persons.

Terrorists derive great psychological benefit from being publicly acknowledged as "freedom fighters" rather than criminals. Terrorism transcends national boundaries through:

(1) foreign support in terms of arms, ammunitions, explosives and resources;
(2) the commission of a terrorist act in a foreign country;
(3) an effort to influence the policies of a foreign government;
(4) the yearning for decolonization make terrorists "champions of freedom" in the comity of nations.

International terrorism has become a serious problem today with the beginnings of widespread attacks on diplomats, hijackings of airlines in foreign lands, hostage-taking and kidnapping of hostages for negotiations having international ramifications. Due to the sovereignty explosion and prevailing power-alignments there has been almost a total lack of agreement on either the cause or the cure of international terrorism. Although there is widespread acknowledgement of the necessity for dealing with international terrorism, power politics and ideological militancy of power blocks continue to make a mockery of the laws of the nations and international law. International connections of terrorists encompass various aspects, doctrinal, financial and technical being the main ones. Besides ideological inspiration refuge, modern weapons, training and intelligence, even forged travel documents and currencies are being provided to the terrorists by foreign countries interested in destabilizing the political system of a particular country. The examples can be numerous. The Khalistan movement for a "Sikh homeland" in northern India, bordering Pakistan, with officers of the "Republic of Khalistan" allegedly established in some foreign land, is believed to be receiving financial support, training and modern weapons from some foreign governments. The outside powers and their agencies play a subtle role by providing ideological motivation, finances, training and resource support to terrorists.

The concept of terrorism is not free from polemical dialectics because victories or defeats can almost overnight turn terrorists like Tito, Sukarno and Castro into "Liberators" and Batists, Idi Amin and Pol Pot into "criminals" of all types. In other words terrorists can be either virtuous or evil, patriots or traitors, all depending on the finale of the terrorist outcome, the international environments and the media role in its mass publicity and its labelling it in a given perspective. Unfortunately the tragedy lies in the emergence of such situation where ordinary common masses start not only approving and applauding the deeds of certain terrorists but also begin to submit to them, accept their ideological cult and support their deeds. In a democratic free society the fear of being accused of employing repressive measures particularly in situations emerging out of religious, ethnic and cultural minorities, haunts a popularly elected government and generally the governments wait till there is a general mass out-cry or breast beating by the citizens. In free and democratic societies, terrorism flourishes in spite of the best of will and all the legislative, executive and judicial measures marshalled by the state authorities.

Changing Modes of Terrorism in India

Subversive sabotage, profitable kidnappings, stunning assassinations, brutal bombings and explosions, aircraft hijackings, are some of the varied ways of terrorism all over the country.

Ravindra Hareshwar Mhatre, India's assistant high commissioner in the Birmingham consulate was kidnapped and later found dead at about 8-30 p.m. on Sunday, February 6, 1984. The Kashmir Liberation Army (KLA) was suspected to be the terrorist group responsible for this act of terrorism. India has witnessed terrorism and insurgency in its varied forms in Tripura, Nagaland, Mizoram and Manipur during its insurgency periods when insurgents committed varied acts of terrorism against government officials, public and the convoys of the armed forces. Such terrorist acts prove effective in removing the people's aloofness and baptise them in the crucible of fire, blood-shed and destruction. Subversive sabotage activities not only undermine the country's production, economy and morale but also inhibit the general helplessness of the masses. The effective stoppage of the flow of petroleum by the Assamese terrorists during their peak agitation in 1980 against the foreigners' issue made the Indian exchequer incur a daily loss of Rs. 30 millions. Naga insurgents disrupted rail traffic by planting explosive devices killed nöumerous passengers and injured many other innocent people. According to Rajiv Madan, during the last three years major killings carried out by the Punjab terrorists were as under.

Date	*Event*	*Dead*
May 10, 1985	Delhi and parts of north India rocked by bomb explosions	42
June 23,1985	Air India's Boeing 747, Kanishka crashes off Ireland following bomb explosion	329
July 25, 1985	Terrorists gun down bus passengers near Muktsar, Faridkot district in Punjab	15
June 13, 1987	Terrorists strike at several points in South Delhi residential localities	14
Nov 30,1986	Terrorists shoot down bus passengers near Khuda, Hoshiarpur district in Punjab	24

July 06, 1987	Bus hijacked and travellers shot near Lalru in Patiala district of Punjab	38
July 07, 1987	Terrorists attack passengers of two buses near, Fatehabad in Haryana's Hissar district.	32

Rural terrorism was started by Naxalites in 1967 and it has spread from West Bengal to Andhra Pradesh, Kerala, Tamil Nadu, Bihar, Punjab, Orissa and Tripura. Naxalites indulged in large scale political murders and between April 1970 to March 1971, approximately 636 political murders were committed and between April 1971 to July'71, approximately 475 political murders were committed. During 1971-72 the number of Naxalites arrested was 6390 in West Bengal alone. In West Bengal 1711 murders were committed by Naxalites during 1969 to 1972 and 153 policemen were killed. 2007 bomb throwing incidents were reported in West Bengal during 1969-72. The persistence of rural poverty and the existence of large masses of landless poor continue to provide a good breeding ground for Naxalites and therefore this rural terrorism may increase in future. These rural terrorists collect money at regular intervals from farmers and businessmen and continue to carry out indiscriminate killings and torture. In rural areas there have been brutal caste and class conflicts resulting in numerous deaths. With the killings of Lalit Maken, his wife Gitanjali, Harchand Singh Longowal and Arjun Das in the short span of five weeks, India has outdistanced even Italy in terrorism. Terrorists in India have boldly proclaimed the identity of their targets, stalked the quarry and then killed the hit list enumerated tragets with frightening casualness. The fear gnaws that nothing can stop the terrorists. Terrorism is now part of the game being dexterously played by both internal and external forces which are interested in destabilising the democratic set-up of the country. Naxalite terrorists waged a virtual armed struggle and unleashed a reign of terror in many parts of the country. The aim of the Naxalite terrorists was the annihilation of the landlords, money--lenders, police and its informers. The Naxalite terrorists provided great impetus to student unrest, agrarian unrest and boycott of elections. Mao has observed: "It was necessary to bring about a brief reign of terror to suppress the activities of the counter-revolutionaries and overthrow the authority of the gentry". Naxalites and other terrorist groups witnessed internecine warfare between different competing terrorist groups and splinter groups. Destruction of controlling centres, purification campaigns, purges, liquidations, forced exiles, blackmails and extortions are some of the common occurrences within the terrorists organisations. There are today alomst more than a dozen splinter Naxalite groups operating independently and sometimes even at cross purposes. Disruption of public utility services by the terrorists causes widespread paralysis over large areas for indefinitely long periods. The extensive fire at the Obra Thermal power station in Uttar Pradesh in October 1983, disruption of railway traffic due to explosions of the track and tampering of railway tracks in Ambala, Ludhiana sections in October 1983, derailment of Jammu bound Sealdah Express causing death of 18 passengers and injuries to 150 persons are some of the well-known instances of disruption of public utility services by the terrorists. Profitable kidnappings for extorting money by the dacoit gangs of Chambal valley, the tragic assassinations of Srimati Indira Gandhi, veteran journalist Lala Jagat Narain of Punjab, Akali Dal leader Sant Harchand Singh Longowal are some of the recent instances of terrorist actions. In spite of all possible protection by guards, influential leaders have often remained vulnerable to the threats of assassination. According to official information issued by Director General Punjab Police from July 1, 1984 to July 27, 1987 a total of 1368 men, 81 women and 22 children have been killed by the terrorists in Punjab. [(11)*]

The invention of plastic bombs/gun-powder, high explosives, TNT and other variations of modern explosives have added another weapon to the armoury of the terrorists. The bomb planted near Samastipur in Bihar on the dais erected for Central Minister L. N. Mishra exploded killing him on the way to hospital. In Assam alone 34 bombs exploded in the year 1980. About 200 bomb explosions were reported in the first half year of June 1982 in Assam. Around 200 bomb explosions were recorded in Punjab during the first ten months of the Punjab agitation ending May 1983. Aircraft hijacking is one of the most powerful weapon of terrorists. India has witnessed a number of skyjackings of its aircrafts. The first Indian aircraft a Fokker Friendship was hijacked on June 30, 1971. Air India Jumbo was skyjacked on Dec. 24, 1974 and a Boeing 737 scheduled for Bombay from Delhi was forced to head for Lahore on Sept. 10, 1967. There have been by now more than a dozen unfortunate cases of successful hijackings by the terrorists in India. The terrorists gain world wide publicity and recognition for their terrorist act. In one of the worst disasters in aviation history 329 men, women and children were killed when the Air India Jumbo flight from Montreal to Delhi/Bombay via London was blown up off the Irish coast on June 23, 1985. [(12)*] The Kirpal Inquiry Committee's conclusion that the Kanishka crash was caused by a bomb explosion confirms the widespread feeling that the gruesome tragedy was a deliberate act of terrorism carried out by Khalistan extremists.

There are endless newly emerging variations in terrorist actions. On September 21, 1985 three persons were killed and one injured when a transistor bomb exploded in a narrow lane in the walled city near the Old Delhi Railway Station. On September 22, 1985 the Punjab state was rocked by bomb blasts in at least seven different places killing three girls and causing damage to about six vehicles. The blasts were reported from Amritsar, Batala, Dinanagar, Dhariwal, Bhagowala (Gurdaspur district), Talwandi Sabo (Bhatinda) and Faridkot in one day. While there is increasing sophistication in the techniques and methods of terrorists, terrorism is being unleashed at local, regional, national and international levels. According to the State Minister of Home Shri, Chidambaram, terrorist acts in Punjab have claimed 410 lives and injured 1180 persons between August 4, 1982 and June 3, 1984. (3)* Some 1,117 persons have been killed in incidents due to terrorist activities in Punjab between October 1, 1985 and August 10, 1987. The number of terrorists killed during the period in the state was 225. (14)* In 1983 terrorist killings in Punjab were estimated to be 54, in 1984, 275, in 1985, 64, in 1986, 520 and upto July 11, 1987 it was 444 as per estimates made by B.K. Sharma. (15)* Some of the common features of terrorism are enumerated below:

(a) Most of the terrorists take the initial offensive by their ability to jump the gun first and thus, the benefit of early initiative.

(b) Terrorism has the demonstrative tactics to make the victims succumb by demonstrating their supremacy over the government.

(c) Terrorism creates impending threat -- imminent and implied of captivity, torture, bloodshed and destruction which forces the victim's behaviour in the desired direction.

(d) Terrorism is generally a group activity.

(e) Terrorism gets unaware victims as the acts of terrorism come as unexpected and unprovoked.

(f) Terrorism creates fear psychosis and violence is resorted generally as the last resort.

(g) Terrorists are publicity conscious and have security orientation.

(h) Terrorists are selective in their selection of targets, but no target is inaccessible and no person invulnerable.

(i) Terrorism makes every incident seen like an exception to the rule that ought to apply. No government can protect everything and everyone everywhere and constantly.

(j) Terrorist groups finance themselves primarily through armed robberies, extortions and kidnappings for ransom.

(k) Urban terrorism is on the increase and is causing serious panic in cities and towns.

Management of Terrorism

Despite the best intentions of governments, action against terrorists is substantially hampered by every state's own network of political alliances. (16)* Any liberal democracy, by its very definition, poses its own restrictions on the battle against domestic terrorism. Security against terrorists attacks is particularly difficult because terrorists can attack anything. We have entered an era where combating terrorism is going to be the primary jobs for the police. Terrorism violates civic liberties and involves a substitution of pain or punishment for reason in the adjudication of political and social ends. Terrorism as a policy is anti-democratic and violates a sense of civil liberties. Terrorism demands instantaneous decision making and has an appeal to elites. Terrorists usually have to foil those people who are innocent, non-combatants and non-participants. Terrorism, by its selective use of fear, subjugation and intimidation, disrupts the normal life of a society. Terrorism has a symbolic perspective, although the vicitims of terrorism are usually quite limited yet the calibrations are usually large because terrorism involves death and destruction by design. In questions of terrorism, the measurements of success cannot simply be its ability to loosen that order symbolically by weakening the legtimate capabilities of the elected officials and the obligations of a democratic state. Terrorism is not an analyzable concept into itself, terrorism is often a tactical function of situational framework and may be part of an instrumental network based on aproximated ends. The solution to the problem of terrorism is invariably beyond the framework of counter-terrorism and security measures. Responses to terrorism has to be necessarily accompanied by the strengthening of the socio-political fabric as a whole and specifically of the economic order.

The following measures can cope with terrorism in Punjab to a great extent:

(1) The entire resources of the state have to be utilized to deal with terrorist violence although the Army should not be used for internal security tasks, there should be no hesitation in employing it when the situation goes beyond the control of the civil administration. (17)* In Holland, Japan and Italy there

are specialised forces to carry out operations against terrorists. National Security Guards have been as an armed force of the union for combating terrorist activities with a view to protecting states against internal disturbances and for matters connected thereinto under the National Security Guard Act 1986 (Act No. 47 of 1986) Central Reserve Police Force is sending officers and men on deputation to national security guards. CRPF, BSF and NSG are the "third force" to deal with terrorists and other extremists.

(2) Tightening of airport security and taking all protective measures against hijacking.

(3) Expanding of intelligence set-up and physical protection to all vulnerable targets.

(4) Building up specialised units and organisations to deal with terrorists and revamping of training of such specialised units and para-military forces like CRPF, National Security Guards and commando.

(5) Improvement in international cooperation to deal with terrorists and improving the skills for negotiations for dealing with terrorists at political level.

(6) Since terrorism is a socio-economic problem, it has to be dealt at socio-economic level along with political front.

(7) Civil police alone cannot deal with terrorists but they must provide required support and intelligence to other forces which are assigned the task of dealing with terrorists.

(8) Effective implementation of legislative measures against terrorists.

(9) The borders of Punjab have to be completely sealed and if necessary, anti-personnel mines should be laid.

(10) A strategy needs to be worked out through intelligent use of radio, T.V. and even newspapers and magazines to insure that the terrorists are denied support from the people.

(11) A third force should be used for anti-terrorist duties and CRP is the appropriate police force.

Today terrorism has plagued many countries including Britain, France, West Germany and the United States but there are no illusions about terrorism in those countries. Somehow India is suffering from some dangerous illusions about terrorism. It is an illusion to think that one or more states, say Punjab, can be cordoned off and the problem localised. Terrorism generally involves many nations. The terrorists "may belong to one country, financed by a second, trained in the third, may have equipment from the fourth and may operate in a fifth. The terrorists who carried out the massacre at Lod airport in Israel, belonged to Japan, were trained in Korea, purchased arms in Italy with money raised in West Germany and had the sympathy of several Arab countries." [18]. At an interstate conference on coordinating anti-terrorist activities, cabinet secretary, B.G. Deshmukh, has made the following recommendations:

(a) the setting up of special anti-terrorist cells in the seven states (Jammu & Kashmir, Himachal Pradesh, Punjab, Haryana, Uttar Pradesh, Rajasthan and Madhya Pradesh) and the two union territories of Delhi and Chandigarh;

(b) upgrading of existing intelligence systems and the more effective coordination with neighbouring states;

(c) increased highway patrolling and speedier methods of communication;

(d) tightening up of security at power stations, railway stations, hospitals and cinema houses.

(e) provision of armed guards on all buses playing at night in the entire northern region. [19]·

It is generally accepted that both politically and militarily the army is a crude instrument for dealing with terrorism. It is wasteful and inefficient to use a high status, technological army as a counter - terrorist force. [20]· It is an illusion to think that terrorism has reached the worst and now things will improve. Modern technology like powerful plastic explosives is placing more and more dangerous instruments in the hands of terrorists and there is bound to be escalation of terrorism in future. It is another illusion to think that terrorism can be fought mainly by para-military forces. Actually terrorism has to be fought by the people themselves with the help of intelligence and enlightened public opinion. It is another dangerous illusion to think that terrorism is a crime apart from other crimes. Terrorists take calculated risk and one of the examples which can be easily cited is the burning of 37 railway stations in Punjab in a single day. In the first 19 months of Punjab agitation, 220 murders occurred in the state, out of which 190 were of Sikhs. By contrast in the last two months after January 26, 1985 there were 96 murders and an overwhelming proportion of the victims were the Hindus. Terrorism in Punjab has many things common with other terrorists. "They destroy, intentionally or not the innocent and the uninvolved. They intimidate. They suppress dissent. They give birth to gory internal clashes. All these consequences seem to be linked inescapably to terrorism". [(21)*] In Punjab there is a need to embark on an all out psychological, political and administrative offensive to resolve the problem of terrorism. The people of Punjab need to be mobilised to fight terrorist violence. A suitabily armed and organised people's militia can be raised to supplement the efforts of security forces. [(22)*] All efforts should be made to win the hearts and minds of the people so that they are weaned away from terrorist ideology. Psychological warfare in the contemporary environment needs to acquire some sociological perspective in order to understand, identify and exploit the social and political base of the society for the effective management of terrorism, a proper strategy has to be worked out in such a way that terrorism can be controlled and fought at all levels simultaneously. The Terrorist and Disruptive Activities (Prevention) Act 1985 (Act No. 31 of 1985) seeks to:

(a) Provide for deterrent punishments for terrorist acts and disruptive activities.

(b) Confer on the Central government adequate powers to make such rules as may be necessary or expedient for the prevention and for coping with terrorist acts and disruptive activities.

(c) Provide for the constitution of designated courts for the speedy and expeditious trial of offences under the law.

The then Prime Minister of India, Shri Rajiv Gandhi, while intervening in the special discussion on the situation in Punjab in Lok Sabha on July 28, 1986 has said. "Terrorists must be dealt with extremely firmly. There can be no doubt about that and there will be no hesitation on the part of the central government. We shall give whatever help and support that the state government asks for, to fight terrorism in Punjab."

To control and contain terrorism, national efforts are required. Police infrastructure has to be revamped and restructured for this purpose. Intelligence set-up has to be reorganised. Trials of terrorists have to be implemented. Scientific information system backed by computer technology is needed for recording, storing and retrieval of information about the terrorists, their associates, their *modus operandi* and their sources of finance and support. Electronic and physical security procedures at airports have to be continuously improved. Enlightened public opinion and mass support can help in controlling and containing the terrorists. While police and paramilitary forces have to carry out flushing operations against terrorists, nothing effective can be done in democracies unless sound public opinion and strong political will are built up against terrorists. Purposive preparations, residential protection, workplace security, personal security, transit safety, area defence, environmental support, security consciousness and institutional aids can effectively neutralise the evil designs of the terrorists. Besides an effective anti-terrorist act and a well-trained internal security force a national conscience is needed to cure the cancer of terrorism. The vast majority of the population should back the efforts of the government to control and eliminate terrorism. "The police officers and anti-terrorist squads need to be trained for combating terrorist activities. Their training should include theoretical knowledge of subjects like (1) growth of terrorism (2) target selection (3) strategies of terrorists (4) threat assessment (5) modern weapons of war (6) developing tactical capabilities (7) analytical techniques on investigating terrorists gangs (8) prevention of terrorist incidents (9) legal armoury available to deal with them and (10) crisis management". [23] Practical outdoor training has to consist of commando training, unarmed combat and physical fitness training for developing quick responses to various situations. At F.B.I. Academy Quantico, Virginia there is a course for 8 months for training anti-terrorist groups and special task forces. Useful lessons can be learnt from the strategies developed in the USA and Britain and special programmes for controlling terrorism should be launched. The crisis management committees at various levels must be formed to deal with developing situations in terrorist infested areas. Wherever there is a risk either of individual terrorist attack, executives and staff must be trained to reduce the risk or should the need arise, to participate in the response. [24] The International Air Transport Association has recommended 8 point security measures against hijacking and these measures should be implemented at all airports. Metal detectors and X-ray screening systems have to be installed at all airports for proper security check of passengers and the cargo. The Anti-Hijacking Act 1982 is a bold action in this direction.

A futuristic assessment of the trends of terrorism is always difficult and hazardous. There seems to be no easy solution or remedy for the growing terrorism. But internal peace and security will remain elusive till violence, extremism and terrorism are not successfully contained and overcome. The under mentioned laws relating to terrorism and disturbances have to be used with imagination to curb and control the terrorism.

1. The Anti-Hijacking Act 1982.
2. The suppression of unlawful acts against safety of Civil Aviation Act 1982.

3. The Arms (Amendment) Act 1985.
4. The National Security Act 1985.
5. The Prevention of Damage to Public Property Act 1984.
6. The Armed Forces (Special powers) Act 1958.
7. State armed police forces (Extension of Laws) Act 1952.
8. The Terrorist and Disruptive Activities (prevention) Act 1985.
9. The Terrorist Affected Areas Act 1984 as amended up-to-date.
10. The Disturbed Area (Special courts) Act 1976.

International cooperation and multi-pronged attack on terrorism can contain and control terrorism in the world. "We have to take appropriate steps", says F.B.I. Director William Webster "to make sure that the terrorist do not succeed in getting a beach-head such as they enjoyed for years in different countries of the world." A series of effective preventive and security measures have to be taken to provide the greatest protection possible to all the known terrorist targets with the help of special task force. Local civil (unarmed) police cannot alone deal with terrorists, special task force consisting of commandos, National Security Guards and Central Reserve Police Force have to be properly equipped and trained to deal with the terrorists. A worldwide "counter - terrorist network" forced the abandonment of 80 " terror operations" and a number of countries helped the United States by providing information and help. Public cooperation and help is very important in combating terrorism. A well trained and highly motivated police force and special task force can effectively cope with terrorism if the tens of milions of people in market, in buses, in trains, in public places and other places give an understanding, cooperation and support to the anti-terrorist operations. "Ultimate success against terrorism is possible only when government and people remain calmly committed and behave normally in the context of their own traditions, ideologies, concepts, strategies and techniques of response against terrorism must be articulated in a manner consistent with popular traditions of the country concerned". [25]

Conclusion

Developing his theoretical model of causation of terrorism, Felik Gross has laid down the following four seminal antecedents for terrorism and extremist politics against a democratic rule.

1. There must be an erosion of shared democratic values, a state of anomie or a crisis of democratic institutions;

2. Presence of a terrorist organisation;
3. A pre-assassination phase directed at subverting and defaming democratic leaders and institutions;
4. Activist personalities to initiate terror.

Democratic societies are easily prone to terrorism in the modern world because there are many constrains and limitations in democratic system. Democratic societies generally tolerate terrorism due to the following main constraints.

(a) Public opinion against use of excessive force against terrorists.

(b) Operation of Rule of Law.

(c) Insufficient intelligence due to secretive nature of terrorist activities.

(d) Complex and slow moving criminal justice system.

(e) Lack of adequate data about terrorists and their activities.

(f) Negative response from public due to mass fear psychosis created by terrorists.

(g) Lack of genuine political will and commitment to take repressive measures against terrorists.

(h) "Toleration is more manifest in democratic societies with constitutional guarantees of right to free media, and a number of sympathetic groups to minimise the brutality of terrorism and glorify the heroism or idealism in it". (26)*

A democratic polity, a quasi-federal constitutional system, and essentially a humane orientation of police provides a fertile ground for terrorism. In fact there is now a clear recognition that for dealing with terrorism, it is the armed police of the states and the centre which are more appropriate. A very strict control over weapons can be an effective measure of checking terrorism. On the pattern of U.K. and Japan strong measures are needed to restrict the supply of weapons to terrorists. The only remedy to fight terrorism is a police force which is efficient, well-trained, motivated and which enjoys the confidence of the people. What is required first and foremost is the setting up of a think-tank which includes not just government officials and politicians but also leaders of the opposition, journalists, academicians, social workers, policemen and other people dealing with the terrorism so that they may produce policy options and lasting solutions to the problem.

Notes and References

1. Rajiv Gandhi's address at the United Nations General Assembly as a part of the commemoration of its 40th anniversary - *The Times of India*, October 25, 1985.
2. Chalmers Johnson – "Perspective of Terrorism". In Walter Laquer (Ed) (1974) – *The Terrorism reader - A historical Anthology*, London, p.268.
3. R.G. Sawhney – International Terrorism - A one sided Debate, *Times of india*, 16 May, 1986.
4. Stephen Segaller – *Invisible Armies: Terrorism into the 1990s*.
5. Paul Wilkinson (1974) – *Political Terrorism*, London, p.16.
6. Jordon Paust – "Terrorism and International Law of War", *Military Law Review* 1974, p.34.
7. Carlos Marighella (1970) – *Mini-manual of the Urban Guerrilla*, Tricontinental Havana 1970.
8. Jay Mallin – "Terrorism as a Military Weapon". In *Terrorism - inter-disciplinary approach* (Eds.) Y. Alexander and S.M. Finger, p.100.
9. Walter Laquer cited by Yonah Alexander -- "Terrorism, The Media and the Police". In Alan D. Buckley and Daniel D. Obson (Eds) (1980) *International Terrorism*, p.90.
10. Roland Gancher (1968) -- *The Terrorist*, London, Seakar and Warburg, p.298.
11. *The Hindustan Times*, 31st July, 1987.
12. *Indian Express*, March 17, 1986.
13. *India Today*, Sept. 15, 1985.
14. *The Hindustan Times*, 26th August, 1987.
15. *India Today*, July 31 1987, p.32.
16. Stephen Segaller, *op. cit.*
17. Lt. Gen. S.K. Sinha "Punjab-Lessons from the Past", *The Indian Express*, 28th May 1987.
18. N.S. Saksena, "Dangerous Illusions about Terrorism", *The Times of India*, 10 April, 1984.
19. *India Today*, July 31, 1987, pp. 31-32.
20. Anthony Burton (1975) -- *Urban Terrorism*, p.222.
21. Raj Mohan Gandhi, "A national failure", *The Indian Express*, 7th May, 1984.
22. Lt. Gen, S.K. Sinha, *op.cit.*
23. Dr. K. M. Mathur (1987) -- *Problems of Police in a Democratic Society*, RBSA Publishers, Jaipur, p.168.
24. Richard Chutterbuck (1985) – *Managing the Episode in Terrorism and Personal Protection*, (Ed.) Brian M. Jenkins, p.247.
25. Anthony Burton. p.212
26. Chalmers Johnson, *op. cit.*, p.255.

CHAPTER-5

GROWING AGRARIAN UNREST IN INDIA AND HOW TO COPE WITH IT

INDIA IS basically an agrarian society since 72% of the people live in villages and agriculture is the mainstay of the Indian masses. The entire economic, social and political structure of Indian society revolves around agriculture although an important characteristic of Indian economy is the "insufficient holding" of less than two acres. 160 out of 189 farmer families in the village hold less than five acres. According to S.C. Dube only 10 per cent of the families have any marketable surplus, 24 per cent maintain a balance between their needs and their production and the remaining 66 per cent families are in deficit. India has attained "green revolution" by increasing agricultural production but the benefit of this production has not reached the landless labourers and marginal farmers. Social factors like caste and "the influence", the economic factors of lack of capital and security and above all the lack of education in the masses, together with political awakening as a result of adult franchise, are all influencing the situation and threatening to increase agrarian unrest in the rural areas. The constitution of India provides for equality of status and the principle of social, economic and political justice to all citizens irrespective of caste, creed, sex, etc. According to the sixth plan documents (1980-85) distribution of land holdings is as under:

Table 5.1
Showing distribution of land

Holding	*Percentage*	
	Number	*Area*
Less than 2 hectares	72.6	23.5
From 2 to 10 hectares	24.4	50.2
Over 10 hectares	3.0	26.3

According to the sixth plan (1980-85) documents, the very substantical' improvement in agricultural production has not solved the problem of poverty (p.8). The document attempts to give a picture of the poor in the rural areas by dividing them into four categories :

(a) Landless labour (generally Scheduled Castes)

(b) Small and marginal farmers (Backward Classes)

(c) Rural artisans (Backward Classes) and

(d) The tribal people.

According to some estimates (1979-80) 50.82 per cent of the rural population has been living below the poverty line. It is against this background that agrarian unrest in India needs to be analysed. Supreme Court of India in *Neerja Chaudhary* vs *State of M.P.* has held, that "poverty and destitution are almost perennial features of Indian rural life for large number of unfortunate ill-starved humans." There is bound to be agrarian unrest when many crore sons and daughters of mother India suffer hunger, thirst, deprivation and indignity in rural India. According to *Yojna* July 16, 1987 there were 253.1 million rural poor in 1977 which came down to 222.2 million in 1984-85. Thus 39.9 per cent of the masses living in rural India are below the poverty line.

A survey of the emerging literature on rural India makes the macro - indicators of agrarian unrest fairly obvious. Agrarian unrest refers to the unrest relating to land or its management or distribution and other matters related to agriculture. The peasants uprising during 1856-61 in Bengal and Champaran Satyagraha in 1917 in Bihar are well known cases of agrarian unrest in Indian history. Unrest signifies a troubled or disturbed state, restlessness, disquiet, or uneasiness. History of the world is replete with examples of agrarian unrest. Frantz Fanon has observed: " The starving peasant outside the class system, is the first among the exploited to discover that only violence pays. For him there is no compromise, no possible coming to terms." (1) The Chinese and Russian revolutions are classical instances where agrarian peasants have played a crucial and decisive role in revolution. Marx and Engels were painfully aware of the fact that if the industrial proletariat was to fulfil its historic tasks by leading the forces of revolution, it would have to mobilize peasant support, especially in countries with predominantly peasant populations. The peasants were given a definite place in the Bolshevik revolutionary strategy under Lenin's slogan of "Alliance of the working classes and the peasantry". Although peasant riots and uprisings were endemic in China, Mao's organizing genius enabled it to reach to new heights in 1925. In India in 1945 peasant movement was the Tebhaga movement of north Bengal for reduction of the proprietors' "Jotedars" share of crop from one half to "one- third". Another peasant uprising was the Telengana movement which erupted soon after Hyderabad became part of Indian Union. The major peasant uprising in independent India was the Naxalite movement started in 1967 under the leadership of Charu Majumdar and Kanu Sanyal in Naxalbari. It is now two decades since the shots rang out in Naxalbari and the Naxalite movement was born. Today the movement's profile is very different; rhetoric has given away to grassroots activisim. [2] Agrarian unrest has been growing and conslidating its strength in widely different regions of India. In Uttar pradesh under the leadership of Mahendra Singh Tikait, the farmers, movement has gained great strength. According to him "Justice to farmers means giving them the right price for their produce. To decide the right price is to equate farm produce with factory goods; the cost of production will determine the cost of the produce." [3] On March 1, 1987, Shri Tikait demonstrated the support of one lakh strong crowd at Shamli, U.P. for his peasants' cause. In Maharashtra the Shetkari Sanghatana was formally launched on January 1, 1982 under the leadership of Sharad Joshi. The agitation for better prices for onion produce in Nasik district, tobacco in Nipani and sugarcane in western Maharashtra successully established Sharad Joshi as the farmer's leader. He has propounded a "Bharat vs. India" (i.e. Agricultural India versus Urban India) theory. He has been able to mobilise about 50,000 farmers in the *Rasta roko* for higher cotton procurement prices and around 45,000 were jailed. About 40,000 women are said to have participated in his rural women's meet at Chandwad in Nasik district in November 1987 which was the largest meeting ever of rural women. In Karnataka in the 1950s Ram Manohar Lohia courted arrest in Shimoga district demanding the peasants' right to land. In the late 1960s and early 1970s the peasants movement in Karnataka centred around the demand for implementation of land reforms and the occupation rights of tenant farmers - share croppers. The Communist Party (Marxist) (CPI-M) and front organisations launched a movement in 1987 for a rational land distribution policy and remunerative farm prices, reasonable and minimum wages to agricultural labourer. Over 30,000 peasants courted arrest in the *Rasta roko* movement. In Gujarat peasant Bardoli movement led by Sardar Ballabh Bhai Patel is a well known event of Indian freedom struggle movement. The farmers' agitation in Gujarat was noticed in October 1986 after two continuous years of drought had considerably impoverished the state's 30 lakh farmers. The current agitation was begun by the Bharatiya Kisan Sangh (BKS) in October 1986 when farmers from north Gujarat, south Gujarat and Saurashtra united in their demands for cheaper electricity and remunerative prices for agricultural commodities. On January 1, 1987 a massive rally was held at Vijapur and about four lakh farmers attended the agitation. On March 18, 1987 K.S.S. organised Assembly Gherao in which ten farmers were killed in police firing and dozens injured in the ensuing lathi charge. In Bihar, Andhra Pradesh and Orissa Naxalite movement has gained stronghold in certain areas. Srikakulum, Khammam, Warrangal, Adilabad, Nizamabad, Karim Nagar, Nalgonda and East Godavari districts in Andhra Pradesh, Gadchiroli and Chandrapur districts in Maharashtra, Bastar, Durg, Bhilai, Raipur, Bilaspur and Surguja in Madhya Pradesh, Koraput, Sunebada and Kalahandi districts in Orissa, Patna, Bhojpur, Rohtas, Aurangabad, Gaya, Nowadah and Nalanda districts in Bihar are strong-holds of Naxalites and are having problems of agrarian unrest and violence. [4]

During the last four decades the conflicts and contradictions inherent in the processes of change in India became manifest and sharp. The agrarian unrest manifested in the form of violence against the Scheduled Castes/Scheduled Tribes in India is not a law and order or administrative problem. At bottom it is a socio-economic problem and arises out of the deeper processes at work in the economic, social and political structures. The sharp increase in the scale and quantum of agrarian unrest in the more recent period is traceable to the differentiation and conflicts taking place in Indian rural society as a consequence of the various institutional and technocratic attempts to transform the agrarian structure in a broadly capitalist direction. [5] There are more spectacular outbursts of agrarian violence, featuring for example, well organised killings of share-croppers, marginal farmers, agricultural labourers belonging to the Scheduled Castes by caste Hindu landlords or rich peasants. Instances such as the Kilvenmani carnage in Tamil Nadu in 1968, Belchi in Bihar, Banda and Narainpura in Uttar Pradesh, Bidar in Karnataka or Kestara in Madhya Pradesh may be cited. [6] According to the latest estimates of the Government of India 50.82 per cent of the rural population have been subsisting below "the poverty line" continuously over a long period. [7] Rural areas are facing tensions due to the implementation of DPAP and IRDP programmes. For the country as a whole the following picture emerges in respect of agrarian tensions :

Table 5.2

	Economic Tensions		*Socio-Religious & Political Tensions*	
1974	928	(29.9%)	2102	(70.0%)
1975	468	(13.6%)	2958	(86.4%)
1976	1019	(27.5%)	2690	(72.5%)

Agrarian unrest needs to be analysed critically. According to 1981 Census the workers in the primary sector formed 70.68 per cent (cultivators 41.53%, agricultural labourers 25.16 per cent, household industry 3.99 per cent) of the total main workers. The agricultural workers constitute the poorest section in the country. Though nearly 80 million rural workers are classified as cultivators, their economic condition is not far from that of the 47 million agricultural labourers, since 17 per cent of them have landholding below an acre and nearly 60 per cent have holding below 5 acres as a result of which the cultivators also compete with the landless agricultural labourers in the rural labour market. Farmers' movements sprang up in the 1970s in various parts of the country as and when the farmers found themselves in "a cash - crunch or a debt trap". [8] The bitter fact about farmers' movement is that only the affluent ones have been cornering all the facilities granted by the governments. Poor and marginal farmers have only been used as cannon - fodder. Remunerative prices for farm produce have enabled the holders of large agricultural lands to acquire financial and consequential political influence. The Karnatka Rajya Raita Sangha has shown the people that only agitational methods can yield results. Srimati Indira Gandhi, however, openly held that "if we yield to such demands (being raised in such peasant agitations), the equilibrium in rural areas will be disturbed and there will be greater inflation and sharper polarisation between villages and towns." Somehow most of the recent farmers' movements are disappointed and disgusted by the politicians for their personal gains and vested party interests leaving the farmers in the lurch after their own aims are fulfilled. The farmers agitations ultimately become an effective smoke-screen for the intensification of the exploitation of wage labour and atrocities on the rural poor at one level and rising pressure for satisfaction of the sectional interests of surplus farmers at another. The surplus farmers at the same time pretend to stand up as undisputed leaders of rural society as a whole.

Another dimension of agrarian unrest is the social conflict arising out of maltreatment and atrocities on Harijans, the weaker sections of the society. The assault on Harijans at social, economic and political levels -- is the result of a complex combination of causes that are perpetuated in many ways. Though the figures are of 1977 and 1978, a comparative picture of the trend of atrocities in 11 states is indicated in the table 5.3. [9]

Table 5.3

S.No.	States	No. of Atrocities 1977	1978	Percentage of Increase/Decrease	
1.	Andhra Pradesh	102	110	7.84	(+)
2.	Bihar	681	1911	180.62	(+)
3.	Gujarat	331	540	63.14	(+)
4.	Karnataka	59	376	537.27	(+)
5.	Kerala	233	767	229.18	(+)
6.	Madhya Pradesh	3366	3240	3.74	(+)
7.	Maharashtra	570	1046	83.51	(+)
8.	Orissa	69	135	95.65	(+)
9.	Rajasthan	261	886	239.46	(+)
10.	Tamil Nadu	54	130	140.15	(+)
11.	Uttar Pradesh	4974	5660	13.79	(+)

In 1981, the government has recorded 11,743 incidents of atrocities in the first eleven months. In 1980, the number was 13,746 and in 1979 the figures were 13, 426 cases. In 1978, there were 15,053 cases of atrocities against Harijans. On June 17, 1988 an armed mob of 55 supportors of the Arvind faction of Mazdoor Kissan Sangram Samiti (MKSS) launched a surprise attack on the Harijan Toli of Nagwa of Nenhai village of Jahanabad district in Bihar and brutally killed 18 Harijans who belonged to Indian People's Front (IPF). In 1987, about 20 people belonging to Alelchak Bhagaura and Chechani villages of Bihar were killed in caste-clashes and atrocities were committed on other villagers. The term atrocities covers cases of murder, rape, arson and violence although the term has not been defined by the penal laws. National Police Commission has noticed the increasing awakening in the rural areas leading to bitter and brutal caste and class conflicts. Rural unrest can be anticipated in future as rural landless workers and small agriculturalists are now organising themselves demanding better wages and better prices for their products. It is anticipated that the most serious threats to law and order will in future arise in rural areas. [10] The problems of the north-eastern region which have caused great concern to the Central Govenment during the last four decades since India's independence are basically economic in nature and can be termed as peasant unrest or agrarian unrest in a limited sense. Insurgency, violence, ethnic conflicts seem to be the apparent causes of unrest in north - eastern region but the basic cause is agrarian and economic in nature. Mizo unrest was the direct outcome of economic backwardness and famine conditions in 1965 and it can be to some extent called an agrarian unrest. In 1965, the district was hit by famine and within the next couple of years a full scale insurgency was on. [11] If we trace the genesis of unrest in Mizoram we find that it was in the year 1959 that there was a serious famine in Mizoram and in order to provide relief measures for the victims of the great famine a voluntary organisation known as Mizo National Front was formed. Thus Mizoram insurgency was basically an agrarian unrest which got political, tribal and ethnic dimensions at a later state. However, agrarian unrest in north-eastern region has been contained by various economic, political and legal measures, under the I.R.D.P. 58.15 per cent of the fimilies could be assisted in the region by the financial institutions during the sixth plan period and subsequent five year plans.

Agrarian unrest in various parts of the country are on the increase due to the following main reasons:

(1) A new set of values centering on consumerism, religious fanaticism, provincialism and gross conspicuous consumption have been taking root in rural areas resulting in agrarian unrest.

(2) The creditability of the institutions which sustain our social, economic and political structures has been seriously eroded in recent years and there is consequently an all pervasive decline in respect of and authority of law in rural areas. Grossly criminal, corrupt and anti-social activities are acquiring legitimacy due to developing ambivalence towards societal norms resulting in agrarian unrest.

(3) Indian villages have never been idyllic abodes of peace. Tensions between different castes, classes and communities in rural India have been always acute; often enough they have led to fearful eruptions of organised violence. [12]

(4) Agrarian unrest has been compound by the grant of adult franchise, spread of education and the growth of political consciousness.

(5) The farmers agitations in different parts of the country has acquired a vigorous momentum on its own due to their muscle - flexing and popular support by various political parties who are keeping an eye on the rural vote-bank.

(6) Concentrtion of jobs as well as good things of life in the cities led to the migration of the rural folk to the cities and their awareness of industrial unions' strength has given rural farmers a new awareness of their strength. Peasants are now asking for abolition of the betterment levy in irrigated areas, cancellation of agricultural

loans, and most significantly an agreement in principle that agriculture would be regarded as an industry and that an attempt would be made to strike a new parity between the prices of industrial manufactures and farm produce. [73]

(7) Caste / Class war is on the increase in Bihar, Uttar Pradesh and some other northern states where upper classes are not able to reconcile to the new balance of power created by the protection to the weaker sections of the society by the Government. Belchi, Pipra, Parasbigha, Masaurhi, Arwal, Darmia and Pelalchak are some of the instances of mounting agrarian violence in Gangetic Bihar and Uttar Pradesh. Naxalite violence, caste - wars and class struggle are all on the increase and it is easy to see that rural violence will not lessen in the near future. No one is able to find an easy and workable solution to the ever-mounting agrarian unrest.

(8) According to Prof. Rajni Kothari, "In rural Bihar, Orissa, Andhra Pradesh, Madhya Pradesh, Eastern U.P. and Haryana life has been rendered so insecure that people have themselves begun to identify their protectors and destroyers and do not hesitate to talk in terms of violence. This is happening both among the landlords and dominant castes (who have lots of firearms and mercenaries in their pay) and the militant sections of the downtrodden communities who, though weaker are also being forced to think in confrontation terms." [14] Rural Bihar and Orissa, like rural Andhra and Tamil Nadu, according to Rajni Kothari, is seething with revolt. The confrontation between the haves and the have-nots in rural areas is maturing and major mass movements, a leading example of which is Mazdoor Kisan Sangharsha Samiti (MKSS) in Bihar are on the upswing and are destined to make themselves felt in the long run for democratic rights and social transformation.

(9) Population explosion is an important reason for agrarian unrest. In rural areas there is demand for land due to increasing population. Inequal distribution of land and defective system of heredity of land have aggravated agrarian unrest.

(10) Agrarian unrest in India is part of the new growing Indian culture of violence, indiscipline and agitational politics. "If the language of violence has become the national language", says K.S. Srinivasan, "it is because governments, all over India, seem to recognise only that language; nothing moves authority until there is loss of life and property." [15] The root cause of agrarian unrest today is the appalling lack of faith, between people and government, between

sections of society, between man and man. An adjunct of Indian politics in the last three decades has been the glorification of the mob. Politicians fan frouble during agrarian unrest for their vested interests.

(11) According to social thinkers agrarian unrest in India is a "Symptom of changing social order." [16] Agrarian unrest today represents the awakening among the oppressed about their rights and privileges and their preparedness to fight for them. They are no more prepared to suffer in silence and would rather prefer to take to arms. When the consciousness grows among the landless labourers about their rights, the tendency among the landlords is to meet it through strong arm methods. The lack of even basic amenities like roads, water supply, communication and jobs for the unemployed is also a factor accentuating rural violence and agrarian unrest. The criminalisation of politics, aided and abetted by the politicians, as evident during elections when booth-capturing becomes the order of the day, also accounts in its own way for the growing agrarian unrest. This is coupled with the easy availability of firearms and ammunitions mostly of the illegal variety in many pockets of the states. Thus the entire social order today is aggravating agrarian violence in India.

The present police organisational structure is inadequate to meet the growing agrarian unrest due to the following main reasons.

(1) Strength of present rural police is inadequate.

(2) The communication facilities in rural areas are poor and unsatisfactory.

(3) Lack of effective leadership at middle ranks namely Inspectors and Sub-Inspectors.

(4) Gross underestimation of future events and failure of intelligence planning.

(5) Lack of commitment and motivation in police force.

(6) Lack of adequate training and lack of preparedness to deal with agrarian unrest.

(7) Lack of proper manpower planning and misuse of available resources.

(8) Partial attitude of police officials.

(9) Corruption in police force and arrogant attitude.

(10) Poor system of communication with weaker section of society.

(11) Inadequate representation of Scheduled Castes/Scheduled Tribes and other weaker sections in middle and higher ranks.

(12) Prejudiced and biased attitude of police towards poor and downtrodden.

(13) Inadequate transport and non-availability of transport for emergency duties.

(14) Lack of proper rapport and communication with representatives of farmers and other weaker sections of the society.

(15) Agrarian unrest is considered as purely law and order problem and not a socio-economic problem.

(16) lack of proper orientation and briefing in rural police for such tasks and inadequate response.

Rural policing of India needs qualitative and quantitative improvements for meeting the growing agrarian unrest. In rural area a police station should have about 50 to 60 thousand of population to cover and from the crime point of view 600 crimes annually is the maximum for a rural police station. It is also necessary that civil police should have only graduates as Sub-Inspectors and there should be no lower ranks in the rural civil police in due course of time. All constables and head constables should be transferred to armed police for sentry and other duties. More police stations should be opened in rural areas. Modernisation of rural police is needed in terms of transport, communication and use of computers. Rural policing needs to be improved by better training and motivation of police personnel. Rural policing in India needs immediate attention. The number of rural police stations should be immediately increased as per the felt needs. Home guards and village defence parties should also be constituted and trained under the proposed village police act. Legislation of a comprehensive act by the state governments to set up an effective village police system is recomended. The challenges of the future will require new skills in personnel management, and a much higher level of professional knowledge, commpetence and leadership from the senior officers in the police. [17] It is however obvious that the problems of agrarian unrest and social violence that beset our nation will not be solved by police measures alone, however necessary these may be. A deeper and long term agenda of thought and action is called for, especially as the deeper malady is being exacerbated by a number of other developments. [18] Police can play only a very limited role of collecting intelligence and controlling and containing violence and agrarian unrest by effective patrolling and other containment strategies, organisational police structure of the rural areas in India must strive to develop an organisational climate that will encourage social justice, democratic values of life, crime prevention and healthy police-public relations. Improved training programmes, individual career development plans, selection of effective police leaders, a more flexible orgainsational structure and effective man-power planning alone can build up a modern rural police in India which will be capable of dealing with growing agrarian unrest in the future.

Agrarian unrest cannot be handled by police alone. The state governments and the entire nation have to play their respective roles to deal with the growing agrarian unrest. In May 1988 about 60,000 Orissa farmers from 4500 panchayats assembled at Bhubaneswar. The Orissa Chief Minister said. " All political parties are exploiting the farmers. The Government decided to bring their representatives together, hear their problems and work out a solution in consultation with them." The highlights of the promises showered on the gathering included the following: (1) 1000 more subsidised fertiliser outlets in rural areas; (2) releasing 80,000 Adivasi and small farmers from the cooperative loan burden by compensating the lending institutions with Rs. 2/- crore from the anti-poverty programme funds; (3) heavy subsidies to dig 50,000 wells; (4) panchayat level crop insurance Schemes covering 1.2 lakh farmers which will cost Rs. 18/- crores of which the state government will pay Rs. 6/- crores and the Centre and insurance companies the rest. [(19)] In Orissa during February/March 1988, over 3,000 farmers and their families courted arrest demanding implementation of major irrigation project. Thus political will is needed to redress the grievances of the farmers. Agrarian unrest can be contained and controlled only by giving farmers their legitimate dues and much needed economic support by the government. For example in Andhra Pradesh state was giving electricity at Rs. 50 per HP per year to the agriculturalists and supplying fertilisers and pesticides at 50 per cent subsidy to farmers during natural calamites. Government of India has launched a number of economic programmes under Twenty Point Programme for the amelioration of the economic condition of rural poor. Special programmes for the weaker sections are : the Small Farmers Development Agency (SFDA), the Marginal Farmers and Agricultural Labourer Development Agency (MFADA) and the Integrated Dry Land Agricultural Development. Bonded Labour System (Abolition) Act 1976 has made all bonded workers free and discharged from any obligation to render bonded labour. The Twenty Point Programme of 1982 emphasises on effective enforcement of minimum wages for agricultural labour. The above measures have to some extent checked and contained growing agrarian unrest in India. Agrarian unrest can be ultimately diffused through political, administrative and social measures aimed at bringing social harmony in rural areas and economic transformation of the undeveloped regions. A suitable strategy needs to be worked out by the state govenments through intelligent use of radio, T.V. and Press to ensure that agrarian harmony is built up in rural areas through various socio-economic and political actions. Masses should be mobilised to keep rural fabric intact and help in building a violence free rural India. A former Planning Commission expert on agrarian reform who drafted the well known Task-Force Report has recently observed : "We are not likely to formulate and implement a meaningful anti-poverty programme until the numerically large poverty groups get themselves together organised and start influencing public policy. [20]

Notes and References

1. Kathleen Gough and Hari P. Sharma -- *Imperialism and Revolutions in South Asia.*
2. Ajoy Bose, "Naxalites : A Change of Focus", Express Magazine - *Indian Express,* June 12, 1988.
3. "Farmers on the March," *Indian Express,* Sunday Edition Magazine Section, February 21, 1988.
4. Ajoy Bose, *op. cit.*
5. For further details see Govt. of India First and Second reports of the Commission for Scheduled Castes and Scheduled Tribes (1978-79).
6. For further details see Express Magazine *Indian Express*, 18th April, 1982 PPI and also M. Shivaraman in H.P. Sharma and K. Gough (1973) - *Imperialism and Revolution in South Asia* pp. 246-64 (Monthly Review Press)
7. Government of India - Ministry of Home Affairs "Annual Report of the Implementation of the Protection of Civil Right Act 1955 for the year 1980".
8. Sharad Joshi, "The Lessons of Meerut", *Indian Express,* Sunday Magazine, March 27, 1988.
9. For further details and special report see *Indian Express*, Sunday Edition, April 18, 1982. p.1.6.
10. Dharam Vira, "Report of the National Police Commission" (Eighth Report) p.20 para 62.20.
11. Banerjee, "The Troubled North-East", *Sunday* (Calcutta) Vol. 12. No.5 - 14-20 February 1988. p.29.
12. K.C. Khanna, "Farmers on the War Path - A New Facet of Rural unrest", *The Times of India,* Nov. 18, 1980, p.8.

13. *Ibid.*

14. Rajni Kothari, "Violence over National Language" *The Hindustan Times,* Sunday Magazine, July 26, 1987, p.9.

15. K. S. Srinivasan, "The Roots of Violence", *The Hindustan Times,* May 2, 1987.

16. A. J. Phillip, "Bihar Violence - Symptom of Changing Social Order".

17. Sixth Report of the National Police Commission Govt. of India, March 1981, p.1.

18. Surinder Suri, "Growing Social Discontent: Clash of Head and Heart", *The Times of India,* December 8, 1986.

19. Farzand Ahmed, "Attempt to Woo Farmers - Orissa's Costly Stunt", *India Today,* June 30, 1988, p.61.

20. See P.S. Appy, "The Phoney War - Reaction to Poverty Symposium", *Financial Express,* dated 1 November, 1982, p.5 also see "The Report of the Task Force on Agrarian Relations", *Kurukshetra* Vol. XXVII No. 13, 1 April, 1979, pp.4-22.

CHAPTER-6

EROSION IN POLICE MORALE

NAPOLEON BONAPARTE once said, "In war, morale conditions make up three quarters of the game; the relative strength of material and balance of man-power account for the remaining quarter". [1] Morale is the general overtone of employee attitude in the organisation as a whole. Morale is an intangible but effective indicator of need satisfaction both of the individual employee and of the group as a whole. *Webster Dictionary* defines morale as "a mental condition with respect to courage, discipline, confidence, enthusiasm and willingness to endure hardship". Morale is a mental condition of groups and individuals that determines their attitude and eagerness to their work, it connotes something highly tangible and subjective. Group morale is a measure of the summed motivations of group members to work together towards a common goal assigned to the organisation while the individual morale is just a measure of an individual's response and motivation to pursue with others the common organisational goals and objectives. Morale can be said to be the sum total of several pshychic qualities that include courage, resolution, fortitude, zeal, enthusiasm, confidence and determination to carry out the expected job in a given situation.

The Concept of Morale

It is pretty difficult to define 'morale' as there is much confusion about the exact connotation of the word. Morale is "wanting to do what you have to do" but it is very vague one. In the words of R.M. Guion, "morale is the extent to which an individual's needs are satisfied and the extent to which the individual perceives that satisfaction as stemming from his total job satisfaction". (*Individual Morale: The problem of Terminology*) According to Blum and Naylor morale can be defined as "the possession of a feeling on the part of the employee of being accepted by, and belonging to, a group of employees through adherence to common goals and confidence in the leadership of these goals" (*Industrial Psychology*). Dalton E. Mc Forland stated that "Morale is basically a group phenomenon. It is a concept that describes the level of favourable or unfavourable attitudes of the employees collectively to all aspects of their work, the job, the organisation, the tasks, working conditions fellow-workers, superiors and so on. Attitudes express what the individuals think and feel about their jobs. The emphasis is on how employees feel denoting the strong emotional elements associated with attitudes (*Personnel Management-Principles and Practice*). Morale is a dynamic psychological phenomenon, it is a subtle environment, formed by the sum total of the attitudes of the people working in an organisation, which has a great impact on the ultimate success or failure of the organisation in fulfilling its assigned tasks and responsibilities. In general parlance the word "Morale" is used very loosely in the sense of enthusiasm, zeal or esprit-ed-corps. It at times refers to a combination of employees' attitudes, towards employment and is a synthesis of how employees think and feel about their jobs, their working conditions, their superior officers, their organisation, their colleagues, their pay, their promotion chance and so on. Morale is generally judged by symptoms such as work stoppages, acts of indisciplines, or strikes, but can be generally appraised through attitude opinion, interviews and surveys. Employees' morale is said to be high when they feel enthusiastic and optimistic about their work and is said to be low or poor when they are dissatisfied, pessimistic and frustrated with their job. The judgements about levels of morale rest on some such evidence as of actions, expressions, oral comments, criticisms and answers to questions and all such evidences have to be correctly and objectively interpreted. Erosion of morale can be said to exist when there are work stoppages, high personnel turnover, lack of interest, absenteeism, disciplinary problems. If the employees seem dissatisfied, irritated, cranky, critical, restless, pessimistic and indisciplined, these reactions can be described as evidence of erosion of morale. In contrast the main four attributes of a good morale are as follows:

(a) Zeal -- the voluntary "plus" which a man gives to his task, over and beyond perfunctory obedience to regulations.

(b) Discipline -- in General Marshall's words "cheerful and understanding subordination of the individual to the good of the team."

(c) Self -- Confidence -- basic sense of personal worth, founded on a realistic appraisal of what the job is like and on confidence in past training and present leadership.

(d) Satisfaction -- freedom from discontent and worry, fundamental satisfaction with one's day-to-day part in the organisation.[(2)] In any organisation the following indicate the presence of high morale:

(i) Feeling of togetherness in an organisation;

(ii) Well defined goals of the organisation;
(iii) Well defined goals of individuals within the framework of group goals;
(iv) Feeling of job satisfaction;
(v) Personal adjustment; and cultural orientation;
(vi) Ego-involvement in one's job;
(vii) Social recognition and status;
(viii) Initiative, regularity and punctuality, commitment to the work;
(ix) Sharing common goals with one's work group and having confidence in the desirability of these goals;
(x) Sound manpower management and organisational health;
(xi) Effective organisational leadership at all levels in the organisation.

The factors enumerated above are the important determinants of morale in any organisation. Erosion of morale starts in the absence or deterioration of some of the factors mentioned above.

Indicators and Determinants of Morale

Broadly the term includes both individual and group aspects of morale; individual morale being the structure of an employee's mental attitudes towards employment, working conditions and organisational goals; whereas group morale is the general tone of employee attitudes in the organisation as a whole or in a particular branch or department. Generally morale in an organisation and the ultimate success of an organisation depends on the group morale of the employees towards the accomplishment of its objectives. In all organisations due to hierarchy system, there are distinct groups. In police organisation, there are distinct and clearly devisible four groups of personnel. Constables to Havildars constitute approximately ninety two per cent of the total police force, subordinate officers constitute approximately six per cent of the force, state police gazetted officers constitute 0.6 per cent of the force and senior police officers of Indian Police Service constitute 1.4 per cent of the police force. Thus there are four distinct groups in civil police force and group morale of each group is determined by somewhat distinct factors, though there are certain common factors also. Erosion of police morale in the constabulary group is reflected by the recent police unrest in Maharashtra, Haryana and other places. The para-military force, Central Reserve Police Force, Railway Protection Force, Central Bureau of Investigation, Intelligence Bureau and Central

Industrial Security Force have also in recent years noticed gradual erosion in morale of their personnel. Erosion, the dictionary defines as "eating away," and "wearing down". The police morale is gradually being eroded and process seems to be very fast and clearly visible. The police strike in various states and central police organisations in 1979, recent Bombay and Haryana police strikes clearly indicate that their morale is eroded and police personnel have adopted the war path out of sheer frustration. In order to get the correct extent of erosion of morale in police, one can gauge from the important determinants of morale which are as under:

1. Individual and group attitude towards the organisations in general.
2. General attitude towards supervision and seniors.
3. Work load, work pressure and work tension.
4. The inter-relationship between subordinates and seniors.
5. Satisfaction with job-standards and job expectations.
6. Treatment to the individual in the organisation in matters of welfare, leave, personnel management and retirement.
7. Pride in the profession of organisation and social status.
8. Satisfaction with salary and allowances and variation with contemporary salary structure system.
9. Intrinsic job satisfaction and motivational factors.
10. General attitude towards formal communication system in the organisation.
11. Satisfaction with and chances for progress, promotion and postings in attractive places or assignments.
12. General attitude towards co-workers and *esprit-d'-corps*.
13. Working conditions and prestige in and outside the organisation.
14. Extent of professional autonomy and scope for specialisation.
15. Professional hazards and risks and the compensation for it.
16. Organisational structure, organisational health and system of human resource development.
17. Organisation polices on pesonnel management and welfare.

Though no authentic research survey has been carried out to analyse the extent of erosion of police morale, high rate of desertion and absentee without leave cases, slackness in dress, and saluting, of misunderstanding of orders, frequent requests for transfers, insubordination, wilful disobedience of orders, court cases and disrespect to seniors are visible indications of erosion of police morale. Poor leadership has been a great contributory factor in erosion of police morale. Two very small surveys on attitude of subordinate police men carried out by the syndicate group of senior officers course of National Police Academy, Hyderabad reveal that the morale of police is gradually eroding. 68.5 per cent of the respondents surveyed held the definite view that Government was not doing what it should for the betterment of police personnel. 87 per cent of police ranks seemed to be disillusioned with the long working hours. 73.5 per cent of the respondents held the view that the people were not friendly and helpful to the police. (For further details please see *Transactions* - S.V.P. National Police Academy, Hyderabad, 1974, pp.11-39.)

Causes of Erosion of Police Morale

Frequent judicial or magisterial enquiries into alleged police excesses while dispersing assemblies of people have brought in very demoralising effect in the police administration. There is now a distinct inclination among the police to avoid using force while dealing with violent crowds and allow arson, looting and murders to happen in order to save themselves from appearing before inquiry committees to defend themselves, against charges made by members of the public. The sub-human standard of existence, the long impossible hours of duty, and the tremendous pressures of a job which is both taxing and unendearing have completely eroded the morale of the policemen. The outdated concept of administrative accountability, the relegation of the bulk of the service to improductive role performance, lack of social status, absence of vertical mobility in carrier planning, a distorted scheme of rewards and punishments, cynical acceptance of corruption as a way of life, communication gap within the police organisation and lack of effective leadership are some of the main causes of erosion of police morale. Irrational and arbitrary postings and transfers of the police officers have contributed to the groupism and intriguing at various police levels and have caused the greatest erosion to police morale. Political interference at all levels of police administration has caused the greatest erosion to police morale. Police constabulary who constitute ninety-two per cent of the police force, put in long hours of work on religious and national holidays without any extra allowance or compensatory leave. They are treated at par with unskilled labourers and eighty per cent of them retire in the same rank after serving the police force for thirtyfive years. Thus they develop " the police sub-culture of a persecuted minority community". [3] Police often have to deal with their clients adversaries and frequently under p.essure to serve incompatible ends. The incompatible demands made on police, and the power dynamics effect the morale of the policemen. In day--to--day life policeman is faced with prejudice, fear, suspicion and sometimes with hostility in his performance of duties and this lowers the police man's frustration-tolerance level and ultimately his morale. Inadequate emoluments, lack of housing facilities, long hours of work, harsh and hostile treatment accorded to the police, insecurity of job, absence of promotional opportunities, social isolation, political interference, low social status, absence of effective machinery of redressal of grievances, statutory disability and restriction on fundamental rights are some of the factors which have caused erosion in the police morale. Politicization of the police and the erosion of the police morale as a result of political interference with the normal working of the force constitute a malaise that is common to almost all states. (4) Favouritism, nepotism, corruption and violation of departmental rules in carrying out duties had eroded the police morale. Change over of Inspector General and Superintendent of Police without proper justification on flimsy grounds have also caused erosion of police morale. Lack of material incentives such as inadequate housing facilities, low pay and allowances, inadequate death and pensionary benefits, absence of good schooling facilities for children, frequent transfers and difficult working conditions with long hours of work all these factors have eroded the morale of police personnel. Mr. Bhagwan Das Shastri, President of All India Non-Gazetted Policemen's Federation has said "that the morale of the police force is at the lowest ebb at present". (5) The liberalised regulations regarding possession of firearms have brought up a new wave of murders, dacoities, extortion and armed robberies and have caused erosion of police morale as they feel helpless (6) in controlling increasing rate of lawlessness, particularly in states of Bihar, U.P., Punjab and Delhi. Defective criminal justice system has also caused great erosion of police morale as courts do not convict the criminals and they manage to be out with bails and petitions. Policemen of all ranks have no forum to properly ventilate their grievances and problems and the police unionisation has not served the desired purpose. (7) It is significant that police administration is still governed by the Indian Police Act 1861 and the crisis of Indian legal system has eroded the morale of the police force. Inadequate and unsatisfactory training in training institutions from disgruntled instructors also causes erosion of police morale. Summing up political interference, poor management practices, difficult working conditions, lack of effective leadership, misuse of privileges by superiors, increased organisational bickerings and formation of informal group (cliques) in the organisation, lack of job satisfaction and negative role of police-- all these factors have gradually eroded the morale of police personnel.

Implications of Erosion of Police Morale for Public

A demoralised and diffident police administration cannot act as the bulwark of law and order and social stability. Erosion of police morale has resulted in the fall of standards of police performance and increase in the complaints against them ranging from cruelty and indifference to duty to dishonest investigation, illegal detention, collusion with criminals, rudeness towards people and what is worse, even corruption and practice of third degree methods. Erosion of police morale has added a very disturbing and infamous dimension during the last decade in which some senior police leaders went out of their way to sing paeans to the people then in power, some braggingly concocted criminal charges were framed against their political rivals and some took a personal part in tormenting persons in their custody even to the extent of eliminating inconvenient political opponents in the name of so-called "encounters", just to please their political bosses. Erosion of police morale has caused lack of confidence by subordinates in their superior officers and subordinates have started cultivating political masters and power that may be. Good work, seniority and good discipline have no more any considerations for promotions, transfers and postings and subordinates have lost confidence in their leaders. Erosion of police morale results in police ineffectiveness. The image of ineffectiveness is a double-edged weapon which brings down the respect of police (i) in the eyes of the people of the community and (ii) in the professional estimation of the policemen and ultimately lead to following consequences:

(1) A bulk of the crime and criminal offences against law go unregistered, uninvestigated and hushed up.

(2) The weaker sections of the society feel insecure and a socio-psychological belief takes over the common man -- that might is right, and thereby threatening the very existence of a civilised life.

(3) Political, economic and social peace is threatened by the few fanatics who take law into their own hands.

(4) It may result in administrative chaos, functional anarchy and failure of a civil government in the ultimate analysis.

(5) Communal riots, political vandalism, social conflicts, industrial and campus unrest become the order of the day and ordinary citizen feels insecure, harassed and helpless and ultimately aggravates the crisis of policing in a pluralistic society.

(6) Erosion of police morale leading to police ineffectiveness will ultimately usher an era of lawlessness and ordinary citizens will lose faith in the efficacy of the democratic institutions.

(7) The demoralised policeman will breed distrust and alienation in the community. On the other hand, professional frustration, bordering on cynicism, will weaken the morale fibre of the police and is bound to create psychological void in the lives of those who live in the midst of crime and criminals. They will develop an indifference to their work and deterioration in the quality of policing.

(8) Analysing the consequences of erosion of police morale, Professor O.W. Wilson of the California University has said, "When the activities of the police are misunderstood and construed as wrong, their morale is damaged, the maintenance of *esprit-d'-corps* is made difficult and they develop a negative mental state that causes them to be fearful of undertaking any constructive work. And faced with a critical, hostile public, the police unfortunately tend to develop a hostile attitude which worsens public relations." [(8)]

(9) Unfortunately not many empirical studies have been conducted about the state of morale of policemen, but it is a commonplace experience that policemen, particularly of subordinate and lower ranks are too frustrated to bother about their own public image and continue to indulge in vulgar display of their power, arrogance, corruption and sadistic tendencies. They even do not make any secrets of their frustrations, dissatisfactions, anguish and obvious failures and continue to act as petty pawns on the chess-board of district, state or central politics. [(9)]

(10) Erosion of police morale has resulted in social isolation and alienation of the police from the society and further strengthening the hold of "police-sub-culture". A policeman feels pariah in social life and ultimately develops a cynical outlook to the society he is expected to serve.

How to cure the Erosion of Police Morale

If the malady of erosion of police morale is to be cured, it is better to treat the malady with proper diagnosis and treatment rather than treating a few symptoms. The erosion of police morale can be cured only if the entire police system is reformed on proper lines with a new police act having trust on policeman. In police administration there is need for police "leaders" and not "bosses". [(10)] There is a clear failure on the part of the police leaders to develop a rapport with the rank and file of the organisation and taking up stand with the government to redress the genuine grievances of their subordinate policemen. Indian police today needs "the nurturant task leaders: who have affection and consideration for subordinates and initiate, guide and direct their subordinates to maintain a high level of efficiency with utilisation of latest techniques of motivation and morale building. [(11)] Police has to build up a healthy organisational climate and opportunities for vertical and horizontal mobility and promotions. The genuine problems and grievances of the policemen have to be looked into and resolved in a most just manner.

Public cooperation and willingness to assist police can stop further erosion of police morale. Public cooperation and public trust can build morale and restore the police confidence of the policemen in their own selves. Morale building is an unending process in an organisation and the following specific steps can help in the process:

1. Sound manpower management.
2. Sound organisational pattern having structural conduciveness for specialisation, professionalism and autonomy.
3. Human relations approach in management and work environment.
4. All ranks participation in management and healthy subordinate-senior relationship.
5. Utilisation of modern motivational techniques by police leaders and building up of effective communication system within the organisation.
6. Job enlargement and job enrichment with opportunities for vertical and horizontal mobility.
7. Establishment of police security committees at central, state and district levels and giving of complete autonomy to police officers by abolishing control of district magistrate over police.
8. Orientation and restructuring of training so that it becomes more practical, field oriented and related to the real job.

9. Building up of high powered police research organisations at each state level to monitor the organisational problems and suggest remedial measures.
10. Police reforms based on principles of autonomy recognition, modernisation, specialisation, professionalisation, decentralisation, democratisation and management orientation. [12]
11. An institutionalised system to protect and safeguard the interests of upright and conscientious policemen who refuse to carry out improper and at time illegal order of politicians and their superiors.

Police morale cannot be built in a day and it is a very slow and gradual process but a bold beginning has to be made immediately. To stop further erosion of police morale " Expert Committee Approach" should be adopted in which experts make a spot survey, talk to the people, write a comprehensive report in which they give advice regarding ways and means to build up high morale. The expert committee should be constituted for uncovering environmental conditions and technical difficulties which in their opinion lowers morale. The expert committee consisting of management experts can provide wise counsel to the government by suggesting concrete steps for building up the police morale. The National Police Commission Report should be published and its recommendations should be immediately implemented as it constituted of many police leaders and experts.

Conclusion

Morale in an organisation does not mean that "people get along together"; the test is performance, not conformance. [13] The first requirement of organisational health is a high demand on performance and a management that does not define performance as a batting average is a management that mistakes conformity for achievement and absence of weaknesses for strength. Performance is the consistent ability to produce high result over prolonged periods of time and in a variety of assignments. Organisational analysis with an eye to improve the social status, working conditions and job satisfaction will go a long way in building up the morale in the long run. Morale can be built up and developed over a long period of time as a result of sound management and personnel policies and procedures, good supervisory practices, effective leadership, better working and living conditions and use of correct motivational techniques. A concerted effort on the part of the police, the public and the government alone can provide a sound basis for refurbishing the eroding police morale.

Notes and References

1. Napoleon, *Correspondence de Napoleon*, Paris 1865, Vol. 17, No. 14, 275, p. 549.
2. Dr. Donald A. Machinnon-"Motivation and Morale". In *Psychology for the Armed Services.* Edwin G.Boring (Ed.) (1979) p.326.
3. Harshad R.Trivedi (1975) -- *Urbanism: A New Outlook*, Atma Ram and Sons, Delhi, p.184.
4. *The Times of India*, August 31, 1982, "Haryana's Police", Editorial.
5. *Indian Express*, 1 October 1982, New Delhi.
6. For further elucidation see Vinod Tuli, "*Menace of Fire Arms*: Need for Stricter Licencing", *The Times of India*, August 14,1982.
7. Dr. Upendra Baxi (1982) -- *The Crisis of the Indian Legal System* (Vikas, New Delhi) has analysed the issue at great length.
8. Quoted in "The Punjab Police Commission Report 1982", Chapter-V, Sub-section-8.
9. For similar views see, "Report of Mahajan Commission", Govt. of India, New Delhi, 1986.
10. Raj Nandy in his article, "Art of Management--Have Leaders instead of Bosses", (*The Times of India*, September 8, 1982), has very effectively analysed the problem in its proper perspective.
11. For fuller details of the concept please see Jai B.P. Sinha (1980) -- *The Nurturant Task Leaders*, Concept Publishing Company, New Delhi.
12. For details on Police Reforms please refer Dr. P.D. Sharma (1981) -- *Police Polity and People in India*, New Delhi.
13. Peter F. Drucker (1978) -- *Management Tasks - Responsibilities and Functions.*

CHAPTER-7

HISTORY AND DEVELOPMENT OF CENTRAL RESERVE POLICE FORCE

CENTRAL RESERVE Police Force is a versatile force, trained and equipped to deal with armed insurgents, infiltrators, anti-social elements, extremists, terrorists, and violent mobs on the one hand and to provide rescue and relief operations against natural calamities and man created contingencies on the other. It has carried out its varied and onerous duties with utmost discipline, devotion, loyalty and efficiency during the last fifty years of its glorious record of history. The CRPF is not only the oldest police force functioning under the Ministry of Home Affairs but is also one of the most reliable, dependable and versatile force that has stood the test of time. The force has come to be reckoned as an important factor for ensuring internal security, peace and national integration of the country. The force has made rapid and praiseworthy strides on various fronts during the last fifty years of its dedicated service to the nation. The CRPF has set very high examples of courage, discipline, honesty, integrity and unflinching devotion to duty and a future historian of India's political and administrative developments will surely record the great and progressively growing role of CRP during the last four decades of our existence as a free, independent, democratic socialist secular republic. The CRP has had a most fascinating and chequered history which can be briefly brought out into various milestones of its long and glorious journey.

The Central Reserve Police Force was originally constituted as the Crown Representative's Police Force on 27th July, 1939. The Force was designed to operate in detachments under the superintendence and control of the Political Agents of the locality in "political relation" with the native States concerned. The force was organised and trained on military lines to come in aid to civil power in Princely States in Pre-independence era. Originally the force was sanctioned with One Commandant, 7 superior officers, 30 subordinate officers, 100 Head Constables/Naiks and 870 Lance Naiks/Constables. The force was to be organised on a class composition basis roughly coming to 375 Hindus, 375 Muslims and 250 Sikhs. Neemuch in district Mandsaur was selected as the headquarters of the Force. Major Peart, a British officer was its first Commanding Officer. Its accessibility to the Princely States of Central India, and its strategic importance as the gateway between Rajasthan and Malwa plateau, together with its commercial eminence as the centre of the largest opium growing area next to Gazipur, must have been factors for its selection as the headquarters of the C.R.P. Its initial recruitment was started, first of all from the disbanded personnel of 4th/2nd Punjab Regiment and from the Mina Corps from Erinpura and Deoli areas and lastly from the retired or released ex-army personnel, from open market in Punjab, the N.W.F.P, Rajputana and Delhi areas. The force of the strength of a Battalion was initially raised by an army officer Major Peart who was its first Commandant. The force was organised into four Service companies, two Tear Smoke Platoons and a Headquarters Wing to provide the administrative and training staff. After its basic training, the CRP provided during 1940 and 1941, detachments to Charkhari State, Mhow and Indore, all in Central India, on duties which normally would have devolved on the Army units 'in aid of the civil power'. Besides, contingents were sent to Abu and Deoli, to provide the vital guards and at the latter place, to guard the political detenus of German and Italian descent. In the year 1942, a small fleet of patrol cars and a wireless contingent was added to the Force and a scheme was adopted as a measure of establishing closer co-operation with the native States; whereby the members of the State Police Forces of Rajputana and Gwalior areas attended the Crown Representative's Police courses at Neemuch. With the arming of the force with P-14 Rifles with peep sights, the scope for baptism of fire on active duty was provided to the force in Khairpur State in Sind, during the Hur trouble of 1942-44. Under the command of Major N.S. Holmes, a detachment of 3 service Coys was sent in March 1942 to Khairpur State to deal with the Hur menace. The Crown Representative's Police captured a large number of notorious Hur outlaws and recovered innumerable weapons and large quantities of arms and also train-wrecking implements. During 1942, George Cross(G) Medal was awarded to Naik Barket Singh of 1st Bn. The names of the two Crown Representative's Police Officers, Messers Stracey and Osbourne, were among those who were mentioned in the despatches by General Wavell, the than Commander-in-Chief "for valuable services in connection with the operations of the Upper Sind Force, 1942-43". The Force carried out their duties in excellent manner for 16 months and then 2 coys were returned to Neemuch in July 1943 and the 3rd Coy was withdrawn in May 1944. The Khairpur Durbar presented the Battalion with a handsome silver salver.

In 1943, another detachment of CRP was sent to Balasinor State in Baroda Agency under the command of Sub. Chanan Singh. This force arrested 64 dacoits and shot down one. It seized four BL and 28 ML guns with lots of ammunition, besides swords, daggers and miscellaneous weapons. The recovery of the stolen properties led to the detection of 23 dacoities, 8 robberies, 4 murders and 4 attempted murders.

Indian Police Medal(Gallantry) was awarded to HC Parbat Rao and Ct Dadu Kolekar during 1944 for capturing armed dacoits in which--on 14th December, 1943 during a raid carried out by the CRP detachment in a village in Balasinor State (Ahmedabad District) with the object of capturing the dacoits operating in the State. HC Parbat Rao noticed one of the dacoits aiming a gun at close range and from the lying position at the Police party under his command. The HC at once rushed and fell upon the dacoit and succeeded in disarming and capturing him. During the same raid one of the armed dacoits aimed his gun at the Jemadar and was about to fire when Ct Dadu Kolekar rushed upon him and brought him to the ground. HC Parbat Rao and Ct Dadu Kolekar by their prompt and courageous action saved the lives of other members of police party.

In 1945, the force was provided with No. 1 Mark III Rifle and the Tear Smoke Platoon was reorganised. The very Light Pistol was also introduced in the armament of the force. A detachment participated in the dacoity campaign in Rajputana, especially in Kishangarh State between December 1945 to June 1946 and rounded up 4 wanted desperate dacoits and lost one constable in the encounter. In fitting recognition for the good work done, 2 King's Police Medals and 3 Indian Police Medals for Gallantry were awarded, one of them posthumously to the deceased constable Soda Ram. The first induction of CRP was made in the undivided Punjab with a small contingent sent to Pataudi for a short spell of 2 months on anti-dacoity operation in 1945 at the request of Nawab, the ex-ruler.

On 24th February, 1946 when the detachment under the command of Sher Zaman Khan was on active duty in Kishangarh State on anti-dacoity operations, they were informed of the presence of a dangerous and desperate dacoit in a village. Immediately Sher Zaman Khan with his party approached and examined the huts suspected to house the dacoits when a shot was fired which gave a clue to the particular hut the dacoits were lurking in. There was exchange of fire in which constable Soda Ram was seriously wounded as it was getting dark and the coy commander's order to the dacoits to surrender was unheeded, he ignited the hut. Before doing so, he gave a final call of surrender to which the dacoits agreed, since one of them was also wounded. On their coming out they were surrounded and arrested with a large number of arms and ammunition. Ct Soda Ram died of his wounds on April 26,1946 in the Victoria Hospital, Ajmer. Sher Zaman Khan and the party acted with commendable promptness, carried out successful operation with skill and courage even when under continuous firing at close range throughout. Nk Pata Ram similarly entered a group of huts in one of which heavily armed outlaws were lurking. Ct Bhabuta Ram and Ct Ganga Ram displayed cool courage in removing their comrade Soda Ram, who gave his life in this encounter, under fire hazard from the dacoits.

During 1946 and 1947, C.R.P. was deployed at a number of places for short duration for maintenance of law and order and dealing with other internal security problems as can be seen below:

1946		
Rewa State	One coy with Tear Smoke	for 2 months.
Pataudi State	2 Platoons	for 2 months.
Dujana State	1 Platoon	for 1 month.
Datia State	4 Pls. & Tear Smoke	for 2 months.
Charkhari	2 Platoons	for 2 months.
Kothi State (Nowgong)	2 Platoons	for 2 months.
1947		
Loharu State	1 Platoon and Tear Smoke	for 1 month.
Ratlam	1 coy	for 2 months.
Ajmer	1 coy with Tear Smoke	for 1 month.
Delhi and Rampur	3 coys with Tear Smoke out of which 2 coys proceeded to Rampur in August. It checked communal trouble and saved the Nawab's palace.	from 30.7.47 to 12.11.47.
Rajkot	1 coy	since 22-8-47.
Junagadh	2 coys	
Nowgong	1 Platoon	for 2 months.
Chamba	1 Platoon	for 2 months.
Virahi	1 Platoon	for 2 months. (approx.)

The independence of the country marked an important watershed in the life of the C.R.P. which was renamed the Central Reserve Police by an Act of Parliament in 1949. This Act constituted the C.R.P. as one of the Armed Forces of the Union. C.R.P played the most glorious role of ensuring merger of small states of Manawadar, Bautwa, Sardargarh, Mangrol of Kathiawar and Junagadh which were likely to become 'Island of Pakistan' in Indian territory. Thus CRP played a most glorious role of carrying out the intricate task of integration of small states to the Federal Republic of India. On Sept. 16,1947 419 Muslim officers and other ranks proceeded to Pakistan and these vacancies were filled up in due course of time by Indian nationals including 150 Gurkhas. After the advent of freedom the force was re-named as 'Central Reserve Police' and was placed under the control of newly formed states' ministry. After independence, the first induction of CRPF in U.P was made in Rampur State then under the Nawab of Rampur in August 1947 due to anticipatory disturbances on the eve of partition of the country. 2 Platoons and one Tear Smoke Platoon remained in the State from Aug. 5,1947 to Aug. 8,1947. Small contingents were also sent to the erstwhile Princely States of Nowgong, Rewa, Jaora, Piploda, Indore, Mandsaur, Bhopal, Pratapgarh and Ujjain for law and order duties and for special anti-dacoity operations. After independence, 5 coys and 2 platoons of CRP were sent to take active part in the integration of Kathiawar States of Manawadar, Bautwa, Sardargarh, Mangral and Junagadh.

Realising the utility and necessity of a Central Armed Force by the Centre, on Feb. 13,1948, the Second battalion of CRP was raised. The first induction of CRP in Orissa was in the month of October 1948 when one coy of 1st Bn. was sent to the State to quell communal disturbances in the district Baripad. The coy was withdrawn in January 1949 after a stay of about 4 months. Henry Osbourne, the grand old man of CRPF commanded 2 Bn. CRPF for over a year and settled down at Neemuch after retirement in 1949.

In 1949, the CRP Act No. LXVI of 1949 was given assent by the Governor General on Dec. 28,1949 which provide for the Constitution and Regulation of an Armed Central Reserve Police Force. The Act has 19 sections and the schedules and was introduced by Sardar Patel with the following important speech:

"The Bill before the House follows generally the pattern of Crown Representative's Police Law. It makes provision for the constitution of the force, appointment of the officers, general duties of the members of the force, its administration and certain liabilities and penalties for the members of the Force. Since the Force has been functioning ever since the 15th August, 1947, we are seeking to give the Bill a retrospective effect. When disturbances of law and order arose, demands came form several provinces and some States also that their Police Force was not sufficient and in some cases not effective and, therefore, they needed help. We found it very difficult to offer help, because our own resources were not adequate. Ours is a vast country, where consolidation has taken place with electric rapidity. So, unless we are very watchful we may find to our cost, difficulties arising for which we may have to pay heavily. Therefore, we have taken care to organise our services, our police force and all the requirements that are considered necessary for keeping law and order in the whole land so that progress may be as effective and as rapid as possible."

On Dec. 28,1949, CRPF was made one of the Armed Forces of the Union. The CRPF was made according to the constitution one of the armed forces of the union, for the purpose of utilisation in the internal security front, and its scope of duty was extended all over India. Side by side, the Central Govt. created the right to confer on the members of this Force, certain power under Cr. P.C. connected with the larger objectives of active duty *i.e.* "suppression of internal distrubances and restoration of order."

On 19th March, 1950, on behalf of the President of India, the C.R.P.F. was presented with colours in an impressive ceremonial parade. From 1950 to 1952 the major part of the CRP was deployed on the Jammu and Jodhpur Indo-Pak border. 2 Coys were also deployed for controlling the agrarian trouble and they were successful in carrying out their assigned task. The CRP was first inducted into erstwhile Nizam's state of Hyderabad in May 1950 when one coy of 1st Bn. was deployed to fight against the communal menace and also to suppress the activities of Razakars. The coy remained in the State upto March 1952. A detachment was also sent to J&K in 1953 to deal with Praja Parishad agitation and deteriorating law and order situation in J&K. They were entrusted with the difficult task of checking and arresting unauthorised entries in J&K area. In 1954, a detachment of the Bn. was inducted in the then Vindhya Pradesh and Madhya Bharat for anti-dacoity operations. Unit stayed in this area upto 1956 with small detachments at Calcutta and Bombay deputed for short duration. The first encounter was in January 1954 in Dargaon in Madhya Pradesh with famous decoit Devi Singh who himself managed to escape leaving 2 dead bodies of his associates, Narpat Singh and Chhakachhi and large quantity of arms and ammunition.

In April 1953, when the most dengerous and wanted dacoit Kartara was lurking in village Kishangarh (Bhatinda district) the CRP contingent on receiving information, rushed to the spot, cordoned off the house where the dacoit was present and the exchange of the fire continued for about 2 hours with no result. Thereupon Subedar Ganpat Ram climbed on to the roof of the house, dug 2 holes in the roof and threw two hand grenades one after another, the second one of which killed the dacoit on the spot. A high degree of personal courage, leadership and disregard of a danger to his own life were shown by the Subedar.

President's Police & Fire Services Medal for Gallantry	1. Ct Kundan Singh 2. Ct Bachan Singh.

On 19th July, 1953 when the CRP were operating in PEPSU, and had combed the jungle area to spot Janga, a dangerous and desperate dacoit, a sharp encounter took place and the party suddenly came under heavy firing from dacoits, concealed in the nearby sugarcane field. Though placed in an awkward position, firing all round, the CRP were ultimately successful in shooting Janga dead after about 20 minutes of heavy exchange of fire. His comrade Chand continued to resist. In this encounter Ct Kundan Singh received a bullet under his right shoulder blade while his comrade Ct Bachan singh crawled down to a very close position, throwing a hand grenade at dacoit Chand from a distance of less than 10 yards. Chand picked up this grenade to hurl back at the police party but it burst before he could do so killing him instantaneously, Constables Kundan Singh and Bachan Singh displayed undaunted courage, leadership and devotion to duty of a very high order.

In the year 1955, the Bn earned laurels by successful participation in liquidation of notorious outlaw Man Singh in Bhind--Morena sector of Madhya Bharat. After long chase, dacoit Man Singh was brought to bay on Aug. 28,1955 in a deadly encounter about 5 miles from Bhind. One detachment of 4 to 6 service coys operated on the Rajasthan-Pakistan border from 1949 to 1953 with Hqrs at Gadra Road, under an Assistant Comdt. with Sub-Headquarters at Jodhpur, Jaisalmer and Kutch as the first line of defence, sometimes in collaboration with the States and sometimes directly under the Western Command. CRPF had to man the frontier patrols from post to post on camels, jeeps or on foot, braving the intractable deserts most of the time under canvas with poor supply of water, and rations and invariably any green vegetables to fill their plates. But more important exploits awaited the force in the North between [1950-53] when the Praja Parishad agitation and the emergency arising out of Dr. Shyama Prasad Mukherjee's death led to an urgent switching off of the three companies from the Rajasthan border to Jammu.

The activities of anti-social elements and outlaws in Nabha and Bhatinda in PEPSU created panic, requiring an urgent despatch of two coys. During a short time after their arrival in 1954, under the command of Shri Maha Singh, the CRP jawans were successful in shooting down Kartara and Gajjan Singh dacoits in their notorious hideout in Kishangarh village in Bhatinda and in a courageous bid costing lot of time and energy rounded up several other associates and restored complete normal conditions in those parts. Another coy operating in Nabha under the command of Shri C.S.Dixit, Dy SP along with the PEPSU Police, displayed even greater zeal and gave chase to Janga, who was called the "Bhupat" of PEPSU and who held sway over the panic stricken inhabitants for 40 miles along the Ghaggar river. In an encounter, both Janga and his associate Chand were killed and the members of the CRP party were granted by the Raj Pramukh a reward of Rs. 4,445/- out of Rs. 8000/- prize declared for Janga alone. Two members of the CRP party were also awarded the President's Police and Fire Service Medal and one Police Medal for gallantry in these operations. On 5th March, 1955, C.R.P. Rules were published in Gazette of India Part-II Section-3. These rules formed solid base for the organisation, administration and working of the C.R.P. and laid the solid foundation for a very viable organisational set-up of the CRPF. In 1955, 1 Bn CRP earned laurels by successful participation in liquidation of notorious outlaw Man Singh gang. Notorious dacoit leader Man Singh killed in an encounter on August 29, 1955 with CRP/ SAF and the area was cleared later of dacoits menace. Late Bakshi Gulam Mohd. Prime Minister of J&K awarded a silver Boat(trophy)- a replica of the Kashmir house-boat to 1st Bn CRPF. In Jammu & Kashmir CRP dealt with anti-national and subversive elements from across the border. In Bhuj they were entrusted with the duties of guarding the International Border.

The Chief Minister of Madhya Bharat awarded a silver trophy to 1st Battalion CRP. By now the Force was being used to guard the International Borders, assist the states in cases of turmoil in addition to serve as the Reserve Police with the centre. The 3rd CRPF was sanctioned on 23 April, 1956 but the unit started functioning under a separate commandant independently w.e.f. 1 September 1956 at Neemuch. 4th Bn C.R.P was raised on Nov. 7,1956 and after training unit was moved to Indo-Pak borders in Kashmir. Prior to November 1956 the ministerial cadre of CRPF was borne on the combined ministerial cadre of the erstwhile Ajmer-Marwar clerical cadre which comprised the District Police and Government Railway Police Ajmer Marwara. The clerical staff for CRP was drawn from the above cadre. On 1st November, 1956, a separate clerical cadre was sanctioned.

1957- CRPF was first inducted in the North-East during 1957 in Nagaland when insurgency had just started in the district of Naga Hills and Tehseng areas. Initially two companies were sent to Naga Hills and two companies were deployed in the foothills of NEFA.

3rd Bn CRP sent in Feb'57 in J&K for law and order and election duties. The first detachment of 3rd Bn CRPF was sent to Delhi on Jan. 4,1957 for law and order duties. CRP did commendable work on the Indo-Pak borders against infiltrators, raiders and cattle-lifters. It assisted the civil administration in the maintenance of law and order during 1957 elections in the State and took part in humanitarian work also time to time. Early in 1957, one coy of CRP 3rd Bn was assigned duties of guarding the Indo-Tibetan Border near Hot Springs in Ladakh.

1958 - Two more Bns deployed on the Eastern Frontier region. Political situation in J&K became tense. CRPF provided assistance to local authorities.

During the years 1949 upto 1958, CRP remained deployed in M.P, Bombay, Jammu & Kashmir and Gujarat. They guarded Bhaba Atomic Energy Centre, Trombay and prevented theft and pilferage of costly and valuable stores equipment and even information. The CRP Battalions remained deployed in Nagaland when the underground activities were at their highest from the year 1956 to 1964 and carried out anti-insurgency operations with remarkable success.

1959 - It was the C.R.P. which faced the brunt of the first onslaught of the Chinese at Hot Springs. One sub unit of 3rd Bn CRPF was sent for duty in Ladakh from September 1959 to July 1966. On October 21, 1959 one CRP patrol of 21 men fought a gallant action against an overwhelming Chinese force at Hot Springs. In the ensuing battle, 10 men of the CRPF laid down their lives and one officer and several others were taken prisoners. The sacrifice of these brave men has been etched in letters of gold in the annals of the Indian Police. The day is observed as the Police Commemoration Day in memory of the policemen who laid down their lives in the service of the country. A memorial service is held at Hot Springs every year and is attended by representatives of all police Forces in India.

Defence of the country necessitated expansion. Raising of two more Bns were sanctioned. Bns were raised at Neemuch and Rampur. To cater to the requirements of stores of the Force a Central Supply Agency was created in 1958-59.

From 1960 onwards presence of CRPF in Assam became a regular feature. Four more additional Bns were sanctioned in June/July '60.

Central Training College Neemuch came into existence on Dec. 1,1960 for basic and inservice training of various ranks of the force. In the initial stages only recruit wing was created but in 1961 cadre wing was added. Upto 1968, CTC Neemuch conducted training of recruits, directly recruited SOs/UOs, Senior Cadre Course, Junior Cadre Course, Weapons Training Course, Physical Training Course and Un-armed Combat with very limited supervisory staff. Earlier training of recruits and others were carried out by respective units themselves. The history of bands in CRPF begins with the year 1960 when the first band was raised in Ajmer under Commandant R.K. Lefearcher. The first band master was Inspector Ujagar Singh and the strength of the band was 41. It was a military band comprising brass reeds and percussion instruments.

For the first time Govt. of India recruited four directly appointed Deputy Superintendents of Police from open market with the help of Union Public Service Commission for C.R.P.F, M.P. Singh, K.R.K. Prasad and S.N. Mathur continued to serve the Force and have been now promoted serving in senior posts of the Force. Their basic training was carried out at C.P.T.C. Mount Abu along with 1961 batch of IPS Probationers. The courageous act of 'A' coy 3rd Bn under the command of Dy S.P. Shri N.K. Das in moving to the buffer zone of ceasefire line and occupying "Sher-Dil Thakeri" in Balkot under heavy and constant fire from Pak hostiles thereby achieving the goal of Jummu & Kashmir Govt. to establish civil administration in the area won the whole hearted appreciation from Government, Army and the State authorities. With the ever multiplying and diverse nature of duties that were being entrusted to CRP, demands for its deployment continued to increase making further expansion inescapable. CRP was grouped into two ranges each under a D.I.G with the overall command resting with the Inspector General of Police, Delhi. A further reorganisation resulted in each Bn having 6 coys instead of 4 coys. The following CRP Bns of 4 coys were made 6 coy Bns in the year mentioned against each :-

7th	Bn	-	May	'63
8th	Bn	-	May	'63
9th	Bn	-	April	'64
10th	Bn	-	March	'66
11th	Bn	-	March	'66
12th	Bn	-	Oct	'64
13th	Bn	-	March	'66
14th	Bn	-	March	'66

This reorganisation of CRP units by addition of 2 more coys brought greater strength in respect of Nos. of each Bn and thus the operational capabilities of the CRP were increased to a large extent.

Two more Bns raised in the wake of Chinese aggression in 1962. MHA recruited a number of candidates from open market as directly appointed Dy. S.P in consultation with Union Public Service Commission and they were initially sent for training at C.P.T.C. Mount Abu for training alongwith IPS Probationers. During the Chinese invasion of our country in September/October 1962, 9th Bn CRP fought rear-guard action and the CRP was the first to fan out as standard bearer to re-establish outposts after the withdrawal of the Chinese from Kameng and Siang Frontier Division. In this venture one of its outposts at Chayang Tajo was treacherously over-run by the enemy who killed eight of CRP men, the base Supdt. and asstt. Political Officer. In Lohit and in Kameng divisions 1st Bn CRP was sent to work for re-establishing the civil administration and tracing out arms/ammunition left behind by the Chinese as well as our retreating troops.

On August 3, 1963 Shri V.G. Kanetkar was the first Inspector General of Police exclusively appointed to supervise and provide highest level leadership to the Force. On 16/17th October, 1963, patrol party of 10 Bn CRP had an encounter with Pak Rangers near Cease Fine Line in which one Pak JCO and 2 ORs were wounded. In July 1963, 6th Bn CRP was deployed in Punch sector under 121 Brigade. One platoon of 6 Bn alongwith 2 platoons of 7 Sikhs defended Gali post when it was covered from all sides by Pak army and its road and air links were cut off. One platoon of 6 Bn was responsible to defend Bangloi post (tactically known as one-one post). HC Sawai Singh, Ct Gurmukh Singh and L/Nk Prabhu Dayal of 6 Bn CRP led the Brigade attack on Sona Gali Pakistani post and acted as Guides during night.

In 1964, Shri Gurbachan Singh Randhawa made a history for the nation by clocking 14 seconds in 110 metres hurdles at 1964 Tokyo Olympics. He was the first Indian to get Arjuna award, the first Indian to win a gold medal in decathlon in 1962 Asian Games at Jakarta, the first Indian to create four national records 6'-6" in high jump and 210'-3.5" in javelin throw at the 1962 Indo--German meet, 6,912 points in decathlon at trials for Asian Games held at Bangalore. He was the second Indian to make the finalists grade in Olympics, Milkha Singh being the first one.

As there was more and more demand for CRPF Bns, the Govt of India sanctioned the raising of three addl. Bns Two Bns 15th and 16th were raised in 1964. The first pipe band of CRP was raised in Durgapur in the year 1964 under Drummer Major Gurdial Singh.

During 1964, following arms and ammunition were captured besides arrest of 15 Pak infiltrators :-

Miscellaneous articles	-	10
Grenade	-	1
2" Mortar bomb	-	1
.303 Fired cases	-	2

Upto 1965 a radio platoon was authorised to each executive battalion and known as platoon No.16 and had one Jem(S.I.), 3 Head Constables, 50 Naiks, R.M-3, R.F-1. A Police Radio Officer was authorised in 1 Battalion for training and co-ordinating and consisted of Asstt. Comdt-1, Sub-1, Jem-1, Havildars - 5, R.M-1, Cts-2, Steno-1 and LDCs-2 with effect from 1.12.65. 1 Signal Battalion was raised vide MHA letter No. F6/8/64.P.II dated 2.6.1965 by withdrawing the Radio platoon from the executive battalions. It was located at Neemuch and was authorised GOs-3, Subs-2, Jems-23, HCs-90. Nks-829, Ct Storeman-2, Ct Tradesman-6, Ct Orderly-21, followers-17 and M/staff-11 thus having a total of 1004. The first induction of CRPF in Tripura took place in the month of July 1965 when 4 companies of CRP were sent to Tripura in view of the mounting tension with Pakistan. 17th Bn was raised in 1965. By the middle of 1965, Pakistan had started sending her armed infiltrators in J&K for sabotage activities and to disrupt communications by damaging/destroying bridges. A number of CRPF battalions were airlifted and sent to J&K to face the grave situation. CRPF did highly commendable job against the Pak infiltrators and guarded vital bridges near the international borders in spite of many heavy attacks from Pak intruders. 4th Bn CRP alone arrested 69 infiltrators and smugglers, laid various ambushes and captured Pak saboteurs. In the Runn of Kutch, during the Indo-Pak War of 1965, the dedication, commitment and professionalism of the CRPF were tested. On 4th September that year, four companies of the CRPF guarding the Sardar post and Tak post repulsed the attack of a Pakistani Brigade. Fighting an unequal battle in terms of numbers and fire power, our men held the post and despite heavy casualties, forced the enemy to retreat, leaving behind 30 of their dead men. The CRP fought bravely although it lost four gallant CRP men and five were wounded. The enemy were able to take way 19 of our CRP personnel but Pakistan also suffered heavy casualties. In the words of the then Union Home Minister: "this battle will go down in the history of Indian Police nay in the history of Military battles" and surely it has secured a place of pride for CRP in the annals of the country's war history.

During 1966 seven Indian Reserve Police Bns from various States were absorbed in the CRPF. One Signal Bn was also raised during this year. This increased the strength of the Force to 24 battalions and one Signal Bn. CRPF was first inducted in the Mizo Hill district of Assam in April 1966 and six companies of 17 Battalion were sent to fight insurgency.

1967 - Another post of I.G.P. was sanctioned. Side by side 2 new posts of Deputy Inspectors General were created and Base Hospital was also sanctioned. In January '67, 6 Bn CRP was moved to Amritsar in connection with Akali agitation. During February 67, the unit was hurriedly moved to Bihar in connection with industrial labour unrest. Its coys performed duties at Ranchi, Hatia, Hazaribagh and Giridih. During March 1967 the unit was deployed in Delhi to deal with D.A.P strike. During Sept.'67 the unit moved to Manipur to carry out counter-insurgency duties.

1968 - 1969 is the most historic year of the CRPF as it completely changed the structure of the Force. Large scale expansion and reorganisation of the Force took place in 1968. Group Centres were raised and to each one of them three or four battalions were allotted. Nineteen India Reserve Police Battalions were absorbed in the CRPF during 1968 and three new battalions were raised. Thus bringing the strength to 46 battalions. During 1969 two India Reserve Police battalions were absorbed and four new battalions were raised making the figure to 52 battalions. Govt. approved the setting up of 14 Group Centres which are to carry out the house keeping functions of Bns and serve as store holding units, as base for the families and as location for battalions for rest after strenuous tenure in the operational area. The construction of buildings at the Group Centres and for the training institutions, signal battalions and base hospitals involves a capital outlay of about Rs. 60 crores. A large number of buildings were constructed at Rampur, Neemuch, Ajmer, Delhi and Jammu. A complete new Group Centre in new building has been set up at Jammu. In July 1968, two additional signals Bns were sanctioned vide MHA letter No.6/25(ii)/67-P.II vol.II dated 31.7.68 and located at Rampur and Hyderabad. Second signal Bn was raised at Rampur w.e.f. 1.9.1968. The CRPF was reorganised and the following changes in the organisational structure were introduced:

i. The headquarters of the Force were upgraded into a Directorate General with a Director General as its Head. Director General was assisted by 3 Deputy Directors and 1 Wireless Advisor as Staff Officers.

ii. For purposes of field command and operational effectiveness, the Force was split into two Sectors each under an I.G.P.

iii. Sectors were further split into 7 Ranges each under a D.I.G.P.

iv. The institution of Group Centre was introduced to look after the provisioning, accounting, book-keeping and other house keeping jobs of its attached Bns so as to relieve the field officers to devote their undivided attention towards the operational role.

v. Ten Group Centres came into existence although 14 Group Centres were sanctioned.

vi. Three more training institutions were sanctioned for training recruits and conducting other training courses for various ranks.

vii. A Central Weapons Store was created.

viii. 2 more Signal Battalions were raised bringing the total to 3 Bns.

Recruit training Centre-I at Barwaha(M.P) was started on 1st August, 1968. Till 1983 end it trained 17436 CRP recruits and 967 SSF, CISF recruits and provided them basic training.

CRPF Football team won the championship in All India Police Games in 1968.

During 1968-69 nearly six battalions were sent to Assam due to language riots. Govt. of India decided to merge 28 Armed Police Bns raised initially by the States with CRPF and the Force was allowed to raise 7 Bns. Induction of CRPF into Andhra Pradesh was done to deal with Telengana agitation. The Central Training College-II, CRP Avadi was established on the 1st Sept.'69 at Avadi under the authority of Govt of India, M H A letter No. F-23/6/68-P-II dated 20.2.69. Owing to paucity of drinking water at Avadi this institution was shifted from Avadi to Neemuch during June 1975 and in February 1978 to Deoli (Rajasthan). The College was reverted back to Avadi during May 1980 and now continue to function there. It conducts nine in-service courses for CRP and Tear Smoke course for all Police Forces.

Recruit Training Centre-II GRP at Avadi was sanctioned vide MHA notification No.F.6/25V/62-P 2 dated 31.7.68 but it came into existence on Feb. 1.1969. Actually training of recruits commenced on April 14,1969. The scheme of centralised pay and accounting system as approved by Govt. of India, Ministry of Finance in consultation with the Comptroller and Auditor General of India was issued under MHA letter No-F-25/65/67 P.II dated 22.5.69 and came into force w.e.f. 1st July, 1969.

1970 - Strength of the Force raised to 52 Bns. Induction of CRPF into West Bengal was carried out following the promulgation of President's Rule. Force saved about, 13,500 lives from ravages of floods in West Bengal. 2. Bns rushed to Gujarat in the wake of communal riots.

Signal units were reorganised in August 1970 vide MHA letter No.O.IV-6/69-W-F(P)-I dated 22.6.1970 and C.T.C. (T)/ Signal Group Centre was raised. The following staff for the signal unit was authorised.

	GO	Sub	Jem	HC	NK	L/NK	Ct	Foll.	M/Staff
(a) Sig Bn.	10	27	42	191	622	18	72	19	11
(b) CTC(T) /SGC	6	5	9	31	40	1	36	17	52

1971 - During 1971 elections to Assembly, 114 companies were deployed in West Bengal, 18 companies in Jammu & Kashmir, 9 in Andhra Pradesh, 8 in Delhi, 6 in Bihar, 5 in Tamil Nadu, 2 each in Assam and Kerala and 1 in Madhya Pradesh. 5 CRPF battalions took part in Indo-Pak war in December 1971, out of which 2 were deployed in J & K and other 3 in Eastern Sector. In December 1971 the CRPF fought shoulder to shoulder with the Army in the Chicken Neck area during the Indo-Pak War.Our boys withstood the onslaught of Pakistani forces and the Brigade Commander complementing their excellent performance said: "the boys of CRPF did not yield even an inch of territory to the ememy". In another sector, an Air Vice Marshal praised the excellent support one of our Bns gave the Air Force and the valiant defence of a forward air strip which made it possible for the Air Force to operate from there without let or hindrance. It is indeed gratifying that the valour and courage of our officers and men have received due recognition by the award of Sena Medals and other gallantry medals. In order to provide more effective supervision, office of S/III was sanctioned in 1971.

Appointments to the posts of one Inspector General of Police and one Dy. Inspector General were also sanctioned. 16 Bn, 20th Bn, 25 Bn, 38 Bn and 46 Bn actually participated in Indo-Pak war side by side with army in the Western Front (Shakargarh and Chicken Neck area) and the Eastern Front in the liberation of Bangladesh. 33 coys of CRPF were allotted security duties at P.O.W. camps at Ranchi, Ramgarh, Sagar, Agra and Gwalior. These CRP coys were released in Aug.'73 after return of P.O.Ws. to Pakistan. CRPF Bns deployed practically in every state and Union Territory, the largest contingent being in West Bengal. In October 1971, under the Ford Foundation Fellowship Krishna Mohan Mathur, Commandant 50 Bn CRPF was sent to the U.S.A. and Japan to study training techniques used in police training institutions abroad. 38 Bn CRPF had the distinction of fighting Bangladesh war and its two coys were moved in Bangladesh on 10.12.71 for mopping up operations and guarding vital installations and these coys remained in Bangladesh till the first week of January'72. They bravely fought and stood against heavy shelling by Pakistan army. 38 Bn earned 2 President's Police and Fire Services Medals for gallantry and 9 Police medals for gallantry for their outstanding role and gallant action in the war. 16 Bn CRPF similarly got 2 Seva Medals and 5 Medals for gallantry. To cope with every increasing demand for CRP by various states of Nagaland, Mizoram, West Bengal and Andhra Pradesh and others, major expansion took place in 1971 when 8 more battalions were sanctioned bringing the total strength to 60 Battalions. Since this expansion cast more administrative burden, the number of sectors was raised to 3 and that of Ranges to 8 in CRPF. During 1971 war 46 Bn captured the following quantities of ammunition in Bangladesh in mopping up operations- 7.62 MM-72, 308 cart. 7.62 bolted- 41000, 303 CTN- 1928, Grenade hand-48, 16 MM bomb HE No. 13-60 nos., 16 MM bomb H E 72 nos., Fuse 35 E 35 nos., Rockets HE-35" - 50 nos., Grenade Rifle head No. 94-14 nos.

The story of CRPF is closely linked with the efforts of the Government in snuffing out the challenges. Whether it was the Naxalbari movement in West Bengal and Andhra Pradesh or insurgency in Nagaland or Mizoram or the agitation over foreigners' issue in Assam or the GNLF in Darjeeling, the CRPF has always played a major role in quelling them. The Force has also successfully put down many communal disturbances in different parts of the country. The fact that there has often been demand from the local population for the deployment of the CRPF to protect the minorities is ample testimony of the impartial and secular approach of the Force.

1972 - In West Bengal since March-April 1970 CRPF assisted West Bengal and Calcutta police in apprehending approximately 46000 extremists. They recovered more than 7500 bombs, 800 guns and rifles and thousands of other lethal weapons. In Oct. 1972, languages riots erupted in various parts of Assam and nearly 6 CRPF Bns were sent for the relief and succour of common law abiding men and rounding up of the anti social elements. In 1972, CRPF men asserted their superiority by emerging athletic championship in the All India Police Games at

Bangalore. CRPF secured first position in wrestling in XXI All India Police Games, 1972. In March 1972, 16 States and 2 Union Territories had Assembly elections in which 10 companies were deployed in Delhi, six each in Kerala and Mysore, two in Goa and one in Pondicherry. There was massive induction of CRPF into West Bengal to help in the elections to West Bengal Assembly. There was further induction of CRPF into Andhra Pradesh consequent on the agitation of a separate Andhra region.

1973 - CRPF was inducted into Uttar Pradesh following the PAC mutiny. A CRPF Bn sent to Sikkim on law and order duties.

1974 - During the All India Railwaymen's strike from 8th to 28th May, 1974, CRP contingents were extensively deployed at most strategic points to guard Railway lines, important Rly. installations and main centres of labour trouble. Statewise deployment of CRP was as under:

1.	Andhra Pradesh	- 13 coys at Vijaywada, Secunderabad and Kasipet Rly. divisions.
2.	Bihar	- 3 coys at Gaya Rly. division.
3.	Delhi	- 6 coys at Delhi Rly. division.
4.	Kerala	- 11 coys at Olvakot and Madurai division.
5.	Maharashtra	- 15 coys at Bombay, Poona, Nagpur, Pune and Bhusawal divisions.
6.	Orissa	- 6 coys at Chakradharpur and Kurda division.
7.	Tamil Nadu	- 11 coys at Madras.
8.	U.P.	- 15 coys at Mughalsarai, Allahabad, Jhansi Moradabad divisions.
9.	West Bengal	- 23 coys at Asansol, Adra, Howrah, Siliguri, and Kathiar divisions.

Govt. of India, Ministry of Home Affairs vide their memo no.M.II.1/73-Prov-FP-II dated 10.6.1974 have accorded permission to combatise the posts of Medical Officers in the CRPF.

1975 - Govt. of India sanctioned a new Range in Mizoram with its Hqars at Aizawl. In the one month of January 1975 CRPF captured 17 MNF hostiles and 16 pieces of arms and 125 rounds of ammunition. Govt. of India took a decision to combatise the doctors in CRP and the first course for combatised doctors was held at Neemuch from Dec.13 to Jan 10, 1975. Internal Security Academy was set up at Mount Abu with effect from 1st February, 1975 when Sardar Vallabhbhai Patel

National Police Academy shifted to Hyderabad. The Academy conducts basic training of directly appointed Gazetted Officers (Dy.SP) and other inservice courses for CRPF officers. Besides it conducts Internal Security Courses for civil police officers of various senior ranks. Directly appointed gazetted officers of Serial no.14 onwards have been trained at I.S.A. Mount Abu whereas earlier few batches were trained at CTC-I Neemuch.

The multi-dimensional duties and the onerous responsibilities which the CRPF has often been called upon to shoulder, have made it a unique and versatile Force - switching roles quickly and efficiently be it a fight against terrorists or communal elements or the insurgents.

1976 - GPF cell started functioning in February 1976 under the charge of Shri M. P. Singh, AD(EDP Cell). Nine digit code number allotted to the personnel would become their GPF number. In a massive rescue operation carried out in Kutturpuram on Nov. 25 and 26, 1976, about 15,000 people were evacuated from Kotturpuram low lying area located in the southern bank of river Adyar. In 1976, 642 CRP jawans posted in Delhi made voluntary blood donations to the Red Cross Society in order to help the suffering humanity. This gesture was very much appreciated by various authorities and the Indian Red Cross Society.

1977 - In 1977, men from all the CRPF units, Group Centres and Training institutions were deployed in various parts of the country during Lok Sabha elections. Some of the units had to travel long distances without proper accommodation, rest or sleep. Shri N.S.Saxena, Director General CRPF retired on June 4,1977. Shri S.M.Ghosh took over charge of Director General, CRPF. Government of India approved promotion of 40 Dy. S.P. to the rank of Asstt. Comdt on ad-hoc basis. RTC-III started functioning at Deoli from Feb.1, 1977. Approval was accorded in 1977 for the construction of residential and non-residential accommodation for CRPF Group Centre at Imphal at a cost of Rs.7,52,32,620.00.

1978 - CRPF companies were deployed all over the country for internal security duties as can be seen from the deployment as in August 78 in various States: Assam - 74, Arunachal Pradesh - 29, Andhra Pradesh - 11, A & N Islands - 2, Bihar - 21, Delhi - 23, J & K - 24, Kerala -1, Manipur - 24, Mizoram - 40, Meghalaya-11, Nagaland - 13, Pondicherry - 1, Tamil Nadu - 1, Tripura-24, West Bengal - 11, Sikkim - 6, Gujarat- 11, U.P. -20, and Rajasthan - 3.

During 1978 following sanctions were accorded for construction works. Construction of 418 family quarters of various types for CRPF GC MKG (Bihar) at a cost of Rs. 1,46,85000/-. (ii) Installation of pumps for augmentation of water supply to CRPF campus at Neemuch at a cost of Rs. 86,977/-. (iii) Advance payment of Rs. 9,50,000 to Durgapur Development Authority, Durgapur for integrated water supply scheme for CRPF campus, Durgapur.

1979 - The deployment of companies as in August 1979 in various states was broadly as under : Assam-28, Arunachal Pradesh- 26, A & N Islands-2, Bihar - 18, Delhi - 24, J & K-25, Kerala -6, Manipur - 24, Mizoram-42, Meghalaya-6, Nagaland-19, Pondicherry-1, Tamil Nadu-4, Tripura-8, West Bengal-12, Sikkim -6, U.P.-9, M.P.-8, Rajasthan -4, Orissa - 8. During 1979 a wave of police forces indiscipline and unrest engulfed the various police forces of the country. The police unrest started in Punjab in May 1979 and gradually spread to many other states and Central Police organisations. CRPF personnel at Group Centres New Delhi, Trivandrum, Bhubaneswar and Neemuch and some other CRPF units were also affected by the unrest but it was quickly and firmly handled. CRP units helped Govt. of India in controlling unrest in many police forces of the country and even in CISF. By and large CRPF jawans deployed a very high sense of dedication to duty and loyalty to the nation.

1980 - In January 1980, the coy wise deployment of CRPF in various states was as under: Andhra Pradesh - 4, A&N Islands-3, Assam-31, Arunachal Pradesh-26, Bihar-31, Delhi-40, Dadra & Nagar Haveli-2, Gujarat-4, Goa, Daman & Diu-2, Haryana-6, J&K-24, Kerala-6, Meghalaya-13, Mizoram-47, Manipur-26, Nagaland-13, Orissa-4, Pondicherry-4, Sikkim-6, Tamil Nadu-14, Tripura-6, U.P.-6, West Bengal-21.

The Govt. of India had in November 1980 decided to raise three peace - keeping Bns and had entrusted the responsibility of raising these to the CRPF. The aim, broadly, was to deal with situations of violence and to provide rescue and relief to the people affected by violence and natural calamities. Consequently, the 3 peace-keeping Bns 69,70 and 71 have been raised at the CRPF GCs at Hyderabad, Durgapur and New Delhi respectively. Each such Bn has a Pioneer platoon comprising 45 tradesmen. It has extra tentage for setting up relief camps and will be capable of constructing temporary shelters providing temporary electricity connections and repairing houses, roads and culverts. Each unit has 22 personnel trained and equipped to extinguish fires.

Kamdeo Singh, a notorious dacoit and smuggler of Bihar who was evading arrest for the last 20 years and carried reward of Rs. 65,000/- on his head was killed by personnel of B Coy 53 Bn in an encounter on April 18, 1980 in village Nayagaon. 9 other members of his gang were also arrested. The CRPF shooting team which participated in the All India Police Duty Meet held at Nasik from April 12 to 19,1980 won the overall championship by securing 1168 points. Shri. L.P. Singh, Governor of Assam paid a glowing tribute to the effectiveness of the CRPF in the following words: "During the troubled times we have gone through in Manipur, Meghalaya and Assam, we have had to depend, in a large measure, on the CRPF to deal with law and order situations, and to give sense of security to peaceful citizens, and in particular, the minority communities. In these crucial roles, the performance of the CRPF has been excellent. If there have been criticisms, the reason has not been any brutalities, excesses or misconduct by the CRPF personnel, for the CRPF has been singularly free from any of these. It is the very effectiveness of the Force that has given rise to these complaints from those who would have liked to use violence against the minority communities, with complete impunity. When the strength of CRPF was increased in the mid-60s from 14 to 56 Bns, it was hoped and expected that it would be the main central instrument for providing protection to the minority communities, and the weaker sections of the population, generally. In the light of my experience in the North-Eastern region during past years, I can say, without any hesitation, that the Force has fulfilled that expectation, admirably."

As many as 1443 promotions of CRPF personnel were announced in the month of July 1980. This sent a wave of jubilation among the other ranks, for about 90% of the promotions went to them. Cts got the maximum benefit; 784 Cts were elevated to the rank of L/Nks, 192 L/Nks were made Nks, 358 Nks promoted to H/Consts and 42 H/Cs ascended to the rank of Sub-Inspectors. Among the class of subordinate officers, 32 Sub-Inspectors became Inspectors and 35 Inspectors got gazetted rank of Dy.Supdt. of Police.

1981 - In January 1981, the coy-wise deployment of CRP in various states was as under : Andhra Pradesh-1, A & N Islands-2, Assam-75, Arunachal Pradesh-29, Bihar-17, Delhi -34, J&K -24, Kerala-1, Meghalaya-15, Mizoram-42, Manipur-24, Nagaland-13, Orissa-4, Pondicherry-1, Sikkim-6, Tamil Nadu-1, Tripura-24, U.P.-14, West Bengal-12, Karnataka-1.

70 Bn CRP came into existence w.e.f. 4.3.1981 with its headquarters at GC Durgapur. The passing out parades of 5 newly raised Bns were

held at various places during the month of October 1981. 5 companies of Delhi based Bns were moved to Chandigârh on January 18, 1981 in the wake of gherao organised by the opposition parties of Punjab Vidhan Sabha on Jan. 21, 1981. The MHA has ordered large scale promotions and confirmations in the Force. 65 DySsP were promoted to the rank of Asstt. Comdts and 26 Asstt. Comdts to the rank of Comdts. As many as 478 officers of the rank of Dy. Supdts of Police, 208 Asstt. Comdts and 57 Comdts were confirmed in their respective ranks. All promotions ordered on ad hoc basis since 1974 have been regularised. As regards subordinate officers and other ranks as many 1,472 promotions were ordered between January and end of April 1981. Of these a major share went to Consts,928 Consts were made L/Nks, 169 L/Nks and 122 Nks ascended to higher ranks. Among the drivers, 118 Cts rose to the rank of L/Nks, 67 L/Nks became Nks, 16 Nks were made H/Consts and 3 Sub-Inspectors were promoted to the rank of Inspector (MT). Among the fitters 2 Consts, one L/Nk, 11 Nks and 2 H/Cs ascended the next higher ranks. Rest of the 33 promotions ordered related to various ranks of tradesmen-Armourer, carpenters and tailors. Govt's contribution towards ration money of CRPF non-gazetted personnel has been increased to Rs. 1154/- per month for the qualifying areas and Rs. 92/- per month for non-qualifying areas as per orders from MHA, w.e.f. 1.4.1981.

CRP units deployed in Tripura captured a number of T.N.V. insurgents and large amount of arms/ammunition. In Assam CRP rendered valuable service to the people during Assam Bandh and maintained law and order and public tranquillity. GC Dimapur (Nagaland) came into existence on July 1, 1981. On the evening of December 31, 1981 Shri R.N. Sheopory, Director General CRPF left his mortal abode.

1982 - The dawn of 1982 saw the CRP personnel in Delhi attired in their ceremonial uniforms to give a tearful farewell to their beloved chief Shri R.N. Sheopory whose body was drapped with CRP flag. Henry Osbourne, the grand old man of CRP who commanded one unit of CRP during 1949 died on July 6, 1982 at the age of 82 years. During the state assembly elections held in May 1982 in West Bengal, Kerala, Haryana and Himachal Pradesh CRPF came under heavy pressure since a strength of nearly 14 battalions had to be mobilised without disturbing the existing arrangements in North-Eastern region, Punjab and communally sensitive pockets in a few states. The raising of this strength required diversion of manpower even from static formations like training institutions and group centres. The role of CRP during the elections was commended by many states. In April 1982 the coy-wise deployment of CRP in various states was as under : Andhra Pradesh-2, A & N Islands-2, Assam-80, Arunachal Pradesh-29, Bihar-21, Delhi-28, J & K - 24, Kerala-7, Meghalaya - 10, Mizoram - 47, Manipur - 24, Nagaland-13, Pondicherry-1, Sikkim-6, Tamil Nadu-1, Tripura-24, U.P-14, West Bengal-10, Punjab-5, Rajasthan-12, Chandigarh-1.

In 1982, the then Home Minister Giani Zail Singh made the following comments about the Force : "The Central Reserve Police Force is the parent Para-military force to perform specific duties. While the force has been dealing with various internal turmoils before and after 1947, it has also constantly stood guard against external aggression. In 1965, 4 companies of the CRPF again shed blood in the Pakistani aggression in Bhuj. In 1970, the happenings in East Pakistan (now Bangladesh) again made the CRPF to tackle border problems. The CRPF is not only engaged during wars but also renders help during peace time. In the natural calamities like flood, famine, cyclone, etc. the CRPF renders yeoman's service. The CRPF is a model of national integration. The personnel who are serving the Force are from all religions, castes and creeds. They are an example of unity. The nation is proud of CRPF men who have laid their lives for the protection and maintenance of order."

In 1982, Shri P.C. Sethi, then Union Home Minister gave an account of the CRPF in the following words : "I am proud to say that wherever the CRPF has been, it has earned for itself a good name through hardwork. The Force is deployed in most difficult areas, particularly in the North East but its men have not retreated from duty in the face of challenge from insurgency and violence. I am proud to say that when the CRPF entered Meerut soon after the recent riots, it was welcomed with slogans by members of both the communities. This shows that Force is endowed with a non-communal, non-partisan attitude. The country today needs security forces which could deal with all sections of the community fairly and equally and with the law-breakers, sternly. In this respect the officers and jawans of the CRPF have created history."

In 1982, in the communal riot torn city of Meerut, the historic performance of CRP was acknowledged by the Commissioner of Meerut Division to D.G. in the following words:

"I feel much pleasure in appreciating the performance of the jawans of 71 Bn(peace-keeping) of CRPF during the current Meerut communal riot. A number of houses and shops were burnt by the rioters during the riot and your jawans were asked to rebuild them.

I have inspected all the houses and shops repaired and rebuilt by your jawans and I must say that they have done it beautifully. They worked with speed and quality of their work has been found very good. The best part of their performance is that they did the job willingly and devotedly. The citizens of Meerut and the local administration have very much liked and praised the work and discipline of your jawans."

In recognition of good work done by the CRPF units in Assam, the Govt. of Assam has sanctioned cash rewards of Rs. 73,500/- towards the welfare fund of various units deployed in Assam.

For operational performance w.e.f. March 10, 1982, 4 Sectors were created in CRPF so that various units deployed in that areas may be operationally controlled by the respective IsGP. Eight CRP sub units were airlifted to Maharashtra to deal with policemen's agitations, CRP units were deployed in Delhi for Asiad 82 at various sensitive areas to control the crowd and safety of foreign dignitaries visiting the country to attend the Asiad.

1983 - In January 1983, the coy-wise deployment of CRPF in various states was as under : Andhra Pradesh - 19, A & N Islands - 2, Assam - 53, Arunachal Pradesh - 26, Bihar - 13, Delhi - 27, J&K - 24, Kerala-11, Meghalaya - 6, Mizoram-48, Manipur-30, Nagaland-13, Pondicherry-1, Sikkim - 6, Tripura - 54, U.P. - 11, West Bengal - 12, Punjab-21. C.R.P.F. performed a commendable role during Commonwealth Heads of Governments meetings. Shri S.C. Tandon, the Commissioner of Police, Delhi wrote "words cannot adequately express the deep sense of gratitude that we in Delhi Police owe to the CRPF for the help and assistance that we received from them during Commonwealth Heads of Governments Meetings held from 23rd Nov'83 at Delhi." On July 30, 1983 Shri Shiv Swarup, IPS of Uttar Pradesh cadre joined CRPF on deputation as Director General of Police. Govt. accorded sanction for raising of 3 additional Bns for peace keeping duties and 2 addl. Bns unattached pattern basis and thus the total no. of Bns came upto 76. No. 810715528 Ct Khalid Kamal Ansari of 22 Bn CRP dedicated his life for the nation and was awarded President's Police Medal for gallantry. In 1983, Govt. of India, Ministry of Home Affairs approved the following Cadre Review proposals of Group `A' posts in CRPF vide MHA notification No. Pt.I-45027/5/81-DO-Pers-II dated 16 July 1983.

(i) Upgradation of 20 posts of the Commandants to the level of Addl. DIG.

(ii) Upgradation of 9 posts of Asstt. Comdts to the level of Comdt.

(iii) Creation of 73 posts of Comdts/ADs in the Selection Grade.

(iv) Redesignation of 89 posts of Asstt. Comdts to those of Second-in-Command.

(v) Upgradation of 93 posts of Dy. SP to the level of Assistant Commandant.

1984 - Peace in Haryana received a big jolt in the month of Feb. 1984 when as a backlash to the happenings in Punjab, there was violence in various parts of Haryana, particularly in Panipat, Karnal and Jind. The CRPF was immediately rushed to the disturbed areas in order to bring about peace and restore confidence among the members of the minority community. Coys of 2 Bns(41 & 49) of the CRPF assisted the local administration in restoring the normalcy.

The CRP coys provided protection to Gurdwaras, guarded vital installations and govt buildings and organised patrolling to guard against any possibility of sabotage and to bring about confidence among the populations in the affected areas. A major rail accident at Bahadurgarh Rly. station on Feb. 19,1984 left 43 dead and many injured. Personnel of GC N/Delhi and peace keeping elements rushed to the site of the accident, where Rohtak-Delhi shuttle had rammed into the rear of Bombay bound Punjab Mail. Heavy damage was caused to three rear bogies of Punjab Mail. Majority of the dead included defence personnel who were travelling in one of the ill-fated rear bogies. CRPF personnel rendered help to Rly. rescue team and local police authorities in controlling crowd at the accident site and in extricating the victims. PKE personnel helped the Rly. rescue team in rescuing two civilians alive from the debris after nearly five hours of gruelling work.

1985 - Personnel of the CRPF were granted promotions on 31 March, 1984. SI to Insp(GD)-65, HC to SI(GD)-81, NK to HC(GD)-2, L/NK to NK(GD)-1, 172, Ct to L/nk(GD)-6, SI to Insp(MT)-2, HC to SI(MT)-3, NK to HC(Dvr)-112, Ct to L/nk(Dvr)-420, NK to HC(Ftr)-14, HC to SI(Armr)-1, NK to HC(Armr)-4, Ct to NK(Armr)-23, NK to HC(Band)-1, NK to HC(Tlr)-5, Ct to NK(Tlr)-11, Ct to NK(Mochi)-2, NK to HC(Carpt)-7, Ct to NK(Carpt)-22 and Ct to L/Nk(Ftr)-2. Govt. of India, MHA sanctioned the creation of 30 temporary posts of General Duty Medical Officers Grade-II vide MHA letter No.O.IV-2/82-Prov-FP-IV dated 16.2.84.

127 volunteers donated blood during a blood donation camp organised in GC Rampur with the help of Rotary Club of Rampur. There was massive deployment of CRPF in Punjab during 1984 and there were 100 companies of CRPF deployed for anti-terrorist duties.

In June 1984, broadly CRP deployment of companies was as under: Assam-63, Arunachal Pradesh-25, Andhra Pradesh-2, A&N Islands-2, Bihar-3, Chandigarh-12, Delhi-23, Haryana-11, J&K - 23, Karnataka-1, Kerala-8, Manipur-20, Maharashtra-1, Mizoram-36, Meghalaya-6, Nagaland-10, Pondicherry-2, Tripura-28, West Bengal-9, Sikkim-5, UP-2 and Rajasthan-1. Thus CRP was deployed all over the country for assisting local police in maintenance of law and order. CRPF has played an outstanding and historic role during "Operation Blue Star" in Punjab. CRP Medical team of five doctors and other para-medical staff attended to more than 10,000 Bhopal Gas victims at Bhopal by Dec. 15, 1984. The CRP team worked round the clock and won gratitude of the gas victims and their families.

The tremendous pressure on the Force was acknowledged by no less a person than the late Prime Minister, Smt. Indira Gandhi, when she addressed senior officers of the CRPF at the Internal Security Academy, Mount Abu in June 1984. She said:- "I am aware of the tremendous pressure on you, whether you are in Assam or in Punjab. There are a number of men who have had no rest for months. At times one feels they may not even be able to stand.Still they are on duty. We wish that our resources should increase so that we are able to strengthen the force further, thereby reducing pressure on them." She further said: " The CRPF fulfilled an essential need which was to have a force which may comprise people form different religions, from different states, speaking different languages and still working together. We have observed that wherever the CRPF has gone, the people have reposed confidence in it and they (CRPF men) too have worked with great courage and dedication."

1985 - CRPF continued to have its widespread deployment in the country during the year. The deployment of companies during July 1985 in various states was as under : Assam-50, Arunachal Pradesh-25, A & N Islands-2, Delhi-28, Chandigarh-16, J & K - 15, Manipur-129, Mizoram-27, Meghalaya-6, Nagaland-10, Pondicherry-2 Tripura-39, West Bengal-8, Sikkim-6, Punjab-137, Gujarat-8, U.P.-2, Rajasthan-6. The CRP deployment in Punjab by November 1985 went upto 187 companies in view of the terrorist activities in the state. During Assam elections, CRPF made a very significant contribution towards ensuring peaceful poll. It was a historic occasion for CRPF when Shri Rajiv Gandhi, the Prime Minister of India witnessed the CRP parade on November 1, 1985 at Group Centre Jharoda Kalan in New Delhi. Shri S.B Chavan, the Union Home Minister addressing a conference of senior officers of CRP in New Delhi said:" C RPF have a very valuable and creative role to play. This old and versatile force has contributed immensely to preserve together the people putting in different directions due to diverse interests. In the long history of its growth and development, the Force has sacrificed many officers and men, won several decorations and awards, captured many anti-nationals, wanted insurgents and terrorists, along with arms and ammunition and above all, offered relief and succour to victims in calamities and disasters. This multiple role of the force has endeared- 'the organisation to the people of India'."

In 1985, eighty men of the CRP lost their lives on duty, 691 extremists and insurgents were captured by CRPF from various parts of the country, 210 arms of the various types were captured and 2562 rounds of different calibres were recovered in operations conducted by CRPF. On November 1, 1985 Shri Satish Dutt Pandey took over charge of Director General of the Force. CRP was to a great extent responsible for conducting a smooth and peaceful poll in Punjab. In a message Shri Purno A. Sangma, then Union Minister of State for Home Affairs wrote : "In CRPF the people see a friend in need. The very presence of the CRP men is a deterrent to trouble makers and source of security to the peace-loving people. They have provided succour to the people in distress in times of natural calamities. In recent years it has won acclaim in combating terrorism." CRPF played its important role in ensuring a free and peaceful poll in the Assembly elections held on March 2 and 5, 1985 in 11 states and one Union Territory. As many as 215 companies were provided to various states for elections. The state wise break up of additional companies was as under : Andhra Pradesh-39, Bihar-563, Gujarat-25, Karnataka-3 coys, Madhya Pradesh-12, Orissa-3, Rajasthan-12, Uttar Pradesh-53, Sikkim-3, Pondicherry-2 and Maharashtra-5. Considering the urgency 23 coys had to be air-lifted, on June 5,1985. Shri J.F. Ribeiro joined CRPF as its Director General but he was later transferred and posted as Director General of Gujarat on July 8,1985. The Govt. of India sanctioned raising of twelve additional battalions of CRPF in the month of May 1985 and these included one Mahila Battalion. Eleven of these battalions were serially numbered 77 to 87 and Mahila battalion was numbered-88. The CRP Mahila Bn has been deployed in various parts of the country and they are generally assigned the following duties:-

(i) Tackle agitations involving women agitators.

(ii) Carry out search/frisking of women when required.

(iii) Route lining and security of women's enclosures during public meeting.

(iv) Law and Order duties during fairs and festivals.

(v) Relief and rescue operations during communal riots and natural calamities.

(vi) Guarding installations and establishments which are less vulnerable from security angle.

CRPF has representatives from various states and is truly a representation of the nation as can be seen from the table given below:-

AS ON 1-1-1985

Sl.No.	State/UT	Strength in CRPF	Population of State/UT	State % in Force.
1.	Andhra Pradesh	1864	53403619	2.11
2.	Assam	1712	19902826	1.94
3.	Bihar	8680	69823154	9.81
4.	Gujarat	919	33960905	1.04
5.	Haryana	11034	12850902	12.50
6.	Himachal Pradesh	3691	4237569	4.18
7.	Jammu & Kashmir	3149	4981600	3.57
8.	Karnataka	1461	37043451	1.66
9.	Kerala	8077	25403217	9.15
10.	Madhya Pradesh	2872	52131717	3.25
11.	Manipur	579	1433691	0.66
12.	Meghalaya	63	1327874	0.07
13.	Maharashtra	3202	62643898	3.63
14.	Nagaland	34	773281	0.04
15.	Orissa	1883	26272054	2.13
16.	Punjab	4569	16669755	5.18
17.	Rajasthan	8242	34102912	9.34
18.	Sikkim	69	315682	0.08
19.	Tamil Nadu	2386	48297456	2.70
20.	Tripura	630	2060189	0.71
21.	Uttar Pradesh	18704	110858019	21.19
22.	West Bengal	2653	54485560	3.01
23.	Andaman & Nicobar Islands .	44	188254	0.05
24.	Arunachal Pradesh	92	628050	0.10
25.	Chandigarh	13	450061	0.01
26.	Delhi	718	6196414	0.81
27.	Dadar & Nagar Haveli	3	103677	0.00
28.	Goa Daman & Diu	8	1082177	0.01
29.	Lakshadweep	-	40237	-
30.	Mizoram	63	487774	0.07
31.	Pondicherry	14	604136	0.02

1986 - Shri G.S. Rathore, Dy SP of 35 Bn CRP and SI Bhagwan Das of 71 Bn were awarded Police Medal for gallantry during the year. CRP continued to have widespread deployment and coy wise deployment in April 1986 was as under : Assam-14, Arunachal Pradesh-24, A & N Islands-2, Bihar-1, Chandigarh-21, Delhi-69, J&K-24, Manipur-29. Mizoram-29, Meghalaya-5, Nagaland-16, Pondicherry-2, Tripura-36, West Bengal-9, Sikkim-3, Punjab-152, U.P.-11, Rajasthan-3.

1987- There has been a massive deployment of 208 companies of CRPF to maintain law and order and to carry out anti-terrorist operations in Punjab. Delhi continued to have a deployment of 76 companies to carry out internal security and anti-terrorist duties in the Union Territory of Delhi. 30 coys in Tripura and 25 companies each in Arunachal Pradesh and Jammu & Kashmir were used for various internal security duties. During the year 1987, CRPF and local police arrested about, 3750 persons and killed 328 terrorists in encounters.

For the first time in the glorious history of CRPF, a CRP Bn was airlifted to Sri Lanka to form a part of Indian Peace Keeping Force. 58 Bn CRPF airlifted on 22.9.87 and subsequently 35 Bn was also despatched along with a coy of Mahila Bn to Sri Lanka. These CRP units performed their duties in spite of very heavy odds posed by highly motivated LTTE guerillas armed with sophisticated weapons in an unknown soil. Yet CRP jawans and mahila coy personnel gave a gallant fight to save the Jaffna Fort from falling to LTTE hands. Ct T. Mohanan of 35 Bn won the 'Vir Chakra'(posthumously) for gallant action in fighting the LTTE extremists despite being seriously wounded.

CRP Bns deployed in Darjeeling district to cope with law and order porblems arising out of Gorkhaland agitation also performed their duties in a very creditable manner.

751172553 Ct Kali Ram and 720160563 Ct J.S.Pillai of 22 Bn CRP and Dy SP. U.S. Rawat, 701290263 Ct S. Shamsudin, 821150999 Ct Rashidudin and 710559198 Ct Bachan Lal Bharti of 23 Bn were awarded President's Police Medal for Gallantry during the year. 7 CRP personnel were also awarded Police Medal for gallantry. Six companies of 58 Bn CRPF were airlifted from Palam airport on September 25,1987 the companies were deployed in various parts of Sri Lanka for policing some sensitive districts. Placed under the operational command of Southern Command of Indian Army, CRP companies were called upon to take part in operations against Tamil militants. Personnel of 35 battalions were also later rushed to Sri Lanka to reinforce the I.P.K.F. The role played by CRPF was lauded by Shri P. Chidambaram, Minister of State for Internal Security, in maintaining law and order in

Jaffna (Sri Lanka). 12 Coys of CRP continued to be deployed at various sensitive points in Sri Lanka during the year Shri. P.G. Halarnkar joined CRP as Addl. Director General on 2 Sept. 1987. The educational standard for recruitment to the rank of constable in CRP has been raised from 8th class to 10th class w.e.f. 1 Sept. 1987.

1988 - During the year 208 companies were deployed in Punjab to deal with terrorists, 78 companies were deployed for internal security duties at Delhi, 24 companies each were deployed in Arunachal Pradesh, J&K, Tripura and Uttar Pradesh. During 1988, CRPF along with civil police arrested approximately 3430 terrorists/extremists and approximately 340 terrorists were killed in encounters. During 1988, 37 CRP personnel were decorated with gallantry medals for their brave deeds. Inspector B.P. Sharma was awarded Sena Medal. Shri S.S. Virk, DIGP, CRPF Amritsar was awarded "Padma Shree" by the Govt. of India. 670180279 HC P.G. Murugeswar and 750550152 Ct Moti Singh Mehta were awarded Prime Minister's Life Saving Medal. Shri P.G. Halarnkar, IPS took over charge as Director General on 31.3.88 from Shri S.D. Pandey who proceeded on voluntary retirement. Constable Thankappan Mohanan is the first CRP man to be honoured with Vir Chakra which was awarded to him for his bravery against LTTE insurgents in Sri Lanka on October 15, 1987.

Amidst records galore, CRP athletes continued to maintain their supremacy in track and field events for the tenth successive year in the All India Police Games held at Trivandrum. A draft for a sum of Rs. 31,80434/- was handed over to Prime Minister Rajiv Gandhi by Director General CRP on March 3,1988. This amount was voluntary contribution of CRPF officers and men towards the Prime Minister's Relief Fund. On February 6,1988 foundation stone of the CRPF Public School in Rohini in New Delhi was laid by Director General, CRPF. Recruitment to newly created battalions of CRPF started on March 15, 1988 and the new units were given number from 89 to 98 battalions of CRPF. Shri M.P. Singh took over charge as IGP, North Eastern Sector in July 1988. He belongs to the first batch of directly appointed officers who joined the force in December 1961. On 1 October, 1988 total number of CRP sub units deployed in various states were as under : Andhra Pradesh-6, A & N Islands-2, Arunachal Pradesh-22, Assam-12, Bihar-5, Chandigarh-17, Delhi-72, Gujarat-21, Haryana-3, Jammu & Kashmir-23, Meghalaya-5, Manipur-20, Mizoram-9, Nagaland-12, Punjab-192, Pondicherry-1, Rajasthan-8, Sikkim-3, Tripura-24, U.P.-5, West Bengal-17, and Sri Lanka-13.

CRPF is a secular force in which people of all religions are represented as can be seen from the table of religion-wise distribution of the force as on 1.10.88.

Rank	*Hindu*	*Muslim*	*Sikh*	*X-ian*	*Budd-hist.*	*Jains*	*Parsices*
D.G.	1	-	-	-	-	-	-
Addl. D.G	-	-	1	-	-	-	-
I.G.P	5	-	2	-	-	-	-
DIGP	17	-	3	1	-	-	-
Addl. DIG	17	-	3	1	-	-	-
Commandants	102	4	39	6	-	-	-
2-I/C & A/Cs	299	17	52	6	-	-	-
Dy.SP	521	15	66	20	-	-	-
Inspectors	802	24	177	21	-	-	-
Sub-Insps.	2536	72	258	77	-	1	-
Head Consts.	10076	308	486	334	4	-	-
Naiks	9388	464	431	546	1	-	-
L/Naiks	9146	663	283	458	1	-	-
Consts	42462	4752	1600	1944	26	4	4
Recruits	13188	593	869	371	22	-	-
Followers	7475	305	53	177	-	-	1
Min. Staff	2738	110	57	189	1	6	-
Hos. Staff	903	64	16	150	-	1	-
Total :	99676	7391	4396	4301	55	12	5

CRPF has been recruiting people from various parts of the country and state-wise number of persons recruited during the last 5 years is given below :

S.No.	State/UT	No. of persons recruited				
		1984	1985	1986	1987	1988
1	2	3	4	5	6	7
1.	Assam	145	377	124	126	204
2.	Andhra Pradesh	303	682	117	259	1443
3.	Bihar	337	1046	287	45	695
4.	Gujarat	213	546	61	147	906
5.	Haryana	310	727	250	345	200
6.	Himachal Pradesh	82	398	63	-	100
7.	Jammu & Kashmir	94	414	156	45	116
8.	Kerala	322	838	104	27	100

1	2	3	4	5	6	7
9.	Karnataka	141	637	87	97	1263
10.	Madhya Pradesh	234	818	211	198	1096
11.	Maharashtra	86	829	181	406	1295
12.	Manipur	121	211	28	29	161
13.	Meghalaya	1	20	-	6	52
14.	Nagaland	-	15	-	-	7
15.	Orissa	155	667	203	124	477
16.	Punjab	154	401	28	89	1411
17.	Rajasthan	197	798	219	340	954
18.	Sikkim	9	7	13	-	-
19.	Tamil Nadu	236	659	65	492	1193
20.	Tripura	91	97	-	29	405
21.	Uttar Pradesh	724	2368	592	234	1268
22.	West Bengal	242	1101	262	375	1058
23.	Andaman and Nicobar(UTs)	10	27	-	-	11
24.	Arunachal Pradesh	1	4	-	-	1
25.	Chandigarh (UT)	-	6	-	35	-
26.	Delhi (UT)	44	124	50	153	371
27.	Mizoram	-	23	-	10	18
28.	Pondicherry (UT)	5	35	16	19	51
29.	Goa, Daman and Diu	-	-	-	-	37
30.	Nepal	-	7	-	-	-

The table below will show the details of family accommodation(Type-wise) constructed for C.R.P.F upto December 1988.

1.	Type-I Family Quarters	-	5219	Nos.
2.	Type-II Family Quarters	-	4068	"
3.	Type-III Family Quarters	-	296	"
4.	Type-IV Family Quarters	-	248	"
5.	Type-V/VI Family Quarters	-	81	"

1989 -5th Signal battalion was inaugurated by CRP Director General Shri P.G. Halarnkar, IPS on 12th January, 1989 at Mohali, Ropar district in Punjab. 10 newly raised battalions have completed their training period and have become operationally functional. Thirteen companies of CRP continued to be deployed at various sensitive points in Sri Lanka during the year. Large number of companies continued to carry out anti-terrorist operations in Punjab. During last fifty years the CRP force has expanded tremendously and from one Battalion it has grown into 93 Battalions with 5 Signal battalions, 15

Ranges, 18 Group Centres, 5 Sector Inspectors General with Directorate General.

The figures given below will show the expenditure incurred in construction works of CRPF from 1970 till March 1988.

Sl.No.	Year	Expenditure (in Rs.)
1.	1969-70	1,79,59,000/-
2.	1970-71	1,62,41,000/-
3.	1971-72	2,98,00,000/-
4.	1972-73	4,97,00,000/-
5.	1973-74	4,59,00,000/-
6.	1974-75	4,68,02,000/-
7.	1975-76	5,23,99,000/-
8.	1976-77	6,55,50,000/-
9.	1977-78	8,99,34,000/-
10.	1978-79	8,42,74,000/-
11.	1979-80	4,95,17,000/-
12.	1980-81	5,45,93,000/-
13.	1981-82	5,13,50,000/-
14.	1982-83	4,16,19,000/
15.	1983-84	4,85,57,000/-
16.	1984-85	2,54,46,911/-
17.	1985-86	2,61,19,574/-
18.	1986-87	5,43,33,515/-
19.	1987-88	4,42,40,000/-
	Total	90,43,95,000/-

Outstanding sportsmen who have national and international recognition with their distinctions are given below :

1.	Shri G.S. Randhawa	Commandant		Gold Medal in Decathlon Asian Games 1962.
2.	Shri Hari Chand	Dy.SP	i)	Gold Medal in 5000 mtrs. Asian Games 1978.
			ii)	Gold Medal in 10,000 mtrs. Asian Games 1978.
3.	Shri Ishwar Singh	Dy.SP		Bronze Medal in Heavy Weight category in Wrestling in Commonwealth Games 1978.
4.	Shri Khajan Singh	Dy.SP	i)	Silver Medal in 200 mtrs. Butterfly-Asian Games 1986.
			ii)	Silver Medal in 100 mtrs

				Butterfly- World Police Games 1989.
5.	Shri Bhanu Singh	SI		Bronze Medal in Super Heavy Weight Judo- Asian Games 1986.
6.	Shri Sukhwant Singh	A/Comdt	i)	Rustame Hind-1970
			ii)	Hind Kesari-1970
7.	Shri Ishwar Singh	Dy.SP	i)	Rustame Hind-1978
			ii)	Haryana Kesari-1975 & 1976.
8.	Shri Suresh Chand	Insp.	i)	Rustame Hind-1983
			ii)	Hind Kesari-1983.

The following 4 persons are the recipients of Arjuna Award in the CRPF.

S.no.	Name	Rank	Discipline	Year
1.	Shri G.S. Randhawa	Comdt	Athletics	1964
2.	Shri Hari Chand	Dy.SP	- do -	1972
3.	Shri Khajan Singh	Dy.SP	- do -	1984
4.	Shri R.S. Bal	Dy.SP	- do -	1986

Progress achieved in construction of buildings in CRPF since the year 1970 is given below:

S.no.	Type of building	Total available family qrs year-wise				
		1970	1975	1980	1985	1989
1.	Family Qrs (Type-I to Type-VI)	1062	1662	6817	9243	9912
2.	Barracks 120 men	11	30	81	81	142
3.	Barracks 40 men	-	-	-	36	36
4.	Barracks for SOs	-	-	16	16	16
5.	Barracks for HCs	2	3	13	16	16
6.	Administration block/ office block.		6	23	24	24
7.	Store block and trade shop	-	5	16	19	19
8.	MT office/workshop/store block.	-	3	15	19	19
9.	Garrages	-	125	723	755	809
10.	Washing platform	-	-	-	12	12
11.	Quarter Guard/Radio Stn/ Armourer shop.	-	4	19	22	22
12.	Re-browning chamber	-	-	2	14	14
13.	Magazine	-	2	45	48	48
14.	Base Hospital	-	1	2	2	2
15.	G.C. Hospital	-	2	10	11	11

1	2	3	4	5	6	7
16.	Education class rooms	-	-	15	27	27
17.	Officers' Mess	-	-	13	15	15
18.	SO/HC Mess	-	8	26	31	31
19.	Men's Club with canteen	-	2	7	12	12
20.	Dhobi Ghat	-	-	34	35	35
21.	Badminton Court	-	-	4	11	11
22.	Family Welfare Centre	-	-	11	13	13
23.	Primary School Bldg.	-	1	9	10	10
24.	Grain godown/shopping centre	-	1	12	16	16
25.	Servant Qtr. for O/Mess staff	-	-	8	55	55
26.	Stadium	-	-	2	3	3
27.	DIGP Office	-	-	-	3	3
28.	Scooter-cum-cycle stand	-	-	-	28	28
29.	Stationery and printing Block.	-	-	1	1	1
30.	AWS Building	-	-	-	2	2
31.	CWS Building	-	-	5	13	13
32.	Base Workshop	-	-	-	1	1
33.	Wireless receiving stn.	-	-	1	1	1
34.	Drill shed	-	1	1	1	1
35.	Squash Court	-	-	2	3	3
36.	Nurses Hostel	-	-	1	1	1
37.	Sand Model Room	-	-	1	1	1
38.	Mortuary	-	-	1	2	2
39.	Wireless Transmitting Stn.	-	-	4	7	7
40.	Officers Suits	-	-	-	15	15
41.	Technical Bldg(Signals)	-	-	-	3	3

Statement given below will show the details of land available to CRPF at various locations, proposed acquisition cases and projects in hand.

a) Land belonging to CRPF at various locations :

Sl.No.	*Location*	*Land(in acres)*
1.	Dimapur	174.00
2.	Pinjore	142.50
3.	Silchar	222.00
4.	Pune	203.00
5.	Neemuch	1190.00

Sl.No.	Location	Land(in acres)
6.	Bangalore	256.00
7.	Gandhinagar	202.00
8.	Pallipuram	137.00
9.	Salt Lake Sector III, Calcutta	4.36
10.	Salt Lake Sector V	19.00
11.	Mahabir Nagar(Delhi)	9.08(9.08)
12.	Wazirabad(Delhi)	60.00
13.	Papan Kalan(New Delhi)	20.00
14.	Aligarh	86.50
15.	Hallo Majra(Chandigarh)	24.00
16.	Nagpur	244.00
17.	Avadi	447.00
18.	Bhubneswar	130.00
19.	Rampur	170.00
20.	Imphal	90.00
21.	Mokam Aghat	147.00
22.	Yusafguda(Hyderabad)	9.00
23.	Jharodakalan(New Delhi)	251.00
24.	Ajmer	236.00
25.	Durgapur	198.00
26.	Gauhati	204.52
27.	Hyderabad	196.00
28.	Jammu	157:00
29.	Ranchi	101.33
30.	Chandigarh	142.50
31.	Awantipura(Srinagar)	50.00
32.	Rambagh(Srinagar)	5.00

(b) *Proposed land acquisition cases: Land in acre : Purpose*

1.	Papan Kalan(Delhi)	20.00	Bn HQr.
2.	Gharauli(Delhi)	9.88	"
3.	Wazirabad(Delhi)	60.00	Tran/Camp
4.	Nehru Nagar	0.70	Dte. Staff camp
5.	Patna	4.00	DIG Office.
6.	Srinagar	10.00 (appx)	DIG office

			1 Bn Hqrs.
7.	Ghaziabad	50.00	88 Bn HQrs.
8.	Delhi	100.00	for 2 Bn HQrs.
9.	Lucknow	150.00	Future GC
10.	Jallandhar	150.00	Future GC
11.	Location yet to decide	150.00	Future GC
12.	Jalandhar	50.00	Bn HQr.
13.	Maneshwar(Haryana)	113.00	Firing Range
14.	Hallo Majra	20.00	Bn HQrs.
15.	Patiala	50.00	"
16.	Agartala(Tripura)	3.50	DIG Office.
17.	In or around Chandigarh	40.00	5 Sig. bn.
18.	Champak Nagar(Tripura)	189.18	Yet to be decided
19.	Pinjore	30.00	Addl. land for GC
20.	Srinagar	12.00	Bn HQr.

c) *Projects in Hand*

1.	Imphal	-	4 Bn GC
2.	Mokamaghat	-	4 Bn GC
3.	Ranchi	-	Signal Gc/3 Signals.
4.	Gauhati	-	4 Bn GC
5.	Silchar	-	4 Bn GC
6.	Mahabir Nagar	-	Bn HQrs.
7.	Biharipur(Wazirabad)	-	Transit Bn.
8.	Aligarh	-	72 Bn HQr.
9.	Hallo Majra	-	Bn HQrs.
10.	Pinjore	-	4 bn GC
11.	Awantipur	-	Mini GC
12.	Bangalore	-	2 BN HQrs and ISA
13.	Pune	-	RTC-3
14.	Shillong/Salt Lake/Hyd.	-	IsGPNE Sec/E Sec/S.Sec.
15.	Neemuch	-	Water Supply Scheme

Statewise representation in CRPF of personnel showing their percentage is given in table below:

S/No.	Name of State/UT	No of persons serving in CRPF	Percentage of representation in CRPF
SOUTHERN SECTOR			
1.	Andhra Pradesh	2,204	2,30

(Contd.)

2.	Karnataka	1,846	1,93
3.	Kerala	7,615	8,00
4.	Madhya Pradesh	3,303	3.46
5.	Maharashtra	3,577	3.74
6.	Tamil Nadu	2,987	3.12
7.	Lakshadweep	4	--
8.	Pondicherry	49	0.05
EASTERN SECTOR			
9.	Andaman & Nicobar Islands(UT)	83	0.08
10.	Bihar	9,782	10.24
11.	Orissa	2,472	2.58
12.	Uttar Pradesh	19,978	20.91
13.	West Bengal	3,723	3.89
14.	Tripura	585	0.61
15.	Mizoram	57	0.05
NORTHERN SECTOR			
16.	Dadar and Nagar Haveli(UT)	9	--
17.	Gujarat	1,525	1,59
18.	Rajasthan	8,026	8.40
19.	Delhi	669	0.70
20.	Goa, Damnan & Diu(UT)	12	0.01
NORTH EASTERN SECTOR			
21.	Assam	2,213	2.31
22.	Manipur	751	0.78
23.	Meghalaya	87	0.09
24.	Nagaland	69	0.07
25.	Sikkim	67	0.07
26.	Arunachal Pradesh	79	0.08
NORTH WESTERN SECTOR			
27.	Haryana	11,009	11,52
28.	Himachal Pradesh	3,847	4.02
29.	Jammu & Kashmir	3,719	3.89
30.	Punjab	4,662	4.83
31.	Chandigarh(UT)	12	0.01

On the occasion of inaugural function of Golden Jubilee Celebration on 6.4.1989 at Vigyan Bhawan(New Delhi) Shri Buta Singh, Home Minister said : "The Force has distinguished itself commendably in the discharge of its onerous responsibilities and presently constitutes one of the elite para-military forces in the country. It is really a credit to the Force that it has been able to adapt itself not only to the multifarious problems but also to the different functional environments. It is, perhaps, the adaptability and the versatility of the Force, which has made it stand out as one of the elite central police organisations in the country today. This is amply proved by the fact that the demand for deployment of the CRPF in various troubled states of the country is growing more and more every day, to the extent that the Central government is finding it difficult to meet such demands."

Conclusion

The CRPF has, with each succeeding year, grown in stature by virtue of its hard, efficient and selfless service to the people of the country. The CRPF has a very distinguished record of valuable service to the nation. Members of the gallant force can look with a measure of pride for its services to the nation over a long span of time. The CRPF has earned a very good name for itself wherever it was deployed. Members of the CRPF are drawn from different parts of the country and from all communities. It is a truly secular and effective police force which has cheerfully discharged the duties assigned to it in all parts of the country, even when called upon to do so under most difficult and challenging conditions. They have throughout its 50 years of existence maintained the highest traditions of integrity, loyalty, courage and dedicated service to the nation. It has earned numerous awards for gallantry and meritorious service. It has given an excellent account of itself whether it has been called to defend the frontiers of the country or to deal with communal disturbances or to tackle internal security problems, or to handle insurgency in the North-Eastern region or extremists in West Bengal and Andhra Pradesh or emergency/relief operations in various calamities.

During various operations against insurgents, terrorists and other anti-social elements, the force has suffered a number of casualties in the past. Operations casualties of the Force from 1946 to 1988 are shown below:

Year	*No. of personnel killed in action*	*Year*	*No. of personnel killed in action*
1946	1	1972	1
1948	2	1973	3
1949	5	1974	5
1955	1	1975	9
1959	10	1977	1
1960	1	1979	6
1961	1	1980	8
1962	2	1981	12
1963	10	1982	12
1964	21	1983	7
1965	17	1984	18
1966	12	1985	8
1967	33	1986	15
1968	10	1987	48
1969	6	1988	45
1970	9		
1971	7		
	Total : 346		

CRPF is one of the most mobile armed force in the world. A glimpse of inter state moves undertaken by the CRPF coys during the last 3 years will give a good account of its high mobility. CRP jawans leaving their family behind move from place to place, district to district and state to state to maintain internal security of the country.

Year	By Air	By Road	By Rail	By Ship	Total coys
1986	132	307	456	-	895
1987	104	290	421	2	817
1988	65	208	297	13	583

CRPF is highly disciplined, mobile and effective police force which comprised personnel drawn from all parts of the country belonging to different faiths but truly secular in outlook and conduct. The splendid performance of CRP over the past 50 years has earned appreciation from all quarters and this versatile force is fondly looked upon by the state police forces as the citadel of strength in restoring normalcy in disturbed areas. There is constant and pressing demand for the CRPF from all parts of the country. This is indicative of the implicit faith and confidence that the people have in its ability to deliver goods, its efficiency, impartiality and fairness. The people seem to have conferred on it the status of a disciplined, effective and mobile elite force. CRPF is a time-tested and dependable national force which has contributed to a large degree in maintaining the integrity and secular nature of the Indian Republic.

CHAPTER-8

MANAGEMENT IN POLICE ORGANISATIONS

THE INCREASING size and complexity of Police organisations, new challenges to policing, technological developments and the increasing turbulent social context of policing in developing societies of the third world have given an increased importance and visibility to the role of police management. Although it is less than thirty years since the police service started to consciously apply management concepts to police problems, this does not mean that previously police leaders and supervisors were any less managers than their modern counterparts in other organisations. There is a need for managerial awareness within the police organisations today. If the senior police officers are responsible for management of police organisations it is obvious that they should look to that body of theory and research which has been developed since the beginning of this century to serve the needs of managers in industry and parts of the public sector. Management theories can provide useful sources of ideas and model for police management. The extent to which management theory can and should provide an appropriate and proper basis for the practice of professional police management is one of the most important questions facing the police service at the present time. (1) Pressure upon the police is mounting everyday and it comes from the Government, politicians, minority groups, local communities, police Unions and from the general public. Today the police have to deal with a population which is aware of its civil rights and therefore police work today needs excellent management. Management theory is an umbrella term referring to a variety of attempts to create a more solid foundation for the parctice of management in police work. Police management has to deal with all aspects of police service and police organisation with special reference to its resources, techniques, objects and policies. A police manager is responsible for motivating, directing and controlling the officers and civilians under his command to achieve results which are determined by the overall objectives of the organisation. A police officer should know the following six vital aspects of his command responsibilities:-

(a) The current performance of his men set against the overall objectives of the police;

(b) The desired level of performance for his subordinates;

(c) The means which are available to improve efficiency and effectiveness, after taking into consideration constraits and limitations which exist;

(d) Goals and objectives which he will use to measure the achievements of his command;

(e) problems of personnel management including problems of motivation and personnel appraisal;

(f) Problems of resource management and time management.

The police officers and managers must adopt a rational management process to identify problems and have to apply the concepts of rational management to policing methods. To proceed from the definition of a problem to its solution requires a system of management to transform ideas into action. There are four elements of the management cycle as shown in the figure below: [(2)]

Figure I: Management Cycle.

Planning-plan policing methods in response to specific problems.

Controlling-Evaulation Monitor the day-to-day progress. Evaluate the long term results.

Organising-identify the task to be performed and organise human resources accordingly.

Implementation-Execute the Policing Method.

The management process moves through four stages of planning, organising, implementation and controlling evaluation and the process continues as a cycle where the lessons of the past are used to improve future performance. Police work demands a system which will encourage initiative, discretion and decision making at lower and middle levels and not a system which tends to destroy these qualities. Despite some enlightened management, the police force remains a predominantly hierarchical, authoritative, bureaucratic organisation which, as Heaton suggests, is a more suitable work environment for "Theory X" individuals. There appears to be strong evidence to conclude that the management system of most police forces is the reverse of that which is required for effective police management.[(3)] Paradoxically constables and other field level functionaries develop "Theory Y" attributes as a necessary response to their work environment.

Police constables gradually learn through socialisation process how to go beyond the organisational rules and procedures while maintaining a facade of conformity which facilitates "the illusion of control". In police organisations the organisational philosophy suits the individuals who prefer directions and control, who avoid responsibility, who are authoritative and follow Mc Gregor's 'Theory X'. (4) In the established models communication goes from the highest level downwards with the behaviour of individuals, being ordered and coerced in ways determined by the higher authority. In this established pattern organisation is imposed from the top down and is managed or administered in an authoritative style and field personnel tend to question the validity and competence of the centralised structure in achieving the goals of the police force. (5)

Personnel Management

Personnel Management in the police organisation is a high priority management area where time tested man-management concepts can be usefully supplemented by the scientific methods of performance appraisal, job analysis, work measurement, motivations, promotions, postings, transfers and job rotation. Personnel management has the following four broad aspects :

(1) Administration of personnel including recruitment, induction, placement, transfer, promotion, and salary management,

(2) Planning and development of personnel including manpower, planning, career planning, performance appraisal, personal records and job requirements records and organisational development;

(3) Welfare management including housing, education, sports, medical, provident fund, risk fund, pension and retirement benefits;

(4) Training and development of personnel by organising in-service training and specialised training programmes for effective career management.

Personnel Management is very important in police organisations because police officers deal with the people of the community as visible symbol of the government. Police personnel management is complex and demanding because it involves the management of the policemen both on and off duty, from the day they are selected to the day they retire. The essence of a dynamic personnel management is getting effective optimum results, not only in the short run but also in the long run through building and maintaning a satisfied, motivated and productive human organisations. The final responsibility for personnel policy must lie with top management to whom the personnel officer acts as advisor and its execution must run through the whole line of management if it is to be effective. [6] In the context of present day requirements there is an urgent need for an independent department of personnel at police headquarters. A broad organisational structure of personnel department with built-in felxibility of multiple tiers may be adopted depending on the size and complexity of the organisation in the state and other Central police organisations and armed police forces. [7]

Community Management

Every police organisation is intimately related to the community in which it is located and in which it serves. The personnel of the police are drawn from the community and have a personal involvement in the life and values of the community. [8] Police organisations are expected to maintain a friendly, cooperative relationship with the community. Accountability of the police in discretionary areas, opening the police agency to enquiry by citizens and news media to ensure freedom of information, citizens' complaints and redress of grievances; internal investigations and supervision of police behaviour, identifying the needs and problems of the community and carrying out service utility tasks are some of the areas requiring attention of police organisations for carrying out effective community management. Proper monitoring of developing situations in the field can pre-empt and defuse a likely outburst; timely feed back can control growing conflicts and tensions. This requires a two way flow of information from the community to the police and back. Police are accountable to the community it serves and therefore community management is one of the most important management task. "The today's community which the police is endeavouring to serve is vastly different from the community of yesteryears. This implies a need for new concepts in police education and police training, especially so to social and behavioural science." [9]

Behavioural Aspects of Police Management

The police manager's role demands a knowledge and understanding of the psychological aspects of management. The police manager, having different types of personnel within his department must attempt to mould them into a productive unit so that higher objectives may be set and achieved within a given frame of time." Only through the understanding of human behaviour as it relates to organisation can the manager make the most effective use of personnel within the department." [10] Dr. Abraham Maslow's Hierarchy of needs, Frederick Herzbery's Motivation hygiene theory, Douglas M c Gregor's Theory X and Theory Y, Chris Argyris Immaturtiy Maturity theory and Management styles on a continuum developed by Rensis Likert are to be understood by police managers so that they may utilise and implement these theories in their organisation with benefit. Police managers must analyse and understand their own organisational behaviour with the help of theories of motivation prevalent in contemporary management and utilise the positive side of each theory to create a more effective organisational environment. While the scientific Management Movement of Frederick W. Taylor emphasized concern for purpose or task, the Human Relations movement of Elton Mayo stressed the concern for people. In essence the police manager who is able to change his style of leadership according to situation and according to the needs of his employees is the manager who is most effective in obtaining both personal and organisational objectives. [11] A great deal of criticism has been levelled at police managers by their rank and file who perceive top managers as aloof, aristocratic and too politically motivated to have the best interest of line-officers at heart. [12] Police managers unlike military managers do not and cannot actively lead or direct their men in crucial situations. "Police managers are not leaders so much as they are cheer leaders. They cannot participate in the game but can only exhort, applaud or rail at the players." [13] Because the police manager is accountable for the conduct of all police agency employees, he should have a direct interface with the internal discipline process. Police management has a profound obligation to provide police officers with a working environment reasonably consistent with individual needs and conducive to the fulfilment of the police mission.

Functional Aspects of Police Management

The police manager who emphasizes Management by Objectives (M.B.O.) in his department assumes that each police officer wants to know what is expected of him and that he wants to know if he is performing upto the optimum level in a given environment. Management by objectives is "the establishment of effectiveness areas and effectiveness standards for managerial positions and the periodic conversion of these into measurable time - bound objectives linked vertically and horizontally and with future planning." [14] Management by objectives can best be described as a seven part process consisting of :-

(1) Recognition of community values and departmental beliefs;

(2) Statement of department mission;

(3) Establishment of long term goals;

(4) Establishment of short term goals:

(5) Development of projects;

(6) Development and implementation of action plans and

(7) Evaluation of the system

Police manager in the implementation of his management by objectives system should determine the time and effort that can be devoted to bringing about change in the department keeping in view the pitfalls of M.B.O. because Management by objectives by no means is panacea for all management ills. The Police manager cannot allow management by objectives to over-ride the responsibilities or caring for day-to-day activities of the police organisation. The police manager in viewing management by objectives must constantly keep in mind its role as a rational tool to aid and assist him in making the broad managerial functions of planning, organising, staffing and implementation easier. [15] Problem analysis and decision making are two most important issues that the police manager faces every day, cost, time and side effects are important - considerations in decision - making process of police managers, planning is the foundation upon which much of police management is based. Planning is necessary to set realistic goals for the organisation, to develop objectives which lead to the accomplishment of these goals, to devise operational strategies to ensure goal attainment, to allocate available resources in the most effective and efficient manner and to evaluate the impact of police operations and programmes. [16] While doing planning police managers must take into account the factors of time, severity, frequency and ripple effects.

Time Management

Time cannot be stockpiled nor it can be recycled. By delegating tasks and distributing work he is able to effectively use the time allotted to him in an effective manner. Police managers have to utilise their working hours time in a most economical, rational and judicious method. He requires time for public contacts, conferences, inspections, weekly evaluations, self-development and other supervisory functions. It is important for the police manager to set aside a time each week when he can be creative, innovative and carefully think out and plan for the future. The police officers have to learn the art of delegation with effective control and monitoring devices built in within the system. The police manager must keep himself out of "activity-trap" by delegating tasks and jobs to his subordinates. It will help ease his job pressure and time pressure and will provide him more time for use in planning, organising, leading and all other management functions and activities that bring about growth of a police organisation. Staff meetings, public contacts and discussion with political bosses all require time and therefore time management is an important requirement for all police managers. Each manager must utilise time consistently, systematically and conscientiously in a most productive manner. Time management is important even for the organisation as certain tasks and jobs need to be completed within a given time.

Communications Management

Communications are mutual interchange of ideas and views by an effective means within and from outside the organisation. Communications in a police organisation are downward, upward, lateral or horizontal. Upward police communication however frequently gets blocked at different levels of transmission channels. Horizontal communication between the police and the public needs to be kept most effective and open at all times. Police-public communication management is of crucial importance to the police managers. All possible barriers to communication network have to be managed in an efficient manager. An imaginative management information system in police organisation is needed for effective communication management. Police Management information system can be gradually refined, perfected and developed into a powerful link between the police chief, his articulate staff and interacting citizenry including the public and mass media. Police managers have to keep proper and effective communication with the mass media to build up police image and to contradict rumours and incorrect reporting about crimes and offences. Management of communication behaviour of police subordinates is an all important task for the police managers. Communicative behaviour patterns can be broadly categorised as under. (17)

(1) Controlling Pattern.

(2) Relinquishing Pattern.

(3) Defensive Pattern.

(4) Development Pattern.

Under the 'controlling pattern' the police manager uses his influence to force his subordinates to do exactly as he desires. The 'relinquishing pattern' allows decision at subordinate levels. In 'defensive pattern' police manager totally withdraws from problem solving process and he begins to move away from the problem. Under the 'developmental pattern' the influence flows between the police manager and his subordinates and is a two way process. Through effective communication, a police manager attempts to establish a specific behaviour pattern in his subordinates. Communication management with the press, mass media, public and the government are also important aspects which police manager, cannot ignore at any time. The Johari Window is an information processing model by which the police manager can judge his effectiveness in dealing with the communicative concerns of feed-back and exposure. [18] The Johari Window model is shown in Figure 2 below :-

Figure 2

The Johari Window

	Exposure	Known to self	Unknown to self
Known to Others		Region I Arena	Region II Blind Spot
Unknown others		Region III Facade	Region IV Unknown

Feed back

Region I represents open communications where information is equally shared and understood. Region II represents the area where information is known by others but unknown to manager. Region III inhibits interpersonal effectiveness but the imbalance is in favour of the police manager. Region IV constitutes that portion of the interpersonal relations where information is unknown by both the police manager and others. Police managers should ensure that communication methods should be open, flexible and responsive to the needs of the organisation. The most damaging characteristic of a poor communications system will be confusion among the officers as to their role and contribution towards the goals of the organisation. [19] Confusion and uncertainty are the hall-marks of ineffective communication management and the predominant means of information dissemination becomes rumour and speculation. Communication gaps or communication break-downs within the police organisations have led to indiscipline and the unrests in the past. Therefore communications management is an important taks of police managers.

Resources Management

Every police organisation has lot of resources in terms of human resources, capital resources, computers, transport, wireless, dogs, forensic science laboratories, training institutions, materials and financial resources which require effective and optimum management. The police managers have the ultimate responsibility for establishing priorities for the allocation of various resources and for linking these priorities to organisational objectives. In some police organisations there is an appalling ignorance of resource allocation priorities at lower and middle levels which run counter to the principles of effective management. Police managers need professional cost accountancy and materials management support. The police chief needs a group of experts to design, instal and operate a modern system of resources management. Fiscal management including financial management is one of the key areas for police managers. Budget is an allocation of scarce resources among competing demands from different branches of the police department. Programme budgeting demands an analysis between cost benefits and cost effectiveness. Budgeting is a planning tool in helping in the every day operation of the police department. Fiscal management is an area that should be carefully studied, analysed and understood by all the commanders in the department so that they might assist the chief of polic in preparation, approval and execution of the police department's budget. The mechanism for monitoring and feedbacks is outdated in most of the police organisations because police managers have remained mostly untouched by the great precision and sophistication which has been introduced in financial management in other organisations. Financial rules and regulations and fiscal discipline are important areas where police officers must get proper working knowledge. A police manager cannot achieve effective controls unless he bases this control upon accurate objectives, programmes, schedules and budgets. The manager should exert the greatest control efforts against a few critical factors and as a result will obtain maximum control with minimum effort and expense. Police officers must know their role in the development, execution and implementation of a department budget. The police managers need to face budgetary processes with an open mind and a positive attitude. An efficient manager must understand the broad distinctions between object budget, performance budget and the programme budget. A successful police manager is one who learns to plan expenditure wisely, operating within the means provided in the budget. Fiscal management is the process of planning and controlling of funds, estimating expenditures, revenues, preparing the budget document, review and adoption and execution at periodical intervals.

Traffic Management

Considerable professionalism is needed in generation, maintenance and updating of traffic safety systems. Efficient and effective traffic management in big cities and metropolitan areas particularly during peak hours and during important occasions is a big challenge to police organisations. It is necessary to employ modern techniques for better husbanding of both human and technical resources of traffic management. The science of traffic engineering is vastly developed today and police organisations must make liberal use of trained traffic engineers to take care of such improvement needs as the installation of traffic control signals, signs and parking kerbs to control traffic flow to avoid congestion in metropolitan and big towns and capitals. Managing the orderly flow of traffic and preventing accidents is a basic and primary responsibility of the police organisation. Selective traffic enforcement is a traffic management practice whereby enforcement efforts are "proportional to traffic accidents with respect to time, place and type of violation." (20) A good police manager first identifies traffic problems and then plans and executes meaningful enforcement strategies for traffic control and regulation.

Emerging Trends in Police Managerial Practices

Successful police managers have to understand human behaviour in an organisational setting. According to Douglas Mc Gregor successful management depends - not alone, but significantly - upon the ability to predict and control human behaviour." (21) Planning plays an important role in the management of police organisations. "Only by committing himself to planning by formulating and articulating policy, by implementing an adequate programme, and by encouraging and supporting planning by personnel at all levels regardless of basic assignment - can the police chief executive assure himself that his agency will perform with increasing effectiveness in a changing environment". (22) It has now been realised that it is for the police managers to create the proper working environment. The concept of reinvigocrting individual managerial environment (RIME) is based on the conviction that personal growth can be achieved only by giving one's best to the organisation. Organisational practices are like religious precepts in that they are infused into the large body of men from above. It is possible for a sensitive police manager to generate for himself and his staff a working environment which encourages the best results.[23] It is the human relationships which determine the climate of the organisation. The trend of increasing specialisation of police tasks has been said to have reduced job-satisfaction among uniformed officers by narrowing the scope of their work. Most of the police organisations are suffering from the problems of organisational climate. Police work and police organisations require a sensitive and flexible management system. Policing by objective (PBO) was developed by Val Lubans and James Edgar following a review of the use of Management by objectives by police forces in the United States.[24] P.B.O. (policing by objectives) is a process built upon three basic management concepts - planning (including organising), implementation and evaluation and can be shown in the Figure 3 given below :-

Figure 3 - (25) - Basic PBO Cycle:

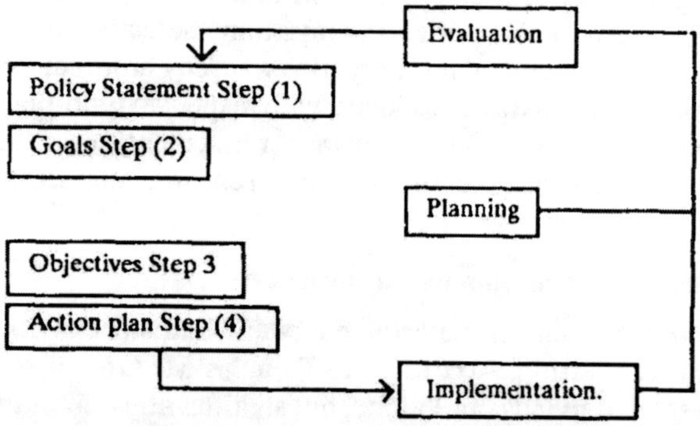

The purpose of adopting P.B.O. model is to allow a greater degree of decentralised decision making within the force with a view to improving police management. The extremely diverse nature of police work creates on the one hand an interesting and challenging management tasks but on the other makes it difficult to provide instructions for every foreseeable eventuality in an ever changing world. The rational management approach is concerned with achieving operational improvements which are likely to be facilitated by improved human relations.

Management Theory for the Police - Search for new Models

James H. Auten has developed a new approach to management for productivity in public service organisations and specifically law enforcement organisations. Law enforcement agencies deal with an intangible that is extremely difficult, if not impossible, to measure in terms of costs- the satisfaction of the tax paying public with the services they provide in the form of combating crime and providing peace and order in the society. Theory "P" - managing for productivity has the following principles :-

(1) People are the most important resources in any public service organisation.

(2) People are capable of growth and organisations will become more productive as their human resources realize their growth potential.

(3) Goals and more specifically objectives, when properly created, motivate people.

(4) People have expectations about themselves, others and work.

(5) These expectations can be translated into tangible, achievable goals and objectives.

(6) People want to be the best at what they do.

(7) Our capacity to do is only limited by our opportunities and capacity to learn.

(8) Effective management is based upon the communication of expectations between employer and employees. To the extent possible, it is the responsibility of the management to identify and develop organisational and individual expectations into tangible, achievable goals and objectives and to then guide organisations and individual growth towards the attainment of these goals and objectives." [26]

In law enforcement organisation it is people whether they function as administrators, managers, supervisors, detectives or patrol officers that determine how productive the organisation is or becomes. Behavioural scientists hold that the average human being only uses approximately 10% of his brain or intellectual capacity. Theory 'P' tells us how do we motivate people to begin to realize their untapped potential for growth. Theory 'P' asserts that if we are seriously seeking to motivate employees to higher productivity through the use of certain incentives, then we need to consider implementing some of the following alternatives.[27]

(1) Improving the work environment so that the employee is called upon to go beyond his present level of performance and productivity.

(2) Making certain that we acknowledge employee achievements towards goals and objectives.

(3) Allowing significant participative decision making in the organisation.

(4) Helping employees in preparing themselves for promotion/advancement opportunities.

(5) Standardising, enlarging and enriching jobs.

(6) Creating a healthy organisational atmosphere of positive attitudes and approval within the organisation.

(7) Providing useful information service that relates to job requirements and needs of the employees.

(8) Setting up an environment of pride and friendly competition for achieving objectives and goals within given target dates.

(9) Providing full opportunities for human resource development within the organisation.

(10) Building up a more conducive and healthy working environment.

(11) Allowing greater innovativeness, inventiveness and creativity on the jobs and within the organisation.

(12) Permitting employees to have a significant voice in determining the criterion on which their job performance should be judged and evaluated.

(13) Involving employees in setting up broad goals and objectives for the organisation.

(14) Making certain that employees understand how their individual contributions are increasing the overall productivity of the organisation.

(15) Delegating responsibilities to employees and building up a proper system of career development for the employees.

(16) Providing intangible incentives to the social, ego/slates and self-actualisation needs of the employees to motivate them for greater productivity.

According to Zangwill work performance is directly related to energy level i.e. higher our energy level, the more productive we are in our jobs and a decline in our energy level often results in a decline in our productivity. [28] Zangwill further held that if we are seeking to create an environment in which the human resource can begin to grow towards its potential, then we need to work hard to eliminate negative emotions and the situations that cause them. But how this quest for increased productivity affects law enforcement has been best expressed by Cronkhite when he stated: " Combating increasing crime with static or decreasing resources is a challenge for today's police administrators." [29]

Police officers at field level have to face many uncertain and unforeseen situations and therefore 'P' theory is not fully applicable to explain their efficiency. Despite certain similarities about common management problems of coping with political influences, fiscal accountability, training, supervising and controlling personnel, each nation's singular matrix of historical and contemporary influences bestows uniqueness of character on its nation's police processes, organisation methods and effectiveness. Japanese police management system applies 'Z' management theory as propounded by Archambeault and Fenwick. [30] Management theory 'Z' is an organisational management model combining modern human organisational management technology and approaches, popularly termed "Japanese management approaches" which produces a highly efficient, flexible and cost effective organisation and which is characterized by team work, "holistic" concern for worker's welfare, defined career paths, use of informal control mechanisms and worker input into decision making. [31] The Japanese National Police Agency has discarded the Weberian-Fayolian para military bureaucracy and has replaced it with a modified management Theory 'Z' organisational frame. Within this frame Japanese police deliver services and live their lives. This approach recognises that workers are part of a larger social - economic matrix of influences, including family, religion, economic etc. Managemet assumes the responsibility for dealing with the whole human being and not just a segmental part which is characteristic of the bureaucratic organisation. Management Theory 'Z' provides the consistency in structure and management processes which allows a national police force to be decentralised into a semi-autonomous neighbourhood - centred system of fixed posts, referred to as "kobans" in urb n areas and "Chuzaisho" in rural areas, this structure positively fost , a high degree of interaction and cooperation between police and neighbourhood residents, fosters cooperation and creates a favourable image of the police. [32] In Japan police work closely with volunteer crime prevention groups and reinforce the importance of public relations, by placing crime prevention as major field of specialization within the National Police Agency on par with criminal investigation, security, traffic and patrol services. The Management Theory 'Z' type work environment creates an atmosphere which encourages team work and collective responsibility, the police officer is taught to see his efforts as contributing to the best interests of the police team which is merely an extension of society itself. [33] Comparative analysis of U.S.A. and Japanese organisational management models can be useful and instructive. Can application of Japanese Mangement theory 'Z' be very useful and effective to other countries.? A comparative study of differentiating characteristics of Japanese and the United States of America can be made with the help of given table :-

Table : Differentiating Characteristics of Japanese and U.S.A. Police Organisations

	Japanese Police		*United States of America Police*
1.	Low Crime Rate	1.	Very High crime rate
2.	Service to Citizen orientation.	2.	Political Survival Orientation.
3.	Oriental Value/ Traditions	3.	Western/Anglo American Values.
4.	'Z' Type Organisation	4.	Weberian-Fayolian Bureaucracy.
5.	Limited Participative Management	5.	Authoritarian Management approach.
6.	Decentralised Control	6.	Centralised Control
7.	Demilitarised pattern	7.	Para-Military Pattern
8.	Emphasis on Non-Coercive Control	8.	Emphasis on Coercive Control
9.	High Police-Citizen interaction.	9.	Low Police-Citizen inter-action.
10.	Holistic concern for Police welfare	10.	Segmental Concern for Police welfare
11.	Positive citizen attitude towards police.	11.	General negative citizen attitude towards police.

Conclusion

How can Indian Police benefit from management approaches developed in U.S.A. and Japan? Can we import their system as a whole or will we require certain modifications? It will take more than one generation of police professionals in India, if ever, to change its present managerial techniques and methods and build up a more democratic, decentralised and effective police management system in the country. Police personnel in India have to be motivated to commn themselves whole-heartedly to the organisation. Management has to take a "holistic" approach towards the police officers providing all basic human and social needs. Police leaders have to learn latest management techniques and create a more flexible, decentralised efficient and effecitive police organisation. "We cannot ape the Japanese system but we can incorporate some of their approach, which will strengthen our areas of weakness." (34) Future thinking and research needs to be directed to this end. There is at present a big gap which exists between management theory and management practice in India. Any attempt to import "a theory of managing" into policing in India which is not based upon an understanding and grasp of the peculiarities of Indian socio-economic legal system is liable to have unintended and unwelcome consequences. What are the handicaps of Indian Police? Why is police image not good in India? Why police organisational reforms have not been attempted so far. Why there is proliferation of posts at higher levels without positive results? There are many more basic questions which need to be analysed before we can find out and suggest a suitable management approach to Indian police system. Improved policing methods should be accompanied by improvements in the interpersonal skills of all officers with managerial responsibilities; police managers in India must have an empathy with lower ranks and must build up a suitable organisational environment responsive to the challenges of the future. Management training and orientation of present police managers will go a long way in improving the police force. Management strategy is a package which only delivers results if all parts are included. Improvement in the effectiveness and efficiency of police forces in India will not occur overnight by accident or chance. They can be achieved by professional, decentralised and competent management which should be capable of learning from the experience of others.

Notes and References

1. David Bradley, Neil Walker and Roy Wilkie (1986), *Managing the Police Law organisation and Democracy* p.35.
2. A.J.P. Butler (1984) - *Police Management*. Gower Publishing Company, Aldershor, England p.15.
3. A.J.P. Butler (1984) - *Police Management*, p.113.

4. Mc. Gregor D. *Human Side of Enterprise*, New York.

5. A.J.P. Butler - "A Study of the occupational perceptions of Police officers." Doctoral dissertation, Faculty of Law, University of Birmingham (1979).

6. *Personnel Management in India: The Practical Approach to Human Relations in Industry* compiled by Indian Institute of Personnel Mangement, - Asia Publishing House, Bombay 1961. P 63-64.

7. Recommendations of the Seminar on Personnel Policies in Police, "Need for Departments of Personnel in State and Central Police Forces", Seminar at S.V.P. National Police Academy, Hyderabad, September 1986.

8. William A Westley (1970), *Violence and the Police - A Sociological study of Law, Custom and morality*, p.19.

9. Louis A. Radelet, *The Police and the Community*, p.14.

10. Ronald G. Lynch (1978) - *The Police Manager - Professional Leadership Skills*, Allyn and Bacon In. Boston. p.47.

11. Ronald G. Lynch (1978) - *The Police Manager*, Allyn and Bacon Boston. p.77.

12. William Boppand Paul Whisenand (1980) - *Police Personnel Administration* W.328.

13. Thomas A Repetto, "Revamping levels of Police Middle Management". An address to the American Society for Public Administration, New York City Conference March 22, 1972).

14. Reddin W.J. (1970). *Effective Management by Objectives*, New York Mc Graw Hill p.12.

15. Ronald G. Lynch (1978) - *The Police Manager*, p.151.

16. Charles D. Hale (1977) *Fundamentals of Police Administration*, Holbrook Press Inc Boston. P.312.

17. Ronald G. Lynch, *The Police Manager op.cit.*, pp.97-98.

18. For further details about Johari Window, see style of Management Inventory - Learning Instrument. Dr. Jay Hall, Dr. Martha Williams Telemetrees Intl. Conroe Texas.

19. A.J.P. Butler, *Police Management*, Gower Pub.Com-Aldershit 1984. p.117.

20. Gordon H Sheehe, "Police Traffic Supervision". In George D. Eastman and Esther M. Eastman (Ed.) *Municipal Police Administration* (6th Ed.) Washington DC. 1969 p.115.

21. Douglas Mc. Gregor (1960), - *The Human Side of Enterprise*, New-York Mc. Graw hill p.4.

22. National Advisory Commission on Criminal Justice Standards and Goals, Police (Washington D.C. 1973 - p.119).

23. A.J.P. Butler (1984) - *Police Management*, p.115.

24. Luban V.A. and Edgar J.M. (1979) Policing by Objectives. Hartford. Conn. The Social Development Corporation.

25. *Policing by Objectives* by V.A. Lubans and Edgar - Based on the model at p.23 reproduced by A.J.P. Butler *Police Management* p.160.

26. James H.Auten - Theory 'P', "Managing for Productivity". In *Police Studies - The*

International Review of Police Development, Vol.8No. 2 Summer 1985. ISSW 0141-2449. p.104.

27. James H.Auten has enumerated 23 alternatives for motivating employees - See Theory 'P' - Managing for productivity 1985 Vol. 8 No. 2 of *Police Studies - International Review of Police Development.* p.108.

28. William I. Zangwill-Success with People - The Theory approach to mutual achievement (Home Wod II : Dow James in 1976). p.23.

29. George Cronkhite, "Facing increased Crime with decreasing resources", *F.B.I. Law Enforcement Bulletin*, April 1983. P.1.

30. W.G. Archambeault and C.R. Fenwick, "A comparative analysis of Japanese and American Police Organisational Management model: The evolution of a military bureaucracy to a theory 'Z' organisation"-*Police Studies - International review of Police development*, 1983 (Fall) pp.3-11

31. See William G.Ouchi - Theory 'Z' - *How American business can meet the Japanese Challenge*, Reading Adison Wesley 1981; Ouch-Theory 'Z'. An elaboration of methodology and findings, contemporary business 1982. pp.27-41; Albernathy, Clark and Kentrow - *Industrial Renaissance - Producing a competitive future for America* 1983; Naisbitt Megatrends - *Ten new directions transforming our lives* - 1982.

32. D.H. Bayley (1976) - *Forces of Order - Police Behaviour in Japan and the United States*, Berkeley, California p.91.

33. For full details and better analysis see W.G. Archambeault Baton Rouge, Charles R. Fenwick, "Differential effects of Police organisational management in a cultural context; Comparative analysis of South Korea, Japanese and American law enforcement", *Police Studies* Vol. 8 No. 1 - 1985 - pp.1-11.

34. Pascale and Athos - 1981 - pp 34-35 - Quoted by Archambeault, Baton Rouge and C.R. Fenwick - *Polic Studies* - Vol. 8 No. 1,1985 - p.11.

CHAPTER-9

POLICE LEADERSHIP

THE LEADERSHIP role asssumes great significance in all organisations because without leadership an organisation is but a muddla pf men and machines. Leadership involves the responsibility of the leader to marshal the forces of the Organisation, to stimulate effort, to capture the imagination,to inspire people, to coordinate activities of the Group and to motivate it towards common goals. The essence of leadership is the ability to obtain from each member of the organisation the highest quality of service he has the capacity to render. Leadership brings success to all the potential that is in an organisation or its people. Leadership is a purposeful behaviour in the act of influencing people associated intimately with an organisation.

There are three schools of thought as regards the concept of leadership:-

(i) one school emphasises the trait approach and defines a leader as possessing certain characteristic traits;

(ii) another school believes that situational factors determine leaders;

(iii) the third group emphasises the behavioural aspects of the group in order to define leader.

Tannenbaum defines Leadership as an inter-personal influence exercised in a situation and directed through the communication process towards the attainment of a specific goal or goals. Leadership is an inter-actional phenomenon and refers to a role or a set of roles whose influence and effects are conditioned by such factors as the personality of the leader, characteristics of group members, the environment in which leadership role is to be performed and the general socio-political climate. Leadership role can be exercised by more than one person or a single individual combining several roles in himself. Leadership in Police Organisations is built-in by institutional arrangements. In the context of Police Organisation; leadership is the process of influencing organisational members to use their energies willingly and appropriately to facilitate the attainment of the goals set by the police organisations. All Police Leaders have to be sensitive to their three main responsibilities viz. (a) contributing to the fulfilment of the department's mission, (b) ensuring that the effort of subordinates is productive and that they are achieving and (c) producing impacts on their areas of responsibility.

Leadership is a most precious commodity that has always been in critical demand and is sought even more in the fast moving world of today. Leadership is a rare quality that is hard to define and even more difficult to explain. Leadership is not a matter of hypnosis, blandishment or high pressure salesmanship.

Leadership, as defined by George R. Terry is "the activity of influencing people to strive willingly for group objectives". An effective and successful leader always aims at the following objectives -

1. to raise the level of subordinates motivation and job-satisfaction;
2. to increase the readiness of the subordinates to accept change;
3. to develop team work, morale and organisational cohesiveness;
4. to improve the quality of all managerial decisions and personnel management;
5. to further the individual development of his subordinates, and achieve organisational effectiveness;
6. to attain optimum level of job-satisfaction and group (rep.) performance for the organisation;
7. to achieve the organisational goals and assignment in the best possible manner;
8. to attain maximum operational efficiency and output from his subordinates;
9. to manage social impacts and social responsibilities;
10. to manage to change with the demands of the new challenges in a turbulent environment.

Police Leaders at various Levels

"The police leader should be tough but sincere; accomplished but basic; formal but approachable; informal but strong; suspicious but empathetic; authoritarian but flexible; democratic but management-oriented". (1) The "formal leader" leads by virtue of his hierarchical position and has followers assigned to him by the police organisation. Physical bearing, moral courage, decisiveness, dependability, endurance, enthusiasm, initiative, integrity, judgement, justice, knowledge, loyalty, tact and unselfishness are considered essential traits of successful police leadership. Leadership is an art and can be acquired and developed in varying degrees by any one properly motivated and possessing the necessary mental and physical capabilities. One's leadership ability is influenced by his willingness to study, practice and apply sound leadership techniques. Morale, sound professional knowledge, *esprit d'-corps*, discipline and proficiency are the indicators of police leadership. Leadership is that unique ability to get others to do what must be done if there is to be efficient and harmonious goal attainment. In police organisations leadership is situational i.e. its requirements vary in time and place due to the nature of police task. Different leadership behavioural patterns are called for in differing situations. [(2)] Police leadership can be divided into three broad categories viz. (i) top level leadership, (ii) middle level leadership and (iii) the first line leadership. Each category requires different personal qualities and tasks. Top level leadership determines policy, directs programme execution, harmonizes varying viewpoints, coordinates the processes of administration and is responsible for the attainment of the organisational goals. Top level leaders must know and understand the general theories of human motivation, psychological analysis of human behaviour and group dynamics. Middle level police leaders translate policies into action and their primary function is to activate the department's policies by adapting the organisation to particular tasks, by maintaining operational control and by setting standards and reviewing accmplishments. The first line leaders have to operate at the performance level and their duties include divising work plans, laying outbeat assignments, maintaining records, developing team spirit and accomplishing given tasks. Station House Officers, Sub-Inspectors and Asstt. Sub Inspectors come in this category. Planning, organising, staffing and assembling resources; direction and control are the organisation. Police policy making is one of the most important function of top level police leaders. Police leaders must have a thorough understanding of sound management principles, organisational theories and administrative techniques and they should be able to apply this knowledge to the practical day-to-day realities of the police organisation.

Directors General of Police and Inspectors General of Police are the policy makers for the police organisations. They have the overall leadership of the police organisation in a State. Deputy Inspector General is responsible for leadership at Range level which constitutes of a few districts and D.I.G.P. is an essential link between Police headquarters and the district police. Superintendents of Police, Asstt. Superintendents of Police, Deputy Superintendents of Police provide leadership to police at District and Sub-divisional levels. Inspectors provide leadership at Circle level which is constituted of a few police stations in a given area. Police station level leadership is provided by the Station House Officers. In Central Police Organisations like BSF, CRPF, ITBP and CISF, similar three-tier leadership can be easily identified. Top level leadership in police is generally manned by officers of Indian Police Service.

In Central Police organisations like I.B.,R & W, C.B.I., also I.P.S. Officers are occupying top positions from DIGP level onwards. Leadership at middle and lower levels in Central Police Organisations is with officers belonging to Central Police Organisations. Police functions differ in the social, economic and political context of its time and place and police leaders have to understand these factors for effective performance. Police leaders have to understand why the Indian Policeman differs from the British bobby and why the police system of the United States differs from that of China, Japan, Pakistan, France or other European countries. Police leaders have to understand why and how present day leaders have different duties/roles and challenges than those police leaders who lived two decades before. Population explosion, adult franchise, spread of education, growth of terrorism, industrial unrest, racial and communal conflicts, political protests and agitations have all resulted in providing new challenges for the police generally and police leaders in particular. The last thirty five years have witnessed an enormous increase in police strength and corresponding increase in police problems.

Police Leadership at Police Station Level

Leadership at the Police station level assumes great importance because the police station is the basic functional unit of the police and improvement in the efficiency is essential to make police organisations more efficient. Police image can only be improved by prompt and correct registration of crime, proper investigation and effective prevention and detection of crime with a public service attitude. For effective functioning of police stations, the status and powers of the Station House officers have to be raised substantially. Good Police leadership is necessary to bring about favourable environmental changes and to reinforce and consolidate upon the environmental changes. It is necessary to provide more positive leadership at every police station. The police leadership has to be more sensitive to the local needs and has to resolve competing demands of rival interest groups through by understanding and moral leadership at local levels. To sum up police leadership at police station level (1) should get more powers and enhanced status commensurate with the responsibilities and duties,

(2) should have powers of counselling, mediation or warning to dispose of petty offences and juvenile delinquency; (3) should provide assistance to weaker sections of the society and protect them from exploitation, (4) should freely interact with local citizens in non-confrontation situations, (5) build up a healthy and good image of police by getting the trust of the local people and (6) develop correct attitude and behaviour towards all citizens of the area.

Evaluation of Police Leadership Role

Making adequate allowance for some local conditions, peculiarities, traditions and stages of political and social development, police leadership finds itself in a turbulent environment in "policing of a perplexed society". There has been no specific crystallisation of ideas regarding an appropriate police leadership system for a plural society such as ours which is committed to secularism, socialism, national integrity and democratic principles. How do we evaluate the role of police leadership in our present day context ? Have they evolved any social philosophy for police reforms? Have they been able to resolve the dilemma for the police from its role expectation as the agent of social change and the protector of human rights ? Have they been able to provide practical guidelines to deal with violent disturbances and public protests ? Have they been able to create institutional devices to protect the policeman for his unwillingness and refusal to obey wrongful, illegal or unjust orders? Has police leadership streamlined personnel management in view of its direct impact on discipline, efficiency, morale and motivation ? Has police leadership been able to build up a satisfactory grievance redressal system in the police ? Has police leadership been able to improve police-community relations and the police image. Has police leadership ensured provisions of amenities and welfare activities in a meaningful manner for the various ranks ? Has police leadership arranged adequate transport and communication facilities for the police system ? Has police leadership provided required material equipment, scientific aids, statistical instruments and proper training for the police personnel ? Answers to these questions are difficult, elusive, inadequate and indefinite. But it can be safely said that above questions are most inconvenient for the police leaders to reply. The real issue is the crisis of police leadership. What is needed in police organisation is enlightened police leadership which has assimilated the implications of the changed circumstances in the country and is ready to take bold measures in keeping with modern management techniques to build up a happy, motivated, trained and dedicated service oriented police force. Police leadership can surely play a live and revolutionary role in motivating the entire organisation for its new and exhilarating role as an upholder and guardian of law. Very few police leaders have been bold enough to make open complaints against the pressures frequently put on them to do things which are either against the law (or rules) or which they would not have done by themselves. The proliferation of senior supervisory posts and diversion of professionally competent police leaders to non-police assignments have disturbed the organisational stability of the police system resulting in pushing up of operational and administrative responsibility. The pyramidal structure of the police organisations has been completely shattered due to too frequent changes of top police leadership and the consequent groupism and intriguings at the highest police levels. The proceedings of the Shah Commission of Enquiry have vividly exposed the helplessness and ineffectiveness of the police leaders.

Most of the police leaders have been reduced to the level of vacillating, fawning functionaries working under the threat of removal due to frequent transfers and political interference. There is no police leader today who can speak for well above one million policemen in the land and be accepted as a father figure. Sooner or later, a Chief of the Indian Police will have to be designated, may be one of the Chief of Central Police Organisations or the director of Intelligence Bureau. According to K.F. Rustamji, failure of the Indian Police Service(I.P.S.) to give correct leadership to the force and the inability to combine in a proper *esprit-d-corps* and service discipline are the foremost causes of the steadily declining efficiency of the police. Barring such acts as police drunkenness and brawling, generally all police actions are ordered and approved by the police bosses, the category of officers drawn form the PSC and IPS cadres. Of the 18 senior police leaders interviewed, 17 admitted that third degree methods could not be done away with. [(3)] Have Police leaders been willing to make sacrifice and share the risks and discomforts of the police job with their men? The tasks of police leaders is to articulate the goals of the police organisation based on the transcendent values of society and to hold the agency to the pursuit of these goals. Institutional leadership is the articulation of the basic desires and enduring social values. Police leaders have to educate public about police problems and police role.

Leadership involves external efforts to minimise *role-abiguity*. The effective grievance redressal system and sound personnel policy are the important factors to build up the police morale. Poor living conditions, turbulent environment, lack of public trust as embodied in the laws, political interference, unenforceable laws, duality of control at district level, inadequate grievance redressal machinery, poor reward and punishment system, media criticism, over-dependence on statistics, poor performance of the criminal justice system and finally the poor leadership have caused erosion of police morale in India. The 1979 police unrest in India and its aftermath has caused further erosion of police morale. The frequent changes in the heads of the police at the top level give the impression to the average policeman that effective and dedicated leadership in police is fast disappearing. "The formal leadership is abdicating its functions, its role to lead; the informal leadership is only too ready to step in to fill the vacuum". (4) Thus the informal leadership emerging through police associations and unions, are in many places able to fulfil the needs and aspirations of their group. Delay in drawal and disbursement of Pay and TA, out of turn allotment of quarters, incivil behaviour, use of harsh and abusive language, forfeiture of pay for overstayal, suspensions without sufficient justification are some of the sensitive issues causing a confrontation between the formal and informal leadership. Present day Police leaders bear a special responsibility for providing good leadership in the force as also for interpreting the problems of the police to the society at large so that the police get the necessary support from the community.

Police Leadership at the Cross Roads

What police leaders have failed to do has been summarised by Di Grazia in the following lines:

"There is one thing few police chiefs are doing- leveling with public about crime. Most of us are not telling the public that there is relatively little the police can do about crime... Rather than speaking up, most of us stand silent and let politicians get away with law and order rhetoric that reinforces the mistaken notion that the police-in ever greater numbers and with ever more gadetry - can alone control crime. The degree to which a police Chief exercises leadership should be judged by the risks that he(or she for that matter) takes by seeking improvement in personnel and the delivery of police services and in educating the public and the politicians about what the police can and cannot do". (5)

During the last three decades, complexities in the society have widened the gap between expectations and actual performance of police leaders. In fact pulling down the structural hierarchy, short circuiting the command and control structure, detestable trade-unionism in police, political interference, proliferation of higher posts in police organisations, defective leadership training, self-seeking interests of retiring police heads, frequent changes of top leaders by politicians, unending frequent transfers and postings, erosion of moral values and mushrooming of senior assignments outside the polic have subverted the essence of police leadership and have brought it at the cross-roads.

A syndicate study carried out by S.V.P., NPA, Hyderabad shows that as many as 77 per cent of the senior leaders of the police possessed a predominantly authoritarian style of leadership. It was surprising to note that not a single officer had the pace-setter style of leadership which means setting example as a leader to the subordinates. The police leadership today is not very effective because of job stress, police sub-culture, and power dynamics at individual, group and organisational levels. There is a great need for introspection and self-evaluation in police leadership. There is a great crisis of obsolescence in the police leadership and to overcome this crisis there is need for new attitudes, new skills in management, new philosophy of work and willing acceptance to acquire new knowledge, concepts and new techniques. The inability to lead effectively is the most characteristic feature of police leadership today. The police leadership in India has the unique opportunity of playing a dynamic role in converting the image of the policeman into that of a friend, guide and protector of the people. Police leadership has to develop and nurture the correct type of close relationship with mass media like T.V., cinema and press including newspapers and magazines editors. Police leaders should evince positive interest in basic function of the police and accord high priorities to prevention of crime, investigation and prosecution of cases and maintenance of law and order in the society. Shri K.F. Rustamji has remarked": "officers even at the highest level have not only become agents of politicians, they have become politicians themselves".

The police agitations clearly betrayed a lack of rapport between the officers(leaders) and men in their forces. [6] Police unrest and strikes raise many a question about police leadership. Failure of leadership is one of the important causes of police unrest. Many of the senior police officers do not still believe in free and frank communication between superiors and subordinates. There is a crisis of confidence in the police leadership,because some of the police leaders of different levels have failed to inspire the confidence in their men. "There is a growing feeling among the rank and file that the senior officers are neither able to protect them from unwarranted attacks from political and other quarters nor effective in getting their legitimate grievances redressed by the Government or appropriate authority." [7] Collective bargaining by the police unions and police associations is going to be a big challenge to police leadership in the future. There are in the country today about 55 associations of policemen and officers. The problem of police associations is a very complex one and has to be handled by police leaders with sympathy, foresight and firmness. Police unrest or agitation does not just take place. It is a gradual build up that explodes. Many police leaders often plead that they were taken by surprise but the truth is that they had neither the time nor the patience nor perhaps the rapport with the men to accurately gauge their mood and their intentions. [8] Unimaginative police leadership, their naked greed for power and jockeying for positions and personal advancement in the police are some of the main causes for the spread of unrest among the policemen. The police leadership is also at many places emasculated and has to look towards secretariat bosses for direction and guidance for even minor matters. Mutual distrust between police leaders and police agitators existed in many places. Where the communication gap was existing, the leadership could not venture to think of talks with the constabulary resulting in a complete paralysis of work and even acts of indiscipline by the agitating policemen. The innumerable accounts of police atrocities during emergency, blindings of persons in police costody at Bhagalpur, fake encounters against dacoits and naxalites, the Rajan episode in Kerala, are just some of the well known instances of police misconduct. The sub-culture of the Indian police is acquiring more and more the characteristics of a persecuted minority community. There is a crisis of confidence in and within the police. [9] It is necessary for the police leaders to treat not merely the symptoms but the disease and get to the roots of the problem and seek effective long term permanent remedies.

Emerging Challenges for Police Leaders

The recent trend of the unionisation of police officers has added a new dimension to the job of the police leadership. The increased employee diversity with the influx of minority and women officers has made the police organisations more broad-based having representation of almost all castes, creeds and religions. Police officers of the new generation want participative management in organisational decisions and do not accept a semi-military, authoritarian hierarchical structure. The public is expecting greater accountability from the police. Technological sophistication of crime, socio-economic crime, white collar crime have added increased responsibility to the police leaders. The turbulent nature of contemporary society requires more skilled police leaders for active adaptation and pro-active management. Democratic policing calls for a deep understanding of the political developments and social changes occurring in the society. Police leaders have to be in tune with "the frontiers of change. To do this they have to develop a new or enlarged range of skills and understandings from those which sustained them as junior practitioners". [10] Police leaders have to learn the science of management and the art of leadership. The contemporary Indian scene presents following challenging factors to police leadership:

1. With the spread of education and increased awareness of masses, the social structure is in a state of ferment and criminal tendencies are on the increase.
2. Economic disparities and regional imbalances are more noticeable and people below the poverty line are clamouring for attention and care resulting in protests and agitations.
3. Bare necessities like drinking water, houses and other essential commodities have not kept pace with the rising population and there is increase in economic offences.
4. The socio-political system is finding it difficult to adjust and respond to the rapid changes in the social and economic environment and the rising aspirations of the masses.
5. Every cross-section of society is demanding more and more share of national cake and pressure groups are resorting to agitations and strikes to manifest their demands. The challenge for the coming decade will be to earn public and official confidence in police performance.
6. Large numbers of educated and uneducated youth, entering the employment market are getting frustrated and disgruntled and police have to handle them.
7. Intermittent disasters, God-made and man-made call for crisis management by the police.
8. Demoralised and overburdend police personnel who are feeling social isolation and feeling of "persecuted minority".
9. Political agiations, insurgencies, terrorism and all kinds of protests and violence are increasing in the society.

10. White-collar crime, victimless crime and socio-economic crimes like Bank frauds, Computer-aided crimes are on the increase.
11. Problems of hijacking, terrorism, sabotage, insurgency and internal subversion throw great challenges to police leaders. There have been 10 cases of hijacking in India so far and our police forces have failed to respond to them effectively. "We have the men, the funds and the expertise to complete this job on a nationwide scale within a few years. But no one is making the necessary effort". (11)

Constraints to Police Leadership

The limiting factors and constraints that operate on police leaders are as follows:

1. Emphasis on seniority and security of service often result in mediocrity and police leaders tend to abdicate their role, initiative and responsibility.
2. Increasing conflicts of direction and control from higher echelons leave the field officers with little or no time or discretion to work out solutions based on their understanding of the realities of the situations.
3. Police leaders often feel helpless due to scarcity of resources, problems of staff and the overbearing control and interference by the political leadership.
4. "The very process of survival and of going up in the system exhausts and dehydrates many of them". (12)
5. Most of the senior police leaders spend their maximum efforts and energy for "(a) surviving on the post, (b) keeping the powers that are pleased, (c) dealing with the dead burden of routine paper work and (d) making arrangements for post-retirement jobs and supplementing their incomes". (13)
6. Insecurity of tenure often prevents many police leaders from delegating, trusting and supporting their subordinates and they have no time to think, study or initiate new ideas and policies in the organisation.
7. Weakening of the position and role of the heads of the police organisations and proliferation of higher posts have resulted in uncertainty of tenure.
8. The lower career value, lower status and lower prospects of pro-

motion in comparison with I.A.S. officers.

9. Cadre management of police leaders being done by I.A.S. officers and absence of any new ideas to improve cadre management.
10. Authoritarian approach of some senior police leaders and absence of a fair performance appraisal system.
11. Frustration and unfair deal to promoted I.P.S. officers and their stagnation at the lower levels.
12. Shortcomings in training, inadequate knowledge and experience of investigation and thereby over dependence of I.P.S. officers upon their immediate subordinates.
13. Lack of professionalism in the senior police leaders and their inadequate representation in policy making forums.
14. Difficult service conditions, increasing professional hazards, lack of prestige vis-a-vis the other services and a sense of uncertainty arising from political situations give rise to frustrations among police leaders.

Police Leadership and Officers of I.P.S.

According to the Sixth Report of National Police Commission, two Central I.P.S. Cadres should be constituted, one for the Para Military Organisations like the B.S.F., CRPF, ITBP and the other for such organisations as the I.B., C.B.I. and RAW. Such cadres could be constituted within the framework of Article 312 of the Constitution. But Central police Organisations like CRPF, and B.S.F. have a very big number of grade A Gazetted officers and deserve a separate cadre for building up professional expertise in the police profession. The present differentials of I.P.S. with I.A.S. are counter productive and it would be cost-effective for the Government to improve the quality of recruitment, emoluments and career prospects of the police leaders by bringing them at parity with those of the I.A.S. [14] The gap between I.P.S. regular officers and State promoted I.P.S. officers also needs to be bridged. Something has to be done to attract better personnel in the middle and lower ranks of the State Police Service, so that, they may communicate more meaningfully with their seniors in the I.P.S. and the people at large. The non-I.P.S. State level police officers of junior levels account for 95 per cent of the total police force in India and their service conditions, pay, and promotions need special attention. The hiatus in recruitment methods, promotional avenues, emoluments, service conditions and even retirement benefits between State Police officers and the I.P.S. are so serious and so obvious that State Police officers (all non.-I.P.S. officers including Dy.S.P., Inspectors, sub-Inspectors) feel demoralised and demotivated to keep their team in good trim. Police leadership at lower levels is too demoralised and frustrated to bother about their own public image - real, fake or phoney. If the structure of All-India Services is to be maintained (as it seems to be the national consensus) there is absolutely no ground to perpetuate the present disparity between the I.A.S. and I.P.S. (15) The Fourth Pay Commission has lowered the career value of the Indian Police Service by tinkering with some of the old scales applicable to the I.P.S. on the one hand and by upgrading the equivalent scales in the other comparable services on the other. The Fourth Pay Commission had compromised the position of the Directors General of Police with their counterparts in other Central Services which would have a telling effect on police morale and efficiency. (16)

Some aspects of Negative Leadership in Police

There are many police leaders who exhibit negative leadership and are prey to nepotism, favouritism, corruption and intellectual dishonesty. Among common failing of police leadership is its obsession with creating a small coterie of favourites who are given the most favoured treatment in all matters. (17) Due to lack of moral courage there is a tendency in some police leaders to delete the names of powerful persons from the list of accused on flimsy grounds. The lack of moral courage in the face of extraneous political pressures influences the entire police functioning down the lines and causes very negative repurcussions on the maintenance of law and order and prevention of crime in the society. Caste and regional loyalties and subcaste affiliations result in various groupings and sub-groupings and ultimately lower the prestige of the police leaders. Intellectual dishonesty, favouritism, use of third degree methods, fake encounters, indulgence in corrupt practices,indecision at crucial matters of decisions-making, sympathy for wrong doers, alignment with certain political parties, dictatorial style of functioning are some of the negative aspects of leadership found at certain place in the police organisations. In-services rivalry and internal bickering, and factionalism created by communal, caste and provincial considerations have eroded the unity and strength of police leadership. In actual terms, police leadership today is mainly confined to the punishment of his subordinates. Police leadership today is merely responsible for the shine of the leather and the polish of the brass. "Most of the ills of the present day Police Forces are due to poor leadership." [18] A study carried out by syndicate group at N.P.A., Hyderabad has showed that 77 per cent of the officers interviewed felt that the trust reposed in them and the support they received in the police from their superior officers were far from satisfactory. What about a bad leader ? He is easily recognised in the police service. He will not accept responsibility; he is erratic in his judgements and decisions; he does too much ordering; he passes the buck - up for decisions, down for blame; he depends too much on regulations and procedures; he is overexacting and demanding; he cannot distinguish between the essential and non-essential; when approached with a specific problem he is given to generalisations; he is aloof and unapproachable, he favours favourites and he almost invariably displays the weak man's initiation of strength - rudeness." [19]

National Police Commission has recommended police association for various ranks in the States. Formation of Police Associations of various ranks have resulted in the rise of Police Association leaders who generally start behaving as representatives of Police Force. Some of these police leaders devote their entire time to association activities only and totally abstain or neglect their official duties. These informal police leaders tend to obtain advice and help from political leaders. The leaders tend to use inciting and unparliamentary language and take recourse to media prematurely. Association leaders start taking up individual cases and obstruct legal and departmental proceedings involving policemen. Some of the leaders of the association tend to form joint fronts with trade unions and other civilian servants' association and tend to disturb the discipline of the police system. These police leaders cause dissatisfaction among police personnel.

Some Suggestions for Improvement in Police Leadership

1. Improvement of technical competence and professional knowledge by in-service training courses.
2. Ensuring inner democratisation, decentralisation and innovativeness by changing attitudes and behavioural modifications.
3. Development of right value system and commitment to the core national values.
4. Use of modern scientific methods and approach to police work including use of computers, modern management principles and modernisation of equipment.
5. Synthesis of vision and reality, harmonisation of public.

6. Support and community participation in police work.
7. Installation of supporting structure, system and subculture for efficient, effective and reliable police work.
8. Constant adequate training and orientation to all ranks for meeting newly developing challenges of police work.
9. Aptitude test for police leaders at the time of recruitment should be introduced at all levels and depoliticisation of recruitment.
10. Police system should be insulated from day-to-day political interference and police leadership should be able to function without political vendetta or harassment.
11. Police vices such as use of third degree methods in interrogation, padding of evidence, police misbehaviour, corruption should be controlled by effective police leadership.
12. Adequate opportunities for self-growth and advancement of middle level and junior level police leaders should be provided in the police system.
13. Establishment of separate cadre for Central Police organisations and providing adequate promotion opportunities to the officers beloging to CPOs Cadres.
14. Establishing parity between I.P.S. and I.A.S. upto reasonable limits.
15. The selection of Directors General, Inspectors General and District Superintendents of Police should be done by a Committee of central and state officials headed by the Chairman of Public Service Commission and their tenures should be fixed.
16. Police leaders should get an opportunity of working in civil organisations of the Government, so that, they get an opportunity to view police set-up from outside and also develop managerial skills and professional expertise to lead the organisations in an unauthoritarian leadership style.

A Syndicate Research Study of Leadership Styles in the Police

A syndicate study carried out by five I.P.S. officers of XXXIX Senior officers Course at S.V.P., NPA, Hyderabad in November 1977 has given the following findings :- [20]

1. No study about the type of leadership styles being followed in

the police organisation and their corresponding effects had ever been undertaken.

2. There was strong evidence of the prevalence of authoritarian style of leadership in the police orgnisations and there is total lack of participation in decision making by the middle and junior level leaders of the police.
3. Lack of delegation of authority is a big demotivating factor for the middle and junior level supervisors.
4. The police organisation is largely a one way communication channel and there is complete lack of upward communication. Even the genuine grievances of the men hardly reach the higher authorities.
5. Most of the police leaders interviewed by the syndicate appeared to be firm believers in the Theory X of human nature and that is why too much stress was laid on punishment and coercion.
6. There is role ambiguity and absence of clarity about organisational goals.
7. The development programmes and in-service training for police officers at various levels are not receiving the attention they deserve.
8. A feeling of helplessness and demoralisation was noticeable among some district Police Chiefs.
9. Police leadership was considerably diluted because of the abuse of the concept of unity of command and introduction of several irksome executive controls.
10. Survey of leadership styles conducted with the help of managerial grid (developed by Blake and Mounton) instruments show an overwhelming concern for tasks than for people.

Conclusion

Leadership in the Police field is becoming more and more complex every day. The management of police departments today requires a broad understanding of the social forces at work in the society as well as an understanding of the application of recent scientific discoveries in the police is extremely important. [21] For improving police leadership, the recruitment, training and placement policies require drastic changes. Effective grievance redressal machinery has to be institutionalised in the police on the basis of the recommendations of the National Police Commission. Police leaders must question traditional philosophies, philosophies, policies, priorities, and methods and must initiate changes in "old ways of doing things". The standards of competence and preformance alone should be the sole criteria for the selection and retention of a chief of police and not political or other considerations. Police leaders of the future must become increasingly committed to active and proactive modes of change, they must learn to re-evaluate rules and policies on a continuing basis, they must encourage communication and shared decision-making among all levels of police personnel and they must learn to view their function in relation to a total system and the total environment rather than to their own police organisation. The whole culture of police leadership in India has to be changed from bureaucratic structure-oriented sub-culture to dynamic and performance-oriented sub-culture. Police leaders have to improve their perception of their correct role in the organisation. They have to develop techniques for approaching the public and the mass media and establishing healthy police public relations. They have to get specialised training and psychological insights into the relationship between police officers and delinquents, gang members, people stopped for questioning, offenders, criminals, suicidal persons, alcoholics, drug addicts, mentally retarded people respectable citizens and political leaders and public in general. Police leader is an educator and a persuader who matches public sentiments to departmental capabilities and then reconciles the two. (22*)

Numerous writers have looked to the police leadership as the primary change agent - one who, through leadership and initiative, can bring about reform and produce measurable results. The police leadership has to be fully aware of organisational and operational shortcomings and recognise what must be done to improve their organisations. The needs, mission, problems, priorities and values of the organisation have to be identified by the police leaders. The police leaders have to recognise the need to re-examine the parameters of the traditional mission as well as the policing orientation in relation to the expectations of the community. Police leaders have to become skilled administrators and effective managers if they want to make a difference from previous routine performance. Organisational leaders have to keep themselves aware of the political, economic, social and organisational environment and the changing pattern of the new challenges. "The most common cause of executive failure in the inability or unwillingness to change with the demands of a new position. (23)

A successful leader accurately understands himself, the individuals and groups, he is dealing with and the broad socio-economic environment in which he operates. The issue of police leadership itself needs to be addresed in the context of restructuring of the entire police system and re-institutionalising of effective leadership from within the organisation based on the principles of professionalism, democratic value system, autonomy, managerial skills and ecommitment to the public service. There is an urgent need for a national debate involving not only the police and the Government but all sections of the society, e.g. academicians, lawyers, politicians, administrators, and leaders of public opinion to evolve a consensus about the role of police leadership in the present day context, to spell out goals and priorities for police leaders and to provide the police leadership with a consistent basis for self-image and effective democratic leadership style. A national policy has to be worked out to provide practical guidelines as to what police leaders should do in response to scurrilous attacks, distortions and just plain mistakes of ignorance that are common in newspapers, books, films and television.

Notes and References

1. David A Hausen and Thomas R. Culley (1971), *The Police Leader : A Handbook*, Charles C. Thomas., p.XV.
2. Donald O. Schultz (1979), *Police Organisation and Administration - An overview in Modern Police Administration*, Gulf Publishing Company, Tokyo - p.10.
3. Javed Faridi, "Police Brutality" p.1. *The Hindustan Times* - Dec 21,1980 -
4. Sudhir Kumar Jha, "Juxtaposition of formal and informal leadership in police." Papers presented at XVIII All India Police Science Congress, 1984 Port Blair, p.18.
5. Di Grazia R.J., 4 (1976), "Upgrading Police Leadership". Remarks delivered at Executive Forum on upgrading the Police - Washington D.C. April 14. Quoted in The *Future of Policing* (Ed) Alwin W. Colin, p.291.
6. Lt. Gen. K.P. Candeth, *Indian Express*, 2-7-1979.
7. Working paper on Police Unrest, "Seminar on Police unrest," S.V.P., N.P. Academy, Hyderabad, 1980, p.18.
8. J.N. Chaturvedi, Leadership's Role in Police Unrest" - Seminar on Police unrest 1980 - S.V.P., N.P.A., Hyderabad - P.145.
9. B.G. Verghese, - System Credibility - Seminar - Police Vol. No. 218 Oct. 1977. p.22.
10. J.C. Alderson "Police Leadership in Times of Social, Economic and Political Turbulence", *The Police Journal*, Vol. XVIX-No.2 April, 1976, p.91.
11. N.S. Saxena, "How to cope with Hijacking" *The Times of India*, August 29, 1984 p.6.
12. Sixth Report of the National Police Commission, Govt. of India, 1981, p.3.

13. *Ibid*, p.3.

14. *Ibid*. p.5.

15. P.D. Sharma, "Parity problems in Public Services of India" *Journal of the Society for study of State Governments* (Varanasi, July-Oct., 1974) pp. 225-46. Also P.D. Sharma, "Ideas And Issues in Police Administration in India", *The Indian Journal of Political Studies* January, 1980, p.172.

16. *The Hindu*, Thursday, July 3,1986.

17. Jaspal Singh, "Aspects of Negative Leadership in Police,"-*The Indian Police Journal* Vo.XXVIII No.3 - January - March, 1982. p.21.

18. N.Rama Iyer - "Leadership in the Police Force", Second All India Police Science Congress, Bombay, September 1961 . p.229.

19. L.Localey, "Police leadership" *Police Journal*, February, 1968. p.99

20. For full details, see Syndicate Report on Leadership styles in the Police, Chairman A.R. Sharma, SVP, NPA, Transactions Vol.26-1978. pp.3-86.

21. John P.Kenny, *Police Management Planning*, p.140

22. Lee W.Potts, "Police leadership;. challenges for the Eighties" *Journal of Police Science and Administration*, Vol X No 2 June 1982 - reproduced in *Indian Journal*, March 1984. p.41.

23. Peter Drucker, *The Effective Executive* p.58.

CHAPTER - 10

POLICE TRAINING FOR LAW AND ORDER AND INTERNAL SECURITY DUTIES

THE INDIAN Police system has been under constant pressure after independence to meet the growing demands of the democratic and pluralistic urges of our nascent developing socialist, secular and pluralistic society. The overall performance of the Indian Police system has been not able to rise upto the expectations of the people and the Governmnet in particular. The police responses to various law and order situations and to internal security challenges in the past have been matters of severe criticism. The present tune calls for a serious reappraisal of the relevance and utility of the existing system of training particularly in the context of police training for law and order and internal security duties. Police training is actually an effective tool for bringing about requisite professional skills, competence, attitudes and behavioural orientation with a view to improving employee effectiveness through exposing them to a carefully formulated training/learning process in a proper training environment. Emphasising the need for police training First Report of the National Police Commission (1977) observed that "the style of police handling of public order situation has had to change from an aggressive mailed-fist attitude to a peaceful and persuasive handling of agitational groups." Police training should be able to provide correct ethical and moral indoctrination that will reinforce appropriate attitudes for the sustenance of democratic institutions and the peaceful co-existence of diverse population groups in our socialist secular democratic society. The United States President's Commission on Law Enforcement and Administration of Justice (1967) bemoaned the fact that many of the training programmes merely equipped a police officer to perform police work mechanically, but did not enable him to understand the community, the police role or the imperfections of the criminal justice system". Institutionally the Indian police stands in urgent and compelling need of change in its training pattern so that it may properly equip its members to tackle various law and order or internal security problems.

"Success in any endeavour" says O.W. Wilson, "is dependent on preparation and the first step in preparation is the evolution of a plan of action". (1) The world is changing today more quickly and dramatically than any time in history. "Police officers throughout the world face challenges without precedent. Never in the history has the police man's job been more difficult. The future in law enforcement belongs to those who prepare for it". [(2)] To prepare the gazetted and non-gazetted ranks of an armed or civil police battalion for internal security duties, adequate planning and its proper execution are required. "The five basic steps in planning are:

(1) Recognizing the need for the plan.

(2) Statement of objectives.

(3) Collecting and analyzing data.

(4) Details of the plan.

(5) Acceptance of the plan". [(3)]

The worst malady which can afflict an organization is the dry rot of contentment with existing practice, and this is usually coupled with suspicion of innovation and suppression of experimentation". [(4)] In order to be effective and useful, there is need for new knowledge, new skills and new attitudes in keeping with the new dimensions that are continuously being added to the traditional tasks of the civil servants and law enforcement agencies. "It has been realised that the new and changing requirements of administration necessitate a well-planned and systematic approach to the problems of training." [(5)] Training is a systematic process involving learning/training which aims at increasing knowledge, skills, attitudes, techniques and behavioural change in the police employees. Entire police training system needs to be revamped to improve the training standards in the police. In order to usher democratic model of policing the entire police training system needs a new strategy and methodology. Training for internal security has to comprehend the following -

(i) Identification of training needs for each category of police officers;

(ii) Formulation of training objectives and aims;

(iii) Designing of training programmes;

(iv) Implementation and execution of training programme in a conducive environment;

(v) Scientific evaluation of training and its follow up measures.

Internal Security Duties

The Internal Security duties in India are increasing every day with the increase in violence, political agitations and large scale disturbances like riots, student agitations, strike by Govt. servants and other civil disturbances. As a result of social and economic changes, millions of people who were subdued and reluctant to express themselves, have become vocal and demanding; millions are packed explosively in slums; refugees have come to India in large numbers and have not yet settled down; large scale industrialisation has led to frequent labour unrests; rise in prices of food stuff and essential commodities, shortages, indiscipline of various types, frustration and above all, the activities of the political parties aiming always to overthrow the constitutionally established Government by force and violence; all these have created conditons in which any type of spark can set off a violent explosion." [(6)] The problems affecting the internal security include "violent agitations, industrial unrest, agrarian trouble, communal tensions, students' indiscipline, espionage, subversive activities, high incidence of crime etc. and it hardly needs to be metioned that the police is held responsible for dealing with all such problem. [(7)] The Internal security of a nation - State broadly refers to the survival, maintenance, preservation and protection of the entire state from all kinds of internal disturbances and serious law and order challenges. The internal security challenges in a democratic political system assume a new dimension and magnitude in the context of our national commitments to the ideals of socialism, secularism, social justice, liberty, equality and economic development. In order to prepare police for effectively dealing with internal security challenges, various demensions and magnitude of the problem need to be understood, appreciated and worked out with clarity and precision by all police officers of various ranks. Internal security duties are generally termed as "law and order" duties but such duties are taking new dimensions in the present democratic set-up of india. The concept of aggression in modern times does include fifth column activities and subversive action by enemy agents aimed at crippling the economic strength that really represents the fighing power of a nation. "The security responsibility of a developing country like India are indeed vast. All anti-national efforts aimed at creating chaos, disorder and destroying the country's vital industries and lines of communication, whether they come from within or outside must be neutralised by timely action. This responsibility mainly rests on the police though in this process of maintaining the integrity of the counrty, vigilance and effort is required from many quarters and all sections of the public". [(8)] The main responsibilities of the police in maintaining internal security are to:

(a) preserve the peace, including control of riots and civil disturbances;

(b) protect the population from intimidation, terror and other forms of insurgency;

(c) prevent crime and subversion;

(d) enforce the laws, and

(e) apprehend offenders". [9]

Para police battalions deployed on internal security duties are normally assigned some of the specific tasks -

(a) patrolling in any of its various forms;

(b) guarding of vital installations and lines of communication;

(c) prevention of unlawful assemblies and demonstrations;

(d) control of mobs and crowds and public meetings during various occasions;

(e) V.I.P security arrangement;

(f) Striking reserve duty at control rooms;

(g) Counter-intelligence activities and particularly identification and neutralisation of subversives; and

(h) apprehension of notorious outlaws and offenders

Police and Central Police organisations have to work very closely to deal with internal security challenges. Local police and Central police organisations have to be in hands and gloves with each other and work out duties in a very co-ordinated manner. Internal security duties are increasing day by day and the role of police in dealing with public agitations needs a discussion on policy of control over agitational activities. [10] It is essentially a political matter but the ruling leadership should see to it that the legitimacy of the Government in power is preserved in consonance with the protection of the sanctity of the rule of law. The police and para police organisations can play an effective and a responsible role but their usual limitations are:

1. The politicians interfere in the process of the administration of law and order in grave situation.[11]

2. District Magistrate continues to be responsible for law and order in the district and law and order is not left entirely as a police affair and police authority is not established in position of trust, accountability and responsibility. [12]

3. The public press and other opinion leaders are callously apathetic, hostile and even credulous and do not come forward to lend a helping hand to the police when they are in distress. [13]

Identification of Training Needs

In order to prepare the gazetted and non-gazetted ranks of the battalion for internal security duties. It is the foremost duty of police administrators to identify the training needs of the battalion personnel. Practically in all organisations,..especially in the Govt. there is multiplicity of job scale, job responsibilities and post designations which stand in the way of an apparent and simple categorisation. In a battalion organisation, coy. commanders and above can be categorised as senior management level. Subedars, Platoon Commanders, Section Commanders can be categorised as middle management level and Naiks/L/Naiks and Constables can be termed as lower level/base level or infrastructure level. Similarly in civil police, training needs of S.S.P. Dy.S.P. Inspectors, Sub Inspectors and Constables are different. While SSP and Dy.SP are required more of conceptional training, other police officers require more field- oriented practical training. The more diverse is the work of an organisation, the more effort and attention it needs to achieve effective planning, rational organisation and smooth control. The identification of training needs envisage analysis work of data collection to be diverted and completed at three distinct plans -

(1) Analysis individual-wise;

(2) Analysis category-wise and

(3) Analysis organisation-wise.

"A careful analysis of data at these three levels would project the academic and the professional profile of the individual, the category and the organisation, so that eventually the training function can integrate those, locate pertinent gaps and then hope to fill them thereby achieving a purposeful satisfaction of the training function. The above effort would throw up the following conclusions:

(a) Specific training gaps in certain distinct functional areas.

(b) Specific training gaps in terms of the functional areas as noticed in certain individuals.

(c) Specific training gaps in the three distinct categories (senior, middle and infra-structure) with specific reference to the functional areas.

(d) Specific training gaps in the organisation as a whole generally and in the organisation in terms of the functional areas in particualr. [14]

During a research evaluation of police training in India, the author reached to the following main conclusions :

(a) There is a great gap between what is done in the field and what is taught in police training institutions.

(b) Training programmes present unrealistic goals before trainees and there is a noticeable gap in the realm of attitudes and values between what they are taught and what trainees find in the field.

(c) Most of the training programmes do not deal with live problems and issues currently faced by the police in the field.

(d) Latest training techniques like case study method, incidence method, and case history method are rarely used in an effective manner by the trainers.

(e) There is great dearth of well-documented case studies on law and order situations and on problems relating to internal security challenges and the required police response to such duties.

During many serious disturbances which have taken place in the various parts of India since independence, serious gaps have often been noticed in (i) the organisation strength, resource and training of police, (ii) the investigation of heinous crimes that were committed, (iii) the macninery for collecting preventive intelligence and its assessment and (iv) the plans for handling such disturbances even when there were adequate indications of the approaching storm". [15] During large scale disturbances and serious internal security situations, the ineffectiveness of the police officers can be attributed to the following among other causes :-

(1) Want of proper appreciation of the issues involved and failure to make preventive arrests in time.

(2) Incorrect assessment of intelligence and lack of correct intelligence of developing situations.

(3) Inadequate planning and preparation by the local administration.

(4) Weakness of organisation and lack of confidence in officers to deal with situation.

(5) Inadequate means of communication and transport.

(6) Unsatisfactory functioning of control rooms at various levels.

(7) Inadequate psychological preparation of officers and inadequate training to face the disturbances.

(8) Demoralised and untrained police officers particularly at middle levels and lower levels of police organisations.

(9) Lack of proper rehearsals and briefing about internal security and riot schemes of the district.

(10) The delayed actions on the part of the local administration and tendency to seek guidance and instructions from police headquarters on phone

(11) Lack of effective and dynamic police leadership at operational levels.

(12) Insufficient and inadequate training and orientation to deal with various law and order situations.

Such shortcomings have been revealed in practically every serious and widespread disturbances that have occurred since independence and yet lessons do not seem to have been drawn from past history to prepare for future eventualities." [(16)] A detailed examination of each serious large scale disturbance needs to be carried out and proper lessons should be drawn to find out where action was belated and not firm enough or where due to premature or too strong action the situation worsened; what defects were noticed in the planning in the training and in the utilisation of available resources and what were the general shortcomings of the police forces deployed. The results of such studies should find concrete place in the syllabus of training. Plans need to be prepared for every city and town for handling different types of disturbances and emergency internal security schemes are required to be prepared for rural areas in vulnerable States like Uttar Pradesh, Madhya Pradesh, Bihar, Assam, Punjab and Andhra Pradesh.

"It is important to realise that a single training programme should not endeavour to prepare the administrators for the entire range of duties he is likely to be called upon during his career. The trainer and the trainee should be able to focus their attention on a specific period of first five or then years of the trainee career and confine the training to the job requirements of the period". [(17)]

The analysis of training needs of a battalion to be deployed on I.S. duties reveal that all ranks of the battalion, particularly gazetted officers require a fundamental knowledge of civil disturbances control, planning and operations. Emphasis is required to be given upon achieving a state of "wareness, initiation of proper preventive and preparatory measures and employment of functional confrontation management techniques during actual confrontation. The old concept of 'riot control' has to be replaced in the minds of the battalion personnel by a broader and more scientific concept of 'confrontation managements concepts and techniques'. The concept of confrontation management seeks to provide more precise, meaningful guidance of civil disorder. "Confrontation management is a strategy counter the attempts of dissident organisations to further their movements through confrontation tactics. It seeks to defeat their strategies of provocation of control forces which may produce an over-reaction on their part and thereby radicalize additional supporters for the dissidents from a disaffected but presently univolved populnce". [18] Confrontation management envisages a systems aproach wherein police operations can be phased out in following six phases :-

1. Preliminary preparations.
2. Deployment and planning action.
3. Timing of intervention and confrontation.
4. Action on withdrawal.
5. Post riot action.
6. Normalcy restoration". [19]

Various principles for confrontation management have to be applied with tact and patience to deal with various serious riot situations. In dealing with communal riots in particular, there have been lot of lapses and mistakes committed by the police in past. Internal security duties in India call for a searching self-analysis by the police followed by intensive preparation in the shape of reorientation of outlook, structural changes and positive training schemes. "There is a growing evidence that absence for inadequate identification of training needs can well make or mar the success of any training effort as the identification exercise can alone provide a scientific framework for imparting training at various levels in an organisation.

The polce training needs to shift attention from drill and regimentation "to the development of proper attitudes through the study of social and behavioural sciences and modern management concepts". [20]

"The solution does not lie in scrapping or reducing the stress of drill and parade. What is required is repatterning of the syllabus and methodology". [21]

In Internal security duties each situation is different from the other and there can be no rigidity of approach though clarity of objectives is required and police approach needs to be mainly guided by law. "There is need for specific training to deal with crowds and mobs in realistic situations of today". [22] Police officers should be ready to change both their strategy and tactics to meet situations in different places and at different times. However, the basic principles remain the same. [23]

The late Prime Minister Srimati Indira Gandhi, while addressing the conference of the Inspectors General of Police in Delhi on the 19th October, 1973 stressed "a very genuine need for introducing some sort of study of crowd psychology" because police men have to face these days a number of different types of unrest. [24] Crowd, mob psychology and mob behaviour need to be thoroughly studied by all police officers.

Training Objectives for Gazetted and non-Gazetted Ranks of Police

For internal security duties separate "specialised courses" are required for all the three categories of ranks of the battalion. For senior level, middle level and lower level different types of "specialisation courses" of at least two months are required and training objectives for each course have to be clearly spelled out. Senior level training needs to be largely oriented towards policy making, programme planning and review and problem solving. It should be divided into two parts: (a) a general study and orientation supplemented by group discussions, seminars and syndicates (b) specific studies of a set of policy problems or a detailed study of the entire policy making process in a segment or area of administrative activity." [25] Senior level training should include Coy. Comdrs, Asstt. Comdts. and Commandants. The middle level training will be meant for young Coy. Comdrs. Subedars, Sub-Inspectors and senior Havildars The lower level training will be meant for junior Havildars and below. General linstructional objectives of the specialisation training courses will be:

(1) to equip unit personnel to efficiently perform their assigned role in internal security duties;

(2) to attune the unit personnel to the new tasks which they may be called upon to perform in a changing world;

(3) to inculcate the right attitude towards the public, never forgetting that civil sevant is the servant and not master of the community:

(4) to sustain the human touch not only in direct personal contacts with the public but also in all confrontation/situations;

(5) to develop and maintain high standard of performance and dedication to the public cause of maintenance of law and order in the community and enforcement of "rule of law".

(6) to develop capacity for patience, forbearance, greater responsibilities, higher work and spirit of public service;

(7) to develop a democratic outlook recognising the fundamental rights of the people and to develop respect for "rule fo law";

(8) to develop resistance to the danger of becoming mechanised by visualising what they are doing in a wider setting and by preserving their own educational development.

(9) to identify and analyse the nature of internal security problems. the patterns of motivation and confrontation, the psychological factors that influence individuals, the methods used by dissident leaders and the need for psychological and physical preparation to participate in civil disturbance control operations;

(10) plan for and conduct civil disturbance management operations using confrontation management principles, and the proper application of management techniques in accomplishment of operational tasks.

The role of police has to change with changing reuquirements, the very quality of the policeman has to change through proper training. (26)

Curriculum and Syllabus for Internal Security Duties Training

The curriculum is the content or subject matter organised in a meaningful sequence. This step of the process requires the training office to take the objectives and identify the appropriate content which is needed to support the objectives. (27) Constitution of India, economic plans, collective behaviour and mob psychology, Organisational behaviour, group conflict and manifestation of behaviour deviation, role of police in the context of social, political and economic changes, laws affecting internal security like Indian Penal Code, Criminal Procedure Code etc are some of the improtant subjects to be incorporated in curriculum. Fundamental rights of the Indian citizens, Directive Principals of the Indian constitution and certain other "core" subjects will provide an orientation in the political, economic and social infrastructure of the Indian nation. Subjects covered in the Foundation course at National Academy of Administration, Mussoorie need to be included in the curriculum for senior level induction course. Terrorism, insurgency, mob-violence, naxalite activities, espionage, subversion, communal riots, political agitation and all other subjects need to be thoroughly discussed and various strategies and techniques to handle these situations must be taught to the trainees. Case studies, and practical field experiences should be shared with the police trainees to provide them realistic training. Use of latest arms and equipments also need to be included in syllabus. We are passing through, in this country, a very big change in the social field. "The rapid development, the various Five Year Plans, the rapid rate of industrialisation and urbanisation, the growing consciousness of the people, our constitution - the fundamental rights, the emphasis on rule of law, all these are factors which impose on all of us, particularly on police, a new responsibility, a new obligation, a new sense of dedication to the cause of the country to help in the establishment and restoration of law and order wherever their services are called for. Police have to change alongwith the changing social sense. And therefore new teaching and new training become absolutely necessary for all of us". [28] The curriculum and course contents will have to undergo constant review and reveision in the light of new developments. Police training for law and order duties and internal security duties should prepare the policemen with a healthy and balanced perspective about the community problems and should prepare them to acquire a high degree of clear understanding of the social purpose of their activity and also develop correct attitudes in consonance with the dynamic concepts of social justice, secularism and democracy. Training should prepare police officers with practical exercises for internal security operations in the special context of our prevailing national environment and should thereby contribute to organisational efficiency and effective performance in the actual field. Training is to be considered not only a means of developing personnel but also of achieving the organisational objectives. "In formulating training programmes, therefore, effort is made to match the objectives of the organisation with the aspirations and capabilities of individuals to be trained. Adult education philosophy is kept in view in developing training programmes by taking into account the aptitudes, talents, skills and interests of the individuals concerned". [29] A country like India cannot afford to develop and run training for Internal Security duties of the type and on the scale in use in U.S.A. and other advanced countries, but we can definitely draw on these programmes for developing our own training programmes particularly in the conceptional areas of systems approach, training priorities and methodology, etc. Training of senior officers and middle level staff (subordinate officers) should cover instructions "on how other countries resolve the conflict between the constitutional right of citizens and the maintenance of public peace, what methods are utilised for enforcing public order, what methods are utilised for actually quelling disturbances and what is the general outlook of the public authorities in such matters". [30] Training syllabus of lower level should include practical training in the full utilisation of the resources available with the police in form of transport, communications, control rooms, weapons, riot drill equipment, use of tear smoke etc. Training of middle and lower levels should be both psychological and physical to prepare the men to face crowds and even suffer casualties without necessarily taking to reprisal measures by opening fire. The training in unarmed combat will also be useful for junior and lower level staff. Jawahar Lal Nehru, speaking about crowd control held that approach of an officer in any situation dealing with crowds or groups or individuals must always be a "friendly approach" and one must develop a human approach". [31] Police officers require highly specialised training for dealing with terrorists and terrorism. For effective combating terrorism, training should include theoretical and practical knowledge of subjects such as (1) definition of terrorism and its growth, external support available to the terrorism and its growth, external support available to the terrorists, (2) targets and strategies of terrorists, civil designs of the terrorists, (3) organisational set-up and weapons of terrorists and their plans and modus operandi, tactical operations to combat terrorists such as road block, nake bandi, patrolling, ambushes, cordon & search & raids on terrorists hideouts, (5) legal armoury to deal with terrorists and how to apply those laws, (6) art of interrogation to get information from terrorists, (7) specialised operations and investigation techniques do deal with terrorists.

Operational tasks and techniques for internal security duties should form important part of training curriculum. Preparatory stage, action stage, and post action stage are the 3 stages of law and order operations and all trainees should have a very thorough training in carrying out these assigned operations. Principles to deal with civil disturbances must be incorporated in the training syllabus. "The principle of minimum force" is sacred to the police but so is its mandatory duty to save life and property. [32] It is suggested that efficiency, vitality and morale of an organisation depend essentially on the calibre of the higher levels. The benefits of training descend they do not ascend. [33]

Administration of Training and Need for Training Staff

Even the most well-thought out and sophisticated training programme cannot succeed unless it has the infrastructure of a sound well-defined organisation meant exclusively for its implementation. For effective training for internal security duties, police trainers must utilize training methods such as (a) simulation, (b) knowledge based practical exercise, (c) experimental management games, (d) role plays, (e) case study methods and (f) in-basket exercises to provide realistic field experience to the trainees. The case study method though in vogue in many police training institutions has not really become popular and hence is not in extensive use. If police training has to really serve its purpose, there is need to constantly check on the validity and utility of specific training programmes. In order to prepare both gazetted and non-gazetted ranks of a police for internal security duties, most important aspect is administration of specialised training courses for the police personnel. Training should be "practical oriented" and what is most important is to impart to the trainees not merely knowledge and understanding of the professional subjects but to give them an insight and practice, of how this knowledge can be applied in the work they will be required to perform in the field.[34] The concept of training administration includes several functions--planning, organising co-ordinating, motivating, controlling, directing, reviewing and supervising. For training of gazetted ranks and middle level staff of the battalion, training responsibility will have to be given to the training institutions who have specialised trainers at their disposal. The training of superior level and middle level staff in internal security duties therefore has to be organised on a range/sector area basis if not on the entire force basis. Training academy has to provide staff for training and battalion personnel of both senior and middle level have to be spared for training. Training of lower level staff in internal security duties can be organised at battalion level, once battalion has a team of qualified gazetted and non-gazetted instructors. Training Department of the organisation has to prepare "training manual" or required literature for internal security training. Training of battalion personnel for internal security duties is ultimately the responsibility of the battalion commander as "training is an integral part of management function and cannot easily be delegated".[35] Effective training of gazetted an non-gazetted ranks of a battalion for internal security duties, should be able to change the attitudes and behaviour of the trainees and it should be able to create a new climate in the organisation. Organisational climate of a unit can be built up by right attitude of battalion officers, particularly the Commandant. Senior officers in the field should display faith and belief in and extend their whole-hearted support to the process of training." [36] Police training has to build and sustain an attitude of service to the poor and the downtrodden and to bring about a behavioural orientation in police to the democratic ideals of service in a welfare state. [37] It is necessary to induct new concepts into police training programmes and to provide training material, which may make police officers aware of the tremendous problems of the minorities and the under-privileged classes.

Police training to deal with public agitations has to develop a different philosophy for work in respect of police officers, constables and sub-inspectors. The administration of training programmes and the orgainsation of training function involve "capability in determining assignments of priorities to the ingredients of a training course. This determination is closely based on a clear understanding of the steps necessary to accomplish the course character. This mechanics has to take note of the identification of course ingredients, selection of background material, identification of course instructors and the necessary time span". [38] Evaluation of training and feedback of results are always essential part of a training programme. The training programme of police personnel for internal security duties, in the above context, has to deal with live issues and problems currently faced by the police officers attending to it with a sustained focus on devising the strategies and styles of solving them. Through proper training to deal with public agitation, it is essential that police develop greater number of more highly trained constables, capable of assuming responsible initiative in day-to-day affairs. [39] Training effort in the field of law and order administration is emphasised every day but much of this is either stereotype or wasteful in its failure to revise the attitudinal value scales of the personnel. [40] Proper training on scientific lines is impossible unless we have properly trained trainers who are themselves motivated and have undergone attitudinal change. Well-developed training programmes in the field of law and order will fail to bring the desired results unless the organisational climate of the police department undergoes revolutionary change and qualified trainers take charge of training function. If training is to be recognised as a viable organisation device, as a strategy of achieving organisational goals and as a means of affecting change, suitable programmes to train trainers should be rigorously and conscientiously pursued. The need for development of trainers potential through carefully planned training can hardly be overemphasised." If the need for more training, both quantitatively and qualitatively exists, the need for developing trained trainers is self-evident. [41] The rapid pace of development in the field of training occasionally underline the acute lack of trained trainers. All efforts need to be made to create a cell of trained trainers.

Logistics for Internal Security Duties

In order to prepare the police for internal security duties, training of gazetted and non-gazetted ranks alone will not meet the organisational objectives. Police organisations have to be equipped with various equipments which are required for internal security duties like protective clothing, portable magaphone, cameras, taperecorder, tear smoke munition, cane shields, lathies and other riot dispersal equipments. A fleet of reliable good vehicles will increase the mobility of the battalion and will enable unit personnel to arrive at the desired place well in time. Battalions on internal security do move too frequently from one place to another and therefore a fleet of dependable motor transport is a very important requirement. To prepare the police for internal security duty, provision should be made for adequate transportation for personnel (including reserves), equipment and prisoners together with arrangements for servicing and fuelling. Provision should be made for special equipment that may be needed such as barriers, generators, flood lights, ropes, tools and meterial for constructing barricades, gas guns, riot drill protective clothing and public address system. A network of wireless sets is also important requirement. In recent years, a number of advanced countries like German Federal Republic, France, the U.S.A, the U.S.S.R, the United Kingdom, Switzerland, Japan, Italy, Egypt, Czechoslovaia have produced Internal Security vehicles, bomb disposal and detection equipment, special anti-riot weapons and equipment, body armour, shields and bomb disposal suits, surveillance, security and perimeter protection equipment and special communications and ADP equipment which are of great utility in Internal Security duties. The United States of America, the United Kingdom, France, the Federal Republic of Germany, Italy, Switzerland, Belgium, Spain and the Netherlands are significant suppliers of internal security equipment. [41] India can import some of these latest internal security equipment for its police forces.

The quality of police service and the success of many police operations are dependent on the means of transport that is provided. Adequate provision of motor transport is a means of great economy as it not only increases the effectiveness of the police work but also that of its limited manpower. The consideration of economy and centralisation should be weighed against considerations of efficiency and the need and desirability of expeditious repairs to the police vehicles. (43) Manoeuvrability is an allied requirement for a police transport which cannot be over-emphasised. In internal security duty, "arrival of police on the spot within a few minutes of the reported emergency, allows little time for miscreants to start any trouble on a large scale or any kind of emergency to develop beyond control. (44) Provision of adequate wireless sets is also an important requirement.

The Final Objective

Objectives of organisation undergo chage in content and emphasis with time. Organisational structure, standards of performance and methods of work need continuous review in the light of changes. (45) In a society gradually settling down to a life of democratic constitutional existence, the police also have to be gradually equipped to transform themselves. This process however cannot be hurried beyond what the improvement in the civic situation permits. (46) When all parties in India are having an increased awareness about the techniques in mass demonstrations, the police mechinery is geared more towards confrontation than precaution or prevention. The police administration must evolve a positive policy in this context. "Our society is passing through what could be termed a revolution of rising expectations, directed to achieve political, economic and social modernisation. And since police touch upon the lives of the individuals at so many points and spend a greater proportion of their time and effort in working with the people, society's expectations from the police have also been steadily rising. As a result the entire gamut of the role of police and its place in society must assume a new complexion. (47) Summarising the duties and responsibilities of police in internal security duties Shri B.N. Mullik has observed You protect the country itself against subversion and foreign intrigues. There is no field of protection which is outside your scope of work and you must arrive in time, again and again, to protect, whenever evil raises its head, whenever peace is disturbed and whenever danger theatens your country". (48) According to David H. Bayley India presents an interesting paradox. It has a far higher level of public protest and violence than any other democratic country and yet it seems to withstand them with greater poise than other democratic countries". For meeting the newly emerging challenges of internal security, police organisations not only need for effective and meaningful training but also latest equipment like bullet proof vehicles for patrolling terrorist infested areas and latest weapons to match the weapons carried by the terrorists. Police officers at all levels require high level of motivation and effective leadership to fulfil their responsibilities. Education and training for the police, enhance democratic values and develop foundations for mutually supportive police-public partnership. [49] According to newspaper reports, on 476 occasions the Army was called in aid of civil power between 1951 and 1970. But between 1976 and 1986 the Army was called in on as many as 374 occasions. It speaks at least partly of the increasing ineffectiveness of the police in handling law and order situation although it partly means increasing violence and virulence of communal, ethical or lingiustic conflicts in Indian society. This calls for more emphasis on police training for law and order duties. Police training must develop in employees the capacity to redefine the problems they seek to solve, redesign - their relations with their changing national environments. The new training programme should aim at "indoctrinating police personnel with concepts of pride in the uniform and hard work, patriotism and "civility to people". [50]

Conclusion

As we approach the last decade of the 20th century, the menacing cloud of terrorism and mindless violence in Punjab, the aggravation of internal troubles in Jammu and Kashmir, the continuing insurgency in the North-East, the growing discontent in the vast tribal belt which encompasses parts of Madhya Pradesh, Bihar, Orissa, and West Bengal, the increasing fury of the caste conflicts in the countryside and the rising wave of communal tension and rioting in the urban areas of northern India and above all the general breakdown of law and order in various parts of the country have thrown the most serious challenges to our infant democracy. [51] It would be wholly unfair to blame the police alone or even primarily, for the present state of affairs. However, there is an urgent need for modernising the police. Police should be given additional vehicles, more sophisticated equipment and weaponry, better communication and better training so as to improve its mobility, fire power and ability to flash meassages instantly and to perform its duties in a more effective manner. Police requires more meaningful and job-oriented training to bring about much needed change in its outlook, orientation and behaviour. We are definitely in the wrong if we give the impression to the police or to everyone else in the land, that the police alone can control or suppress serious crimes like rioting, terrorism, insurgency, communal tensions and other law and order situations. True the police have to play a part, even a big part perhaps but the task of securing peace in the land can only be fulfilled if each man in the administration plays his role, consistent with his role and is effective in his own way. Adequate and constant support has to be provided by the armed forces (including Central police forces), the mass media, the legislatures and the powerful voice of public opinion.[52] However, it cannot be denied that a period of great stress and strain is clearly ahead of us and properly trained, highly motivated and properly led police officers can be our great assets.

Notes and References

1. O.W. Wilson (1986), *Police Planning*, Charles C. Thomas, Publisher Springfield, Illinois
2. Evelle J. Younger, 'Challenges to police in changing world', *The Indian Express*, February 21, 1969.
3. O.W. Wilson - *Police Planning, op.cit.*
4. J.H. Pfiffner, *Public Administration*.
5. "Training of civil servants in the United Kingdom" by M. Wadhwani. Training Monograph No.12 Training division Department of personnel - Cabinet Secretariat, New Delhi 1972.
6. S.K. Ghosh (1969), *Law Breakers and keepers of Peace*.
7. N.M. Supnakar, "Police Administration and Security of the State", *The Indian Police Journal*, January 1973.
8. D. Haldar, "Security Responsibilities - Police Planning for the tasks in 1975" - A syndicate study by officers of the XII Advance Course, National Police Academy, Mount Abu.
9. "The Police and Internal security" - Training material published by office of public Safety, Agency *for International Development*, Department of State, Washington.
10. Bayley D.H, *The Police and Political Development in India*.
11. Gorwala A.D, *The Role of the Administrator - Past, Present and Future*.
12. Curry J.C., *The Indian Police*. Wood Suff, *The Man who Ruled India*.
13. Dr. Prabhu Dutt Sharma, "The role of Police in Public Agitations", *The Indian Police Journal*, July 1973.
14. Shri A.P. Saxena, "The Training Function - Identification and Implementation" - Training Monograph No.6 - Training Division - Ministry of Home Affairs, Govt. of India, New Delhi.
15. Shri B.N. Mullik, *Civil Disturbances*, the Manager of Publications, Delhi - 1966.
16. *Ibid.*
17. R.P. Khosla "Training the Administrator" - The Problem of Motivation - *Indian Journal of Public Administration* Vol.X, Oct.-December-1965.

18. Major Warren K. Rus - "Confrontation management" - Lesson prepared for civil disturbance Orientation Course - United States Army - Military Police School, Fort Garden Georgia- USA. For lucid explanation of concept, see Dr. K.M. Mathur (1989) *Internal Security Challenges and Police in a Developing Society* pp.-55-64.

19. Dr. K.M. Mathur (1989), *Internal Security Challenges and Police in a developing society, op. cit.* pp 58 - 62.

20. Shri A.A. Ali, "The role and Range of Training" - *National Police Academy Magazine,* Silver Jubilee issue 1973.

21. Shri S.C. Misra, "My six years at the Academy"-*N.P.A Magazine*, Silver Jubilee issue 1973.

22. Shri N.S. Saksena, "How to deal with planned disturbances". Article published in the Crapler CRP Newsletter and Magazine-October 1974.

23. Shri N.S. Saksena - "How to face food riots" - Article published in the Crapler April 1974.

24. Shri O.P. Grover, "State Police Chiefs confer", *The Indian Police Journal*, April - June, 1974.

25. Administrative reforms commission on personnel Administration, April 1969. Training Monograph No.2 - Training Division, Ministry of Home Affairs, Govt. of India.

26. W. Wood - "Development Administration - An objective" *Indian Journal of Public Administration,* October-December 1967.

27. Leonard Nadler, *A process of Training*, Leadership Resources, Washington.

28. *Ibid*.

29. Shiv Nath, "Training and Development of postal personnel selected overseas institutions"- Training Monograph No.17 Training Division, Department of personnel and Administrative reforms (Cabinet Secretariat), New Delhi.

30 Shri B.N. Mullik, Civil Disturbances, *op.cit.*

31. B.N. Mullik, *Nehru on Police*, Palit and Dutt. Dehradun 1970.

32. Shri N.S. Saxena, "How to deal with planned disturbances". The Crapler October 1974.

33. Shri M.V. Narayana Rao, "Reforms in Police Administration since Independence", *The Indian Journal of Public Administration,* September 1963.

34. Shri A.A. Ali, "The role and Range of Training", *op.cit.*

35. Alex Baveles-Role playing and Management Training - Massachussets Institute of Technology - Department of Economic and Social Science - *Publications in Social Science* - Series 2 No. 21.

36. Shri S.G. Gokhale, "Police : Attitudes. Training Institute, Organisational climate", *N.P.A. Magazine,* 1973.

37. Dr. K.M. Mathur (1987), *The Problems of Police in a Democratic Society*, RBSA Publishers, p-27.

38. Shri A.P. Saxena, "The Training Function, Identification and Implementation", Training Monograph No.6.

39. David H. Bayley, *The Police and Political Development in India.*

40. Report of West Bengal Police Commission.

41. Shri A.P. Saxena, "Management Training for Trainers - Training Division", Govt. of India. Training Monograph No.3.

42. For further details and specifications of various equipments see Michael Dewar, *Weapons and Equipment of Counter-Terrorism*, Arms & Armour Press, New York - 1987.

43. The Mehta Sub Committee on Police Transport, 1956-57.

44. Report of the U.P. Police Commission 1961.

45. N.K. Panda, "Work Study in a Developing Economy", *The Indian Journal of Public Administration*, March 1963.

46. Prof D.G. Karve, "Police Administration in India - A Re-appraisal of the aims and means", *The Indian Journal of Public Administration*, October-December 1956.

47. Shri G.C. Singhvi, "Recent Trends and Development in Police Administration in India", *The Indian Journal of Police Administration* - July - September 1971.

48. Shri B.N. Mullik, *A Philosophy for the Police*.

49. Dr K.M. Mathur, *Internal Security Challenges op.cit.*p.357.

50. Similar experiment has been recently started by Delhi Police. See O.P. Sabheerwal, "Delhi Police - New thrusts" *The Tribune*, Chandigarh, 29-9-1989.

51. Madhu Limaye, "Will the Indian State degenerate into a coercive one ?" *The Times of India*, 13 Oct 1989.

52. K.F. Rustamji, "Police administration - Victim of backseat driving", *The Hindustan Times*, New Delhi. 20 August 1987.

CHAPTER-11

PERSONNEL POLICIES IN POLICE

Introduction

THE MANAGEMENT of human components is the central and most important task because all else depends on how well it is done. The concept of personnel management is primarily concerned with the recruitment, training, career-planning, promotion, performance appraisal, discipline, grievances, welfare, placement, transfers and all other aspects of development of police personnel. Police personnel management is an awesome responsibility that has taken on new significance after the publication of National Police Commission Reports. The co-ordination, control and administration of human resources is a major management responsibility that is central to the success of a police organization's mission in the present day context. The changing nature of the plural society, the demand for greater liberty, the need for greater security, the concern for human dignity and human rights, the requirements of enlightened peoples' police would all require a sound personnel policy for the police. At a time when the country is poised to enter the twenty first century, a national level seminar on personnel polices in police is most appropriate and timely. The growth and development of police personnel administration owes its origin to Sir Robert Peel's London Metropolitan Police Act (1829) and the twelve tenets of Peelian Reforms. Half the principles articulated by Sir Peel related to what today would be termed "personnel administration". The radically innovative ideas of Sir Robert Peel on the recruitment, selection and training of competent policemen serves as a foundation for police personnel administration today. In the modern day world police thinkers have enlarged the concept of personnel administration by introducing the following ten major responsibilities: (i) job analysis and position classification, (ii) recruitment, (iii) examination and placement, (iv) appointment, (v) orientation, evaluation, promotion, and transfer, (vi) compensation, (vii) training, counselling and improvement of working conditions, (viii) employee relations, (ix) discipline and sanctions and (x) maintenance of personnel records. [1] Traditionally personnel management has been conceived of as a staff function. Dynamic and alert organisations constantly need to re-evaluate its personnel administration. Personnel administration, because of its unique perspective, sensitivities and contacts can identify newly emerging trends requiring new or modified policies to meet the ever changing requirements of the society. Personnel management objectives can be broadly classified into the following five categories -

1. Planning manpower requirements by anticipating vacancies and carrying out recruitment;
2. Organizing the manpower resources by carrying out selection and classification of employees;
3. Staffing through induction, transfers, promotions, employee development, and training;
4. Motivating employees by conducting social, recreation and sports activities, welfare measures, effective communications, collective bargaining, employees discipline and regulations of working relationships; and
5. Controlling through performance evaluation, employee counselling, safety procedures, medical services, protection and security and personnel research.

The functions of personnel administration have to keep pace with prevailing social values and attitudes. In India, there are civil and armed police personnel in the States and Union Territories besides a number of Central police organisations like CRPF, BSF, CISF, Coastal Guards, RPF, Intelligence Bureau and other Central Organizations performing police duties. The personnel administration of these police personnel is looked after by the respective police Chiefs and their other senior functionaries. Police forces in India have very large strengths varying from a few thousand in smaller States to nearly a hundred thousand in some of the bigger States like U.P., Bihar, West Bengal and Maharashtra. Planned growth, development and better utilisation of these police personnel deserve an indepth study by the Police scientists and Police leaders. It is high time that the contemplated re-organized set-up of police organizations in India takes a serious view of the place for a progressive and dynamic police personnel policies for the police forces both in the Central police organizations and in the State police forces. Some of the inherent problems of the Indian police organizations can be traced to an inefficient, ill-trained, negative and an inadequate personnel system. Police administration in India suffers from an almost complete neglect of the vital function of "human management" and total absence of well formulated personnel polices. A great deal of criticism has been levelled at police leaders for their neglect of personnel administration by not only the rank and file but also by the social scientists who often perceive top police manager as aloof, aristocrat, authoritarian and too politically motivated to have the best interest of police personnel at heart. It is tragic and ironic that while police leaders are working so diligently to improve the relations between policemen and citizens, the relations between police managers and police personnel are deteriorating. The 1979 agitations by the policemen in different parts of the country and indifferent police organisations call for a scientific analysis and closer introspection. Even the most serious acts of indiscipline by policemen, and the police strikes in various states and some central police organizations have failed to arouse a genuine concern to modernise the police personnel system and personnel policies in India. It will be a most unique and everlasting contribution of this national level seminar organised by S.V.P. National Police Academy, Hyderabad, if the Seminar could recommend all round reforms in personnel management system covering such fields as human resource planning, job analysis, recruitment, selection, promotion, training and education, police personnel relations, performance appraisal, discipline, job satisfaction, motivation and other related fields.

The Basic Tenets and Concept of Personnel Policies

Personnel policies are vital to the management of personnel and permit employees to enjoy a certain sense of security by enabling them to know what treatment to expect. Personnel policies are generally formulated by the professional personnel staff but it is essential that these policies receive approval and support of top management. Once personnel policies are formulated, these are formalised into written statements to serve as invaluable aids in administering it on the whole organisations in various matters. Administration of personnel policies provide an identical and uniform treatment for various categories of employees. Personnel policies have to be integrated closely with policies relating to other functional areas. Personnel policies however must have certain degrees of flexibility in order to allow for the particular conditions or circumstances, surrounding the problem in each case. Personnel procedures serve to implement policies by indicating the chronological sequence of steps to be followed in carrying out the policies. Personnel policies, academically can be split into three :

(i) the personnel aspect concerned with recruitment, placement, remuneration, promotions, incentives, performance etc.,

(ii) the welfare aspect concerned with working conditions and amenities such as canteen, housing, recreation rooms, educational facilities for children of employees; and

(iii) the employer-employee relations aspects concerned with collective bargaining, discipline, grievance redressal machinery, and other matters concerned with human relations.

Personnel polices are written statements of an organization's goals and intent concerning matters that affect people in the organization. Policies are stated in broad, long-range terms that express or stem from the philosophy or beliefs of the organization's top authority. (2) Personnel policies help personnel managers in effective manpower planning, human resource development and long term organizational planning. Personnel policy help men and organizations to live and grow together. Increasingly during the last two decades there is an emergence of personnel specialists whose function is to design and administer personnel management programmes in all bigger organizations as staff advisers to top management. The investment in human capital--often the largest single involved is not appreciated fully unless a senior manager of the organisation is charged as personnel manager with the responsibility for tending and nurturing human capital to attain maximum organizational efficiency. The personnel policies can be formulated and implemented only with the full support of the top management and the department of personnel administration. Personnel policies are concerned with the human aspect of the organization and are framed with a view to providing a high sense of satisfaction to the employees in their work.

The famous Hawthorne plant of Western Electric, where the well-known "Hawthorne Experiment" was conducted, Elton Mayo and his colleagues of the Harvard School of Business Administration formulated "Ten Commandments" of personnel policies which are as follows :

"It is the policy -

(1) to pay all employees adequately for services rendered,

(2) to maintain reasonable hours of work and safe working conditions,

(3) to provide continuous employment consistent with business conditions,

(4) to place employees in the kind of work best suited to their abilities,

(5) to help each individual to progress in the company's service,

(6) to aid employees in times of need,

(7) to encourage thrift and put the employees in touch with those best qualified to advise on matters of home buying or building, use of banking facilities, insurance programmes and other personal financial problems,

(8) to cooperate in social, athletic and other recreational activities,

(9) to accord to each employee the right to discuss freely with executives any matters concerning his or her welfare or the company's interest, and

(10) to carry on the daily work in a spirit of friendliness." [3*]

The above mentioned personnel policies have actually laid the basic foundation for a happy and well-looked after employees and constitute the core of a welfare State. The six basic principles of personnel policies enunciated by "the General Motors" are given below :-

1. Put the right people in the right places.
2. Train everyone for the job to be done.
3. Make the organization a co-ordinated team.
4. Supply the right tools and the right conditions.
5. Give security with opportunity, incentive recognition.
6. Look ahead, plan ahead . . . for more and better things.

In the words of Ordway Tead: "personnel administration is the utilisation of the best scientific knowledge of all kinds to the end that an organisation as a whole and the individual composing it shall find that corporate purpose and individual purposes are being reconciled to the fullest possible extent, while the working together of these purposes realizes also a genuine social benefit". Personnel policies have to be stable yet should possess sufficient flexibility to meet changing conditions. Personnel policies are generally influenced by many factors such as tradition in the organisations, technological development, the prevailing personnel practices in other organisations, government regulations and the ideals of the management. Personnel policies should generally take account of relevant personnel concepts e.g. that every employee is a whole person, with characteristically human needs, which are partly unique and that inner motivation can be more powerful than any externally imposed controls in achieving organisational objectives. In recent years the following changes have been among the most significant for personnel administrators and managers :

1. changes in the composition of the work force,
2. pressure for equal employment opportunities,
3. varied life styles,
4. rapid spread of computer based information and retrieval systems,
5. the economic environment with high rate of inflation,
6. the turbulent socio-political environment,
7. the awakening of political consciousness and political rights,
8. changing attitudes and value systems,
9. increasing expectations in life and recognition of employees' psychological needs,
10. organizational changes and changes in the managerial roles,
11. increasing unionism in workers and greater stress on collective bargaining, and
12. changing concepts of human resource development and increasing demand for professionalism in personnel management from the employees.

Although the personnel functions existed in the form of an employment activity, the personnel department as such did not emerge until about 1912 in the United States of America. One of the pioneers in industrial psychology was Huge Munsterberg whose book *Psychology and Industrial Efficiency*, published in 1913 made the notable contribution to personnel management in the areas of employment testing, training and efficiency improvement. In 1915, the first College personnel course consisting of a training programme for employment managers was organised by the Tuck School at Dartmouth College and by 1919 at least twelve Colleges were offering training programmes in personnel management in the U.S.A. [4] The growth in the status of personnel departments within the organisations is due to the pioneering contributions of early leaders such as Elton Mayo, T.N. Whitehead, F.J. Roothlisberger, W.J. Dicksen, Whiting Williams, Walter Dill Scott, Walter V. Bingham, Ordway Tead, Harold E. Burit, Arthur W. Kornhauser, Morris S. Vitelos. These leaders, by advancing the professionalism of personnel management, helped the services of the personnel specialist to become accepted more by line managers and top bureaucrats. Gradually personnel specialists were employed to assist managers with such activities as training, wage, salary, fringe benefit administration, personnel research, grievance redressal and employer-employee relations. Although all managers and supervisors are responsible for performing a wide variety of personnel functions, personnel departments are being developed in bigger organisations due to their desire to work on long range and broader questions relating to the personnel function.

Personnel Policies in Police organisation in India: a close scrutiny

Carefully developed policies are vital to the management of personnel because each person is sensitive to any differences in the treatment, no matter how slight, that he or she may receive as compared with other persons. [5] Policies provide the means for carrying out the management processes and as such are aid to decision making in all organisations. Police personnel administration is complex and demanding because it involves the management of the policemen both on and off duty, from the day they are selected to the day they retire. Even after retirement, police personnel need looking after in terms of retirement pension, gratuity and other post retirement benefits. In the United States of America and other Western countries, most of the police organizations have fullfledged personnel departments or police personnel administrative bureau. Due to increased emphasis on human resources management, a police department should be able to justify a full time personnel officer when it reaches a size of 200 employees. Thereafter a ratio of one personnel specialist for every 200 employees is in order. [6] Personnel department of police headquarters, should be constituted in all the State police forces as well as in Central police organizations for effective personnel management of police personnel in India. Selected Police Officers should be sent to attend two weeks course on Personnel Administration at Indian Institute of Public Administration, New Delhi or three weeks course on personnel administration at National Institute for Training in Industrial Engineering, Bombay and later utilised in personnel department.

It is both surprising and unbelievable that in India, police personnel policies have not so far been properly enunciated and even formalised in scientific manner. The eight volumes of National Police Commission Report have made a thorough study of various aspects of police personnel management in India. The various subjects falling under the scope of personnel management as dealt in the various reports of the National Police Commission are as under :

First Report - 1. Pay structure, 2. orderly room, 3. machinery for redressal of grievances of police personnel, 4. recruitment, training and career planning, 5. modalities for inquiry into complaints against police.

Second Report - Welfare measures for police families.

Third Report - 1. Corruption in Police, 2. Modernisation of law enforcement.

Fourth Report - No subject relating to personnel management.

Fifth Report - 1. Recruitment of Constables and Sub-Inspectors, 2. training of personnel in the civil police, 3. code of behaviour for police officers, 4. women police.

Sixth Report : 1. Police leadership - The Indian Police Service, 2. training of Indian Police Service officers.

Seventh Report - 1. Organisation and structure of Police, 2. performance appraisal of police personnel, 3. disciplinary control.

Eighth Report - Accountability of police performance.

Some of the noticeable observations on some important aspects of police personnel management as contained in Police Commission Reprots as reproduced below : [7]

(1) "The basic and fundamental problems regarding the police today is how to make them function as an efficient and impartial law-enforcement agency fully motivated and guided by the objectives of service to the public at large, upholding the constitutional rights and liberty of the people." (1.1)

(2) "The police attract only a very unsatisfactory kind of candidate who has not been able to get any other job . . . unless the emoluments and service conditions of the subordinate staff were improved and better personnel recruited, no improvement in the police system would be possible." (2.11)

(3) "The promotional structure within the police system is not conducive to the fulfilment of the legitimate career ambitions of the constabulary . . . a large majority of constables retire as constables without even one rank promotion in entire career." (2.14)

(4) "An average constable works 14 hours every day without any respite under extreme conditions of stress and strain." (2.19)

(5) "Among the police personnel yet to be provided with Government accommodation of any kind, as many as 89.1% are in the ranks of Head Constables/Constables". (4.2)

(6) "The present quantum of house rent allowance is unrealistic compared to the actual amount. Police personnel are obliged to pay for renting private house." (4.23)

(7) "There is an urgent need for devising satisfactory system through which grievances can be effectively voiced and what is more, some solutions can be found with a proper understanding and assessment of the issues involved." (7.1)

(8) "Expeditious sanction and payment of increments and such other allowances as fall due from time to time, prompt settlement of leave, pension, provident fund, gratuity etc. are matters that require close and constant attention from the Supervisory officers." (7.41)

(9) "Governments have tended to accord low priority to funding of police welfare measures." (13.2)

(10) "Among the many deficiencies that got exposed in the situation following the recent agitation by the policemen in some states, one relates to the inadequacy of welfare measures for police families." (18.1)

(11) "The implementation of the recommendations of the Committee of Police Training 1973, despite the lapse of more than five years (and now thirteen years) is disappointing and frustratingly slow." (43.26)

(12) "A demoralised leadership lacking motivation and professional expertise is bad for the police." (44.37)

(13) "Special efforts will be needed to cure the IPS of the ills owing from imposed inferiority and the frustrations arising therefrom because the challenges of the future will require new skills in personnel management and a much higher level of professional knowledge, competence, and leadership from the senior officers in the police." (44.3)

The above observations quoted from National Police Commission Reports clearly indicate complete lack of personnel policies in the police in India. Although police personnel policies have been analysed by many police thinkers, Indian police has failed to formulate and implement any sound personnel policies so far. This deficiency clearly indicates the need for a department of personnel in police forces. Personnel administrators can be most useful when they :

(1) function as policy advisers to top management; (2) serve as 'link pins' e.g. by interpreting personnel policies as they talk with operating managers, (3) refrain from making operating decisions, (4) maximise human resources development through personnel research - Police personnel policies. All police organisations whether they belong to State or Centre, will have to develop and build up an effective

personnel department to cater for the proper mobilisation and development of human resources. Police personnel departments will have to initiate career development programmes for the police personnel and link it with computerised personnel record system.

The Department of Personnel in Police Organisations

An independent department of personnel in State police headquarters and CPOs is an entirely a new and novel suggestion as propounded in the background paper circulated by the National Police Academy, Hyderabad. A close scrutiny of Report of the Kerala Police Reorganization Committee 1962, Report of the Tamil Nadu Police Commission 1971, Report of the Maharashtra Police Commission, 1964, Report of the Delhi Police Commission 1968 and National Police Commission Reports (Volumes 1 to 8) reveals that no report has made any specific recommendation for establishment of a separate department of personnel in the State Police Headquarters or in the headquarters of the Central Police Organizations. However, in the context of present day requirements, the author strongly feels the need for an independent department of personnel at police headquarters. The background paper prepared by the S.V.P. N.P.A., Hyderabad for the seminar has very brilliantly brought out the functions of the department of personnel and the proposed structure of the department. There can be no two opinions about the need for the department of personnel in police. The structure has to be slightly flexible to suit the requirements and demands of the various police organizations. However, there is only one basic question which needs some discussion. Should the department of personnel be manned by police officers themselves or it should be manned by "personnel specialists"? This is a most basic question and needs a detailed discussion. The personnel function began as an employment and record keeping function but gradually it is charged with carrying out programmes developed by management. More recently it has shown signs of maturing as evidenced by more goal-oriented appraisals, centralised and computerised personnel records, more emphasis on planning and police direction. It is gradually becoming a more and more specialised job and personnel management is becoming a career due to the following four related changes of significance. (8*)

(1) The personnel function will assume a more signficant role in the management of the organizations.

(2) The personnel function will become more creative and less mechanistic.

(3) The personnel function will be responsible for furthering the organization, not just maintaning it.

(4) Top management will become more directly involved in the deployment and development of human resources.

Thus there is a possibility of hiring personnel specialists for various larger police organisations. Personnel management and personnel consultancy is a growing business now and police organisations can seek their professional expertise for specific personnel problems. Though personnel specialists will carry out personnel duties and functions, police leaders at all levels will have to undertake some functions and objectives of human resource management. The job of personnel management is too complicated to be left to the police generalists and police leaders alone.

Conclusion

Periodical review and evaluation of personnel policies are needed to keep them flexible and dynamic to meet the newly emerging challenges. The concepts of social responsibility and social audits have given a new dynamics to the personnel functions. In the future in all organisations specialists and executives of the personnel department are expected to play a larger role in the organisation, be broader in their outlook and become more involved in the larger areas that concern top management. Personnel executives will have to concern themselves with the impact that the external environment has on the organisation, including the influence of technological and socio-economic changes. The success of personnel policies is determined by the following three factors:- (9)

(1) The success of the government and top management in formulating and determining policies wisely.

(2) The success of the personnel manager in interpreting these personnel policies properly, in achieving their execution through the line executives and in making the personnel division render as nearly perfect service as possible to the line executives.

(3) The success of the line executives themselves, particularly the first line supervisors in fulfilling their obligations to management and to the employees by interpreting policies wisely, and interestedly and in promoting the effectiveness of their employees by dynamic leadership.

Dynamic personnel policies can build up organizational health and carry out periodical review of personnel procedures to match changing needs and opportunities by formulating integral policy system. As a systems approach, personnel management strategies needed to change in order to match specific situational variables. The essence of a dynamic personnel management is getting effective optimum results, not only in the short run, but also in the long run through building and maintaining a satisfied, motivated and productive human organisation. The final responsibility for personnel policy must lie with top management, to whom the personnel officer acts as adviser and its execution must run through the whole line of management if it is to be effective. (10)

Notes and References

1. Milton M.Mandell, "Responsibility and Competence". In Fritz Morstein Marx (1959) (Ed) – "*Elements of Public Administration*", 2nd ed. pp.500-524.
2. "National Industrial Conference Board, Studies in Personnel Policy" No.169, New York. Quoted by George S. Odiorne - In *Personnel policy Issues and Practices* - Charles E. Merrill Books, Columbus 16, Ohio, p.8
3. For full details and elucidation see Walter D. Scott, Robert C. Clothier and William R. Spriegel (1977) - *Personnel Management - Principles, Practices and Point of View* – Tata McGraw Hill Publishing company, New Delhi pp.55-57.
4. Henry Eilbirt, "The Development of Personnel management in the United States". *Business History Review*, Vol. 33, No.3 (Autumn 1959), pp.10-11.
5. Herbert J. Chruden and Arthur W. Sherman (1976) – *Personnel Management*, South Western Publishing Co. Cincinnati-Ohio, p.86.
6. For further justification see William J. Bopp (1977) – *Police Personnel Administration - The Management of Human Resources*, Holbrook Press Boston, p.79.
7. Extracts from various National Police Commission Reports of Govt. of India.
8. For further elucidation see Frank E. Fischer, "The Personnel Function in Tomorrow's Company" *Personnel*, Vol.45 No.1 January-February 1968, pp.64-71.
9. Scott, Clothier and Spriegel (1979), *op.cit.*, p.59
10. "Personnel Management in India, the Practical Approach to Human Relations in Industry," compiled by *Indian Institute of Personnel Management*, Asia Publishing House, Bombay 1961, pp.63-64.

CHAPTER - 12

OFFENCES AGAINST WOMEN

IN GOING through newspapers and magazines of the past so many months the things that stand out are the Muslim Women's Bill, Roop Kunwar's murder under the guise of "Sati" and the almost daily reports of women being burnt for dowry, committing suicides as a preferable alternative to the torture and the degradation faced in our Indian society. The social, economic and sexual exploitation and harassment of women, wife beating, exploitation of widows, selling and trafficking of girls for immoral purposes, eve teasing of school going girls in buses and at college gates, are today's insignificant matters of daily newspaper reports. Today eighty per cent of patients visiting gynaecologists are only interested in sex determination tests of the foetus so that female babies could be aborted. What is the future of a girl born into a home that despises and rejects her? This is the greatest indictment of our society that women feel it better to die than face the ignominy, insecurity and degradation of our society. The condition of Indian women in subsistence and agriculture sector deserves special attention because of "increasing pauperisation of women". (1) Women folk living below the poverty line are much greater in number than the men-folk today. Thousands of women are oppressed every day. The fact that suicide is considered better than being a miserable, unwanted widow or be a burden on one's parents like the three Sahu sisters in Kanpur, is a serious blot on our present day society. Some 89 per cent of the people in India work in what is called the unorganised informal sector and more than 60 per cent of these must be women. Women work as agricultural labour and also render their services by working as head-loaders, cartpullers, domestic hands, construction workers and in numerous other kinds of jobs where they do not get fair wages and fair deal and often subjected to various kinds of exploitation, injustice and ill treatment. "Not only is the woman condemned to domestic slavery but when she goes out as a labour to earn wages though she works harder than man she is paid less." (2) Persistent factors continues to exploit women negate personality and potential of Indian womenhood and some of these factors can be enumerated as under :

The sex ratio at 933 women per 1000 men (1981 census) continues to favour men and by 2000 A.D. there will be 480 million females against 500 million males.

Nearly 25 per cent of the women are literate and 75 per cent continue to be illiterate, ignorant and deprived of fruits of education and enlightenment.

Nearly 90 per cent of the women (1981 census) work in the unorganised sector which offers no regularised basis for fair wages and reasonable conditions of work including regulative and protective provisions of labour laws.

Women's 10 to 14 hours of hard work in collecting fuel, fodder, water, farming and animal herding gets no formal recognition in computation of work at the planning level and she remains mostly unpaid for this work.

Uncontrolled, unwanted, frequent and at times forced maternity continues to pose a health hazard to women with the result that in India one mother dies every six minutes.

The abortion of the female foetus with the help of modern medical technology is a new introduction in the list of atrocities against the women.

Deprivation of reasonable maintenance to Indian Muslim women after divorce and long delays in court for grant of maintenance under section 125 Cr.P.C.

Pitiable condition of poor divorcees and widows and their ill treatment by their relatives.

Burning of brides for dowry and ill-treatment and harassment of newly married girls by their husbands and in-laws.

Discriminatory treatment of girls and women in jobs and employment opportunities due to social bias and prejudices.

Offences and crimes against women have been showing a singular increase over time.

Almost fifty per cent of pregnant women suffer from anaemia and do not get adequate medical care.

Only 7.5 per cent of the membership of trade unions consists of women.

For every 100 boys who enrol in schools only 65 girls are able to do so. Drop out in school girls is estimated at 60 odd per cent at the primary level and about 75 per cent at the elementary/higher secondary state.

Emotional oppression and harassment of women and girls continues in social order.

Eve teasing, molestation and even rape continues to throw indignities at women.

Assignment of tasks to the female servants by the housewife perpetuates the prejudice of keeping women confined to demeaning tasks.

Bigamy is openly being practised and even glamourised by cine-heroes and rich people.

Prostitution and 'call-girl' rackets thrive in all big cities and towns.

There are many girls and poor women who are betrayed in the name of love and unwedded mothers have to bear the intolerable stigma of social disgrace due to deceitful acts of the men.

Incidents of mass rape and gang rape in some parts of the country continue to be reported in the press.

Eve-teasing, involving the verbal and physical harassment of women in buses, market places, college campuses and parks continue to be allowed in big towns and cities. Some new forms of this despisable acts are as follows:

(a) Indulging in cat calls, waving, wolf-whistling, winking and uttering indecent remarks;

(b) Nudging past hurriedly;

(c) Ogling amorously;

(d) Teasing women on telephones in lewd language;

(e) Mailing anonymous love letters in most filthy language;

(f) Bottom pinching and other indecent acts by men to cause harassment and embarassment to women. (3)

Indecent exposures of human body, exploitation of women, commercialisation of sex, immoral trafficking and prostitution continue to be the destiny of women.

How long will women suffer these indignities and harassments? Has it got anything to do with our cultural traditions? Is there a connection between female weakness and backwardness in education? What are the deeper psychosocial, economic and cultural cross - currents that allow such offences against women even in democratic society having adult franchise? Why there are no nationwide drives against injustices to women? How far are women themselves responsible for their own victimisation? Is there a tendency on the part of women to submit meekly to the offenders? Are our laws effective and comprehensive to deal with offenders? There are numerous such questions which crop up in the mind. A review of constitutional provisions and legislative developments in the last four decades reveal a significant attempt on the part of the nation to protect women. The philosophy of the Indian constitution as embodied in its Preamble and Articles 14, 15, 39(a), (d) (e) and 51 A(e) *inter alia*, proclaim that the state shall ensure a just social order for women. Hindu Marriage Act,

Special Marriage Act, Child Marriage Restraint Act, Code of Civil Procedure, Dowry Prohibition Act, Equal Remuneration Act, Factories Act, Maternity Benefit Act and Criminal Law (Amendment) Act 46 are some of the important landmarks in the history of legislation. The Committee on the Status of Women in India (1971) expressed its concern about:

"... the absence of adequate enforcement mechanisms that have made many of the laws ineffective" as also the inadequate efforts of the social organisations to educate women about their legal rights. In the words of Justice V.R. Krishna Iyer: "We have neither sufficient laws nor efficient implementation of laws." The National Committee on Implementation of Legal Aims Scheme has recognised women "as a class who have been subjected to deprivation, brutality and extortion," and has evolved a model scheme where women are entitled to free legal aid irrespective of their economic position. The reality regarding the enforcement of laws relating to women in India is very complex. According to Sulochana Vasudevan, "there is a need to create suitable infrastructure to cope with the increased demand of quick remedial actions against crime committed on women. The long delays in processing cases and obtaining concessions have resulted in loss of faith." (4)

Four persons were arrested on March 14, 1988 in connection with a call girl racket in Delhi. Delhi has registered the largest number of rape cases among all the Union Territories. Such cases in Delhi have shown an increase during the last three years. While 89 cases were registered in 1985 the number rose to 92 in 1986 and 103 in 1987, the Minister of State for Home P. Chidambaram told Rajya Sabha on March 29, 1988 (*The Hindustan Times,* New Delhi - Wednesday March 30, 1988).

The crime of rape is almost a universally occurring crime. While in India the volume of rape case per lakh of population increased from .4 in 1971 to 0.7 per lakh in 1978, in England and Wales it increased from 1.6 to 2.5 and in U.S.A. the increase was from 20.5 to 30.8. In France it rose from 2.0 to 3.0 from 1971 to 1972 and remain at 3.0 upto 1978. In Japan it fell from 4.4. to 2.5 from 1972 to 1978. In legal terms rape is defined under section 375 of Indian Penal Code. Though compared to other countries India has a very low rate of rape, but within india there is a high variation in volume of rape from one State to another as can be seen in table no. 1 ahead :-

TABLE 1

Incidence of Rape in India 1981 - 1985

Sl.No.	State/U.T	1982	1983	1984	1985
1.	Andhra Pradesh	245	309	274	338
2.	Assam	198	168	272	168
3.	Bihar	348	339	475	413
4.	Gujarat	97	89	140	135
5.	Haryana	90	85	114	90
6.	Himachal Pradesh	25	29	24	27
7.	Jammu & Kashmir	115	146	142	207
8.	Karnataka	60	85	97	988
9.	Kerala	78	103	124	120
10.	M.P.	1113	1221	1305	1428
11.	Maharashtra	504	557	675	674
12.	Manipur	20	9	13	18
13.	Meghalaya	17	8	14	17
14.	Nagaland	9	8	5	10
15.	Orissa	137	146	150	163
16.	Punjab	53	56	70	85
17.	Rajasthan	339	378	379	522
18.	Sikkim	4	4	7	3
19.	Tamil Nadu	169	191	207	204
20.	Tripura	22	28	19	35
21.	U.P.	77	700	955	800
22.	West Bengal	489	488	594	521
	Total States	4905	5147	6055	6169
23.	Andaman and Nicobar Islands	-	4	3	3
24.	Arunachal Pradesh	6	8	7	5
25.	Chandigarh	5	3	2	4
26.	Dadar and Nagar Haveli	2	1	1	1
27.	Goa, Daman and Diu	-	10	7	9
28.	Lakshadweep	-	1	-	-
29.	Mizoram	35	39	35	53
30.	Pondicherry	4	7	8	9
31.	Delhi	69	78	85	73
	Total U.Ts.	121	151	!48	158
	Grand Total	5026	5298	6203	6326

Even after the offence of rape, the victim women has to first convince the police, and then subject herself to medical scrutiny and finally face a crucial and humiliating cross examination in the Court. Both during and after the rape the woman is humiliated, dehumanised and degraded. It is a most despisable phenomenon which has the worst repurcussions on the mind of the victim. Vimala Veera Raghavan has analysed the victims' response to the inevitable situation of rape in her study of rapes in Delhi. [5]

TABLE 2
Victims' Response to Inevitable Rape Situation

	Respones	*No. of Victims*	*Percentage*
1.	Submitted meekly	42	49.41%
2.	Fought ferociously	25	29.41%
3.	Became unconscious	1	1.18%
4.	Resisted the Rapist	1	1.18%
5.	Diverted the Rapist's attention	1	1.18%
6.	Overwhelmed with fear	1	1.18%
7.	Gagged and tied so could not respond	13	15.28%
8.	Do not remember	1	1.17%
		85	

The rape victims generally do not report at all because of the undue publicity which may ruin their future lives in various ways. The reasons for not reporting incidents of rape to the police include:

(1) Woman's psychological condition forbids quick post rape planning in a rational manner;

(2) Lack of knowledge of procedure and not knowing how effectively to inform the police;

(3) Fear of retaliation from her offender;

(4) Desire to conceal the matter or to deal with the matter privately;

(5) Fear of further humiliation, shame or embarassment to herself family, relatives and friends; and

(6) The avoidance of the rigours of vexatious cross examination in the court;

(7) The inconvenience caused by numerous adjournments by the Courts;

(8) Knowledge of futility of long court procedures and remote chances of offender's conviction.

Women in India are also victims under Suppression of Immoral Traffic in Women and Girls Act. A total of 15890 cases were registered under this Act during 1982 as against 15658 cases registered during 1981. The main contributors to these cases were Tamil Nadu (8919), Karnataka (2753), Andhra Pradesh (2177), Maharashtra (924) and Uttar Pradesh which accounted for 98.5 per cent of the total offences registered under Suppression of Immoral Traffic in Women and Girls Act. Cases under this Act in various States during 1982 are as under:-

TABLE 3

Cases Under Suppression of Immoral Traffic in Women and Girls Act in 1982

S.No.	State/U.T	Incidence of Crime	Volume of crime per lakh of population
1.	Andhra Pradesh	2177	4.0
2.	Assam	2	Neg.
3.	Bihar	17	Neg.
4.	Gujarat	12	Neg.
5.	Haryana	1	Neg.
6.	Karnataka	2753	7.2
7.	Kerala	22	0.1
8.	Madhya Pradesh	2	Neg.
9.	Maharashtra	924	1.4
10.	Manipur	4	0.3
11.	Orissa	5	Neg
12.	Punjab	3	Neg
13.	Rajasthan	8	Neg
14.	Tamil Nadu	8919	18.0
15.	Uttar Pradesh	880	0.8
16.	West Bengal	55	0.1
	Total (States)	15784	2.3
1.	Delhi	85	1.3
2.	Goa, Daman & Diu	9	0.8

3.	Pondicherry	12	1.9
	Total (U.Ts)	106	1.0
	Grand Total	15890	2.3
	Bangalore	205	7.8
	Bombay	893	10.4
	Calcutta	55	1.7
	Hyderabad	25	1.2
	Kanpur	95	6.2
	Madras	1314	38.6
	Lucknow	501	54.5

Neg. - Negligible i.e. less than 0.05.

The cases under Suppression of Immoral Traffic in Women and Girls Act were not registered in Himachal Pradesh, Jammu and Kashmir, Meghalaya, Nagaland, Sikkim and Tripura. The Union Territories of A & N Islands, Arunachal Pradesh, Chandigarh, D & N Haveli, Lakshadweep and Mizoram also did not register any cases under the said Act. Cases reported from 1976 to 1982 under the said Act were as under :-

TABLE 4
Cases Under S.I.T.W. and G .Act
During 1976 - 1982

Year	Total Cases in India
1976	16150
1977	13924
1978	15448
1979	14196
1980	14308
1981	15658
1982	15890

The above statistics may fall short of the actual dimension of the problem as many a case go unreported to the police. The immoral traffic in women and girls "has patronage from a diverse section of society – administrators, businessmen, politicians, professionals, students and workers." [6] In Bombay and other big cities, call-girls racket is also increasing. The call-girl category evokes little sympathy from social reformers because of their obscurity as well as comparative affluence.

Black money is the backbone of this immoral traffic and the whole immoral system needs a clean up. There is need for their resettlement through marriage and restoring of their dignity by rehabilitation of prostitutes through social organisations like "Savdhan". Women volunteer organisations like the Centre for Women's Development Studies (CWDS) supported by ICSSR conducts research on women problems and influence of government policy on women welfare. Although much is made out of high respect accorded to women in Indian society, facts present a quite different picture. In 1985 in India there were 6189 cases of rape, 13952 cases of molestation and 7652 cases of kidnapping of women and 802 cases of dowry deaths were registered upto July 1986 in Madhya Pradesh alone which heads the list for crime against women there were 904 cases of rape, 2732 cases of molestations, 1621 cases fo kidnapping, 280 cases of eve-teasing and 310 cases of dowry according to official reports. (7) Between 1979 and 1981 there were 1,133 cases of unnatural deaths of young brides. In 1982 alone 372 dowry deaths were reported in various parts of India -- 141 from U.P. 40 from Delhi, 47 from Punjab and 24 from Rajasthan to cite a few.

Today in many developed and developing countries, women do not feel secure and safe on the street. More than two thirds of the women in Britain are afraid to go out at night for fear, they might be attacked, according to a new opinion poll Xinhua reports from London. The survey undertaken by the Poll organisation "Mori" found that 70 per cent of the women aged between 15 and 24 were afraid they would be raped and almost all thought sexual abuse of women and children was the most serious single form of crime in Britain. In Delhi and many other cities of Uttar Pradesh and Bihar, in certain areas, women feel insecure and unsafe after dusk in the market and lonely streets. Some recent cases of India indicate that crimes against women are also being committed or being abetted by people from professions like lawyers, doctors, civil servants and politicians. Generally the women against whom the crimes are perpetrated are always at the lower or middle level of the socio-economic power base. The harassment and psychological torture of married women by their husbands and the members of the husbands' family has of late caused much concern to the nation. "As many as 1319 cases of dowry deaths were registered during 1986 and 1418 during 1987 in the country, according to Union Home Minister Sri Buta Singh. In a written reply in Rajya Sabha he said that 10 cases of murder for dowry were reported in Delhi and one in Chandigarh during 1987." (8) The emergence of wife beating as a social problem is also growing in India though no figures are available. According to

National Crime Survey in U.S.A. in 1976 as many as 18 million wives were subjected to assault at the hands of their husbands. About one in five Australian adults believe that a man is justified in beating his wife in certain circumstances. According to Federal Government survey released in Canberra, 22 per cent of Australian men and 17 per cent of the Australian women believed that a man had a right to shove, kick or hit his wife if she did not obey him, wasted money, failed to keep the house clean, refused to sleep with him or admitted to sleeping with another man. (9) In India harassment and ill-treatment of women by middle class and lower class families for not bringing enough dowry is well known although no figures are available. In India with a crude birth rate of 32 per 1000 we have about 25 million births in a year and at a maternal mortality rate of four per 1000, 100,000 mothers die every year or one every six minutes. (10) Thousands of women in India have been dying annually due to complications during pregnancy and child birth because of lack of adequate medical care and hospital facilities. A recent survey in Anantpur district (Andhra Pradesh) showed only 50 per cent of the deaths in women of reproductive age group and only 40 per cent of the maternal deaths were recorded. These maternity deaths are due to (i) clinical or medical causes (ii) lacunae in the health services and (iii) social factors like female illiteracy, malnutrition, parasitic infestations, unplanned pregnancies and post maternity negligence. In India about 75 per cent of the maternal deaths are directly due to complications of pregnancy and child birth, 20 per cent due to associated anaemia or heart disease which gets worsened with pregnancy and 5 per cent due to other causes like haemorrhages, eclampsia and jaundice. In India hardly 45 per cent of the deliveries occur without any nurse or physician in attendance. Therefore as a social scientist one can clearly see the tragedy of maternal deaths. The maternal mortality is a neglected tragedy involving mostly poor and rural women and those with least power and influence over how national resources should be spent. Preventing of this tragedy requires commitment both at the professional level and at the political level. There are many areas of crimes against women which need to be researched. A fresh code for these crimes against women has to be achieved with a far reaching aim of diluting the crime density, punishing the offender effectively to avoid recurrence and rehabiliting the victim by creating new social horizons. As an essential pre-requisite for this, it is important to have a separate code for crimes against women.

Need for Protection and Better Deal to Women

In 1952, the U.N. General Assembly evolved the first legal instrument dealing exclusively with women's right in a convention on political rights of women. The year 1975 was celebrated all over the world as the International Women's Year and subsequently the decade 1976-1985 has been declared as the United Nations Decade for Women. March 8 is the International Women's Day which churns out fancy aspirations and declarations in favour of women. A perspective plan for Indian women going upto the year 2000 prepared by the Department of Women in the Ministry of Human Resource Development has made far reaching recommendations. The perspective plan envisages mass media to emphasise women's identity and sensitisation of administrative machinery to the needs, urges and problems of women. The perspective plan report suggests measures to rehabilitate victims of crimes like dowry, rape and sati. (11) There is a need for creation of a women's unit in the Planning Commission for data collection and to process programmes for women's uplift and rehabilitation of victims of crimes. Police officers particularly at subordinate ranks and grass-roots level need to be sensitisized through proper training and orientation to the problems of women and particularly to their role in detection and investigation of crime against women. There is an urgent need to increase the percentage of women police to at least 10 per cent of the police force in a phased programme. The National Expert Committee on Women Prisoners headed by Justice V.R. Krishna Iyer has recommended induction of more women in the police force so as "to obviate complaints of indignity and misbehaviour towards women." (12) The total number of women in the police forces all over in India is a little over 3000 which is hardly 0.4 per cent of the entire police force while according to International Crime Police Organisation (ICPO) Argentina has 11 per cent, the U.S.A. five per cent, England and Wales seven per cent and Singapore 12 per cent. The effectiveness of police women's work would be greatly enhanced if they receive special training in social work so that they could be qualified to diagnose and treat social ailments and to effectively perform their duties concerning women and child victims of crime. The victimological perceptions of offences against women open a vast vista for the social researchers to probe into. What can be done for prevention of sexual offences and self-defence for women? How the marital abuse and dowry deaths can be prevented? How neglect and ill-treatment of pregnant mothers can be stopped? How gang rape, molestation of women and suicides by young women due to harassment by husbands and members of his family can be prevented or minimised? These are important issues which need our closed scrutiny and examination. How far victim compensation in cases of offences against women is practical and feasible and can legislation alone help us in this matter? At present there is no agency to assist the victims of crimes against women. Some agencies need to be built up to provide psychological counselling and social case-work to the victims to reduce their trauma, to increase their moral stamina and to relieve them from a total psychological break-down. Victim rehabilitation centres for women can be set up in each state and adequate compensation provisions need to be made by suitable amendments in various laws of the land. The mass media can play a significant role in educating the public to prevent becoming victims of various offences against women. Srimati Mrinal Pandey's T.V. Serial "Adhikar" is a very bold and novel experiment which deserves commendation and attention. The newspapers, films and T.V. serials could project the extent of suffering undergone by the victims of dowry problem, whereby the attitude of harassing husbands and mothers-in-law could be changed.

It is a matter of great concern for social scientists to analyse why there are numerous offences against women. Why there is torutre of women resulting in more and more broken homes? Why torutre and injustices to women are committed by women or under their instigation or support? Why mothers-in-law demand dowry at the time of marriage? There can be a number of causes for increasing offences against women. Indifference to women by women permeates all levels of our society. Why women do not revolt against injustices and ill-treatment meted out to them? Our traditional male oriented society and value system is responsible to a very large extent. In reality the status of women in our traditional Indian society negated her personality and potential. Offenders generally take advantage of women's frailty and submissive nature. In India from the vary beginning a girl is brought up to think that tolerance is the virtue and she should develop qualities of submissiveness, surrender and sacrifice. Child-bearing, child-rearing, domestic chores, cooking food and management of family house-hold work are considered the only responsibilities of women in Indian traditional society. Service to family and husband, obedience to elders of the family and submission to the wishes of the male members are considered virtues of women. Illiterate and socially backward women naturally develop an inferiority complex. 90 per cent of the Indian women do not know about International Women's Day or any movement for their uplift. For an average Indian woman in villages, in slums, in jungles nothing is likely to change nor there is any will to fight against oppression, injustice or ill-treatment. What is the future of a girl born into a home that despises and rejects her? Certainly illiteracy, seclusion, lack of economic independence, lack of social awareness, traditionalism and purdah system are common causes for the sorry state of women plight and exploitation in India. The injustices to women are the symptoms of social, economic and moral decadence setting in our society. Offences against women are due to lack of religious education, erosion of values of life and the absence of the sobering effect of happy family life and spiritual teachings. The effect of western civilization, the pernicious influence of the cinema, the cheap pornographic literature is partly responsible for eve-teasing and harassment of women in Indian society today. There is lack of public consciousness and lack of fear of punishment in the minds of the offenders. The social malaise of dowry deaths and bride burning is due to rotten social system in which women are treated with social discrimination and prejudice. The press and the mass media are also not playing positive role. Today there is too much emphasis on feminism and this is making women a "weaker sex". There is a need to create a suitable and congenial environment for developing the proper personalities of the girls today. There is need for social locomotion in support of social welfare legislation for women. Role of voluntary organisations, enlightened judiciary and effective law enforcement machinery in preventing and curbing offences against women need to be properly highlighted. The awareness of rights in women, accompanied by faith and public support alone can save women against injustices and harassments. Educationists should revise text books with the object of removing a sexist bias.

Conclusion

The time has come when women complain about their exploitation, voice their grievances and draw the attention of an otherwise unsympathetic society. [13] The time has come when offences against women have to be minimised by more effective implementation of existing laws and suitable amendment in laws where needed. Suitable amendments should be carried out in Hindu Succession Act to the effect that female heirs be given the same rights in their father's property, compulsory registration of all marriages, national ban on sex determination tests and proper legislation to protect women's rights in the home and all acquisition, movable and immovable property, acquired after marriage should be owned jointly. There is need for more enlightened sex education and progressive views on widow remarriage, women educations and equal rights need to be propagated. The traditional police organisation of India is "not structured to deal with women be they victims or perpetrators of crime" (14) The entire police structure and the criminal justice system need to be restructured to meet the newly emerging challenges. The social service agencies and non-governmental voluntary organisations can play an important role in building up public opinion against injustices to women. The real solution of the problem can be found in rousing social consciousness and in mobilising public opinion for effecting necessary attitudinal changes so as to strengthen the will of the public to resist such evil practices.

Notes and References

1. For further details see Maria Mies -- *Indian Women in subsistence and Agricultural Labour,* Vistaar Publications.
2. Lotika Sarkar, "Status of women and Law as an instrument of social change". *Journal of the Indian Law Institute,* April/June 1983, p.263.
3. For details see. Dr. Puran Batria, "Eve-teasing : causes and cures" - Agenda papers for XV All India Police Science Congress, Simla 1980 - pp.71-76.
4. Sulochana Vasudevan, "Neither sufficient Laws nor efficient interpretation." *The Hindustan Times,* 13th March, 1988.
5. Vimala Veera Raghavan (1981) – *Rape & Victims of Rape: A socio-psychological Analysis,* Northern Book Centre, New Delhi, p.67.
6. "Prostitution Thrives in Bombay", *The Times of India,* Bombay, April 7, 1987.
7. "Crime against Women", *The Times of India,* 1st April, 1987
8. *The Hindustan Times,* New Delhi - March 2, 1988, p.9.
9. *The Times of India,* 11th March, 1988.
10. "Tragedy of Maternal deaths" by Dr. K. Bhaskara Rao, *The Hindu,* March 27, 1988. Author is grateful to Dr. Rao for his informative article.
11. "Behind the Scene - Better Deal for Women", Promilla Kalhan, *The Hindustan Times,* New Delhi, Monday March 7, 1988.
12. "More Women COPs' urged", *The Times of India* Tuesday, Bombay, February 16, 1988.
13. Justice D.A. Desai, Chairman Law Commission in Seminar on "Economic and property rights of Women", *The Hindustan Times,* New Delhi, 10th March, 1988.
14. Eighth and Concluding Report of the National Police Commission, Government of India, May 1981, p.18.

CHAPTER - 13

VICTIMOLOGY : NEED FOR A FRESH LOOK AT THE CHILD - VICTIMS IN INDIA

VICTIMOLOGY IN India is gradually getting some academic recognition, but there are large areas which are still unexplored. While in India victimological predilection is yet to be a factor in deciding issues, in England it has led to the formulation of the Criminal Injuries Compensation Scheme and the National Association of Victims Support Scheme. In West Germany, Italy, The Netherlands, Norway, Sweden and France legislations have been made for guaranteeing the state compensation for certain categories of physical injuries resulting from crime. In the later half of the 70s even in the United States certain provisions of restitution for an offence have been incorporated in the criminal laws. In India compensation to victims are restricted to Section 357 Cr.P.C., 359 Cr.P.C. Section 5 of the Probation of Offenders Act 1958 and Section 110(B) of the Indian Motor Vehicle Act. Benjamin Mendelsohn, a famous victimologist has mentioned completely innocent victim (e.g. children) in his six types of victims in his book, *The Origin and the Doctrine of Victimology* (1963). In the present paper a study of child victims is proposed in the interest of social justice. It has been estimated that there are at least 100 million children the world over who have no homes and live on the streets being exploited by criminals in every fashion possible. In Europe and the United States there is today a flourishing market in child pornography. According to I.L.O. estimates there are 58 million children in the world who are earning and are under 16 years. In India the number is unaccountable since many of them are sold by their parents in an attempt to keep their home fires stocked. In Delhi itself there are over 100,000 vagrants most of whom are little children from the poor families who are most often ruthlessly exploited even sexually and many of them land up in brothels or as pimps or as child beggars. There are now thousands of children in Punjab and elsewhere who have become orphans due to terrorist killing of their parents or whose parents have become victims of riots. There is an urgent need to look after the orphaned children in the interest of social justice and national commitment to equality of opportunity and justice. There are thousands of children who are working as bonded labour particularly in rural areas and are being deprived of their right to grow as a normal citizens of India. There are hundreds of child workers used as domestic servants by the rich people. There is sale of children for sexual exploitation and begging. There are all important social issues which need a fresh look in the present day context. There are criminal gangs who kidnap children and induct them into profession of thieving, pick-pocketing, prostitution, begging and bootlegging. There is exploitation of children by many sections of the society which generally goes unnoticed or ignored. The children's Act 1960 has made various legal provisions including setting up of children's home, child welfare board and observation homes. The Juvenile Courts where the cases of neglected and abused children are dealt with can do a lot in the matters of safeguarding the interests of the battered children. However, the realities of the ground are very different and need to be seen to be believed. In order to provide justice to the child especially to the downtrodden, an all India survey of the plight of children needs to be done. General statistics on child labour conceal the considerable greater disadvantage at which the female child worker is placed. The country which has enacted the Child Labour (Protection and Regulation) Act 1986 is unable to implement its provisions due to lack of effective political will to implement it. Few of the hazardous industries have set up the designated projects on child welfare. The carpet industry of Jammu & Kashmir showed no interest in taking remedial measures despite the known occupational hazards which include paralysis, deformities, anaemia and tuberculosis. Gujarat refused to set up regulations for its diamond-cutting industry by blatantly lying that there were very few children employed in it - despite a 1987 study clearly showing that 1.6 per cent of those working in the trade were below 14 years of age. Of the 55 million working children in India in the age group of 6 to 14 years, at least 10 million are bonded and half of them are children of bonded labourers. India employs world's largest number of children and continues to be among the most exploitative, despite the constitutional guarantees. The Child Labour (Protection and Regulation) Act 1986 and the subsequent formulation of a national policy on the subject. We still remain in the Dickensinian age so far as the plight of our children is concerned. Millions of them are forced to work. What is worse is the dreary or hazardous conditions under which many of them labour. The task force on child labour headed by Dr. L.M. Singhvi, an eminent jurist, in its report has pointed out utiquity of a child having to work at all. "It is sad but true that since independence the lot of child workers has only deteriorated. It is high time we make a good beginning and make more serious and meaningful efforts to stop the exploitation of child labour." Of the 55 million working children in India in the age group of 6 to 14 at least 10 million are bonded and half of them are children of bonded labour."[1] Majority of these bonded children work for 15 to 18 hours a day but they are neither paid by their employers nor are they governed by the Bonded Labour Abolition Act for the facilities of release and rehabilitation.

Prisoners of Gender-Exploitation and Abuse of Girl Child

Bachi J. Karkaria has analysed the condition of the most deprived section of the society -- the girl child--in his article "Prisoners of Gender" published in *The Illustrated Weekly of India,* February 11-17, 1990. According to the author girl children "are prisoners of their gender, hopelessly, painfully, pathetically even literally so. These are the nowhere child girls. Girls looked up to languish forgotten behind stone wall, and iron bars for being the victims of crime, while the penetrators of it roam free. The girls thrown into prison or brutal state-run homes because they have been raped, and need to be called as witnesses after the case has been settled; the family no longer wants them. **Kidnap victims:** Minor girls who have married against the wishes of parents who viciously register a case of abduction against the groom. Or run away women who escaped dreary village lives to pursue a gossamer dream in the city but ended up in the nightmare which is for ever." The above description has summarised the tragic fate of many girl children born in India. In an investigative study carried out in 1987 by Sister Rita Rozario it was found that those who were exploited or sold are in fact usually children (i.e under 18 years of age) at the time of their initial exploitation. Thirty-five per cent of the sample (sample covered 1100 respondents) were even at that time below 18 and 19 per cent had been sexually exploited as children. The Devadasis of Karnataka, the Kalvanthulus and Basavis of Andhra Pradesh all dedicate children to goddess Yellamma and all girl children thus dedicated are sexually exploited in the name of religion. *The Illustrated Weekly of India* February 11-17, 1990 issue has brought the frightening tale and stories of girl children who were victims of our society. All child labour is damning and tragic but female child labour is more so because it is often more hazardous, unseen, unacknowledged, unaccounted and is carried out in addition to back-breaking domestic tasks on emptied stomachs and sexual harassment.

The Girl Child--The Helpless Victim of Rape

On March 26, 1972, a 16 year old girl Mathura was raped by two policemen in the Desarganj Police Station of Maharashtra's Chandrapur district. It took seven and a half years before the highest court in the land delivered its judgement generally known as the "Mathura Judgement" in 1979. The Supreme Court acquitted the accused on grounds that there were no marks on her body to show that she had put up a fight, neither had she raised an outcry, so it was not proved beyond doubt that she had not consented. Once the judgement was made public there was an uproar and bowing to the public pressure a bill to amend the law was introduced in Parliament and in 1983 an amendment was made to the rape law, which stipulated that in cases of custodian rape-- the minimum punishment would be ten years and the onus of proof would be on the man. In another case of 1980 in a slum in Andheri Bombay an eight year old girl was brutally assaulted by a man with sticks when he found that actual penetration was impossible. The child ruptured her uterus and was in hospital for two weeks. Yet this was looked upon as a lesser offence than rape. In another case reported in 1984 a seven year old Harijan girl was raped by a boy of 18 years. She was severely injured and left unconscious. Jaipur bench of Rajasthan High Court upheld 5 years imprisonment to the rapist. Since child victims of rape require treatment, counselling, shelter and an emotional buffer, social work organisations have a major role to play. Unfortunately mass media and cinema are glorifying rape. There are films like *Zakhmi Aurat* which go all out to exploit the subject of rape. What is needed is a system of criminal justice trial in which the already traumatised victim is not intimidated and harassed but given a healing touch, a sympathetic and assuring hearing in camera.

Case Study

The Hindustan Times dated 13 February, 1990 published the news item: "Mother ties kids to rails : four killed" - Madurai. According to the report 30 year old women Pettakokku who had a quarrel with her husband over his illicit relationship with several woman, left her house at Thurumbuvanam in Madurai district and decided to commit suicide along with her four children. In the gruesome tragedy three male children in the age group of 2-8 who were tied alongwith their six months old sister to the rails by their mother were chopped to pieces when the Madurai bound Rameshwaram Passenger ran over them in the early hours of February 11, 1990 while her mother and her last child escaped with serious injuries and were later hospitalised. It is a matter of serious study as to why such crime against innocent young children should occur in our society? What our community can do to stop such offences against children?

A Case Study of Domestic Servant - Nanku - Mystery shrouds the death of a 10 year old domestic servent, Nanku whose decomposed body was found lying in the bedroom of his employer's house in Mayur Vihar 268 B-Pocket C-Phase-II at New Delhi on January 23, 1990. The police reached the spot after reportedly informed about the alleged murder by some unidentified person over phone and found the decomposed body with head injuries lying on a jute mat in one of the bedrooms of the first floor house. Both the legs of the deceased were reportedly burnt. The neighbours alleged that Mrs. Shivani Pandey used to frequently beat Nanku and on several occasions they had heard the shrieks of the young boy. According to them they had seen Nanku tied to the balcony door sometimes back. They said Mrs. Pandey used to beat him a lot and sometimes even did not give food to eat. They said that a case of murder of a domestic servant needs to be investigated thoroughly by a good investigator.

The Murder of Childhood

Andro Linklater in his article "The Murder of Childhood" published in the *Reader's Digest* April 1989 issue has brought out many startling facts and uncovered the outlines of an international trade in child pornography involving hundred of pedophiles in at least 18 countries. There is tremendous ignorance about the scale of sexual exploitation of children all over the world. Recent researches in the United States of America came to the conclusion that 45 per cent of the female drug addicts, 75 per cent of the female prostitutes and 80 per cent of the rapists were sexually abused as children. One raid found over 4000 photographs of at least 100 different children -- some as young as six years old -- shown in a variety of sexual and sadistic poses and from photographs it was evident that these were taken over a period of several years. [(2)] Child abuse and sexual exploitation results in devastating psychological trauma upon abused children. Abused children react with a wide range of abnormal behaviour and amounts to murder of childhood. Detailed studies suggest that as many as one child in ten may be abused and in approximately one case in three, in fact the crime is committed by a father, uncle or grandfather or some close relative of the child. Although there are few precise statistics but victimologists agree that the problem of child abuse is massively underreported and generally ignored or concealed by ignorance and indifference. Unfortunately the subject of child abuse is so disgusting that society is very much reluctant to handle it and acknowledge it as if it were afraid of being smudged. When two paediatrics in Britain diagnosed 121 cases of child sexual abuse within 5 months in 1987, their conclusions were met with incredulity and charges of hysteria. [(3)] The law enforcement agencies, social organisers, teachers and parents must recognise the seriousness of the problems of child abuse. Preventive measures need to be directed at child abuse by friends and close relatives as well as by strangers. There is a definite need for legislation to adopt a minimum punishment for child abusers and police must devote more resources and trained manpower to deal with crimes against children. Los Angeles police department has set up a special squad specifically concerned with child sex abuse. One of the biggest trade offer in the world today is that of the child prostitute and according to the reports and statistics available, it is a growing market. In the United States there is today a flourishing market in child pornography and it has been estimated that the spin off from this business runs to several million dollars. West Europe, the United States and the oil rich countries serve as the market for this dirty business. It is very much necessary that parents must be made aware of the danger to their children and the need to protect them.

In the context of Indian legal system, section 41 of the Juvenile Justice Act 1986 reads as under :

(A) Whoever, having the actual charge of, or control over, a juvenile, assaults, abandons, exposes, or wilfully neglects the juvenile or causes or procures him to be assaulted, abandoned, exposed or neglected in a manner likely to cause such juvenile unnecessary mental or physical suffering shall be punishable with imprisonment for a term which may extend to six months or with fine or with both.

(B) No court shall take cognizance of an offence punishable under sub-section--

(1) Unless the complaint is filed with the previous sanction of the state government or an officer authorised by it in this behalf

"These legal provisions, according to Sheela Barse contravene Article 2 of constitution of India, protecting life and property and Article 14 guaranteeing equal protection of laws to all." When in India a child is lacerated with a knife, or scalded with burning cigarettes or beaten black and blue by a maid, a school teacher, the staff of an orphanage or a custodian institution, a parent or a guardian, can the police take cognisance of the offence? No. Can a court take cognisance of the crime ? No" [(4)] It is surprising that Section 41 of the Juvenile Justice Act 1986 has modified the conditions of ill-treatment and cruelty as earlier defined in children's Act and reduced the punishment for cruelty from two years to six months. Depriving a child of food, clothing and medical care and dumping her/him in a wretched place are no longer acts of cruelty according to Juvenile Justice Act 1986. According to Sheela Barse several provisions of the Juvenile Justice Act 1986 are oppressive, regressive and unconstitutional. [5] Section 31(3) of the Act seeks to restore the conjugal rights of the husband of a child bride after she is de-infested of contagious disease.

The centre of concern for child labour demanded on January 27, 1990 police registration of every child working as a domestic servant in Delhi with immediate effect and also mechanism for providing health care and welfare schemes for such labour by the administration. Government should appoint a Protector General for child labour in the country where grievances of domestic servants could be heard and investigated. At present there are millions of child labourers without any forum to complaint. Often various brutalities on domestic child labourers by their employers go unnoticed. The domestic child workers are not only ill-paid but also ill-fed and daily subjected to worst brutalities. When they became disease-stricken due to malnutrition, they were left to die in the streets. These deaths caused by malnutrition really amount to "murder". The Akhil Bharatiya Bandhua Mazdoor Mukti Sangh has demanded the release of all bonded labourers, medical test on the teenage girls amongst bonded labourers and the arrest of bonded labour owners for allegedly raping the minors and illegal detention of bonded labourers. [6] The report and recommendations of the task force set up by Central Advisory Board on Child Labour should be implemented at the earliest. The recent task force had to admit that most of the provisions of Child Labour (Protection and Regulation) Act 1986 and the subsequent formulation of a national policy need to be further implemented with full sincerity. Certain provisions would have to be redesigned or modified to bring the ideal down to the level of achievable. The carpet industry of Jammu & Kashmir showed no interest in taking remedial actions despite the known occupational hazards. Gujarat refused to set up regulations for its diamond-cutting industry. There is an urgent need for effective steps to improve the working and living conditions of child labour all over the country. Proper education, welfare and rehabilitation of child bonded labour which is estimated as 50,000 by conservative estimates should get national priority.

Child Labour in Match and Firework Industry

There are numerous laws to deal with child labour ranging from the children (Pledging of Labour) Act 1933, the Employment of Children Act 1938, the Minimum Wages Act 1948, the Apprentice Act 1951 and the Child Labour (Prohibition and Regulation) Act 1986. The law specifically prohibits the employment of children below 14 years in fireworks and match units but the implementation of these Laws/Acts tells a story of official apathy and tacit collusion with the mighty match and fire works lobby. According to Govt. estimates there are approximately 45000 children working in the factories situated in Sivakasi town and panchayat, Sattur town panchayat, Thiruthangal and the near-about villages. Unofficial estimates place the number at 1,25,000 in the three districts of Sivakasi belt. The Tamil Nadu Government has been claiming since 1987 that child labour is no longer employed in fireworks units and is on the decline in the match industry as a result of strict implementation of legislative and welfare measures. The Department managed to launch prosecution under the child labour Act against 23 match and eight fireworks units in 1988 yet there have so far been no convictions. While 22 cases resulted in acquittals the rest are pending. However, any visitor, if visits these units incognito can see number of children working in different chores. There are countless rural households that supply child labour to these match and firework units. These children work from seven a.m. to six p.m. bring home soiled notes of six or seven rupees, clutched in their little palms, to supplement the family earnings. The child labour in the arid poverty stricken tracks of Kamaraj and Thirunelveli districts, form just another raw material to be consumed by the industry. Child labour generally fills empty paper rolls with gun powder, puts fuses into crackers and makes them into bundles upon which labels are stuck. These children are eternally condemned to a sisyphean existence, eternally filling match frames and boxes only to find a fresh pile after the end of each exhausting, working day. It is a matter of great happiness that Govt. has started the National Child Labour Project (NCLP) in Sattur, Sivakasi and Venbukottal blocks of Kamaraj district. The scheme is a major policy initiative by the Central Government to wean children away from match units by providing vocational training and basic education (primarily in language and arithmetics) as well as a mid-day meal through special schools. At present fourteen schools have been set up by voluntary organisations with grants from Central Government. An incentive of Rs. 100/- per child is given to parents who send their child to these schools. Besides about 330 child labour families have been helped with loans amounting to Rs. 5.98 lakhs. There are other schemes under the NREP, the RLEGP and Jawahar Rozgar Yojana with a subsidy of Rs. 25/- lakhs which are likely to provide succour to about 200 child labour families. The real problem lies in the non-cooperation of parents of child labour who are clearly reluctant to bite the hands that pay them. They want their children to work to supplement their family income to make at least one meal a day for the family and to keep them merely at the subsistence levels. The child labour question is essentially an economic one and only later political. Unless parents of child labour co-operate, prohibition of children from engagement becomes difficult.

Case Study of Victims of Terrorist Crime

On 9/10 November, 1989 some students belonging to Kanpur and Kurukshetra were staying at Thapar Engineering College, Patiala (Punjab) for attending some cultural programme. On the night of 9th/10th November, 18 students were shot dead by the terrorists and 6 students were seriously injured. These students were all non-Sikhs and were promising young boys doing engineering course at Kanpur and Kurukshetra. Khalistan Commando Force Chief Gurjant Singh Budh Singhwala, Babbar Khalsa International Chief Sukhdev Singh and Daljit Singh, convenor AISSF in a press note claimed responsibility of this atrocious crime against innocent students. The basic issue is whether the law and order administration of the country is helpless to stop such crimes against children. What strategies and tactics should be adopted to stop such crimes in future? The terrorists wanted to have ban on admission of Hindu students in six educational institutions of Punjab namely, Guru Nanak Engineering College, Ludhiana, Thapar Engineering College, Patiala, Govt. Engineering College, Chandigarh, Govt. Medical College, Patiala, Govt. Medical College, Faridkot and Govt. Medical College, Amritsar. The terrorists carried out shootout at Thapar Engineering College to create fear in the minds of the Hindus. How can such terrorist activities be allowed and how can Hindu students be denied right to admission. These are some very complex issues which require critical analysis and policy formulation at higher level. How can a sense of security be instilled in the minds of Hindu students of these colleges of Punjab?

Victims of Terrorist Crime

Whether it is communal riots or terrorist killings the ultimate result is the pitiable plight of orphaned children whose parents die and who are left to the world to fend for themselves. *India Today* in its issue dated November 15, 1989 has given a heart rending account of 8000 children orphaned by terrorist bullets. Harinder Baweja writes :-

Q - What happened to your father?

A - Uggarwadis (terrorists) came to the shop and killed him.

Q - Why did they kill your father?

A - I don't know.

As Rajiv Kumar, a 5 year old child says these words his eyes transmit confusion, pain and fear, symptomatic of the trauma faced by the 8000 odd children in Punjab orphaned by the terrorist gun, left fatherless, economically vulnerable - together with their widowed mothers - present the most tragic face of terrorism. (7) Terrorism in Punjab has left many children orphaned who live to narrate their traumatic memories that haunt their everyday existence. There is an urgent need for a proper rehabilitation of all orphaned children who are victims of terrorist crime in Punjab and elsewhere.

The Surviving Children of various Communal Riots

India has been witnessing in various parts of the country communal riots from time to time and each riot leaves a large number of orphans whose fathers are victims of communal frenzy. *The Illustrated Weekly of India* dated November 5-11, 1989 has brought out the weekly cover story of survivors of anti-Sikh riots in Delhi which needs our attention. A nine year old boy, Trilok who was only four year old then, witnessed the death and burning alive of his father by the rioters. They first hit him with iron roads and then set him on fire. He was screaming. Sukhwinder Kaur recollects "they (rioters) hit my father, my grand father, my uncle. I saw the blood flowing. Then they took them away." (8) There are thousands of children in rehabilitation camps who were eye witnesses of riots and are riot victims. During anti-Sikh riots the worst massacres have taken place at Trilokpuri, Sultanpuri, Nangloi, Jehangirpuri, Uttamnagar and Bhajanpura, etc. and were estimated 2733 deaths according to official figures released while according to All India Sikh Conference there were at least 5135 people killed. Certainly a large number of children have been made orphans by their deaths. All over the country there are thousands of children, Hindus, Sikhs or Muslims who need protection, care and rehabilitation. Child victims need at times new homes if they are completely orphaned. A positive healing touch and a practical rehabilitation scheme of riot victim - children should be drawn by the State Governments. A national level survey of such riot victim children also should be carried out so that the true dimensions of the problem may be known in right perspective.

Children Working as Bonded Labourers

Indian Express in its issue dated 25 January, 1990 brought out details of some children working as bonded labourers. Miss Sagin, a 10 year old girl was found among the bonded labourers found at the quarry camp of a Faridabad contractor Mr. Sant Lal. Sagin's parents were paid an advance of Rs. 4000/- by the contractor and therefore the agent kept the little girl in his jhuggi almost 6 years, living on crumbs and breaking stones from dawn to dusk. Sagin is only one of the many children in the age group of 7 to 16 working as bonded labourers in extremely hazardous circumstances. (9) The Akhil Bharatiya Bandhua Mazdoor Mukti Sangh has recently (on 13 February, 1990) demanded the release of 62 bonded labourers, of village Dabota in Solan District of Himachal Pradesh. The Sangh members visited the site with S.D.M. and other officials on February 10, 1990. "On seeing the team the bonded children cried loudly, women wept and the teenage girls revealed that they have been gang raped. They were given food only once a day and not allowed to leave the place." (10) There are many children who are spending their precious lives as domestic hands, workers in all kinds of obnoxious factories, industries, restaurants and elsewhere. Not only are they deprived of basic education but even of square meals and clothes. There is no dearth of legislation, the latest being the Child Labour Act of 1986. Though some lacunae exist in this, we still remain in the Dickensinian age so far as the plight of our poor children is concerned. Millions of them are forced to work. Children from third world especially from rural areas often start as bonded employees because of the initial debts of their parents which they find difficult to shake off. (11) It is very important that the various provisions of Bonded Labour (Abolition) Act should be truthfully implemented and rehabilitation of all bonded labours should be carried out. Those who have violated the provision of Bonded Labour (Abolition) Act should be severely punished and if necessary the legal lacunae in this Act should be removed by necessary amendments in the Act. The constitutional guarantees and commitments must be implemented on the ground.

Exploitation of Children

Children are today being sold for purpose of sexual exploitation.

Reports tell us that in Paris there are at least 5000 boys and 3000 girls according to some estimates who are working as prostitutes. In India thousands of children are kidnapped every year or lured away from home and sold for sexual exploitation. A big percentage of prostitutes in brothels is children below the age of 15 years. "Eight girls were brought from various places in Bengal and forced into prostitution. Four were sold at the rate of Rs. 3000 to the brothel owners while the price for four more was being negotiated when they were rescued." [12] According to Anima Basak, in Dec. 1985 about 50 children were sold from south Syria and south Yugoslavia. These children were between 10 to 15 years and were bought from their families for about $ 30 (about Rs. 390) each and sold to leaders of criminal gangs in Italy for about $ 7500 (about Rs. 97500). Child Sex offenders often entice their victims by offering them lift. A growing number of children have been enticed into physical and psychological rituals that culminate in sexual abuse, magic and rituals fascinate and brainwash the child into a consenting association leading to repeated abuse. 75 to 85 per cent of sex crimes against children are committed by someone the child knows, loves or trusts. [13] Some 45 per cent are relatives, fathers, brothers, uncles or grown up cousins. Another 30 to 40 per cent are close or well-known acquaintances, baby-sitters, teachers, clergymen, doctors and neighbourhood friends. Sometimes the emergency lure is designed to disarm, confuse and worry the child or even kidnap the child from school.

Chained Childhood

The Supreme Court had issued notice on February 13, 1990 to the U.P. Government and its police authorities on the writ petition seeking ban on handcuffing of children. The petition was based on a photograph published in *The Times of India* on January 19, 1990 showing the Lucknow police taking a 12 year old boy Aslam in handcuffs. [14] The Supreme Court had issued notice to the Union Government on February 19, 1990 for a judicial inquiry into the allegations of torture of 250 blind girls and their continued detention in the hostel by the Principal of the Rashtriya Virajanand Andh Kanya Vidyalaya. [15] Uttam Sengupta in a special feature on Bihar has reported that though the law prohibits minors from being sentenced to more than three years, around 500 children have been languishing in jails and remand homes for many years, rubbing shoulders with hardened criminals with no hope in sight. [16] The Indian law prohibits minors from being sentenced to more than three years behind bars but the story of Bihar is different. Twelve year old Amar Lakshman has spent the last seven years in the Patna Remand Home for boys. Kabir, a 12 years old boy was kidnapped and taken to Bombay when he was five but the abductors soon deserted him and later he was put in a Bombay Remand Home. In August 1989 a divisional bench of Patna High Court ordered the release of over 500 children in different jails and remand homes who had been awaiting trial for more than three years. According to some estimates there are at least 500 minors who have spent more than nine months in detention without the police even filing charge sheet against them in complete disregard of a 1983 Supreme Court order that all such cases should be dropped. There are a large number of children charged with petty theft who have spent more than 10 years in detention. [17] Juvenile delinquency is often attributed to poor and orphan children and sometimes they are compelled to commit petty offences to make their living. Slum environment, lack of recreational facilities and crimogenic atmosphere at times induces them to petty crimes. Rehabilitation of juvenile delinquents need to be carried out in a well planned manner.

Need to educate Children about Sex Offenders and Child Abusers

"The sex abuse of children is a social time bomb with the potential for destroying many futures. To stop victimisation of our children, we must educate them." [18] Teaching children about the tricks that molesters use could save them from grievous harm and even death and Kenneth Wooden started widely acclaimed Child Lures Prevention Programme in schools, churches and corporations in the United States of America and Canada. The following are some of the basic lessons :-

1. Children should be told that although most of the people are good and do not harm children yet there are also 'bad' and psychologically 'sick' people who are harmful and dangerous and have to be kept away.
2. Children need to be told that no one should touch them in a way that makes them feel uncomfortable or embarrassed and that each child has a right to keep certain parts of his body private.
3. Generally children should be encouraged to travel with friends and classmates to school and around the neighbourhood and "safety in numbers should be stressed".
4. Children should be taught and urged to think about way of escaping and surviving if abducted by unknown persons. Running and screaming for help must be taught to children.

5. Children must be taught to be careful about the motives of any adult -- even a family member especially overnight and such advances should be brought to the notice of parents/guardians immediately. Children should be told the importance of telling parents about the improper advances made by others.
6. Children rarely lie about sexual molestation and therefore parents should encourage them to confide all their problems with them. Mutual trust should be built up.
7. Children should move out of reach and be ready to run and scream for help whenever anyone particularly adult seek for guidance, direction or help and/or acts in a suspicious manner.
8. Children should be told not to accept gifts, sweet, toffees or other eatables from a stranger and tell parents if such an offer has been made.
9. Tell children not to get allured by fame, lure or a modelling job or the chance to compete in a beauty contest which are made by unknown or only acquainted persons. Parents should accompany children in talent pursuits.
10. Parents should keep their homes free from all forms of pornography and children should know that bad people sometimes try to trick children and allure them by job lures, fun or games lures like tickling, wrestling, hiding the coin or hiding under a cover and trying to bring intimate body contacts, children should recognise when there is "a bad touch" by someone.
11. It is necessary that children should be intelligently and in a language which they can comprehend get the correct message of saving themselves from abuse and should be explained about the various tricks which molesters use to entice and allure them. The Child Lures Prevention Programme needs to be given to children. [19]

Conclusion

Dr. L.M. Singhvi's "Task Force" is a welcome step towards improving the plight of these children who are spending their precious lives as domestic servants, workers in all kinds of obnoxious factories, industries, restaurants and elsewhere. Not only are they deprived of basic education, but even of square meals and clothes. Some of the children employed as sweepers, porters, domestic servants etc. have been found extremely intelligent but owing to their helplessness this tremendous wealth is being wasted. What the child deserves is at least basic education, good food, clothing and proper rehabilitation in the form of fair wages and reasonable hours of work without exploitation of any kind. A national law should be enacted that all working children should get education for sometime every day and they should be given affectionate care and rehabilitation by the employers. There must be mandatory provisions for recreational facilities, socio-economic safeguards and for legal and administrative arrangements to ensure that they are not exploited by the employers. An ombudsman is of paramount importance to redress the wrongs done to the child. If a child is exploited or abused, public spirited organisations, neighbours and the child must have the legal right to lodge a complaint in the same way as an FIR and provisions of Juvenile Justice Act need to be amended to make it more effective for delivering quick justice to the children. Efforts need to be made at grass-roots level by helping individuals or the organisations that have a genuine and sincere interest in the child welfare. The first and foremost efforts should be made to make them literate and conscious of their rights and privileges as a child labour. It is sad but true that the lot of child workers during the last forty years has not improved at all and has probably deteriorated. Setting up of a child labour ombudsman is important in this context. The two priorities have to be the enforcing of the prohibition of child labour in hazardous occupation and processes and progressively eliminating their abuse and exploitation with the objective of eventually ending such work. Child abuse or exploitation should be treated as public interest litigation and direct intervention of courts should be made. There are more than 2000 children homes all over the country and an inquiry into their functioning is essential periodically to prevent these homes being used as the source of trafficking in children or their oppression. Since it is not practically possible to completely ban child labour since these kids contribute half of the family income, their working and living conditions need to be improved and they should be given opportunity to educate themselves. The first need is for the political will sincerely to champion the cause of child victims and orphans who have no political voice but are future citizens of the nation. A comprehensive legislation for the care, protection, welfare and compensation of child victims is needed to provide required help to the child victims in India. The Juvenile Justice Act 1986 needs to be thoroughly revised and modified so that it can help in providing quick and cheap justice to the juveniles and child victims.

Notes and References

1. *The Hindustan Times*, 27 January, 1990. H.T. Corresponent - "10 million children are bonded".
2. For details See Andro Linklater, "The Murder of childhood", *Reader's Digest*, April 1989. Vol. 134 pp.37-41.
3. *Ibid.*, p.40.
4. Sheela Barse, "Law denies Justice to child victims", *Indian Express*, 3 February, 1990.
5. For further details see Sheela Barse, *op.cit.*
6. *The Hindustan Times*, February 14, 1990. "Release of 62 bonded labourers demanded" - H.T. Correspondent.
7. *India Today*, November 15, 1989 - "Rescuing an orphaned future", pp.96-99.
8. *The Illustrated Weekly of India*, November 5-11, 1989. "The Survivors" Anuradha Dutta.
9. *Indian Express*, 25-1-1990, S. Kumar, "64 bonded labourers rescued."
10. *The Hindustan Times*, February 14, 1990, H.T. Correspondent - "Release of 62 bonded labourers demanded."
11. "Survey of Exploitation of children", *The Hindu*, 7-3-1988.
12. *Police Research and Development Quarterly-1*, 1988, p.27
13. David Finkelhor, "Sexually Victimized Children."
14. *The Hindustan Times*, February 15, 1990.
15. *The Hindustan Times*, February 21, 1990.
16. *India Today*, February 15, 1990. "A Chained childhood" - Uttam Sengupta, pp.74-77.
17. *Ibid.*
18. Kenneth Wooden - "How sex offenders lure our children" adapted by *Reader's Digest*, October 1988, Vol. 133 No. 798 from *Child Lures Family Guide*.
19. For full details see Kenneth Wooden (1958) -- *Child Lures Family Guide*, Wooden Publishing House.

CHAPTER-14

POLICE TRAINING IN INDIA THE CHANGING PERSPECTIVES

Introduction

TO UNDERSTAND the real importance of police training particularly in the changing perspective, it is necessary to discover its correct foci which undeniably are : the policeman, the police job and the police environment. The whole concept and the range of human resource development has undergone a sea change over the years and with them, the whole substance, perspective and objectives of training. During the last few decades there has been an unprecedented boom in police training institutions and police training programmes in India. India has the rare distinction of being the first country in the world to institutionalize police training by starting training school for police constables in the year 1859 at Vellore in Madras Presidency. [(1)] The earliest police training institution in a foreign country was the one started in France in 1883. India has approximately 7.20 lakhs of civil police and 2.78 lakhs of armed police, besides having para-military forces like B.S.F., C.R.P.F, I.T.B.P, N.S.G, C.I.S.F. and the like, who require in-service training. There are approximately 124 police training institutions imparting training to police officers of various ranks in India. [(2)] The task of police training in India is challenging and very complex in nature and dimensions since the training needs of various levels of police officers are different and different states have their different socio-cultural milieu in which police officers have to operate. Police training in India has received considerable impetus since the Gore Committee was set up by the Government of India in 1971. National Police Reports (Dharam Vira Report) have further highlighted the need for implementation of various recommendations of the Gore Committee on police training. There have been some noticeable developments both qualitatively and quantitatively in the field of police training as a result of implementation of some of the recommendations of the Committee on Police Training(Gore Committee). The evolution and implementation of new training programmes is not an end in itself, and should not provide any room for complacency in India. The nature, level and content of the courses, the methods of instruction, the quality and quantum of the training staff, objectives of police training and its effectiveness, training environment and training facilities in various institutions -- all need a periodic review with the objective of constantly improving the total training efforts to achieve the desired goals. Those charged with the responsibility of organising and conducting police training in India have a task of exceptional complexity due to the most challenging responsibilities and duties of the police. A democratic polity, a quasi-federal constitutional system, an ancient people in the process of social transformation, historical legacies and diversities, conflict of traditional values with modern ones, of secularism with religious fundamentalism and coexistence of rural with urban culture, increasing violence and agitational politics mixed with adult franchise, increasing crime with intermix of politics, and last but not the least pressures of economic planning and developmental administration all pose new challenges to the people of India. In view of the above mentioned newly emerging challenges to objective, training objectives need to be defined and new focus has to be brought on training programmes. These issues need to be addressed squarely if schemes of training are to be devised in a manner which will be truly useful and evoke genuine enthusiasm among police personnel who will be required to undergo the training courses laid down for them in various police training institutions and elsewhere. The need for adequate training of public service staff is now universally recognised. [3]

Police Training in India - A Brief Review

The organisation of police training in India is much more diverse and plural than in other countries like Japan and Great Britain. [4] There are six kinds of training institutions engaged in the task of training of police personnel in India.

(i) National level institutions like S.V.P. National Police Academy, Hyderabad, and Institute of Criminology and Forensic Science, New Delhi for training of I.P.S. officers and other senior level officers;

(ii) Training institutions of central police organisations such as Internal Security Academy, Mount Abu, B.S.F. Academy, Takenpore (M.P.) and others for training of central police organisational personnel;

(iii) State police training colleges for the training of Dy. Supdts of Police, Inspectors and Sub-Inspectors of State;

(iv) Police training schools for training of Head Constables and Constables;

(v) Armed Police training centres for the training of junior members of the armed police battalions;

(vi) Specialised training institutions like Central Detective Training Schools, and North-Eastern Police Academy, Shillong.

In 1971, there were approximately 60 police training institutions but the number has gone upto 124 by 1982. Police training courses of the various training institutions can be broadly categorised as under :-

(i) Basic course for various ranks on their first appointment;

(ii) Refresher courses for various ranks;

(iii) Promotional courses for various ranks;

(iv) Specialised courses on criminal investigation, crime prevention, traffic control, police community relations, commando training;

(v) Management and Behavioural Science courses for senior police officers;

(vi) Vertical interaction programmes for I.P.S. officers from the rank of Director General to I.P.S. Probationers and Addl. Supdts. of Police.

In terms of total number of training programmes for the police, India conducts the maximum number of police training courses in the world. The quality of training imparted however varies from one training centre to another. During the last one decade there has been a proliferation in the number of training institutions and the number of police personnel receiving training. The growing network of police training in India includes some newer types of institutions and modes of training. During 1970s and 1980s a number of management and behavioural science inputs have been introduced in police training syllabii for senior police officers. Based on the recommendations of the Gore Committee, the contents of police training programmes have undergone substantial changes. [(5)] Value orientation and attitudinal changes were two important facets which were given great importance by the Gore Committee on police training. The following considerations, according to Gore Committee on police training, deserve special emphasis in the training of police in order to enable them to play their role in economic development and social welfare : [(6)]

(i) Loyalty to the constitution, commitment to the goals of the nation and the concepts of an egalitarian society and the need for national integration.

(ii) Awareness of the problems that arise in the wake of developmental process, including conflicts, social disorganisation, scarcity and control, regional imbalances, etc.

(iii) A deep social awareness for comprehending and reacting to complex situations.

(iv) Development of analytical and innovative skills since situations will continue to change and no ready-made solutions can be described.

(v) A new orientation in dealing with the masses, who came from various strata of society, divided among many contours such as religion, caste, region, and income as may lead to the correct response in individual cases.

(vi) The need for the application of scientific techniques, management concepts and skills and constructive attitudes and values in police work."

Emerging Challenges

After almost one decade of the publication of Gore Committee's Report on Police Training and its acceptance by the Central and State Governments it is high time to review and analyse its real impact on police training in India. Has there been any marked improvement in police performance or police behaviour or has there been any improvement in "Police image"? Has police training become more relevant and realistic? Has police training been an instrument of change? A number of other supplementary questions arise : What are the basic objectives of police training in the context of a secular socialist democratic Republic like India? What are the basic training needs for which police should be prepared? What type of new training courses should be devised for their role and job satisfaction ? What should be the core contents of their new courses and where should they get it and so on. Answers to these questions are neither easy nor straight. Despite the proliferation of literature on training in the last four decades, knowledge in these areas is still vague, uneven, incomprehensive and debatable. In order to cope with the complex challenges of socio-economic changes, we have to; as described in *Alice in Wonderland* "run as fast as we can, even to stay where we are." Indian society has changed vastly in recent years and is changing continuously while the police system has not shown required flexibility and adaptability. Democratisation, modernisation, secularisation, urbanisation, economic development and peaceful transformation towards a new social order are some of the important variables of the changing Indian society today. Police plays an important role, in a dynamic society by serving as "a bridge between the old order and the new order." [7] The following dimensions of changing Indian society are relevant from the point of view of police training : [8]

1. Increased pace of rapid urbanisation and industrialisation, causing rise in white collar crimes, economic offences and mass violence.
2. Social disorganisation, anomie and lawlessness, leading to a higher rate of juvenile delinquency, alcoholism, permissiveness and social disorder.
3. Threatened political instability resulting in public protests and demonstrations on a massive scale.
4. Acceleration of mobility giving birth to new patterns of law - breaking and criminal acts.
5. Higher aspirations in the masses due to adult franchise and mass education resulting in youth frustration.
6. Declining standards of morality and degeneration of ethical values.
7. Gradual decline of rule of law and increasing lawlessness at all levels.
8. Political extremism, political corruption and political interference in police administration.
9. Increasing collective violence, campus unrest and terrorism.
10. Increasing agrarian unrest and peasant agitations.
11. Proliferation of social legislation and increased burden of social responsibilities to the police.
12. Increasing internal disturbances and law and order problems.
13. Increasing crime induced by social disparities, social factors, developmental administration expenditure.
14. Smuggling, espionage and subversive activities along the international borders and in border States.
15. Virtual breakdown of criminal justice system due to large backlog of pending cases.
16. Increasing traffic problems due to increase in transport facilities.
17. Drug addiction and drug trafficking.

18. Increasing crime and violence against women and worker sections of the society and increasing dowry death cases.
19. Rampant corruption in society and erosion of moral values in society resulting in divorces, suicides and other crimes.
20. General decline in public service ethics and erosion of nationalistic feelings.

Need for Redefining Training Objectives

The traditional objective of training is to attain "the greatest possible degree of efficiency and effectiveness", the Assheton Committee (U.K. 1944) has laid down the following objectives which are valid for our country also :-

(i) To equip the civil servant with the precision and clarity in the transaction of business.

(ii) To attune the civil servant to the new tasks which he will be called upon to perform in a changing world.

(iii) To develop resistance to the danger of becoming mechanised by visualising what he is doing in a wider setting and by persevering with his own educational development.

(iv) To develop his capacity for higher work and greater responsibilities.

(v) To develop and maintain staff morale.

(vi) To inculcate the right attitude towards the public never forgetting that the civil servant is a servant and not the master of the community.

(vii) To sustain the human touch not only in direct personal contacts with the public but also in handling correspondence which demands a proper sense of urgency and due consideration for the man at the other end. [9]

Apart from the functional and technical components of the skills, knowledge, expertise or professionalism required, all police training programmes should invariably have the following training objectives:

(i) Develop among police officers proper norms of accountability, responsibility and responsiveness and making them aware of their moral and ethical obligations towards the police and the nation;

(ii) Develop a maximum awareness of the political, social, legal and economic environment in which police officers operate;

(iii) Develop among all levels of police officers a secular outlook and positive attitude of dedication and commitments to development goals and national interest;

(iv) Develop a scientific temper and willingness to utilize computer technology and other latest scientific tools and equipment to promote highest level of police professionalism;

(v) Develop an enquiring mind receptive to new ideas and the ability to anticipate situations and innovate in order to achieve the overall mission of the police organisations;

(vi) Develop the trainees' total personality in order to achieve maximum human resource development in the organisation and ultimately at the national level;

(vii) Training should aim at humanising the police in the democratic values of the society and should solidify foundations for a mutually supportive police-public relationship ensuring secularism, socialism and social justice; [10]

(viii) Develop a total man with new cultural attributes operating in the realm of personality, character and behaviour and thus totally transform the ruler appointed policeman into "People's-Police".

(ix) Develop in police officers a very great, in terms of Honadle and Hannah "capacity building", an expertise and ability to find their own solutions to various management problems rather than imposing external ideas upon them. [10] It is about the enhancement of individual ability to absorb, modify and apply skills and knowledge to the task of management.

Current Tendencies and Problems of Police Training

Effective police training can only be the final outcome of a desirable series of interactions between the police trainees, the trainers, the training environment, training strategies, and the training programmes. A study of twenty five training institutions, carried out by the author has revealed that 60 per cent of the police training institutions in the country do not have adequate living accommodation for trainees and even minimum physical facilities are not available in more than 70 per cent of the police training institutions of the country. The author found that latest training tools and equipments for police training are not being used in majority or police training institutions and very little innovative effforts are being made by trainers in imparting training. There is an urgent need for scientific evaluation of police training in

India. In most training programmes, particularly basic courses, there is an input-overload with the result that trainees do not grasp the various subjects thoroughly and trainers have to rush through the subjects to cover the given syllabii. Training programmes present unrealistic goals before trainees and there is a noticeable gap in the realm of attitudes and values between what they are taught and what trainees are expected to do in the actual field. Police training programmes seem to be irrelevant to jobs when basic issues of police world are not sorted out correctly. Can the police control the criminals without the use of third degree methods? Can police contain and control terrorism by following due processes of law? Can crime figures be kept below a certain level only by police efforts? Can the suspects be really broken down by interrogation, without resorting to third degree methods? Such questions can be numerous which cannot be easily resolved by training alone. To keep the training on the rails, it is necessary that trainers should keep in live touch with the realities of the field. Present evaluations of police training seldom go beyond a questionnaire survey of trainees at the conclusion of training which essentially measures reactions. There is at present no internal evaluation of the training programmes in terms of its objectives and procedures nor external evaluations in collaborations with sponsoring agencies. A scientific and comprehensive evaluation of training programme should include context evaluation, input evaluation and even cost evaluation. There is a noticeable mismatch between theory and practice in police work. The mismatch has emerged because our expectations from police training programme are based on wrong premises and expectations. Training as a mechanism of transmission of social goals has serious limitations and inadequacies. A mismatch exists between the premises of training and the reality of training because training has been treated as an Alladin's lamp to deal with the totality of the presonality of the police officer. In spite of all training efforts, no noticeable improvement has been noticed in the police officers in the following areas:

(a) Police image has not at all improved,

(b) Police-community relations have not at all improved,

(c) Police behaviour continues to be autocratic, authoritarian and apathetic to the needs of the poor and the weaker sections,

(d) Police corruption has not been controlled,

(e) Police lawlessness has not heen controlled and contained,

(f) Police officers have not succeeded in containing and controlling increasing crime particularly against women and weaker sections of society,

(g) Communal riots and tensions have not been controlled and contained,

(h) Law and order situations have not been appropriately dealt with,

(i) Collective violence has continued to raise its ugly head,

(j) Rural policing continues to be neglected and ignored,

(k) Use of third degree methods of interrogation continues to be the rule at police stations,

(l) Police indiscipline has been on the increase,

(m) Police have not yet become "Friends, Philosophers and Guides" to the people.

Close analysis of the trainees' behaviour during training has identified the following categories of blocks to learning :-

1. *Perceptual* : Police trainees perceive the problem from their own stand- point and do not find training relevant and practical for their actual field work since expectations of seniors are different in the field. Since he is not convinced, he is in no position to move towards change.

2. *Cultural* : The police culture has not yet been changed and therefore trainees avoid a range of behaviour options because of their cultural script. Authoritarianism, arrogance and use of third degree methods continue to be the integral parts of police culture.

3. *Emotional* : The police trainees feel insecure due to their "impossible mandate" and numerous responsibilities and are therefore reluctant to act on new ideas and suggestions.

4. *Intellectual* : The police trainees find themselves at sea with various scientific kits and computer technology and lack the intellectual competence to resolve the situations. Paulo Freire calls this "semi-intransitivity of consciousness." (12)

5. *Expressive* : Due to hierarchical structure in police, there is no freedom of expression and trainees do not freely express their problems and dilemma. Police trainees do not ask for explanations of what they cannot follow because they do not feel free to express their views and opinions on a given subject.

6. *Environmental* : The police organisational climate inhibits the exploration of new learning opportunities. Police officers are chary of trying any novel ideas learnt during training when they are

back to their field. Most of the police trainees are not able to identify and 'Own'--their own learning blocks.

Feedback from police trainees indicates that they find training programmes theoretical, irrelevant and highly academic away from realities. Poor trainers' preparations, boringly delivered lectures, the impersonality of the large classes, rigid adherence to the letters of the law, overloaded syllabii, emphasis on traditional examinations testing merely formal role learning and stress on teaching instead of learning, lack of realities and too idealistic approach were enumerated as some of the reasons for poor police training outcome. The failure to appreciate the real responsibilities, expectations and role of the police officers lies at the core of unsatisfactory police training. Police training programmes are mostly irrelevant to jobs as they are currently expected to be performed. Many trainees held that de-militarisation of training could go a long way in making the policemen less authoritarian. Police training alone cannot bring change in the behaviour and attitudes of policemen unless it is reinforced by organisational environment. While training could certainly initiate and facilitate attitudinal and behavioural change, an integration of training with the entire systemic effort would be necessary for change efforts to succeed. There is a need to develop institutional structures for a supportive climate in police training. [(13)] Most of the trainees felt the need for faculty improvement since value orientation and attitudinal changes cannot be brought about by incompetent, disgruntled and demotivated trainers. Current status of training suggests -- that a wide gap still exists between various measures recommended for strengthening the training machinery and the extent to which they are practised. According to one research study, police training has been heavily concentrated on pre-entry and post-entry courses for seniormost police officers to the utter neglect of in-service training and the training needs of the middle and lower level police personnel. It is a well-known fact that training has been frequently done for the wrong reasons and in the wrong way. People are sent on courses to get them out of the way or to find a temporary placement for those awaiting transfers or postings. Too often the persons who can be spared are not the most appropriate for training. Most of the trainers should have self-education to develop appropriate expertise in organising training and they must have constant and close interactions with two poles -- the knowledge of his subject and the evolving realities of the field. Police trainers, while selecting appropriate training strategies, must take decision about the range i.e. the extent of content to be covered; the time i.e. the length of training programme; and the depth i.e. to what extent the content is to be treated. Most of the police trainers do not utilize correct and appropriate training methods and strategies due to various reasons like indifference, demotivation, lack of organisational support or the general training environment. Case studies, business and management games, behavioural exercises, project assignments and other latest training techniques are generally not being used in most of the police training institutions in India. There is generally no follow-up of police training programmes.

Police Training and Career Planning in India

Career planning and management enables an organisation to meet its current and projected human resource requirements through provision of career opportunities for its employees, which basically aims at optimising the effectiveness of human resources of the organisation through planned development of their knowledge, skills, attitudes, expertise and behavioural response and securing commensurate promotions, status and salary hike. Career development perspective has the following implications :- [14]

1. Improving human resource planning and development activities in the organisations;
2. Improving individual career planning and helping people who are caught in difficult situations to cope more effectively with these situations;
3. Problem of improving the matching process at all stages of the career so that early, mid and later career crisis can be dealt with more effectively by both the organisation and the individuals caught in this crisis;
4. The problem of obsolescence, demotivation and levelling-off which occur in mid or late career;
5. The problem of balancing the family and work concerns at different life stages; and
6. Problem of maintaining productivity and motivation of all employees who are individual contributors and/or who are not motivated towards climbing the organisational ladder.

Police organisation in almost all states including central police organisations have not yet started career management on any scientific lines with the result that individual are deputed on courses without any forethought. Career management has not yet been accepted as a worthwhile goal for junior and lower rank police personnel in most of the police organisations. Constables, head constables, sub-Inspectors, and Inspectors in most police organisations are not sent out for various courses as a part of their career planning. I.P.S. Probationers are required to undergo a number of courses at various training institutions as a part of career planning. [15] Police personnel below the rank of sub-Inspectors constitute approximately 90 per cent of the police force and their institutionalised inservice training is in great neglect at persent due to absence of proper career management of them. An impression has been gained over the years in police that only inconvenient, easily dispensable and indisciplined officers are sent for training. [16] There are no fixed criteria for deputing candidates for training nor their postings after training are properly utilized in various police organisations. Career planning and training have not been properly harmonised or matched in various police organisations in India.

Need For a Comprehensive Training Policy

Recently Government of India have sanctioned thirty per cent of pay for trainers as trainers' allowance to attract qualified and good persons to training institutions and a number of new training courses has been started to provide training to senior police officers. Such adhoc arrangements need to be replaced by a comprehensive training policy. A comprehensive training policy should outline the scope of "all training activities, approaches to training needs, assessment of the priorities and financial arrangements, the roles and functions of different categories of training institutions and mechanisms for co-ordinating their works, linkage of training to career planning and development and guidelines for the monitoring and evaluation of training." [17] A comprehensive training policy for the police organisations must become an integral part of the government's personnel function. Various types and categories of training should be properly related to each of the personnel function--recruitment, placement reassignment, promotion, transfer requirements of the people and thus training should help in effective development of the human resources of the police organisations in India. A comprehensive dynamic training policy would also evolve a system to absorb new training strategies, techniques and innovations at regular intervals and co-operation with well-known national and international training institutions and agencies for sharing a variety of experiences in training for development. It must incorporate a programme of research and development for training. There is no machinery in existence at present which can devote full attention to the training of police officers, even though there are a number of training institutions both under the Centre and the States. [18] Police training in India can be made more broad-based and qualitatively better by seeking collaboration with universities and other academic institutions in the field of research, publication work and training.

Some Suggestions and Recommendations

Considerable attention should be devoted to the constant evaluation of the effectiveness of training so that police organisations may improve their image and effectiveness. Greater clarity is needed in the objectives, scope, methodology and training strategies of various training programmes. More training programmes need to be organised and conducted at regular intervals for middle level and lower level police functionaries. A massive training or re-training, programme for middle and lower level functionaries is certainly needed. Training for trainers should receive high priorities -- better salaries, training fellowships and opportunities for specialised studies should be provided. Police training institutions need more stable leadership and greater autonomy. To become real catalysts for change, training institutes need more finances, more physical facilities and more qualified trainers and administrators. National level police training institutions should play a larger role by offering research facilities and consultancy services to the police forces. The Bureau of Police Research and Development must also revitalize its role and performance and act as a store-house of training literature for the training institutions. Police training has to build and sustain an attitude of service to the poor and downtrodden and to bring about a behavioural orientation in police to the democratic ideals of service in the welfare State. However bringing an attitudinal change through training may be futile if the environment after training was unable to sustain it. [19] Since it is very difficult to provide training opportunities to all police officers of various ranks in training institutions, suitable and well structured correspondence courses for various ranks should be organised by police headquarters in each state for officers upto the rank of Inspectors and Bureau of Police Research and Development should conduct such correspondence courses for gazetted officers of all ranks. The inherent constraints and limitations of police training have to be realised and taken into account while formulating a training policy. Administrative deficiencies, role dilemma, systems defects and resource inadequacies are the four maladies which cannot be cured by police training alone. [20] Police science chairs should be started at a few well known universities and police science should be adopted as a full-fledged subject for Bachelor and Master's degrees under social science faculty on the pattern of the United States of America. Perspective long term national training policy should be drawn up by the Government of India to cope with the future challenges and emerging new requirements for the police forces of the country. Universities and Research Institutions should take up serious and systematic research on various aspects of police training in collaboration with International Police organisations and Bureau of Police Research and Development. [21] Indian police must devise and develop a comprehensive training system which analyses the work elements, the new job environment, the relationship patterns, the social network, behavioural dynamics, training needs, training methods and techniques, training environment, future job requirements and the total training perspective by realigning the attitudes, widening the horizon of outlook and developing the new value-system based on democracy, secularism, social justice and a humane approach to various police problems.

Notes and References

1. For further details see Dr. K. M. Mathur (1987) - *Administration of Police Training in India* - Chapter IV "History of Police Training in India", pp.46-70, Gian Publishing House, New Delhi-2.
2. For list of Police Training Institutions in India See Dr. K.M. Mathur, *op.cit*, pp.362-66. Also See Gore Committee Report on Police Training - MHA Govt. of India, Appendix XXXVI pp.291-302.
3. Report of International Labour Organisation - Joint Committee on the Public Service, Recruitment Training and Career Development in the Public Service pp.47-61.
4. For organisational pattern of training in various States see Dr. K.M. Mathur, *op.cit.*, Chapter-V- pp.72-134.
5. For further details about specific recommendations see Report of the Committee on Police Training (Gore Committee) MHA, Govt. of India particularly Chapter XVII "Summary and Recommendations," pp.111-152.
6. Report of the Committee on Police Training (Gore Committee) MHA, Govt. of India, p-19.
7. Daniel B. Kennedy and Bruce Kennedy - *Applied Sociology for police*, p.116.
8. For a comprehensive treatment of subject see Dr. K. M. Mathur, *The Problems of Police in a Democratic Society*, RBSA Publishers, Jaipur 1987, pp.234-35.

9. Quoted by Report of the Committee on Police Training (Gore Committee) p.11.

10. Dr. Krishna Mohan Mathur, *Administration of Police Training In India, op.cit.* p.361.

10(a) G.H. Honadle and J.P. Hannah. "Management Performance for Rural development : Packaged Training or capacity building". *Public Administration and Development*, Vol.2, 1982, pp. 295-307.

11. See Paul Temporal - "The Nature of Non-contrived learning", *Management Education and Development*, Vol.9, 1978, pp.96-97.

12. Paulo Freire (1974) – *Pedagogy of the oppressed*, Penguin and Cultural - Action for freedom, Penguin.

13. For similar concepts see Lynton, Rolf P.F. and Pareek Udai, (1967) – *Training for Development*, D.B. Taraporevala & Sons Bombay, pp.332-62. Also Harbert A. Teralen (1954) – *Dynamics of Group at work*, Chicago Press, pp.91-92.

14. Edgar H. Schein (1978) – *Career Dynamics--Matching Individuals and Organisational Needs*, London, Addison. Wesley.

15. For further details See Dr. K.M. Mathur (1987). *Administration of Police Training in India, op.cit.*, pp.139-140.

16. See SVP NPA. Hyderabad *Transactions*. Vol XXIV April 1977 XXXVII, Senior Officers Course 1977, Syndicate study on Manpower planning.

17. Samuel Paul (1983) – *Training for Public Administration and Management in Developing Countries*, Washington, World Bank Staff working Paper No.584.

18. Report of the Committee on Police Training (Gore Committee), MHA GOI, p.80.

19. S.G. Gokhale, "Police : Attitudes, Training Institute, Organisational climate" *NPA Magazine*, Vol XXVIII Nov. 1973, p.59.

20. See Dr. Krishna Mohan Mathur (1989) – *Problems of Police in a Democratic Society*, RBSA. Publishers, Jaipur p.150.

21. Please see, "Vistas for Future Research", Dr. K.M. Mathur, *Administration of Police Training in India, op.cit.* pp.359-360.

CHAPTER - 15

THE POLICE CULTURE: NEED FOR A CLOSER SCRUTINY*

The Concept of Culture

CULTURE REFERS to all the shared ways of thinking, believing, perceiving and evaluating that emerge in the course of group experience and that are transmitted from one generation to another. [1] Culture is the superorganic environment and comprises the socially transmitted system of idealised ways in knowledge, practice, laws, customs, conventions, traditions and beliefs along with the artifacts which are acquired by man as a member of society. Culture is a system of acquired and learned behaviour shared and transmitted among the members of a group. Culture generally consists of three components; (i) cultural traits (ii) culture complex and (iii) culture pattern. Culture makes man a human being and provides solution for complicated situations. Culture keeps social relationship intact and broadens the vision of the individual. "Culture is the distinctive way of life of a group of people, their complete design for living." [2] Cultural values and norms are the widely held belief or sentiments of a group of people which are shared by generation after generation. Culture is the design for living, it is the symbolic order which produces a distinctive way of life. Culture provides an unquestioned context within which individual actions and responses take place and thus culture forms the unconscious premises of thought and action.

A culture may be based on occupation especially one that provides a total context for everyday life. Thus police culture is supported by intensive training and socialisation in the organisation. Leonard Broom and Philip Selznick have talked of sub-cultures having patterns, a discernible identity, values, perspectives or life styles peculiar to itself. [3] Such sub-cultures are based on residential, ethnic or social-class criteria. Robert Reiner, Lundman, Skolnick, and many modern sociologists have preferred to call it as "culture of the group". Westley, Bittner, Rubinstein, Cain, Manning, Chatterton, Van Maanen, Brown, Ericson and Fielding have done considerable research work on Police culture. Police socialisation is the process whereby new police entrants learn the values, behaviour pattern, attitudes and actions characteristic of their work group. Police acculturalisation is a continuous process

* The author is thankful to the Editor of *Indian Journal of Public Administration* for granting permission for allowing re-printing of the article in the form of a Chapter in this book.

and can be broken down into three general stages: (i) recruitment and selection, (ii) academy training and education and (iii) early on the job training and field experience. There is a near consensus among social scientists that authoritarianism, suspicion, racism, hostility, insecurity, conservatism and cynicism are the main characteristics of police culture. Policemen, from the beginning are taught not to talk about police work with any one outside. Past experience has indicated that to talk is to invite trouble from the press, the public, the administration and their colleagues; every culture emphasises its particular values and thereby not only affects the emotions, perceptions, feelings and thoughts of the individuals but also characterises a different way of life.

The Development of the Concept of Police Culture

Doctors, engineers, lawyers, judges, politicians, businessmen and academicians all develop distinctive way of perceiving and responding to their environment and gradually develop an occupational culture. Similarly police officers also develop "a working personality" and certain distinctive cognitive tendencies and "style of life". William Westley was the first to identify such identifiable traits of police culture in 1951 in his Ph.D. dissertation "The Police - A Sociological study of Law, Custom and Morality," University of Chicago, Department of Sociology and later perfected it in his paper "Violence and the Police" in *American Journal of Sociology* 59 (July 1953 - pp 34-41). It was however, Jerome Skolnick who wrote about police culture in his chapter "A sketch of Policeman's working Personality" in his work *Justice without Trial* in 1966. As participant observer Prof. George L. Kirkham got an opportunity to penetrate highly covert interactional membranes and develop insights into the social psychology of the policeman. He could discover a danger filled occupational world where there is no perceived omnipresence of danger at every step. Constant encounters with symbolic assailants (Skolnick 1966), the steady highpitched beep of emergency calls and the personal knowledge of violence routinely directed against policemen create a profound sense of insecurity and consequent bonds of mutual support between policemen. In the words of George L. Kirkham, "To be sure, I became in the most literal sense of primary group membership, part of the sub-culture I was studying, In doing so, I took on same strong affects of loyalty and affection for the membership of the group. With the very patrolmen whose attitudes and behaviour I seek to understand as a social scientist, I have shared the deepest of human emotions and experiences; we have been frightened, angry, humiliated, and disciplined together and have fought side by side in situations where our safety depended entirely upon each other. We have cursed, got drunk, laughed and shared the excitement of "good busts" and "chases"."

Police culture however is bound to have variations and difference in different countries. It is only in the United States of America that scientific study has been carried out on police culture. Duncan Chappel and John C. Meyer have carried out an exploration in comparative research on cross-cultural differences in police attitudes of the U.K., Australia, New Zealand and U.S.A. While America has small locally controlled police, Australia and New Zealand have adopted centralised, organised and administered police organisational system. Banton (1964) has recognised some factors that explain the greater perceived isolation of the English police from the public as compared to the American situation. As regards great respect for the police, a survey has revealed the following data(4) :

Table 1

(In per cent)	U.K. Per cent	Australia Per cent	New Zealand Per cent
Great Respect for the Police	82.7	64	72
Little Respect for the Police	0.5	2	6
Mixed feeling about them	15.9	29	19
No answer	0.9	5	3
Total	100.0	100.0	100.0
Number of Informants/Respondents	611	1032	766

These data show that the English public has greater respect for the police than either Australian or New Zealand publics. In British police culture, bobby never carries a firearm, while in American police culture policeman always does. Similarly in Japanese police culture a policeman never carries a weapon when going out on duty.

How Police Culture develops

The new entrants to police service from civilian life get "culture shock" when they join the police organisation. Gunnar Myrdal has described four stages in the "culture shock syndrome". (5)

(i) A kind of 'honey moon' period when individual is fascinated by the novelty of a strange culture.

(ii) The individual settles down to a long-run confrontation with the conditions of life in the strange culture. He becomes hostile and aggressive.

(iii) If he survives stage two, he is on the way to recovery from shock and starts opening away into the new cultural environment.

(iv) The individual adjusts completely and embraces new way of living and doing things."

All new recruits undergo culture shock before they finally adopt and embrace the police culture. The process is slow, gradual and at times takes a few years. There is always "a gestation period" before final adoption of police culture. Training at the Police Academy, selection process for the police and early field experiences provide police socialisation and acculturalisation. There are six environmental factors of police occupation which produce pathological effects, the sordidness of the occupational environment, public hostility, boredom, the potential for danger, the requirement to wield authority and isolation from the rest of the society. Consequently it results in cynicism concerning prospects for positive change in their sordid world, stereotypal labelling of clientele, suspiciousness, defensiveness, in-grouping and anxiety concerning one's personal effectiveness in wielding authority or power in such a turbulent environment. George L. Kirkham has admitted that it is inevitable that even the best and most dedicated of officers will often transgress departmental regulations and will sometimes even violate the law in the course of doing his job. The process of development of police culture has been beautifully brought out by George L. Kirkham, a criminologist who became a policeman to have participant observation study. It is the dynamics of the occupational culture of police through early socialisation which develops the demeanour of suspicion, danger and isolation in the working personalities. This police culture also brings "occupational deviance" which allows police officers to accept activities such as "mooching, chiselling, favouritism, extortion, bribery shakedown and premeditated crime". (Stoddard 1968) - *The Informal Code of police deviance group approach to Blue-Coat crime*). Mooching involves receiving of free gifts as a favour. Chiselling entails demanding free admission to events and discounted prices, shakedown includes the appropriation of expensive items for personal uses and attributing it to criminal activity when investigating riots, arson, looting, break in burglary etc. Secrecy, lying, misuse of authority and power, deviance and other forms of misconduct by the police have been identified by Paul Chevingny (1969) in his book *Police Powers* as part of police culture.

Police culture is the particular set of values and the outlook that police officers develop. New police officers go through a kind of initiation procedure in which they are told by old-timers to forget what they believed before entering police work and what they had been told in the police academy and to learn from them how police work really is done. [6] (Westley 1970, Mc Namara 1967, Niederhoffer 1967). Socialisation of recruits consists of inducting them into "the common Core". Police streses are parts of police culture and police streses are usually divided into one of the four set of stressors: (i) external (ii) internal (iii) task related (iv) and individual (Stratton 1978). Police occupational socialisation creates and nurtures police culture. Police culture can be defined as the meanings, values and behaviour patterns that are unique to the police personnel in any society. Personal rigidities, emotional "loading", experiential limitations and cultural myopia are the results of police culture.

The Core Characteristics of Police Culture

Police culture has several easily identifiable characteristics such as cynicism, personal isolation, occupational solidarity, defensiveness, group coalescence, fascination for the police job and "one track life" (Kenneth N. Frontier in *Police Chief,* Feb. 1972). The police officer develops "a working personality." [7] Two principal variables of danger and authority work as constant pressures on the policeman in the street. Danger and authority are two interdependent factors in the police world to which police culture develops as a set of adaptive rules, recipes and rites in all communities. External and internal pressures on police demand "results" in the form of clear-ups and an important element producing police culture is the pressure put upon policemen to "produce results" to look efficient even at times by stretching their powers and using third degree methods at the cost of violating suspects' rights. Police culture develops by public expectations of the police as professional "crime-fighters". Police officers intrinsically dedicated to the goals of "maintaining order" and fighting crime at all costs as professional policemen consider it as "their core mandate." [8] Police work is not just a job but a way of life with a sense of mission, "it is like a religion, it is a sect". A central feature of police culture is "a sense of mission. The mission of police work is the protection and preservation of a valued way of life and essentially safeguarding social order. Policemen are notably conservative, emotionally and politically and generally possess auhoritative personality.

Police Work - A mission, a commitment and action-centred culture

Police culture is hedonistic and action centred and police work is full of thrills of the chase, the fight, the capture and has "the machismo syndrome". There is a myth of police indispensability in all societies. The essential mission of the police is "to protect and serve". Policemen generally say "we are responsible people, who are not likely to turn around and jack the job in and leave the country open to anarchy". Sir David Mc Nee once concluded "you have to be emotionally committed or you can't stand the policeman's life . . . . This is not just a job; it is a cause, a commitment, a mission." Police officers generally develop "One track life" and tend to restrict their mental and intellectual development. Their reading is usually limited to police journals and books or only things which attract their eyes such as "Our", crime, offence, judgement and law and order problems.

Cynicism and Pessimism

Police culture has cynicism and pessimism as two unavoidable elements. Policemen do develop a hard skin of bitterness, seeing all social trends of deviance in apocalyptic terms. They develop pessimism by seeing erosion of legally accepted values from all sides. The essential core of the police culture is the subtle and complex intermingling of the themes of mission, hedonistic love of action and pessimistic cynicism, cynicism becomes part of policeman's culture when he sees examples of human weaknesses and vagaries during the course of his work. He sees the normal human vagaries such as stealing and lying.

Defensiveness

Police culture of defensiveness is displayed most graphically when the policemen are reluctant to explain police actions to non-police persons even those with a legitimate interest in them. Defensiveness is manifested when police show a hypersensitivity to criticism, even of a constructive type and generally tend to defend their work under restricted and classified information not to be divulged to outsiders.

Suspicion and Secrecy

Suspicion is one of the most important part of police culture. Suspiciousness to a product of the need, to keep a look-out for signs of trouble, potential danger clues for offences and search for potential or real criminals. Suspiciousness is deliberately encouraged by training and futher reinforced by practical field experience. Kona Ram Chandra

Reddy Report of the Police Commission 1984 has correctly observed that the police culture appears to suffer from an excessive dose of secrecy that surrounds its functioning. A part of it is definitely justifiable in the interest of the profession but it should avoid the extreme of shutting itself from any possible open access to the community." (Para 3.39. p.25). Policing is a practical and down-to-earth task. In far too many instances police officers usurp the functions of judiciary and seek to personally define the guilt or innocence of suspected criminal . . . they often resort to practices that range all the way from illegal detention, faulty interrogation, false imprisonment and to the open use of third degree.

Occupational Solidarity and Isolation Syndrome

Many sociologists like Clark, Westley, Cain, Reiner and Skolnick have noticed the marked internal solidarity coupled with social isolation of police officers. Social isolation is a direct product of recruitment policies aimed at severing officers from their local communities and policy of elevating police as a symbol of impersonal authority. Internal solidarity of the rank and file of the police is often aimed at concealing minor violations of law and also giving a protective armour shield to the police as a whole from public knowledge of infractions. Police solidarity is the result of their threat awareness from various elements. "We have got to stand by each other because we are getting it from all angles. We get it from outside, the general public, we get it from solicitors, from QCs, we get it from our own bosses.(Reiner - *The Politics of Police,* 1985 p.97). William Brown has observed that police respond to their various current pressures by withdrawing from the professional arena to the blue collar world. John Pfiffner referred to the isolation syndrome of the police which is born out of self-pity and the failure to make personal adjustment to extreme vocational tensions. [9] Policemen, as a part of a coalescent group, always stick together, learn to work together, fight adversaries together, live together socialize together and protect each other when so required.

Organisational deviance and Corruption

Police Commissions in Delhi (1966-68), Bihar (1961), Madhya Pradesh (1965-66), Uttar Pradesh (1970-71), West Bengal (1960-61), Punjab (1961-62), Maharashtra (1964), Assam (1969-71), Tamil Nadu (1971) and Rajasthan (1972) have extensively dealt with the problem of corruption in police and its causes in their reports. National Police

Commission has observed: "the position has worsened with more rampant corruption in police today with the active connivance of numerous local dadas and unprincipled men in public life." Corruption is an integral part of police culture all over the world though the degree of corruption varied from country to country and time to time. Thomas Barker and Julian Rocbuck view police corruption as a form of organisational deviance. Corruption of authority, kickbacks, opportunistic thefts from arresters, victims, crime scenes and unprotected property, shakedowns, protection of illegal activities, and internal pay offs occur within a number of specific deviant (corrupt) patterns and vary according to several situational dimensions. Some police organisations are reluctant to expose, label and publicly punish their own members for violations and thus encourage it by indirect cover up tactics. The consistent norms of secrecy inherent in police system support police solidarity and simultaneous corruption. "It is an unwritten law in police departments that police officers must never testify against their brother officers" (Westley 1970). Gilbert has used a number of terms to describe police deviancy: mooching, chiselling, favouritism, prejudice, shopping, extortion, bribery, shakedown, perfury and pre-meditated theft. Generally the new recruits are socialised into "code of silence", by "old timers" and the "code" operates under conditions of secrecy and organisational solidarity. Deviant conduct of police officers generally is the result of the structure and organisation of police work, their occupational turbulent working conditions as well as result of police culture. (Albert J. Reiss 1971). The Knapp Commission 1972 has described policemen as falling into two basic categories: "meat eater" and "grass eaters". "Meat eaters" earn huge pay offs and amounts while "grass eaters" simply accept petty favours and very small amouts for their favours. Grass eaters are the heart of the problems because meat eaters represent a small percentage of all corrupt policemen.

Conservatism

Partly this is a function of the nature of the police job to "uphold the right". In their public order role, the police are routinely pitted against radicals, extremists, organised labour and the left. Process of selection, method of training and tightly disciplined organisational structure all lead police officers to be conservative. The police force attracts conservative and authoritarian personalities.

Alienation

Alienation has been defined as a sense of social isolation and self-estrangement. Alienation results in further lowering the self-esteem of the members of the police organisation, resulting in undesirable work response. In an organisation like police, with its role ambiguity, role conflict and role overload, a sense of alienation is bound to come after an individual has stayed in the organisation for some years. According to D.H. Bayley the capacity to acculturate depends largely on isolation from the surrounding community. Nonetheless like any occupational group police develops a distinctive sub-culture. Because the police so often come to feel like a group apart, the opportunities for acculturation to a divergent pattern are probably greater than for most other operational groups in the society. Policeman suffers at times because of his social alienation. We are cut off; we are not like every one else. Some civilians fear us and play up to us; some dislike us and keep out of our way but ot one - accepts us as just ordinary like-them". (Mac Inne)

Machismo

The police world is one of "old fashioned machismo", there is "the masculine ethos" with its propensities for alcoholism, sexual indulgences and corruption. Professional frustrations, bordering on cynicism, weaken the moral fibre and morale of the police personnel. Bayley and Mendelsohn has found policemen as familymen with more stable families. According to them "Policemen represent family men, who value family stability highly and who rely on their families for emotional and psychological support against a populace which they often regard as hostile, indifferent or apathetic. [10]

Rigid hierarchical structure, Authoritarianism and Pragmatism

One important element of police culture is the very pragmatic, concrete, down-to-earth, anti-theoretical perspective which is typical of the rank and file in the police. "Is authoritarian" leadership a product of the police sub-culture or does police attract men with natural tendencies in that direction ? Is there an equitation complex among the police, using that term as symbolic of the survival of outmoded procedures?(Pfiffner 1967). These issues provide us with a deep insight into police culture of authoritarianism, rigid approach and para-Military character of police organisations. There are marked value gaps between police and the policed. Policemen develop indicators of suspicion by a method of pragmatic induction and past experience.

Impact of Police Culture on the Psychology of Police Officers and its aftermath

Police work has been called the most emotionally dangerous job in the world. (Roberts 1977, Wambaugh 1975). Police culture is characterised by cynicism, overseriousness, emotional withdrawal and coldness, authoritarian attitudes and special tunnel vision. Balch (1972) has discovered a fixed police personality constellation as differentiated from mere attitudes and other surface representations. Tifft (1974) found that police officers' perceptions of people were affected by type of assignments and there is multi-variable relationship between personality and police work. Data from medical, sociological and psychological sources indicate that members of the police profession are subject to higher than average rates of psychosomatic illness including circulatory diseases, arthritis, ulcers, diabetes and allergies. Richard and Fell (1975) found the disproportionate frequency of psychosomatic illnesses and premature deaths due to stressful pattern of police occupation. Police officers have been found to have the third highest rate of suicide of all occupations (Richard & Fell 1975). A number of scholars (Kroes, Margolis and Hurrel 1974, Reiser 1974, Caplan 1975, Sarason, Johnson and Berberich 197 Eisenberg 1975) have listed a number of occupational stressors for police officers. Among the most frequently cited are the frustrating relationship with other elements of criminal justice system, excessive responsibilities for the lives of other human beings, negative public image, job complexity and fear and anger provoking duty situations. (Erza Scotland and John Berberich - *The Psychology of the Police*)

The threats to authority of the police officer are a primary source of police violence. (Westley 1970). Toch (1965) notes that machismo syndrome and lack of social skills can be prelude to police violence. Due to the police culture the police stations cause fear in the minds of the public. Research study by Alphonse L. Earayil and James Vadackumchery shows that 74.85 per cent of public respondents believe that the atmosphere in a police station in India is one causing fear in the ordinary citizens of the community - more so in the minds of the weaker sections of the community. One of the problems inherent in the training and development of policemen is the assimilation of the new officer into the established police culture which has several distinct characteristics. Police exert a formative influence by socialising people who serve with them. They teach one another to become thing different from what they were. This reinforces police culture and encourages new style of life and new ways of thinking. Their training and subsequent posting encourage certain values and working styles. Each country produces policemen suited to its national ethos and needs. Examples of the people's police can be found in Great Britain, Japan, Canada, the United States, Australia and some other countries. The police in Soviet Russia and China are typical examples of ruler appointed police.

The culture of the police depends not on individual attributes but elements in the police functions itself as well as in the social and political context in which police have to operate. There are significant differences in the culture of policing between different areas and different countries. "The police culture and its variations are reflections of the power structures of the societies policed". [11] The occupational specialisation and the emergence of police culture have created "a police personality" that is characterised with suspicion, conventionality, cynicism, prejudice and distrust of the unusual.

Police Brutality, and Frustration

Police brutality covers the following common police practices -- (i) the use of harsh, profane and abusive language, (ii) commands to move on or get home, (iii) stopping and questioning people on the street or searching them or their vehicles, (iv) practices of "street justice", (v) threats to use force if not obeyed, (vi) prodding with a 'night stick' or approaching with a pistol, (vii) the actual use of unwarranted physical force or violence itself under encounters. Generally police brutality, according to thinkers, comprise all practices that degrade citizens' status, restrict their freedom, annoy or harass them or use unwarranted or unnecessary physical force. It is the sense of frustration, helplessness and failure to control crime through socially approved channels of administration of justice that generates the police culture of cynicism, police brutality and counter-violence. Case studies of police barbarity as witnessed at Narainpura, Baghpat and Bhagalpur are the results of psychological distortions and undue stresses and strains of defective criminal justice system. The pent up frustration against the limitations of the outdated criminal justice system sometime finds expression in the most outrageous violations of the law by the police. Police lawlessness begins with small irregularities or illegalities; police arrest a man and do not show the arrest in registers; do not inform the court, keep the men in illegal detention or waiting for months without trial, police do not file the challan in time. Police pad evidence, register false cases or make non-cognisable cases cognisable. [12] Ganging up is another sub-culture as all police personnel instinctively rush to the rescue of each other as all are bound in interlocking webs of mutual complicity and internal solidarity. The Supreme Court in special leave petition (Criminal) No. 393 of 1980 *Narain Singh and others* vs. *Prabhakar Rajaram Kherote* has observed: "The disquieting syndrome of police committing crime, of killing and making up perfect paper work cases of innocent discharge of duty should not be ruled out." The Punjab Police Commission (1961-62) headed by Justice Mehar Chand Mahajan observed: "Considerable evidence has been led to the effect that police make out false encounters with criminals and shoot them because they cannot obtain sufficient evidence against them to bring them to justice before the courts of Law". It explains police lawlessness as part of police sub-culture built up by various external and internal factors. In a police culture taking short cuts to solve cases and making short shrift of criminals is regarded as the only way to survival. Police lawlessness is to some extent a result of a criminal justice system which is "terribly cumbersome, expensively dilatory and cumulatively disastrous." [(13)] Report of the United States Commission of Civil Rights 1978 has observed: "Allegations of police abuse, brutality and harassment of citizens, particularly minorities, have for too many years constituted an unresolved and galling public problem in America." Instances of police misconduct, beatings, shootings and intimidation of citizens undermine public safety, trust and confidence in law enforcement. Excessive use of unnecessary force, corruption and misconduct are some of the usual charges against police officers by the public who see these behavioural patterns as part of police culture. Self-protection and self-defence are the first priorities of policemen arriving at the scene of an encounter because the policeman brings to almost all of his encounters some degree of suspicion and uncertainty. Police culture provides policeman with rationalisations or justifications that neutralize commitment to ethical actions. (Stoddard, 1968). Norms emphasising solidarity, secrecy and organisational loyalty contribute to the building up of police culture.

Alcoholism

Alcoholism is a complex chronic psychological and nutritional disorder associated with excessive and usually compulsive drinking. Skolnick has observed that the policemen were by no means total abstainers from the use of alcoholic beverages. Many studies in the U.S.A. have noted that alcoholism is a greater problem for law enforcement than for most other professions. Policemen generally drink because of occupational strain, cultural mores and isolation syndrome.

Police misconduct as organisational deviance

The observations of several social scientists about police misconduct as organisational deviance of the police can be summed up as under :

The policemen in many instances -

(i) Employ third degree and unfair means to elicit confessions and statements from criminals during interrogation.

(ii) Pad up and fabricate evidence in criminal cases.

(iii) Tell lies in courts for getting convictions.

(iv) Produce false witnesses and tutor them to speak lies in Courts.

(v) Use third degree methods in police lock ups.

(vi) Conceal and hush up complaints made against the police.

(vii) Detain arrested persons beyond the statutorily permitted time in their custody.

(viii) Behave with common man in arrogant and authoritative manner amounting to discourtesy at Thana level.

(ix) They are indifferent, suspicious and at times abusive to witnesses.

(x) Police are reluctant to register offences for various reasons and often minimise the offences. They are reluctant to register petitions and complaints in many cases in rural areas

(xi) The rich and the affluent, the social higher ups and the influential, get favourable and partial treatment at various police levels.

(xii) There is certain amount of corruption of some sort at various levels.

Out of a sample of survey of 3416 respondents, 61.68 per cent strongly considered that the use of filthy language and third degree methods have become part and parcel of the police culture in Indian democracy.[14] The police culture that existed in the pre-independence period continued to operate and permeate even after India became independent and no worthwhile breakthrough to change it was ever tried or attempted in a systematic manner.

Variations in Police sub-Culture

Police culture is an end product of professional socialisation, professional training and early field experiences but at the same time it shapes police practices of using discretion in enforcing laws in accordance with situational exigencies and "the working Codes" of the organisations. The culture of the police is neither monolithic, universal or unchanging. The organisational styles and cultures of the police force vary between different places and periods. It varies according to such variables as personality, generation or career trajectory and structured variations according to specialisation, assignment or rank of the policeman. The police culture has developed as a patterned set of understandings, informal codes and routine practices which help to cope with and adjust to the pressures and tensions which confront the police in the socio-political environment of any country. The police culture survives because of its elective affinity, its psychological outfit and practical working rules of the police milieu. Even within the police culture there are four types of sub-cultures adopted by the fourfold typology of police officers.

i) The bobby sub-culture in which policeman believes in applying the law with discretionary commonsense in a peace keeping role;

ii) The uniform carrier sub-culture wherein completely cynical and disillusioned time servers who avoid work and shirk duties;

iii) New centurian sub-culture in which policemen are dedicated to a crusade against crime and disorder and believing policeman to be the repository of all truth, wisdom and virtue;

iv) The professional sub-culture in which policemen are career conscious, liberal, educated with an appropriately balanced appreciation of the value of all aspects of policing with emphasis on police-community relations and professional pride.

A number of social thinkers like Broderick (1973), Muir (1977), Walsh (1977), Reiner (1978), Brown (1981), Shearing (1981) have developed their own independently constructed models and typologies of variations of police sub-cultures. Although these typologies of police sub-cultures, constructed for different purposes and with reference to different police forces are remarkably similar. Police sub-cultures provide evidence about differences in police culture between police forces and between police personnel working in different branches/ areas of a country. Police sub-cultures are the products of individual personality variations and policy choices, which can effectively be made in areas with different social and political structures and cultural traditions. Police of each country is the product of its own requirements and needs. Police of one country cannot work in another country. It is said: "A Berlin Schultzmann in Trafalgar square would provoke a riot in two hours and the peaceloving courteous bobby would be overwhelmed in U.S.A. in no time. If a British policeman were to perform duty in New York he would be kidnapped within a few hours." The above remarks explain the socio-cultural and political dimension of policing. The development of police systems in the present form in various countries depended naturally on the trends of political evolution in those countries, the genius of the people and the cultural patterns of those societies.

Inadequate Knowledge of Police Culture

There are several factors which can be identified as contributory to inadequate study of police culture -

1. Public ignorance of the extremely low level of public accountability, performance and productivity.
2. Public tolerance for minimal levels of public service effectiveness.
3. Inadequate measures to monitor qualitative - quantitative accountability.
4. A paucity of energetic, professionally competent police leadership willing to encourage self--study and self--criticism.
5. Non-availability of dedicated academicians to engage themselves in police research with basic concepts like police culture, police productivity and police control systems.
6. The curtains of secrecy and non-availability of adequate research facilities on the pretext of public interest and national security.

Need for a Proper transformation of Police Culture

Dr. P.D. Sharma has rightly recommended the need for a break-through in police culture. [15] Police culture is an end-product of professional socialisation and a total transformation of police culture is needed if police organisations wan't to elevate their professional status in democratic societies. By being humane, committed to the rule of law, having the underlying philosophy of citizen's police, the police organisations can improve their credibility and bring out a total transformation in the police culture through various behavioural modifications and correctional strategies. It is high time that police steps out of the "isolation syndrome" and seeks the hand of friendship from the people whom they serve by building healthy and cordial relationship with the media and the community. A modest but bold beginning has to be made to manipulate the factors which are within the control of the organisation with a view to bringing total transformation in police culture in the desired direction. "In fact we are very anxious that the entire police philosophy, culture and attitude should be such as to make a police station appear and function as a ready source of relief for any person in a distress situation more so in regard to the weaker sections of the society" (Fourth Report of the National Police Commission, Govt. of India, June 1980).

Following measures will help in transformation and breakthrough of present police culture:-

(i) Civilians should work into administrative positions and training institutions to give them a more sociological and holistic view of human beings.

(ii) Revelations of scandals and police misconduct by the media particularly newspapers are fundamental to effective transformation and organisational reforms.

(iii) Organisational deviance can be checked by introducing required changes in criminal justice system, police organisational rules and regulations and organisational reforms at all required levels.

(iv) Police should be made more accountable to the public and the police leaders.

(v) "Bad Apple" theory for police corruption, brutality and misconduct should be replaced by theory of organisational deviance.

(vi) Indian police must stop the present culture of use of filthy language and third degree methods to get the break-through.

Indian police must develop a culture of respect for human dignity and reorient its attitude towards the public. Attitudinal change is necessary to build up a correct and democratic image. In order to bring total transformation in police culture, policeman should be encouraged to develop into total human beings aware both intellectually and pragmatically of the entire world around them. It is readily apparent that certain stifling aspects of police culture have to be removed and replaced by more positive aspects such as greater social intercourse with the members of the community, liberal outlook of life and wider perspective of the total world. In order to develop a wiser and healthier perspective in police culture, training will have to play an important role. Vertical and horizontal mobility of leaders of the organisation will also help in developing a new police culture. At present police organisations in India tend to show a cultural lag in the acceptance of democratic moves of the Indian Republic. The police themselves must modify many of their own values that conflict with those of their clientele and should make positive efforts in changing or modifying behaviour. The present Indian police culture still possesses a set of values, standards and job goals which were built up in pre-independence days and have not brought any radical change or transformation in them after independence. There is a general conflict between "soft" and "hardline" ideologies for the police culture. Humane approach, public service orientation and citizen's police are the core areas for transformation of new police culture giving its own values of legality, integrity, responsibility, accountability and over-all democratic ethos.

In order to build up a more democratic police culture, police officers need behavioural modifications, psychological counselling, training and even traumatic experience sharing. Police organisations should offer personal stress management courses as in-service training to officers. Periodical medical checking and compulsory leave with full pay for rest and recuperation are essential to keep up good health of police officers. Police agencies can conduct special stress alleviation programmes. In the context of police of a democratic society it is necessary to have a significant change in the philosophy of police and police culture so that police professionalism is built upon values of a democratic polity, secularism, social justice, human dignity and service to the community with a deep human dimension.

Notes and References

1. Broom and Selznick (1975) – *Essentials of Sociology*, p.54.
2. Clyde Kluckhohn - "*The study of Culture*". In Daniel Lerner and Harold D. Lasswell (1951) (Eds.) – *The Policy Sciences*, Stanford University Press, p.86.
3. Leonard Broom and Philip Selznick (1955) – *Principles of Sociology*, Harper and Row, New York, p.71.
4. Duncan Chappel and John C.Meyer, "Cross Cultural differences in police attitudes : An exploration in comparative research". In *Police: Perspectives, Problems and Prospects* (edited by Mac Namara & Marc Riedel), p.72, Table 74.
5. Gunnar Myrdal (1944) – *An American Dilemma*, pp.50-64.
6. Ezra Scotland and John Berberich - "The Psychology of the Police". In Hans Toch (1979) (Ed.) – *Psychology of crime and criminal Justice*, p.32.
7. Skolnick J. (1966) – *Justice without Trial*, New York, Wiley, Chapter 3.
8. Manning P. (1977) – *Police Work*, Cambridge Mass, M.I.T.

9. John M. Pfiffner, "The function of the Police in a Democratic Society", Occasional Papers, Center for Training and Career Development, Los Angeles 1967.
10. Minorities and the Police Confrontation in America.
11. Robert Reiner (1985) -- *The Politics of the Police*, p.109.
12. Dr. K.M. Mathur, "Police Lawlessness : How to Police the Police". In *Essays on Police Community Relations* published by S.V.P., N.P.A., Hyderabad, 1985, p.179.
13. Justice V.R. Krishna Iyer, *Criminology, Law and Social Change*, p.92.
14. Alphonse L. Earayil and James Vadackamchery (1985) -- *Police and the Society*, Kairali Books International, Trivandrum, p.69.
15. Dr. P.D. Sharma (1981) -- *Police, Polity and People in India*, p.182.

CHAPTER - 16

CHANGING ROLE OF THE POLICE IN INDIA

Introduction

"THE CHANGING role of the Police in India" is a subject which needs indepth analysis and scientific study today. The police, being the living symbol of administration, has always been an object of criticism by the press and the politicians, the bench and the bar, the lawyers and the legislatures, the rogues and the reformers, the criminals and the citizens. Without going into the merits and demerits of such criticism it becomes necessary to properly identify "the changing role of the police in India" and to find out how far it is able or unable to perform its changing role. If the role is not being performed to the general satisfaction, what are the reasons, problems or handicaps with the police and what can be done to improve the present stalemate. Police in India, according to some thinkers, is unable to even think of changing role because the police organisation is seriously suffering from numerous maladies and serious symptoms of an unhealthy sick organisation which require medical and surgical treatment at the hands of highly qualified experts.

The Concept of 'Change'

Change is the process by which the future invades our lives and it is important to look at it clearly, not merely from the grand perspectives of history but also from the vantage position of living, breathing individuals who experience it. Today we are witnessing political changes, economic changes, social changes, cultural changes, demographic changes, technological changes and ideological changes -- all simultaneously but at different speeds and directions. In india particularly after independence, changes in all spheres of life are invading us at a very fast speed.

In a changing, developing and democratic society, police also have to undergo structural and organisational changes to cope with the changing aspirations and demands of the society to which they belong. "The policeman stands at the storm centre around which many of the tensions of the modern society are working themselves out. He tries to exercise a stabilising influence at a bewildering period of our national life when everything is in a state of change". (1)

Meaning and Nature of Role

The concept and exact connotation of the word "Role" needs a proper identification for purpose of the analysis of the subject. "The term 'role' is used to designate the sum total of the culture patterns associated with a particular status. It thus includes the attitudes, values and behaviour ascribed by the society to any or all persons occupying this status." (2) In the opinion of Osburn and Nimkoff, "a role is a set of socially expected and approved behaviour patterns, consisting of both duties and privileges, associated with a particular position in a group". (3) In the words of K. Young "what the individual does or performs, we call his role". According to G.H. Mead, "How an individual actually performs in a given position, as distinct from how he is supposed to perform we call his role. The role then is the manner in which a person actually carries out the requirements of his position. It is the dynamic aspect of status or office and as such is always influenced by factors other than the stipulation of the position itself." Broadly, role is a concept which -

(a) denotes an obligation;

(b) points to his individual capacity of doing things;

(c) indicates division of labour; and a number of norms which an individual is expected to act;

(d) denotes the manner in which a person actually carries out the requirements of his job or position;

(e) signifies activities and responsibilities which a person should do, and it is a number of inter-related behaviour patterns clustered together;

(f) indicates the pattern of behaviour expected of an individual in a certain given situation;

(g) represents a fairly stable complex of behaviour patterns.

Role can be given to a person or group of persons or a profession. A person's role is a pattern or type of social behaviour which seems situationally appropriate to him in terms of the demands and expectations of the society, state or the government. "Social roles regulate and organise behaviour and provide means for accomplishing certain tasks." (4) Roles provide social life with order and predictability, and are important part of the guidelines and directives necessary for an ordered society. In every society, all members forming it, are supposed to share the same values, follow the same norms and play a variety of roles, adopting the appropriate behaviour to each other as an aspect of common culture. Roles provide the means whereby values and goals are translated into action. The content of roles is structured in terms of norms which define the rights and obligations applicable to each particular role. George H. Mead has expounded the concept of "Role-Taking" process which involves the individual taking on the role of another by imaginatively placing himself in the position of the person with whom he is interacting. In order to survive, all organisations with professional roles must adapt to their changing environment. Nelson Foote's theory of "empty bottle of formal behaviour" and his concept of role motivation has acquired wide acceptance in the modern times because one limits his real behaviour to a few selected roles that he knows and defines as his own although he learns many more roles than he ever plays overtly. [5] There are generally considerable gaps between role expectations, and role enactments in every changing society.

Police in Post - Independence Era

During the last four decades, in the wake of rapid rise in crimes and public disorders a great amount of structural proliferation has been witnessed in the organisation of police, especially in the emergence of specialised staff agencies at the Centre. Central Reserve Police Force, Intelligence Bureau, Border Security Force, Central Bureau of Investigation, Central Industrial Security Force, National Security Guards, Indo-Tibetan Border Police, Special Service Bureau and State armed police units have not only come into existence but have increased in large numbers causing problems of coordination and personnel management. Proliferation of a number of police organisations have caused question of their respective roles, jurisdictions and interservice rivalry of both healthy and unhealthy nature. However police, being a state subject, continues to be primarily state based. The Central police agencies like CRP, BSF, CISF, NSG, CBI, RPF sometime give semblance of an emerging national police force in the country yet the basic police organisational structure at the police station level, district level, range level and zone level continues to be state based under state governments. The Indian police belongs to a special and unique mould which differs significantly from police organisations in the West. [6] Forty years of free India have witnessed all kinds of administrative and reformative reforms but literally nothing significant has been accomplished in terms of reforms or improvement of Police Administration. CRPF, BSF, CISF, Assam Rifles and ITBP have more or less specified roles, CRPF has a quite diverse and versatile role. The role of CRPF is so diverse and fast changing that it is at times mind-boggling. CRPF carries out anti-terrorist role, anti-insurgency role, relief and rescue operations, striking force to deal with communal violence and normal police duties of guarding VIPs and other vital installations. However for the purpose of this essay, only the changing role of "civil state police" is proposed to be analysed and discussed due to limitations of space and other considerations. Police, in the essay, will mean civil police organised under the Police Act 1861 and having hierarchy of state police organisations. The actual strength of civil police in India, according to latest available data was 944052 in 1983 and there were 287 policemen per hundred square kilometre area in the country. The number of policemen per ten thousand of population was 131 for the country as a whole in 1983. The work-load of IPC crime per civil policeman was 1.9 for the country as a whole. Constables of civil police are at the cutting edge of the police hierarchy (i.e constables who form 96 per cent of the police population) which bear the maximum police contact and which has the least understanding of their expected roles in a democratic society. It is a paradox of the criminal justice system that the policeman, who enjoys the greatest discretion in enforcement of laws and in performing their ambivalent role, has the lowest of status and prestige. [(7)] Police is generally considered by many as the "*laissez-faire*" apparatus for perpetuating the interests of the establishment or as an agent of the government being the strong arm of the executive. Even though the emphasis and perspective keeps changing with the values of the society, there has not been much change in the conventional police roles of prevention and detection of crime, maintenance of law and order and regulation of traffic.

The Changing Indian Scene

In a fast changing society which is undergoing fundamental changes, the "police often face emotional ambivalence and normative contradictions in the choice of alternative in decision making and role performance". [(8)] In India, today we notice that the socio-economic and political scene of the country has changed considerably due to the following factors:

1. Constitution of India and its subsequent amendments from time to time.
2. Planned economic development and successive five year plans and their implementation.
3. Sociological change with modernisation.

4. Spread of education and knowledge.
5. Political awakening and social awareness in the masses.
6. Party politics and its indirect influence in various fields.
7. Criminalisation of politics and politicisation of crime.
8. Demand for dignity of individuals and security of the state at the same time.
9. Communalism, regionalism and linguistic demands and their impact on community.
10. Erosion of morale and social values and changing social pattern.
11. Increasing terrorism and other internal security problems.
12. Awakening in rural masses.
13. Increasing collective violence and crime.
14. Indiscipline in schools and colleges.
15. Economic development and its impact on the masses.

Scientific and technological advances have not only conditioned and influenced society, it has also given a new turn and dimension to *crime and crimsonic factors. Drastic dimensional change in the role of police are needed today. In India police have a big role to play in* combating terrorism, insurgency, internal disturbances and all kinds of law and order problems with the assistance of para-military forces. During war police have to adopt and enforce civil defence measures and even black-out exercises in order to defend the towns and cities. Aviation security, industrial security, VIP security, security of vital installations are some of the new dimensions of police role. Traffic regulation, investigation of computer offences, video piracy, economic offences and organised crime are all responsibilities for the police. Economic development has increased corruption, misappropriation and organised economic crime. Special economic wing of police with special training are needed to deal with such new variety of offences. Hoarding, smuggling, adulteration of food articles, bank robberies, bank frauds, narcotic offences, misappropriation and defalcation in cooperative societies, theft of power and water, evasion of taxes, contravention of controls and regulatory measures imposed by the government are some of the new areas where police has to play a very important role.

What are the Assigned and Expected Roles ?

What is the role assigned to the police in India by the Police Act, Rules, Manuals and Laws of the land? What are the expectations from the police by the society? What is the police role as perceived by the police itself and whether it is different from the role as perceived by the community or society in general ? It is seen that in many cases the role expectations from police are greater than the legally assigned role. An obvious example of such a situation is provided by the complaints of a non-cognizable matter made to the police where, under law, police cannot take cognizance of such complaints. Inadequate resources, lack of training, lack of legal sanction and organisational sub-culture are some of the constraints which come in the way of effective role performance of the police. There is role ambiguity as various thinkers, philosophers and people perceive different roles for the police. Today the police role can be broadly categorised under five major heads :

(a) Police as a law enforcing agency;

(b) Police as an arm of the executive government;

(c) Police as the protector of rights and liberties of citizens;

(d) Police as a social service and agents of social change,

(e) Police with a role in political development. [9]

Some basic Issues

Before analysing police role, certain basic issues need to be considered in proper perspective. The police indiscipline and series of police mutinies in 1979 could draw attention of the government and the people about the genuine problems, difficulties and dilemma of police forces in the country. How do you expect police to perform new, emerging and expanding roles when they are not properly looked after and even denied basic minimum amenities of life required for a decent living. Instead of indiscriminate expansion of numbers, they should have more housing, transport, communications, latest weapons, reasonable pay and allowances and proper career mangement. Only a well contented and motivated police can deliver the goods and can fulfil their assigned roles. Role of police can be of immense value to the nation-building, consolidation of democratic socialism and secularism. Role of police as friend, philosopher and guide is well known to all educated people. What role expectations can we have from the Indian police when;

-- The organisational leadership has no professional freedom to act and manage.

-- The organisation is required by its charter of work to serve conflicting interests of the people and the rulers.

-- When the organisation is governed by an old Act which was framed in 1861 by British rulers.

-- When organisation lacks adequate resource back-up.

-- When people's cooperation and trust is not available due to various historical and other reasons.

-- When organisation has inadequate legal back-up and support.

-- When issues of police reforms and restructuring for the improvement of its quality of service are not accepted and implemented.

-- Organisational problems are not even discussed openly in public due to the misconception of official secrecy and public interest.

-- When other partners of the criminal justice system are almost dysfunctional and ineffective.

-- Organisation gets no priority in the list of national issues.

-- Who will finally decide the changing role and what will be its acceptance by the organisation?

Before discussing role of police in India, it is necessary to examine the challenges before police. Indian police face a number of challenges today and some of the main challenges are as follows:

1. The challenge of expanding democratic process and growing political awakening.
2. The challenge of changing social ferment in which weaker sections are demanding their due share.
3. The challenge of rural masses who have realised their potent power of bargaining.
4. The challenge of national integrity and national security.
5. The challenges of increasing crime, white collar crime and organised crime.
6. The challenge of terrorism and insurgency in the border states.
7. Criminalisation of politics and its aftermath.

8. Rampant corruption and increasing materialism.
9. Drug addiction and drug trafficking across international borders.
10. The increasing challenge of mass violence and disorders.
11. The challenge thrown by the growing consciousness of rights amongst women.
12. Increasing police unrest and agitational approach amongst policemen.
13. Challenge built up due to inadequacy of law, increasing disrespect for law and gradual decay of criminal justice system.
14. Bank frauds, computer crime and organised crime.
15. Increased involvement of women in crime.
16. Increasing crime against women and weaker sections of the society including bonded labour.
17. Inadequacy and inefficacy of legislative measures.
18. Complete or near complete breakdown of criminal justice system.

In the words of Jai Prakash Narayan (1978): "The police in India have continued to remain hamstrung to the procedures and norms of the erstwhile colonial administration." The police force in India seems to be riddled with a multitude of problems, corruption, inefficiency, brutality, inadequacy and lack of effective leadership. If the police are to play a socially purposeful role they ought to be given more training, better wages, better working conditions, more responsibilities and greater recognition. Civil police today is a severely damaged instrument and cannot work without the help of paramilitary forces. Shri S.C. Misra retired Director, National Police Academy once observed: "The police have been moving for quite some time on crutches provided by the paramilitary forces and now their limbs have become so weak that the armed forces have to prop them. These are signs that the civil police will have to be scrapped as an organisation for protecting and serving the people."

Identifying the role of police in India the then Prime Minister Rajiv Gandhi has said: "In any democracy the police must be both guardians of law and the respectors of law. There is no place in a democracy for illegitimate methods, abusive language or oppressive behaviours. The people must look to the police for protection, not in fear, they should not hesitate in approaching a policeman or a police station. The police should be a friend in need". [10]

Changing Role Perceptions

There is an urgent need for a nation-wide serious search to discover the changing roles of police in India. "Society will soon redefine the police role to include ideas, perceptions and insights which will bring the police into the area of dealing with social pathology on a scale larger than the present holding and containing operation". That role has not yet been spelled out and is not even dimly preceived by many police administrators indeed, perhaps most would be feelingly deny it to be within the police purview. [11] It is also at the same time necessary to ensure that "the police service should be put on its guard to ensure that it is not manoeuvred into a position where it promises much but in the final analysis finds existing commitments preventing it from delivering the goods." [12] The police have to perform according to modern thinkers a subtle role in acting as "a controlling radar calculated to keep a society within structural confines, limits and boundaries". The police are expected to act as barometers of the current state of a society gauging the pressures and forces that are arranged in the uneasy equilibrium which characterizes any social structures. [13] Police role can be performed effectively when police personnel not only get a well defined role but also necessary human resources and other infrastructure to perform that role in an effective manner. "Today with increasing social complexity and intra - as well as inter-community conflict, society has to pause and take a close look at the role of the police. [14]

Factors for consideration in formulating New Roles

Changing role of the police has to be analysed in the context of (a) changing dimensions of crime and criminality, (b) the inadequate and incomplete nature of the police organisation in respect of recruitment, training, living conditions, working conditions, equipment, communication, transport, logistics, legal handicaps and lack of support from the public, (c) perpetual shortage of resources in terms of manpower and resources as against increasing demand for various duties and responsibilities, (d) social responsibilities of the police and its limitations, (e) changing social development and social conflicts, (f) political processes requiring police involvement like elections, Assembly meetings and VIP visits, (g) changing economic scenario including developmental programmes requiring police involvement and (h) increasing social legislation demanding enforcement from the police.

What do the police require to effectively fulfil their assigned role? In my humble opinion, they require a well identified role, effective criminal justice system, responsive and active public cooperation. genuine and good leadership, freedom of professional action, better professional equipment, improved conditions of service, proper and correct standards of recruitment, continuous training and reorientation and effective political will to effectively enforce laws according to rule of law. In order to carry out expected role the police must get public cooperation and support, laws should be amended and modified to provide trust and confidence in the police functionaries. Unless police organisation is thoroughly reformed and restructured, unless selection process in police is changed, unless police training is revolutionaised and police leadership becomes professional, competent and dynamic, police will not be able to take up new emerging roles. In Punjab, police have a very crucial role to play in fighting terrorism. In North-Eastern regions police have played crucial role in fighting insurgency and secessionist movements of the tribals. In Bihar, U.P. and Madhya Pradesh police have to provide full support in implementing anti-dowry laws and anti-Sati laws. Protection to weaker sections of the society is now a well accepted role of police in India. For dealing with internal security problems, police have the most important role to play in collecting intelligence and carry out various internal security measures. The role of police has become increasingly diverse, challenging and complex in a fast changing democratic society like ours. "Only a police force which understands correctly its role in the society, identifies itself with the aspirations of the people it serves, and its actions accordingly, can win the faith and respect of the people. [15] The policemen today must have a fully awakened social consciousness of his new role in building a real socialist democratic republic. The policemen die unwept, unhonoured and unsung fighting terrorists, guerrillas, black-marketeers, smugglers, armed dacoit gangs, communal riots and other such law and order situations. In the words of late U.S. President J.F Kennedy: "their success are never sung but failures are heralded" .Since police work is generally carried out under the gaze of public eyes, public easily notices their failures and weaknesses. It is incorrect and injustice to police profession if their efficiency is measured only in terms of crime rates, cases cleared by arrest, the percentage of stolen property recovered, the conviction rate or the number of traffic incidents, injuries and fatalities per inhabitants or registered motor vehicles. If ninety five communal riot cases are contained and diffused in time by the efficient and timely police action no one will recognise it, but 5 cases of communal riots which cause violence and communal hatred in the society, these cases are highlighted by the public, press and the mass media. There is however genuine need to expand the role of police in the context of our democratic socialist set-up. According to Bayley, police must outgrow its role as passive instrument of government and without ceasing to be responsible, should begin to play a creative role as well. A creative role that perhaps no other agency of the government is so critically placed to assume in a developing democracy." [16] In India there are social law like Suppression of Immoral Traffic in Girls and Women Act 1958. *The Civil Rights Protection* Act 1976, Central Children Act 1960, the Probation of Offenders Act 1958, Young Persons (Harmful publication) Act 1956. Anti Sati Act, Anti Dowry Act and others which require effective enforcement by the police. One of the most important role of the police is effective enforcement of social legislations. The present structural organisation of the police did not provide necessary cushion for accommodating multi-dimensional changes to its role which is expected from a law enforcing agency of a democratic developing society.

Role of Police as Strong arm and Agent of the Government

Police are the most ubiquitous, visible and important of governmental agencies for the average citizen. Police as the executive arm of the government, have to act in accordance with the directives and instructions of the senior executives. They are called upon to help the government in the implementation of Twenty Point programmes can be cited as example. Arrest of political leaders at the behest of the politicians in power can be another instance. In the name of law and order and security of the state, the political leadership tighten their rings round the police. Police officers often carry out orders, instructions at the behest of the politicians in power because their postings, transfers, promotions, annual reports, etc. are ultimately controlled by these political leaders. The democratic functioning of the Indian polity has made the police personnel a special pawn on the chess boards of district and state politics. [17] There are a few politicians in India who do not seek the assistance of local police officers to promote their self or party interest and in doing so, it is inevitable that some of the demands made are, strictly speaking, not legal or they are at least against propriety. [18] In actual practice, the policeman is the most visible symbol of the authority of the state. Under the cloak of legality police is sometimes used as an instrument of tyranny in the form of physical detention, harassment and wrong prosecution for attainment of certain objectives. Police are generally seen in the role of "the strong-arm of the government" because both in the negative as well as positive sense, the police have the obligation to carry out the orders of the competent authorities and the government.

Role of Police in Political Development

Political development is closely related to social change and therefore police get a role in political development of the country. Police affect the political life of the nation by directly participating in the top level policy making and by supporting the implementation of policy decisions. According to D.H. Bayley the police have unlimited ability to intervene in politics and policy implementation by merely standing aside. Police, in a democratic society, play a very important role in conducting elections for parliament and state legislatures and feeding political masters relevant data and intelligence for making critical decisions in various fields of public administration. William Kumstler feels that policemen are the victims of a system that utilizes them "to play political roles". The concept of "committed police force" in the states has often reduced the police to being a private army of the ruling party. [(19)]

Role of Police in National Integration [(20)]

"The role of police in national integration has indeed been glorious and has no parallel in any other arm of administration. This must be kept up till we are emotionally fully integrated and reorganisation or reform of police should not omit to keep this in view." [(21)] Police during the last forty three years have performed a catalytic role in aiding in the process of social cohesion and national integration by controlling and containing anti-national and fissiparous tendencies in various parts of the country particularly in Jammu & Kashmir, North-Eastern states of India and elsewhere. Police have a very positive role to play in preserving national integration by fighting the disruptive forces. Espionage activities of the foreign nationals, communal clashes, insurgencies and terrorism, subversion and sabotage, political agitations are some of the sensitive areas where police alone can serve as the watchdogs of national interest.

Role of Police as a Social Service Agency

As a social service agency, police generally act as most easily available agency particularly after 5 a.m. and on weekends for the impoverished, the sick, the old and the lower socio-economic classes. Police can provide counselling to the juvenile delinquents, school boys, unemployed youths, drug addicts, and others. Police can also educate members of the society to protect themselves and their property and on such matters as will increase society's understanding of the functions of the police, their limitations and areas where public can help police. Police service can provide assistance to those who are in state of disorganised mental state or are in need for psycho-emotional stress requiring immediate care. As an agency for social defence it has to play its part in crime prevention, civil defence measures, internal security schemes and village defence measures in border areas. Police play an important part in providing rescue and relief operations during floods, droughts, famines and other natural calamities or disasters. The police must accept their service oriented role to the community and must strive to improve the quality of social life by initiating a continuous programme to infuse in the public security awareness, acquaint them of safety measures and precautions and demonstrate various emergency facilities available to the community. Police role in the police boys clubs and police youth centres can be of great value to the community. Police can play its service oriented role by stepping up their involvement in helping people in distress such as drug addicts, alcoholics, misguided youths and other suitable referrals. Even police schools on the pattern of Sainik schools can be helpful in building up police image. In the U.S.A., policemen assist stranded motorists, give direction to travellers, rescue lost children, respond to medical emergencies and help people who have lost their keys in unlocking their apartments. [22] In Sweden policemen run detective clubs for teenagers, give instructions to students on law and Swedish police cars on patrolling duty carry extra gasoline, spark plugs, and other material designed to assist motorists who develop defects in their vehicles on highways. In Sri Lanka police organises cultural events, sports meets, recreation and reading rooms affording opportunities for the youth to spend their energies and the rural population to enjoy themselves. [23] Some of these newly emerging roles as people's police can be adopted by Indian police if they want to come closer to the Indian society.

The role of police in fighting social evils is unlimited, particularly in a system in which qualitatively and quantitatively police is the only social service agency capable of dealing with such problems effectively. To deny police role in social service will be denying police a positive and constructive role in social development of the country.

Role of Police in Social Development

The role of police in social development is yet to be properly identified. Social development refers to the process of planned institutional change to bring about a better fit between human needs and aspirations on the one hand and social policies and programmes on the other. [24] Implementation of social legislation likely to induct a more human dimension to police work. Social legislation accords to the police a good opportunity to casually and slowly loosen the placental bond with the rulers and evolve their own free identity as a service organisation. The police are one of the privileged institution chosen to motorise social legislation and play the crucial role of the catalyst of the social structural change. It is essential to recognise the vitally important role of the police forces as agents of change and catalysts in the process of development. [25]

Police can expand its role to include environmental health and safety. Martina A. Greenberg held that "policing could be expanded to include the enforcement of laws and regulations concerned with the protection of food we eat, the air we breathe, the water we drink and the products we use." [26] John Pfiffner contends that police should develop a geo-political approach to law-enforcement and must be concerned with recreation, housing, welfare, health of the society and aggressive cultivation of police-community contacts. Police functions now embrace many fields of human activities--rendering first aid, ensuring safety on the streets, combating fire, flood and other natural calamities etc. Police in some countries actively assist and cooperate with the psychiatrists, probation and peace officers and prison authorities in the process of rehabilitation of delinquents. [27]

Police Ambivalence between Conflicting Values and Conflicting Roles

Police have very difficult and exacting roles which are conflicting with each other most of the times. In our democratic developing society, the police role is rightly comparable to tight rope walking on which the tilts and tensions are often determined by the political leadership, police subculture, politico-socio-economic environment and general value orientation of the society and the police personnel in particular. While one section of society wants stern action against terrorists the other section wants a more humane approach. There is a conflict between policeman's legal duty and his sense of compassion when he finds a semi-naked, sick and feeble starving man committing theft of a few loaves of bread to feed his famished children. Value conflict in police work has been explained by Ben Whitaker when he said "we expect a policeman to be human and yet inhuman, we employ him to administer the law and yet ask him to waive it. We resent him when he enforces a law in our own cases, yet demand his dismissal when he does not elsewhere, we offer him to be a member of society, and yet not to share its values." [28] Why police is not able to perform its "expected role" needs a systematic analysis. A police house officer is supposed to control a fire at 6. a.m, provide assistance to injured scooter driver at 7a.m, investigate murder case at 8 a.m, collect intelligence about terrorist activities at 9 a.m., supervise VIP police *bandobast* at 10 a.m., provide dynamic leadership to deal with student agitation at 11 a.m. and intercede in a quarrel between the wife and the husband at 11-30 a.m. and attend to the grievances of public from 2 p.m. How do you expect police to do so many roles? Is the present day police psychologically and situationally equipped to deal with kaleidoscopic array of human problems with their present state of training, behavioural orientation and equipment ? The answer is certainly "No"

Why Crisis of Role Expectations ?

It is erroneous to think that police can be omnipotent, omnicompetent and omniscient. Police is always limited in its role and performance by the quality and quantity of its human resources, their training, their deployment pattern, their equipment, time constraint and cooperation from the public. A low percentage of apprehension, recoveries, and convictions does not reflect the true efficiency or otherwise of the police. There is crisis of role expectation in all developing societies because the public and the police do not share the same norms of propriety and values. Roles of police in such a society remain in a constant state of flux, uncertainty and confusion. Whenever we are looking for a paradigm of police role, an egregious error is commonly committed in ignoring the existing social milieu which is a critical determinant of any group behaviour, as well as the conditions under which he works, which is the essential variable to be considered while contemplating a change. [(29)] Each society creates a police force in accordance with its needs and value system. It is said "what grammar is to language, police is to the society." The police originated in all societies as the repositories of the security and law enforcement functions of the society. Police system are the products of necessity for control mechanism to ensure stability, cohesion and order in all societies irrespective of their cultural, social, economic and political orientation.

Shri E.N. Mangat of I.C.S. once stated that the basic problem is the dichotomy in political perceptions of the role of police at the national and the state level. All the Prime Ministers and the Presidents have been telling us to be responsive to the social change and to the aspirations of the people. Most of the Chief Ministers would also say it but none of them would permit any policeman the luxury of such an action. When the state level leaders urge us to be responsive to the people's aspirations, they are, in fact saying "You silly cop what do you know about the aspirations of the people?" I am their elected representative and I know what they want. Do as I tell you to do." [30]

The police in the world are therefore no longer treated as mere agents of law and social legality, they are now very much the agents of social defence and social welfare. [31] H.G. Wells envisaged : "Any history of police would have to note continuously the steady increase of directive duties and the relative diminution of the more primitive responsive functions. Less and less does a modern police force constrain us to do this and that and more and more does it become a service of specialists associated with the lay out of roads and habitations, dissolving congestions, arresting annoyances, averting dangers, assisting people to do what their education has presumably disposed them to do." [32]

Role perception of Committee on Police Training (Gore Committee)

In India a number of non-enforcement functions have devolved on the police due to the rapid growth of social legislation, economic planning and other socio-political developments. "In the changed circumstances of our society, a wholly law and order oriented force has to be transformed into one which, while retaining a keen appreciation of its legal responsibilities to safeguard life and property, has also an understanding of the larger social issues involved in its day-to-day work. [33] Unlike the pre-independence days when the role of the police was essentially repressive and protective and it was supposed to serve the interests of the alien power, the role of the police today has become promotive, and ameliorative as well as protective. [34] In a developing society committed to the ideals of secularism, socialism and social justice, the expanding functions of the state with its implications for the police, have all but led to virtual redefinition of the role of police. The Committee on Police Training has brought implications of the changing social and political processes and emergency pattern for the police in the following words: "What is new in the situation today is that many of the agitations have a claim to social legitimacy because they are undertaken in furtherance of goals which are recognised by the constitution. The police therefore run the risk of being cast in an anti-people role." [35] Police, in independent India, committed to the ideals of social justice will have to learn to apply the law with a deep appreciation and understanding of the changing needs of the pluralistic society which moves towards a democratic and egalitarian social order. Role expectations from the police in such a social order are different and very ambivalent. Broadening the role of police would contribute to law enforcement by making the police more active and more valued members of the communities. (36) Gore Committee on Police Training has held that "no aspect of the role of the police is more important than their active and purposeful participation in programmes of national integration based on the principles of equality and secularism.

Does Society Demand too Much from the Police?

Professor George L. Kirkhan, after gaining practical experience as a police officer has observed: "As a police officer myself, I found that society demands too much of its policemen, not only are they expected to enforce the law but to be psychiatrist, marriage-counsellors, social workers, and even ministers and doctors.

Certainly it is unreasonable for us to ask so much of the men in blue (khaki in India) yet we must, for there is simply no one else to whom we can turn for help at the time of crisis and problems police deal with." (37) If some one asks this question: "Does society expect too much from its Police?" The answer from an overworked, underpaid policeman would probably be a heart felt "Yes" they jolly well do. (38) The magnitude of the police responsibility becomes too much when analysed objectively.

Practical Constraints and Handicaps in Effective Role Performance

Effective role performance of any police organisation depends upon the following factors :

1. Quality and quantity of staff and their time management.
2. Legal framework and social milieu which forms working environment.
3. Basic training, in-service periodical training and orientation to prepare police for their role performance.
4. Organisational infrastructure, equipment and logistics which facilitates effective role performance.
5. Financial support and economic feasibility for role performance.
6. Social value system and orientation and its support to police in role performance.
7. The scope and limitations of the expected role and its practical feasibility.
8. Organisational environment and its sub-culture with reference to role performance.
9. Police leadership at various levels and their leadership role.
10. Level of motivation and value orientation of policemen for their expected role.

11. Priorities in role performance and role of personal discretion.
12. Organisational reforms and reorganisations necessary to facilitate changing role performance.
13. Level of police professionalism and organisational development task force for sensing and the changing role and predicting the proposing new structural arrangements for ensuring role effectiveness.
14. Organisational health of the police is very unsound. Due to various factors the general organisational health of the state police organisation is not sound as can be inferred from the following examples:

"(1) recruitment and promotion on basis other than merit;

(2) lack of attention to training;

(3) poor leadership at the level of senior gazetted officers mainly IGs and DIGs;

(4) poor morale due to various causes;

(5) lack of adequate strength and equipment." [39]

Indian police has not yet been able to carry out changing new role in the desired manner due to various handicaps and ineffectiveness in role performance of Indian police can be attributed to the following factors :-

(a) Lack of clarity of role expectations and role performance at various levels.

(b) Lack of support of top management;

(c) Lack of organic linkages with other sub-systems of the organisation with perform to their own role performance.

(d) Attitude and behaviour of field performers and their training, level of motivation and own role performance;

(e) Absence of organisational policy, systems and procedure and their impact on role performance;

(f) Absence of adequate training and orientation with regard to tasks, individual assignments and responsibilities;

(g) Lack of public support and cooperation;

(h) Lack of mass media support to the police for its role performance;

(i) Lack of political will for effective police role and political interference or direction/support causing hindrances in performance of its proper role;

(j) Organisational subcultural and value systems with reference to role performance;

(k) Absence of coordination and cooperation between different functionaries and the support from staff and auxiliary sub branches;

(l) Defective policies, procedures and system of human resource management in the organisation.

Police cannot perform its changing roles without a political will to back and reinforce it. Delinking of police from politics is necessary for effective role performance. National Police Commission (1977) has observed "a police force which does not remain outside politics, but is constantly subjected to influences and pressures emanating within the system from the politicized police personnel themselves will in turn seriously disturb the stability of the duly elected political leadership in the state itself and thereby ensure serious damage to the functioning of the democracy." Due to various reasons police is unable to perform its expected role properly and is a victim of the vicious circle of corruption, inefficiency, low motivation and low effectiveness. There is a need to prevent the loss of motivation among those who feel that they are merely cogs in wheel which is forever grinding them closer towards "occupational burn out". The police organisations, being non-plan items do not get adequate budget for expansion, modernisation and building up required infrastructure. Police get more roles to play but supporting budget and manpower is not made available. According to William H.Welstor "we would all like to have increased budgets, more manpower, and more equipment, yet the fact remains that we must meet our responsibilities both expected and unforeseen with the resources that we have." [(40)] From the managerial point of view for effective role performance, police must develop organisational capacity and organisational commitment. Organisational capacity can be built by better training, modern equipment, better financial resources and high professional skills. Organisational commitment can be called a sum total of high state of morale of the personnel flowing from the organisational environment of belongingness reinforced by (a) high level of motivation, (b) the value system of sacrifice and hard work and (c) the altruistic goals of social good.

Limitations of police role need to be explained to the public which expects everything from the police without giving it the necessary training, equipment and orientation. Political interference in police administration has actually destroyed the very fabric that they are supposed to protect. "Bihar had 11 Inspectors General of Police in five years. U.P. has 12 in 14 years. The fact is that the Chief Minister wants to have his Director General of Police imports into the system a personal factor and makes them more amenable to the Chief Minister's wishes and desires legal or illegal. Malaise is no longer confined to the states." (41)

Conclusion

The world is a stage and every one of us is an actor playing one's assigned role or "actor's part". Policeman as an actor in his world theatre has been assigned "a changing role" in every scene. He is not a "hero" but a "supporting actor" expected to play the role of a "Jack of all trades". August Vollmer has once observed that he is supposed to play the varied role of "a soldier, doctor, lawyer, diplomat and educator with the remuneration less than that of a daily labour." (42) By his selection and training, policemen in India are not fully capable for performing various roles which are expected from them in an effective manner. Any tall talk of lofty ideals and expanding role will remain empty shells unless government, people and the state create suitable environment and conditions in which police is allowed to play its given role.

There is collossal ignorance, indifference, apathy and even miseducation about the policeman's changing role, problems, predicaments, frustrations, deprivations, dilemmas and limitations. Changing role of police in India has not been properly analysed, researched or even discussed in a pragmatic and realistic manner so far. Who should define the policeman's role? Politicians, government, administrators, bureaucrats, public, community, laws, traditions, social scientists, political leaders, policemen or all of them together ? Different sections of society have different concepts about the changing role of police. Different governments in different states with different political parties in power will have different views about the role of police. In different countries of the world different nations have different roles for the police. Police in U.K. USA, Japan, Germany, China, USSR have different role for their police forces. Can we borrow or ape some other country's police without any changes? It is very important to have a national consensus about the role of police and its priorities. What precise roles should get priorities over others? Explicit priorities for different roles should be clearly laid down for the police so that the police may get clear directives for channelising their energies and proper training could be arranged to prepare them for their expected roles. There is an urgent need for a national debate to evolve a consensus about the changing role of police in India. The government, the political parties, the intellectuals, leaders of the public opinion, journalists and all other sections of the society must get involved in the national debate in a time bound frame about the changing role and priorities of the police for the democratic secular socialist republic of India.

Notes and References

1. T.A. Critchley, "A History of Police in England and Wales 900-1966" Quoted by Dr. K.M. Mathur in *Problems of Police in a Democratic society,* 1989, p.52.
2. R. Linton (1945) -- *The Cultural Background of Personality,* New York, p.264.
3. W.F. Ogburn and M.F. Nimkoff (1960) -- *A Hand book of Sociology,* London.
4. M. Haralambos and R.M. Herald (1981) -- *Sociology Themes and Perspectives,* Oxford University Press, Delhi p.8.
5. See Nelson. N. Foote, "Indentification as the Basis for a Theory of Motivation", *American Sociological Review* 16(Feb 1951) pp.16-17.
6. Dr. P.D. Sharma (1984) -- *Police and Political Order in India,* p.32.
7. P. Bayley, "Comparative Police Practices in Democracy", note to the National Police Commission of India - 1978, p.2.
8. "Emerging Social Processes and Patterns in India and its implication for Police Training". A Report of the Task Force set up by the Committee on Police Training (1971-72), p.6.
9. Dr. Krishna Mohan Mathur (1987), *Administration of Police Training in India*, Gian Publishing House, New Delhi-2, p.32.
10. Shri Rajiv Gandhi at Dikshant Parade of IPS probationers at SVP NPA on 8th August, 1987. See *SVP NPA Magazine,* Vol.39 No.2 July-Dec 1987.p.1.
11. John M. Pfiffner "The function of police in a democratic society". Quoted by Dr. K.M. Mathur (1987) -- *Problems of Police in a Democratic Society,* RBSA Publishers, Jaipur p.33.
12. P.O. Neivens, "Police and the Young People". In *The Police We Deserve* (Ed.) J.C. Alderson and Stead, p.144.
13. Arthur Nieder Lioffer and Abraham Slumberg (1976), *The Ambivalent Force - Perspective on the Police,* p.197.
14. Maureen E. Lair (1973) -- *Society and the Police Man's Role.*
15. Working paper of seminar on "Role of Police in Redressal of Grievances of Weaker Sections of the Society" SVP NPA, Hyderabad, 1975, p.6.
16. D.H. Bayley, *The Police and Political Development in India.*
17. Report of the Mahajan Commission, Govt. of India, New Delhi, 1968.
18. Sharad Chandra Misra (1970) -- *Police Administration in India,* p.209.
19. Eshwar Anand, "Towards a New Police Culture", *Indian Express,* 8 April 1988.
20. Trilok Nath, *Indian Police - A case for New Image,* p.164.
21. For detailed treatment of the subject see Dr. K.M. Mathur, *Problems of Police in a Democratic Society,* Chapter VIII, pp.116-125.

22. "The Challenge of Crime in a Free Society". Report of the President's Commission on Law Enforcement and Administration of Justice 1967, Washington, p.97.

23. "Police in a Changing Society--Sri Lanka" by Sri Rudra Rajasinham DIG(Admn) PHQRS - Resource Material No. 10 UN APEO, TOKYO J'APAN' Oct 75. pp.56-66.

24. John Jones and Rama Pandey in Preface to *Social Development - Conceptional Methodological and Policy Issues,* 1981.

25. The National Police Commission has observed that police performance is fundamental to overall development. See Fifth Report of the National Police Commission Chapter XXXIX pp.30-40, Nov. 1980.

26. Martina A. Greenberg, "Introductory Guidelines-The Police Role in Environmental Safety." *The Police Chief,* November 1979. p.48.

27. E.D. Greff, "Criminologist and the Policemen" *International Police Review,* April 1957, p.105.

28. Ben Whitaker, *The Police,* p.216.

29. Letter to the Editor, *The Statesman* dated 8.4.1977. Written by Shri E.N. Mangat Rai, ICS (Retired Chief Secretary).

30. *Ibid.*

31. Report of the Working Group on Police Administration (1966). Administrative Reforms Commission, Govt. of India. p.26.

32. H.G. Wells. Quoted in the centenary Issue of the *Indian Police Journal,* p.10.

33. The Report of the Committee on Police Training, Chapter IV, p.18.

34. Emerging Social Processes and Patterns in India and its Implications for Police Training. A Report of the Task Force set up by the Committee on Police Training (1971-72), p.16.

35. Report of the Committee on Police Training (1971-72). Ministry of Home Affairs, Govt. of India, p.46.

36. "The Challenge of Crime in a Free Society." *op. cit.*

37. George L. Kirkham - A Professor's Street Lessons, *FBI Law Enforcement Bulletin,* March 1974.p.89.

38. Inspector Peter Mc Laren- Queen's Police Gold Medal Essay Competition 1978. Ist Prize Winning Article- "Does the Public expect too much from its Police?" *The Police Journal,* July-September 1979, p.218.

39. Shri N.S. Saksena, "Police: A severely damaged instrument". In *Terrorism: History and Facets in the World and in India,* Abhinav Publications, New Delhi, 1985, p.209.

40. *F.B.I. Bulletin,* June 1978, p.2.

41. For details and exhaustive treatment see P.R. Raj Gopal, *Violence and Response,* Uppal Publishing House, New Delhi.

42. Norval Morris and Gordon Hawkins (1970) -- *The Honest Politician's Guide to Crime Control,* The University of Chicago Press, Chicago, p.80.

APPENDIX A

SANCTIONED STRENGTH OF CIVIL POLICE (INCLUDING ARMED)AS ON 1-1-89

S/No.	State/U.T.	DGP	IGP	DIG	SSP	S.P	Addl. S.P.	Asstt. S.P.	Dy.S.P	Inspector	Sub-Inspector	Asstt. Sub. Inspector	Head Constable	Constable	Total sanctioned strength.
1.	Andhra Pradesh	126				Included DSP				239*	3749		NA NA	48961(@)	53075
2.	Arunachal Pradesh	-	1	2	-	8	-	-	33	40	245	115	268	1835	2547
3.	Assam	1	5	12	5	76	66	3	243	453	2783	2830	1864	13339	21680
4.	Bihar	528				Including DSP				759	4487	5151	6864	35860	53659
5.	Goa	-	1	-	-	3	2	-	13	20	92	85	350	1361	1927
6.	Gujarat	2	12	15	-	57	-	-	143	513	2117	-	8876	20101	31536
7.	Haryana	160				Including DSP				237	779	1418	5266	16236	24116 ***
8.	Himachal Pradesh	1	1	8	-	47	12	6	78	130	428	547	1200	4966	7324
9.	Jammu & Kashmir	1	3	10	-	52	-	-	113	321	813	1050	3329	12239	17931
10.	Karnataka	229				Including DSP				419	1635	447	5577	21319	29326
11.	Kerala	1	4	10	-	41	4	-	135	312	1216	571	5359	20629	28282
12.	Madhya Pradesh	1	22	35		124		-	463	996	3147	3294	11065	39161	58308
13.	Maharashtra	509				Including DSP				1415	5230	2933	13524	45223	68834
14.	Manipur	1	-	4	-	39	9	9	81	145	402	585	427	3692	5394
15.	Meghalaya	1	4	4	1	11	7	2	28	100	408	512	456	4286	5800
16.	Mizoram	1	1	3	-	10	6	-	29	54	171	237	296	1171	1979
17.	Nagaland	70				Including DSP				40	112	224	306	3120	3872
18.	Orissa	1	5	16	16	57	30	19	166	456	2188	2521	2226	18349	26050
19.	Punjab	1	4	15	15	51	9	22	161	408	1102	2687	5197	21945	31617
20.	Rajasthan	1	8	15		128	75	-	277	356	1844	2253	3338	24343	32638
21.	Sikkim	29				Including DSP				15	106	29	199	1302	1680
22.	Tamil Nadu	1	8	19	-	62	40	-	319	1301	4016	-	5968	46538	58262
23.	Tripura	1	2	6	-	12	14	-	75	105	546	666	520	4390	6336
24.	Uttar Pradesh	NA	NA	NA	NA	NA	NA	NA	NA	979	9814	28	9117	65743	85681 (*)
25.	West Bengal	3	8	17	——	59	35	(**)	222	869	4834	5697	1613	32816	46173
26.	A & N Islands	-	1	-	-	1	-	-	7	15	34	168	86	238	550
27.	Chandigarh	-	1	-	2(1)	2	-	-	9	31	173	136	670	2213	3236
28.	D & N Haveli	.	- (1 AIG)		-	1	-	-	(1)	1(1)	(5)	2	27	81	119
29.	Delhi	1 CP	-	9 ACP	33DCP	(DCP)	8 ADCP	-	ACP 152	568	3554	3432	9263	22781	39821
30.	Lakshadweep	-	-	-	-	1	-	-	1	5	20	28	65	227	347
31.	Pondicherry	-	1	-	2	-	-	-	13	22	58	18	180	706	1000

Note :-
* Excluding DSP and above
@ Includes ASI and HC also
(**) Included in DSP
*** Including 4726 personnel of HAP

APPENDIX B

THE ANATOMY OF VIOLENCE

(D.H. Bayley, *The Police & Political Development in India*, p.255)

Occasion	*Target*	*Catalytic Agent*	*Organisation*	*Duration of growth*	*Visibility of growth*	*Manner of growth*	*Participants*	*Location*
1. The violence of remonstrance	Autho-rity	Police	Organised	Prolonged	Clear	Definable	Modern social & political groups	Urban
2. The violence of confrontation	Private group	Another private group	Loose & informal	Indeter-minable	Not visible	Indefi-nable groups	Informal traditional	Primarily rural
3. The violence of frustration	Society	Inpersonal experience	None	Short, abrupt, instanta-neous	Clear	Indefi-nable	Any one	Urban

INDEX

(B) Books & Periodicals :

(C) General:

D

E

F